Big Screen
Little Screen

BY THE SAME AUTHOR

Do You Sleep in the Nude?
Conversations in the Raw

Big Screen Little Screen

Rex Reed

THE MACMILLAN COMPANY
NEW YORK, NEW YORK

The Macmillan Company
866 Third Avenue, New York, N.Y. 10022
Collier-Macmillan Canada Ltd., Toronto, Ontario

Library of Congress Catalog Card Number:
77-123526

First Printing

Printed in the United States of America

Contents

Big Screen
Little Screen

Women's Wear Daily

Television Reviews

January 26, 1968

Up to now, the television week has proved only that if Lee (Harvey) Radziwill, working her new gig under the name Lee Bouvier, is to have any kind of professional future at all she'd better turn to stripping. (*Laura* had a big audience, composed mainly, no doubt, of the kind of people who always rush to fires and public hangings. Can Lady Bird Johnson in *Lady Windermere's Fan* be far behind?)

But the week isn't over. Tonight on NBC viewers with taste, admirers of good acting, lamenters of the long-lost days of network drama when TV was still a medium worth getting excited about, and people who still care about the industry's future (I assume there *are* some, although television rarely seems to care about *them*) will get living-room proof that television can still cut the mustard when it gets up off its puny hind legs, stops playing safe, and devotes some of its prime evening network ice cream time to intelligence instead of brainless junk.

Flesh and Blood is a new play by Broadway's William Hanley, which he sold to NBC for a cool $112,500 because it was too uncommercial for Hollywood yet too important to fight for its life in the theater, where art comes and goes through the heads of Hadassah parties and bridge clubs with the quick swish of a windshield wiper.

Few critics (TV criticism being in the sorry state it's in today) and even fewer series-addicts will be amused by *Flesh and Blood*. It has a lot of talk and no guns going off. Nor is it likely to interest all those chic vultures who threw dinner parties Wednesday night to watch Lee Baby and Little Truman make fools of themselves by turning the only good movie Otto Preminger ever made into one of the most agonizingly amateurish evenings TV ever produced. Too serious for them.

But Hanley is a writer, not a computer with a built-in laugh track, and if there is any justice left in such matters, his play may find its public yet. (Just one of the many reasons NBC should be praised for producing it is the fact that nobody forced him to write down for the medium itself—a suicidal act which makes me happy, but also leads me to wonder what's going on at NBC.) Anyway, I'm in there rooting, because here at last is a play that sweeps away the absurdly conventional gauze surrounding the myth of the American family and probes the reasons why people do agonizing and unforgivable wrongs to each other in the name of love.

Christmas tree lights flicker against the fallout-filled air of a New York night. High in the Tic-Tac-Toe design of a tenement marked for demolition, a family waits for New Year's Eve. Like most families that look respectable on the outside, this one has skeletons in its closets: Father is a Willy Lomanish bridge builder whose loss of nerve in the sky looks like the end of a glowing career on the ground and also the end of a false-front pose at manhood; Mother is a ruined graveyard who, like one of Chekhov's three sisters, hides the torture of a wasted, worthless life in fantasy dreams of a day when everything will be better; Uncle is a sickly old turnip living on injections, ready to die, wanting to claim his legacy (a child he once produced by the mother in a moment of desperation and loneliness), instead hiding his truth in four crucifixes to remind him God is near in his own inevitable death and a ragged teddy bear to remind him of the child who has been raised as someone else's. The child, now twenty and graduating from college, has her own growing pains; the older daughter, married in Chicago, is breaking up with her husband for reasons not even she understands (the mother is too selfish and stupid to help her anyway), and the son is a vegetable rotting away in a Veteran's Hospital.

Pretty? Fun? No, just grim and depressing and sad, like life. But truthful, too. Everyone is a potential Peeping Tom and watching these people whine and prick each other is like watching worms on the end of a fork. Hanley knows life is a crap game, that mothers don't have all the answers for the children of mankind. (When Suzanne Pleshette tells Kim Stanley her husband wants to be a "swinger," to indulge in group sex with two of their married friends, Miss Stanley snaps: "Don't ask me what to do—that's not fair.") Hanley also knows that women do think of other men while in bed with their own husbands just to make their own marriages last. He knows that more relationships last through stick-to-itivity than wedding-cake romance, that men are not queer because they cry, and that love is never the same thing to any two people.

In the screening room where I saw the play, high above Rockefeller

Plaza, safe from both commercials and the nauseatingly bad reception that plagues any New Yorker who happens to live on the wrong side of the Empire State Building, *Flesh and Blood* was two hours of searing, disturbing truth. Yet one jaded critic turned to me and said: "These problems exist in lots of families, but this silly play has all the problems in one family." True, but this is not a play about a family. It's about the human race, about time and the passing of it, about growing old before you're ready, about dying before you have the answer to why you've lived. It is shocking in its kitchen sex talk, inconclusive in finding easy solutions to its problems, desperate in its attempt to turn frailties into strengths, lies into truths. I saw myself in it and most of the people I know. I only wonder how many people who tomorrow will mistakenly consider it a two-hour soap opera will have seen themselves.

If for no other reason, see *Flesh and Blood* for Kim Stanley's devastating work as the mother. Touching her daughter's earring with love in the middle of a speech, placing her hands over the vegetable's ears when her husband raises his voice to curse, rubbing an eye when somebody utters a truth she doesn't want to hear, and listening—always listening—she is an actress for whom adjectives become about as forceful as water dropping on gasoline.

No longer the darling Cheri of *Bus Stop*, her face is now a roadmap of human suffering—bags under the eyes, red streaks in the eyeballs, lines in the chin. Where have you been, Miss Stanley? The world has lamented the absence of your genius.

The others—Edmond O'Brien, E. G. Marshall, Kim Darby (perhaps the best young actress on TV), Robert Duvall, and especially Suzanne Pleshette (a powerful, subtle, many-faceted actress almost criminally neglected by Hollywood)—are first-rate.

And although I am still not a member of the fraternity that thinks Arthur Penn is the American Truffaut, I found his direction a rare phenomenon almost never encountered on TV—a masterpiece of subtlety. (Even though his closing and best scene, in which the camera moves away from his characters pacing their rooms and their rooftop like caged jaguars, exposing the darkness of NBC's Brooklyn color studio like the universe around their cagelike world, is a direct steal from Sidney Lumet's last scene in *Long Day's Journey Into Night.*)

But what a finish to an extraordinary evening. Penn's cameras minimize the absurdity, concentrate on the essence of human weakness and the lack of understanding every man knows, and the audience is left, in much the same way as that last scene from *The 400 Blows*, with its own truth to face as Hanley's people watch New Year's Eve on Times Square on a TV set with the volume off: "Look at them screamin' their heads off and nothin's coming out—*nothin'!*"

It's not an evening for *Bonanza* fans, sleepy TV critics, or people with charge accounts at the Electric Circus. For the ostriches, there are other shows. But there's no sand in *Flesh and Blood.*

February 2, 1968

TV has been invaded by blabbermouths. During the day, Helen Gurley Brown smiles sweetly and says, "Tell me dear, are you a Lesbian?"

Virginia Graham flashes her molars from behind her pomegranate lipstick and licks her lips, "Dish the dirt, girls."

These are harmless blabbermouths. All brownie and no pot.

But later, at night, the insomniacs, neurotics, and sado-masochists climb into bed, turn up their electric blankets to five, and watch the Big Three: Joe Pyne, Alan Burke, and Les Crane.

Each has a gimmick:

Pyne drags on the creeps, the simpletons, and the crippled and makes fools out of them while the audience laps it up. He has a particular fondness for whores ("Say, can you really make any money these days when everybody is giving it away?"), homosexuals ("Tell me, Mr. X, what do you really do in bed, I mean, what do two guys SAY to each other?"), or complete mental cases.

This week he presented some poor moron who claimed to be in direct contact with the spirit world and, as a side titillation, insisted he knew Hitler personally: "Tell me, Charlie, where is Hitler now?" "He in hell." "What is hell like for our viewers who may never get to go there?" "It a swamp fulla alligators." "Do the alligators bother Mr. Hitler?" "Oh yeah, dey try to bite his astro-body." "How much does an astro-body weigh?" "Oh, about a pound and a half." "What does Mr. Hitler do there?" "He pray. Dey got some presidents dere too, who din't do no good for Amurrka."

"What do THEY do?" "Dey study, go school." "Are you a spirit, Charlie?" "Oh yeah, I been back lotsa times." "What were you the last time?" "A Catholic bishop." "Do you remember any Latin?" "No, I forgot everthang awreddy. Before dat I raised race horses in Vienna." "We'll be contacting the outerspirit world, folks, after these words from our sponsor . . ."

Alan Burke's gimmick is to invite well-known personalities, like Joan Baez, then berate, insult, harass, belittle, and drive them into a psychotic state bordering on hysteria, hoping they'll walk off the show and prove he's better than they are. He is a prissy, pompous, little man who looks like a dropout in Freud 101. I'm not qualified to decide which of these blabbermouths is more repulsive (a draw?) but they both have a special section in my file marked "Cretins, Etc."

Les Crane's trip to the top of the dung pile is taking longer because he's so busy putting everybody on along the way. He avoids the stars and the creeps and sticks to "highly controversial" guests—Timothy Leary, Rap Brown, the Sexual Freedom League, acquitted ax murderers, etc. Then he bounces on armed with research folders, looking like a post-pubic Junior Babcock, goading the crowd on with a pitch that goes something like "Gee, Pussycats, I could've been a gorgeous moom-pitcha star like Rock and Troy but I bombed out in my first Norman Mailer flick and now I gotta make a living just like you guys, so let's get these kooks steamed up and maybe get a super-keen show going here if we use the old noggin, you know what I mean?" Result: instant nausea, and a guaranteed bonus rating for Johnny Carson.

On a recent trip to California, I was holed up in the Beverly Hills Hotel one night with a smog-cold and, having nothing else to do, tuned in on a typical Crane interrogation. This instalment (which was broadcast this week on New York's clear-channel blabbermouth station, Channel 5) featured Mrs. Dorothy Healey, chairman of the Communist Party of southern California. (Crane's requirements are not stiff: one headline in any paper with a circulation of more than 50,000 and you're IN.) Crane steps out in a zoot suit and a peppermint stripe shirt open at the throat, exposing a tuft of Baby Leroy fuzz shortly south of his Adam's apple, his moom-pitcha star hair greased down with messy kid's stuff, and starts right in, no mincing around.

"You're a COMMUNIST! I mean, you're a card-carrying, dues-paying . . ."

"... we don't pay dues ..." "... dues-paying COMMUNIST! I'm very naive about these things, but ... I'm embarrassed to ask you ... uh ... are you supposed to be in jail or something? I mean, isn't it against the law to be a COMMUNIST?" "I was arrested under the Smith Act and jailed for five months, but they had to prove I attempted to overthrow the government, so I was released." "I just can't believe I'm talking to a COMMUNIST! Do you still call each other COMRADES?" "Yes, it's a beautiful word, just as the word RED is the beautiful color flowing through the blood of every human being." "Are your meetings secret?" "Maybe you can help us find an auditorium that will rent to us ..." "Do you pledge allegiance to the flag?" "The American flag is an artificial artifact to demonstrate false loyalty. I COULD quote Mark Twain ..."

Heaven forbid. The ratings would go down. Instead, Crane breaks for a commercial in which an Eskimo learns to eat Jello for the first time in an igloo. I brushed my teeth.

Crane came back with his second guest, the "noted lecturer and spokesman" R. H. Darden. (I told you he goes in for names.) Now he was really in trouble, because R. H. looked like Robert Wagner with lockjaw. "May I call you Randy?" asked Crane. "Yes, may I call you Les?" "No. You're pretty, but not THAT pretty." To which the insulted R. H. haughtily announced, "I'm the voice of sweet reason. Ask me my opinion on certain questions and I'll give you my maverick, conservative opinion, but I don't have time to philosophize ..."

Before I fell asleep, I learned that Communists pay no Social Security (the hippies in the audience loved that), the war in Vietnam is "immoral and illegal," there are only twelve thousand Communists in America and most of them are Mexicans (HA!), Victor Riesel is "no accurate source of information on Black Power or anything else," and the *New York Review of Books* is a "kook-left publication whose pretenses at intellectualism lead it to be immediately suspect as a Communist front." I closed my eyes at the point where the Yin and Yang of California extremism were really getting down to blows ... closeup of Mrs. Healey, smiling like a lemur, puffing violently on a cigarette ... closeup of "Randy," twitching his left eye and saying, "Philosophically I think the Communist Revolution and its attitude toward the totalitarian structure of our society needs a reevaluation. Philosophically I feel ..."

When I woke up, Ann Miller was tap-dancing her way through Central Park with what appeared to be four hundred young men in sailor costumes. I don't remember the name of the movie, but it was sheer Heaven.

February 9, 1968

Elizabeth the Queen, on NBC's Hallmark Hall of Fame, was a clumping bore, but I was amused by the way Judith Anderson played the title role, like some sort of monstrous cactus. I suppose it was a tribute to her artistry that you were able to survive her spray of poison gas and thorns long enough to suspect there might be cactus milk flowing inside her deadly stalks.

Good support by Alan Webb and Charlton Heston and George Schaefer's customarily well-organized and controlled direction helped take my mind off the sad fact that Maxwell Anderson's script is beginning to show wrinkles in its skin. But it was Dame Judith's night, and although she still looks like the Statue of Liberty, it was good to see her back at the old ax handle.

The real star of the week was George Plimpton, whose NBC special on the New York Philharmonic was a major surprise. When I first heard about his well-publicized request that the orchestra allow a jet-set dilettante with no more talent or musical ability than a bare working knowledge of cocktail-bar piano to join its Canadian tour playing gong, triangle, and sleigh bells in Ives's Second and Mahler's Fourth Symphonies, I was outraged. This jerk, I said, is just trying to cash in on some personal publicity because he is a forty-year-old non-person so unsure of his own identity that he wants to make a celebrity out of himself by acting like a stand-in for everybody else's dreams.

If you're a member of Jackie Kennedy's in-circle, you can even get your laundry list published, so what does a *Sports Illustrated* article on how squash balls are splitting prove? A swinging Walter Mitty indeed! Cocktails with Jane Fonda. (Even I've had cocktails with Jane Fonda!) Scrimmaging with the Detroit Lions. (So what?) And who cares if he plays golf with Arnold Palmer? (My uncle plays golf with Ben Hogan every Friday in Fort Worth, Texas, and he's never even had his name in Suzy.) Resistance to Plimpton's charming impersonations turned to such hostility that I was beginning to think of him as a male Lee Baby Radziwill, an El Morocco version of *The Great Imposter*.

But *The Secret Musical Life of George Plimpton* on the Bell Telephone Hour changed the melody. By participating instead of merely observing, what could have been an obnoxious portrait of a bewildered amateur swinging elbows with the pros became an hour of meaningful TV reportage. George got his story. But by promoting the gag with taste and what appeared to be a genuine thirst for knowledge, Plimpton became friendly enough with the orchestra's personnel to turn his profile of the Philharmonic into a scientific experiment as personal as an evening with friends and as well documented as the study of a beehive: there was wonderful stuff on Leonard Bernstein as the Queen Bee, hamming it up for the cameras in an unbuttoned pink shirt, calling the superstar musicians by name, like drones, and addressing the ensemble collectively, like lowly workers. You got the feel of a 10:30 A.M. rehearsal, when the hall is an empty shell, and the nervous clamminess of sweating it out under Maestro Lennie's baton. You also got the feelings of the stars, the frustrations of the ensemble players, and a kind of magic when they're all put together you'd never get from an orchestra seat.

And you learned something. I didn't know the various instruments had so many characteristics. I didn't know that musicians applaud soloists by shuffling their feet in the privacy of the orchestra pit. I didn't know the Philharmonic oboe player makes his own reeds—thirty a week. And I didn't know the cellist had eleven kids. (Did *you* know the piccolo player started in a rodeo with Hoot Gibson?)

Plimpton came on with natural charm, like Mr. Deeds before he went to town, and the musicians respected him for his goofs. They told him funny stories about famous conductors and beamed like proud papas when he hit the gong right for the very first time in the Ives. He captured the tension that builds up, even among the pros, when three thousand people show up expecting to hear perfection, and, best of all, he proved that long-hair musicians are dear and real and hardly the ethereal types you find in conservatories.

One thing he did not do was shed any light on George Plimpton. I still don't know if he can play the triangle. I don't even know if, behind the facades, there is such a thing as a *real* George Plimpton. I'd be interested now in a show about the psychology behind a man who wants to live his life in the spotlights of others. Any attempt to expose himself without the posture of whatever part he happens to be playing at the moment is something he avoids like diphtheria.

But even if he does still remain a dilettante with big ideas, George Plimpton has now stirred in me a curiosity to know more about George

Plimpton. Anyone Marianne Moore likes can't be all bad. David Wolper, who produced the show, is now talking to him about using his involvement technique on a filmed excursion into the world of haute cuisine chefs. I can hardly wait to see how he makes out with his first *caneton à l'orange.*

February 16, 1968

The Gala opening night of the NEW Madison Square Garden was a mess dreamed up by hacks, which proved that even Bing Crosby and Bob Hope can be shamefully amateurish when their material fails them.

"That's one of my early ones," said Der Bingle, finishing a song so ancient it threatened to fall apart in his throat and looking like Anita Louise's grandfather.

"Early is right—you sang it at Georgie Jessel's bar mitzvah," quipped Ski-Nose.

And people paid up to $250 a seat for this hackwork, just to have it turn up the very next night on NBC, proving, of course, that New Yorkers are silly enough to pay money for anything.

Chrysler (Hope's mentor and pocketbook) obviously saw an easy way to kill off an obligation cheap by televising the whole soggy pudding, but what the audience got was an unflattering portrait of two tired, flat-voiced old men singing "Road to Morocco"—not exactly my idea of a swinging evening. Cameras revealed everything—people walking out of the Garden in droves with their coats slung over their arms, vast quantities of guards roaming around shaking their fists at pushy gate crashers and press agents, and—most embarrassing—cue cards, which ruined most of the Dynamic Duo's stale jokes even before *they* did.

There was one knockout number by the indefatigable Pearlie Mae Bailey, followed by a shabby production bit involving Barbara Eden (who would best be advised in the future to restrict her singing to the bathtub) and what appeared to be a gaggle of dancing Santa Clauses in a musical history of the Garden that seemed to be thrown together with fifteen minutes of rehearsal over coffee and a Danish at the Stage Deli. Miss Eden gargled her way through a silly song about running for mayor while the camera showed a close-up of her sequined derriere being carried aloft by ten men in tuxedos holding tennis racquets. (It didn't make much sense to me, either.)

Then Crosby refereed fifteen rounds of a make-believe heavyweight championship of the world bout between Rocky Marciano (bald with an enormous pot belly) and Hope (drinking Platformate in tangerine sateen trunks). I never thought I'd see the sad day when Bob Hope would sink to such rotten burlesque, but the whole world watched him cross the line of zany nerve and slip into the area of crummy tastelessness when he pulled off his clothes and ended up dancing on a stage full of other Senior Citizens all dancing with each other—Gene Tunney dancing with Ed Sullivan, Jack Dempsey dancing with Marciano, Crosby waltzing with Hope in his sateen trunks—all of them revolving and all of them looking like casualty victims from Chicken Delight.

Not even the Hope-Crosby fiasco quite prepared me for what followed: NBC's telecast of the Foreign Press Association's 25th annual Golden Globe Awards. This ludicrous event is so suspiciously corrupt even NBC and the Federal Communications Commission have sent lawyers to have it investigated. But award giving, pointless as it is, is still big business, and it also gives viewers a chance to see their favorite stars make fools of themselves in public, so the Golden Globes were back, minus some of their sponsors, who backed out at the last minute. After a few boring words from the FPA's president Howard Luft (no relation to Sid—this Mr. Luft comes on like a Sid Caesar take-off on Erich Von Stroheim, interspersed with shots of the stars laughing at him from their tables), emcee Andy Williams summed up what followed: "If you're a winner or a loser, it really doesn't matter too much."

Then Mary Tyler Moore, looking like a buck-toothed Dorothy Lamour, and Peter Lawford, looking like a retarded court jester with his new baby bangs, presented the Best Director award to Mike Nichols, who didn't show up. Nancy Sinatra (no matter how she spends her father's money, she always looks like a pizza waitress) gave the Supporting Actor award to Richard Attenborough, who didn't show up either (tough-broad closeup of Janet Leigh with a cigarette hanging from her lips).

Carol Channing, accepting the Supporting Actress award, thanked "Julie Andrews and her wonderful cast," whatever that means (closeup of Julie Andrews, telling somebody a story and not listening). John Wayne staggered onstage to present the Best Actress in a Comedy award to Anne

Bancroft, who didn't show up (closeup of Roman Polanski and Sharon Tate, eating). Sally Field, "delicious, delectable, delightful" star of *Flying Nun*, flew in from the top of the ceiling, got tangled up in her wiring, and was left hanging there. Her award went to Best Actor in a Musical or a Comedy, Richard Harris, who didn't show up. "He isn't here," said Faye Dunaway, who didn't win anything. "For once in his life common sense prevailed."

After some interminable Pagliacci-like suffering from Jerry Lewis, the Best Comedy or Musical Film Award went to *The Graduate* (closeup of Warren Beatty cursing). Then after an insipidly limp medley of song nominees, Andy Williams introduced his wife Claudine, with something hideous in her hair that looked like stringed popcorn. She gave the Best Song of the Year Award to a six-year-old song from *Camelot*. Rod Steiger did show up to get his Best Actor in a Dramatic Film Award, although presenter Jim Brown called it *In the Heap of the Night* (closeup of Warren Beatty cursing). Natalie Wood, looking like the Maharishi in drag, gave the Best Dramatic Film of the Year Award to the same film (another closeup of Warren Beatty cursing). Candy Bergen, in a riding habit, looked alternately shocked and amused (as well she should be) when her film *Live for Life* won Best Foreign Film of the Year.

It was the one genuine reaction in an evening of hypocrisy and ho-hum boredom that included a Best Male TV Performer Award, a Best Female Newcomer to the Screen Award, a Best Favorite World Performer Award and, as if determined to prove once and for all what trouble movies are in, there was even something called the "Female World Film Favorite Award." It went to Julie Andrews, who stopped talking long enough to say a simple "Thank you." The whole blooming agony looked like it would never end.

Just last week *Newsweek* magazine reported denials from the Foreign Press Association that its members give awards to the stars who throw the biggest feeds. "We are not influenced by a glass of champagne," snapped Luft; "Kirk Douglas threw a party last year, and what did he win? Nothing." This year there was even a special category called the Cecil B. De Mille Humanitarian Award. Who won? You guessed it. Kirk Douglas.

The only award the Golden Globes didn't hand out was an All-Time Worst Evening in the History of Show Business Award. But I guess that wouldn't look nice. You're not supposed to give prizes to yourself.

February 23, 1968

Though her appearances are rare, Angela Lansbury blossoms on the television screen like a bright yellow chrysanthemum in a season of drought. She showed up Friday night on CBS in the springtime-fresh 1964 film *The World of Henry Orient* (butchered earlier this season in a mercifully short-lived Broadway version called *Henry Sweet Henry*) and revived my memory to the tune of two hours of happiness and charm. Boris Kaufman's photography, all smoky grays and snowy whites and butterscotch autumnal colors, was a cinematic valentine to New York, a city that needs every valentine it can lay its grubby hands on. There was nice work by Phyllis Thaxter (one of the most attractive and neglected women in pictures) and Tippie Walker and Merrie Spaeth, as two teen-age autograph hounds with hopeless crushes on a Liberace-ish pianist, were everything fudge-faced kids should be. But it was Miss Lansbury who stole the film right out of the heavy hands of such outrageous fakes as Peter Sellers and Paula Prentiss with her sheer artistry and personal magnetism. Even as a howling caricature of the American mother seen as half-Lorelei, half-gargoyle, she was a brilliant enough craftsman to actually step out of the caricature and become a character. It must have been a shock to the people who waited until *Mame* came along to wake up and discover her wonderful vibrancy that was around all the time, right under their noses. Why, I wonder, does it take so long for some people to find oil in their own backyards?

Reduced to its simplest terms, TV can still warm the heart when it puts aside its success formulas, ditches its gimmicks and produces unplanned moments of joy and discovery. Such a candid moment occurred accidentally and unrehearsed last week on—of all places—*The Joey Bishop Show*. Ordinarily I would practically insist that this lazy, poorly organized excuse for a late-night variety show be calculatedly avoided by anyone with even the slightest pretension to taste, but lucky indeed are the fortunate people who caught this particular segment. There was Joey the Inept, Slob of the Sixties, struggling vainly to interview Julie Harris and making it clearer by the minute that he was out of his Little League simply being in the same room with a woman of talent, breeding, and class.

Then, after breaking into the middle of an intelligent point she was trying to make by clearing the way for an insipid soap pad commercial, he produced some glossy photographs from *The Member of the Wedding*. Wonderful archive stuff, with twelve-year-old Frankie and little John Henry nestling their heads in the time-worn bosom of Bernice Sadie Brown. "This," reminisced Miss Harris, "was the greatest moment of my life. Carson McCullers had planned an entirely different song (she sang some of it), but when Ethel Waters heard it she said, 'This doesn't mean anything to me; I'd like to sing "His Eye is on the Sparrow," the song I used to sing to my grandmother.' She sang it to us all on an empty rehearsal stage and as the tears ran down our faces we knew it was the only song we would ever hear in the part. Miss Waters is the greatest actress in the world and one of the greatest human beings I have ever known."

Then Joey announced the surprise: waiting in the wings, for their first reunion in many years, was Ethel Waters herself. Julie Harris became hysterical. The Aunt Jemima of the universe shuffled onstage, arms outstretched, her white old hair streaming from beneath a bandana like petrified moss, wearing loafers and a cotton washdress. Magic time. The audience went wild, Miss Harris wept tears of astonishment and happiness and Miss Waters turned the one-dimensional boundaries of black-and-white television into wide screen, Technicolor, and stereophonic sound with the spotlight warmth of her face and spirit. She is a bit of a religious fanatic now, and on occasion took leave of the conversation to lift her head toward the ceiling and hold private chats with God ("I saw my baby's name in the TV Guide and I said, 'Oh, give me the courage Lord to pick up the phone and call those people and ask if I could be on with her' and you were listening, weren't you Lord?") If it had been anyone other than Ethel Waters, I wouldn't have believed it. But the woman was sincere, her heart was bursting, and when she clutched Julie Harris, still in tears, to her mammy bosom and sang "His Eye Is On the Sparrow," the tube turned into instant, spontaneous alchemy. It was Frankie Addams and Bernice Sadie Brown, together again as you've always loved them, folks, and you were transported once again right back to the kitchen of a decaying Southern house in the dying heat of a magnolia summer.

Joey Bishop seemed so visibly alarmed at this genuine display of uncluttered sentiment on his cornball show that he switched immediately to another routine by one of his boring, sledgehammer stand-up comic "discoveries" and Miss Harris and Miss Waters were never shown again. But those who saw it happen will never be the same.

Footnote to the George Plimpton Special: a letter from Hollywood informs me *The Secret Musical Life of George Plimpton* was not produced by David Wolper, whom I credited, but by Mel Stuart, one of Mr. Wolper's vice-presidents. Sorry about that.

March 1, 1968

If America is off its bird, television is partly to blame. And if TV's Saturday morning cartoons are any guide to where it's at with the dollhouse set, we should stop worrying about our teen-agers off at *Bonnie and Clyde* and seek psychiatrists for our children. Having none of my own, I usually sleep late on Saturday mornings, missing the sado-masochistic bloodletting running rampant all over the dial. But last Saturday I was not so fortunate. Relatives with monster munchkins in moppet disguise descended upon me and we were all subjected to the Radio City Music Hall Grand Guignol of the Cheerios set. These shows come hard and heavy, one after another, on all three networks—so many they cause confusion and anxiety just reading the program listings. But these were sophisticated little monsters to whom Auntie Mame's list of words for kiddies is truly as obsolete as Grapette. They had their schedule of events mapped out early.

The horror began at 8:30 with ABC's *Davey and Goliath*, a pseudo-sick cartoon about the fearsome Bible duo in which Davey is befriended by something that looks like Clarence the Cross-Eyed Lion while Goliath sounds like Truman Capote reading "Children on Their Birthdays." Not much action here. Only three savage murders in thirty minutes. Shucks.

This was followed by *Casper the Friendly Ghost* (strictly kid stuff), so we switched to CBS's *Frankenstein Jr.*, a gruesome orgy for monsters only involving one little outcast peg-head who wants to be loved. ("Aah," sighed the kids.) I'd have preferred the Laurel and Hardy movie on Channel 9, but nothing doing. "Might as well watch one of those movies with writing on the bottom as those grodies."

Vetoed, I survived something called *Super President*, which is NBC's sneaky way of teaching kids how bad off they are, since most of the villains look like LBJ in wigs. (Passed up in this 9:30–10 slot as "too corny" were

The Herculoids and *Fantastic Four.*) The real action didn't start until 10, when one of the real super-sick heroes, *Spider Man,* hit the waves on ABC. This bizarre oddity stays in bed a lot in the form of a sickly newspaper copy boy (I know that because his editor is always calling him up at home wanting to know where the layout for page one is). But at night when the moon is full this frail sissy turns into—zowie!—a giant spider who kills off everything in sight to save mankind! Previews indicate that next week he fights singlehandedly a whole battalion of knife-throwing Lesbians who want to enslave the men of the world. The kids loved that. "Sock 'em, Spider Man," they yelled.

At 10:30 CBS's *Space Ghost* got knocked out of the running by ABC's *Journey to the Center of the Earth,* about four people and a duck named Gertrude trapped in the center of the earth on an expedition to Atlantis and terrorized by a Neanderthal cretin named Tor and an evil Count Somebody-or-other. They battled a river of hot sulphuric acid (so that's what's down there), Destruction Canyon, suspended animation gas, dinosaurs, giant man-eating spiders, and a hideous man-eating fungus. ("This looks like the end," cried the professor, as the show broke for a Ronzoni Pastina sing-along.)

At 11, *Moby Dick* (in which Melville's pre-Lassie animal hero turns good) and *King Kong* (in which Fay Wray's primate lover still has not discovered the magic of underarm deodorant) were quickly bypassed for NBC's *Birdman,* in which a very psychologically disoriented man who flies, and his trusted eagle Avenger, absorb solar power from the sun to stop missiles from angry planets, thwart evil, and avoid war. (In all these cartoons, the word "war" always refers to hostile attacks on America from outer space and by thugs, monsters, and assorted "destructive forces"—there is never any mention of Vietnam. Let's not get the little darlings any more stirred up than they are already. And for God's sake, let's not start them asking embarrassing questions.) In this episode, Birdman and Avenger get sealed up in glass tubes by a Frankenstein type called Mintauck, who sends them to the White House to destroy the Pentagon. ("Birdman is under some kind of spell," a U.S. Senator casually observes.) The kids were, quite oddly, rooting for the evil Mintauck, and so was I.

This show was interrupted by an unannounced appearance by Space Girl and Meteor Man, who rule the Inter-Galactic Courts of Justice battling such perils as orgons, unknown tranquility zones, metallic monsters ruled by King Dracmor, nuclear super-subs, atomic reactor plants, and super solar energy bolts. "Let's show these drones we're not here to play games," cries Space Girl, who looks like a hyperthyroid Christine Jorgensen. "Right," I said aloud. "Shhh!" said the munchkins, shooting me hard looks.

At 11:30, *Atom Ant and Super Squirrel* (NBC) lost out to *The Superman-Aquaman Hour* (CBS). Superman you already know about if you're a George Reeves-Noel Neill fan, but Aquaman has got to be seen to be believed. Aquaman and Aqualad are two obvious Marine Marvel underwater homosexuals who, with their friend Tusky, the Walrus, protect the sea from Abnamar, King of the Mole Men, remote control ships, diamond drills, torpedo tubes. ("I'll set it on fire in 7 seconds," yells Aquaman to Aquaboy, who looks on lovingly—"if I'm lucky!") Together this daring duet rides jet-propelled seahorses and comes equipped with an incredible new sponsor more mind-boggling than any of the ocean-floor denizens they fight off each week—a toy that looks like a miniature waffle iron into which a child can pour "gobbly-goo" and produce instantly edible candy tarantulas, snakes, turtles, and monsters. The kids at my house all wanted one before the show was over. "Is the A&P open this early?" asked their mother, wearily.

Because Aquaman and Superman never die, their show raves on for an hour, canceling all possibilities of watching *Top Cat* (NBC) or *The Beatles* (ABC). But at 12:30 CBS's *Johnny Quest* arrived. This was the Big One. And, I must admit, the best of the lot. This comic strip is not only drawn well but it has real scripts that follow an H. P. Lovecraft story line and voiceovers that do not sound like they are being read from IBM cards. Johnny, his scientist father, an unexplained blond Tab Hunter type who is always offering to sleep in Johnny's room to keep him safe from harm, an Indian boy named Hadji, and a dog named Bandit battle a new foe each week—black panthers, flying dinosaur bats, vampires, and hunchback gargoyles.

There are many others: *Road Runner* (a rain-bath of violence, physical brutality and sadism in which a poor pea-brained piece of poultry sketched to resemble Hermione Gingold, gets electrocuted, stampeded, knocked unconscious, and crucified week after week to gales of sweet childish laughter); *George of the Jungle; Cool McCool; Kimba; Marine Boy* (Aquaboy's Third Avenue cousin?), etc. In last Saturday's lineup I counted 37 brain concussions, 25 felonies, 40 criminal assaults, and 20 brutal murders. Fine heritage of stalwart virility we're teaching to the people in whom we're placing the future hopes of our country, right all you guys at the networks?

And you can't excuse this kind of lunatic wholesale mind-bending TV slobber by saying, "At least it keeps them off the streets." Last week I saw a man walking down Fifth Avenue scaring the living daylights out of three young matrons. He looked exactly like Spider Man and all the kids on the sidewalk applauded with joy.

March 8, 1968

A Hatful of Rain, last Sunday night's play on ABC, saved David Susskind's reputation as a producer of serious and meaningful television drama and provided, for discriminating tastes (no, nobody expected Jack Gould to like it), two hours of solid dramatic thunder in a week of drizzle. Updated to include references to hippies, LSD, and the Beatles, Michael Gazzo's play remained one of those rare, unbeatable dramas in which everything works, but more important, it has never seemed more pertinent in its exploration of America's drug-addicted youth and what happens to the people waiting for them to come home at night. The slow, labyrinthian course by which the script made its way was encouraging for TV, and John Moxey's introspective yet clinical direction actually gave his actors enough time to develop themselves fully enough for the audience to actually watch them think. Result: viewers were sucked right into those four furnished rooms where, for two hours, they lived with Gazzo's people like one of those glass anthills you used to be able to buy at Schwarz.

There were several parallels to *East of Eden* I hadn't noticed before that I suppose could be classed as clichés—the father showering his love on the good son who turns out to be the bad son; the bad son who turns out to be the good son who loves his father more; the good girl pledged to love the bad son and sheltering the truth about both—but the script seemed as real as the hair on the human head.

Credit for much of the show's success must inevitably go to a brilliant cast. Peter Falk and Herschel Bernardi, as the misunderstood son and callous father, were splendid, and although he looks annoyingly like Laurence Harvey and mumbles like James Dean, Michael Parks added a childlike weakness to the heroin-addicted son that was heartbreaking.

Drug-withdrawal sequences are always good for trapping an audience of laymen into thinking an actor is better than he really is, but Parks handled his well, with a minimal amount of scene-chewing. (I only saw him bite the sofa once.)

Sandy Dennis was the evening's real sorceress. I long ago gave up trying to analyze her work, arriving at the conclusion that you either like her or you don't. Count me among her most fanatic supporters. Sometimes her mannerisms (Pauline Kael calls her a "Babbit Rabbit") make her a sort of distilled and ventilated country bumpkin imitation of an early Kim Stanley. But like Kim, she is continually polishing her craft and improving her technique. In *A Hatful of Rain* she surpassed all hopes, giving what was perhaps her best performance to date. Her portrait of the drab but caring wife was many things—soft, feminine, sensitive, awkward with pregnancy, feet on the ground. Wonderful, genuine moments of quiet splendor, slender girlishness and great strength blossomed from her patchwork quilt portrayal that added up to a total panorama of a certain kind of girl everybody knows, caught like a sparrow in a bear trap. She can take a simple line like "I don't wanna talk about the baby because I don't wanna get emotional," break it up into beats, like pieces of a mental arrangement, and mold the images in such a resulting way that the audience sees life being lived instead of performed. For my money, she is the best actress America has produced in the last ten years.

I don't know how *A Hatful of Rain* fared with the mail-order brains out there in the great unwashed unknown, because I have never seen a rating in my life and never intend to. Only the lemmings at ad agencies and TV networks allow anything as foolish and pointless as a rating to lead them suicidally into a tidal wave of insecurity about their own products. But one critic at the screening I attended said, "Nobody will watch this. It's too intelligent for the public, Sandy Dennis is not a big enough name to carry it, and most of them will think it's *The Rainmaker* and switch to *The Smothers Brothers* or *Bonanza*." A moment of silent prayer for us all if she was right. Anyone apathetic enough to the world at large to be brainwashed by the slobbering trivia of either of those crappy shows deserves exactly what he gets.

There was nothing "special" about last night's Debbie Reynolds "special" on ABC. I've always considered Debbie one of the most criminally underrated performers in show business. She is a fine actress (anyone who doubts it need only catch the way Richard Brooks directed her in

The Catered Affair), she dances like a dream, and contrary to what people who know nothing about voices may think (it's chic to put down naturalistic singing in this age of electronic singing Medeas), she has a beautifully controlled, meadowlark-lyrical voice and a happy tuneful style.

There aren't many things she can't do. But by some freak-out, she managed to do most of them last night. Instead of doing her own thing, she did everybody else's. She looked like a million bucks in Jean Louis gowns and Sidney Guilaroff hairdos, but instead of the meat and potatoes one gets in her night club act (the best act I've ever seen in Vegas), Debbie fed us soggy bites of sassy soufflé.

She's a great mimic, but her opening bit, a Streisand take-off in red chiffon and putty nose, doing three pinched nasal endings to "Happy Days Are Here Again," was enough of that scene. We didn't really need an entire parody of *Grand Hotel* with Debbie playing Garbo, Judy Holliday as Billie Dawn, Bette Davis, Mae West and Barry Fitzgerald in *Going My Way*. The other skits had a pretension to cleverness, but went on too long. There was one really boring disaster that started off on an original note as a comment on military troops too exhausted from twenty-four hours of straight audience duty to ever get around to active duty—but it turned into a channel for Bob Hope's gags and ended up in the bottom of the vinegar barrel when Jim Nabors sang "Mame" like something in a jar.

Another skit with possibilities, in which Debbie and Bobby Darin took off on Sonny and Cher as hippies who turn out to be backstage phonies in a counter take-off on Noel Coward's "Red Peppers," also failed because (1) they were such accurate imitators and (2) their kook clothes, like rejects from a Salvation Army rummage sale, were really designed by Sonny and Cher. So they only looked and sounded every bit as repulsive as what they were imitating. Not funny, Debbie.

Near the end, the show came briefly alive when Debbie and Donald O'Connor recaptured magic moments from old MGM movies. But it was already too late. And Debbie was certainly ill-advised to close her show with the song "I Think I Like You" from *Dr. Dolittle*. This song is only palatable when performed in a bossa nova tempo and its last line, sung after the credits—"I think you like me too . . . do you . . . do you? . . . DO YOU?"—only gave the Debbie Critics who still think the only thing she can do well is sell Girl Scout Cookies the perfect opportunity to shout "NO!" right back at their TV screens.

March 15, 1968

Many things happened last week worth talking about with so little space to talk about them in, but here's a potpourri as judicious as room allows:

The Undersea World of Jacques Cousteau, Part 2 (ABC). Narrated by Rod Serling. A fascinating trip to an underwater coral reef with cameras swimming like Esther Williams in subterranean sets that would boggle the mind of Jo Mielziner. Giant flattened mushroom corals, Christmas tree corals and carousel pink and orange sherbet-colored monoliths 15,000 times as big as the pyramids of Egypt became Technicolor backgrounds for predatory rays, scary urchins, murderous sharks, and phosphorescent starfish. Herds of bumphead parrot fish attacked a coral reef for plant food like buffalo, spitting out enough residue for five tons of sand. Clown fish sought food for their partners, giant carpets of scaly living cells, existing side by side in a Frankenstein-Dracula symbiosis never before captured on film. And more. I don't know how Monsieur Cousteau does it, but his ABC specials are fish ballets, enlightened scientific experiments no aquarium could ever conduct, and hairy visions of an underwater way of life few people know, all rolled into one. I find them absorbing and awesome, and I can hardly wait for the next installment.

The Virginian (NBC). After swinging his super-cool nose off on *Carol Burnett* earlier in the week, the incredibly talented Mel Torme turned up on this oatmeal operetta for toothless nags playing a Percy Kilbride-type ranch hand secretly moonlighting from his notorious past as a—are you ready?—dangerous dead-eye gunfighter. This show gets worse all the time, but Torme had a ball. Notable especially for its Tabby Cat Food commercial in which a white cat licks Jane Russell in the mouth while she's trying desperately to sell Tabby Cat Food. You've got to see it to believe it.

Worst Show of the Week Award: To ABC's Wednesday night special on Mia Farrow, billed as "an engaging, sensitive young woman" under a soundtrack being screamed to death by the tiresome howls of Lou

Rawls. It was a pilot film for a projected series narrated by Ryan O'Neal called *The Now Generation*. Not a bad idea, but O'Neal was a big flop as an interviewer, nervous and scratchy as a chicken pox fatality. Terrible photography, soundtrack practically obliterated by the sound of airplanes overhead (or maybe it was tractors, or maybe it was a lawn mower?). Sample Mia dialogue: "I figured by reading the *New York Times* I'd learn a lot more about Vietnam, but I didn't. It's all so complicated but it's all so simple." (Did you get that, Scotty Reston?) O'Neal: "Mia, you have a most definite personal philosophy in life." (She never told what it was.) Mia: "I found people like Salvador Dali and Bette Davis who did it along with me." (Hmmm.) Mia on meditation: "I'm on this Indian thing. Every morning and every night I find time to meditate." (Easy as washing your face with Dr. Laszlo's sea mud soap, girls, and not half so expensive.) Mia on religion: "God is only a short word for GOOD, so Buddha and God and all those people were really God because they were good." She ate flowers, chewed her fingernails, scratched her nose, played with her hippie beads dressed in something that looked like an old 1936 Myrna Loy bedspread, and avoided any mention of the subject of Frank Sinatra. A very revealing picture, wot, with no mention of the man who has made a celebrity for life and one of the world's richest child brides out of a nobody with the sex appeal of a fried leek. Very deep. What did emerge, however, was the snapshot of the kind of girl Mia really is, a girl who went to London to make *A Dandy in Aspic* and asked where Aspic was, only to be super-stunned to discover "it's something they make Jello with." C'mon, for Chrissakes. This girl needs help, not prime time TV.

Grace Kelly's Tour of Monaco (ABC). A travelogue that would have welcomed even Fitzpatrick. Not a tour at all, but a perfectly ghastly waste of everybody's time turned into a feeble excuse for a series of agonizingly dull songs, some silly, pointless comedy routines by the glaringly unfunny Terry-Thomas (he's not even French, which shows how much thought and preparation went into this mess of a show), and some totally irrelevant dance numbers in the streets. Grace looked wonderful in her Dior gowns and photographed in a pseudoromantic camera style I have no fondness for (sniffing roses in slow motion while sultry breezes blew her jewels and chiffon gaily at high noon), but she rarely appeared at all unless she was in the audience of a nightclub listening to Françoise Hardy or Gilbert Bécaud. Tedium set in early and I was left with the impression that sixty minutes was too long to spend in a place that can be covered in ten. Surely there must be something better to do in Monaco than go to the Grand Prix one day a year and to nightclubs the other 364. No matter. Monaco still looks like a nice place to have a nervous breakdown in. And if you plan on spending any time there, I'd suggest you have one. Relieves the monotony.

The Rise and Fall of the Third Reich (ABC). A three-hour swan dive into hell without passing Go. An ambitious undertaking, massively assembled and brilliantly produced by the David Wolper people, this chronicle of Hitler's rise to power defies description, so I won't attempt any, except to say it is one of the best examples of how television can sometimes reach heights of undreamed-of greatness. Probably the television event of the year.

Not surprisingly, the best series show of the week turned out to be a *Run for Your Life* segment about abortion that did more to press for passage of the law on legalized abortion than anything I've ever seen on the subject. It was shocking, ugly, hard-hitting, and brutal. It said a lot about the corruption of American life and it spared nothing. It also provided further exposure to the rhapsodic acting talents of Kim Darby, one of the few young actresses in television worth building a show around, whose intensity and sincerity never fail to make my twelve-inch screen look bigger than life and twice as engrossing. And it cemented my opinion that *Run for Your Life* is one of the few decent weekly series still left on the air that is dealing with life head-on. Naturally NBC has canceled it for next season. So what do you want, Alfie: intelligence, creativity, talent, a mature vision, and a rating, too?

March 22, 1968

My Saturday night "treat" last week on CBS was an hour of stupefying agony with Jane Morgan. "Would you like to fly in my bootiful balloooonn . . ." Only Judy Garland can hit flats like that and get away with it. Jane Morgan's popularity mystifies me. She sounds like one of those tone-deaf sopranos in their silver-dyed fox stoles who used to fade into the white clapboard walls of old 1940 Humphrey Bogart movies. You know, the ones who sang boring songs by Mack David in the bar scene with Hoagy Carmichael playing the piano while Bogart had all the best sultry dialogue in the closeups. But here she is, in the middle of the turbulent Sixties, and as out of place as an alligator on Madison Avenue.

On this monstrous excuse for one of those "Evening With" specials, Miss Morgan warbled her way through a corny melange of songs several light years beyond her range and ability, in hairdos that appeared to have been rained on and gowns designed for a vampire in search of a transfusion. No shading, no idea what lyrics and phrasing are all about, no stage presence. Waving her arms wildly and moving her mouth like Lizabeth Scott with a novocained upper lip, she sang "Jar-ja on My Mind," Tevye's song from *Fiddler on the Roof* in spangles and boots, and "Ten Cents a Dance" like Vaughn Monroe ("It's a queer rumance . . . customers crush my tosh . . ."). I'm not suggesting she has a lisp, but I feel certain her career would be over if she ever had an adenoid operation.

At one point she raised her hands in a long black cloak, like a mock-Crucifixion, with a spotlight forming a halo behind her head, while she déjà-vued her way through a tribute to Edith Piaf. But the best was still to come: On "Born Free" a movie screen lit up with lions roaming the tundra across her forehead as her orchestra, which sounded like it was being conducted with a pitchfork, crashed its way through "The Battle Hymn of the Republic." Go figure that one out.

Helping Miss Morgan make this the most easily forgettable odd-ball event of the television season were the monotonous Doodletown Pipers, ten men and ten women who should know better, weighted down in baggy sweaters and sunlamp smiles, who doop-doop-dooped and ooo-ooo-oooed their way through everything from "California Dreaming" to "Georgy Girl" without precision, coordination, or technique. At one point they sang the Beatles' song "Yesterday" lying on their stomachs, and for their finale they all took their shoes off and threw them at the audience. (One Doodletown Piper fell down onstage in the middle of the fracas.)

Just what medieval torture CBS had in mind by perpetrating this massacre of good Saturday night time on an unsuspecting public is anybody's guess. But I do know one thing. Jane Morgan is to modern music what Vera Hruba Ralston used to be to Republic movies. There is only one way to stop Jane Morgan. Drive a stake through her heart.

The Actor (ABC) got off to a good start when Alec Guinness promised to storm the bastions of the actor's terrain and show what really goes on behind the proscenium. The actor and his adversaries, the audience—

he promised—come together out of a common need for something in their natures. We came together. But all he did was take us on a Yorkshire pudding-drenched trip through London's snobby Garrick Club and show us some Royal Academy students learning how to cross their eyes and mumble.

The best thing on the show was a visit with England's irascible young Heathcliff, Nicol Williamson, who thumbed his nose at British traditions with a few well-chosen right hooks. Loping like a wounded bear: "How well did *you* do those six hundred performances of *The Bells*, Henry Irving and Edmund Kean, and how do we really know you were such good actors, anyway?" I liked that. I also liked the delightful go-to-hell attitudes of Joan Littlewood, the high priestess of London's off-Broadway, taking delinquents off the streets, sitting on the edge of her little stage in a reconverted slum in sneakers and a cocky pillbox hat, looking like a cross between Brendan Behan and Saint Joan, puffing cigars and teaching the little buggers how to act. "The famous ones can take care of themselves—these are the ones I'm interested in."

But some of the famous ones didn't do such a good job of taking care of themselves. Joan Plowright looked frightened to death as she announced nobody writes parts for women anymore. Peter Bull discussed backstage superstitions ("If you whistle in the dressing room, you must go out and knock three times before entering again.") Fascinating, wot. And Harold Pinter came off as a pompous, nondescript little bore, whose only contribution was a personal put-down of Peter Brook, the only real genius among England's new directors. Pinter also told a pointless story about Sir Donald Wolfit that should have been deleted entirely. It only wasted time.

There were nice shots of the buskers in Piccadilly Circus, the nuts at Hyde Park Corner, women in feather boas walking poodles, bobbies directing traffic—all people dramatizing their existences by dressing up and calling attention to themselves. And proving, of course, that all the actors in the world are not on the stage.

But mainly it was a richly encrusted, expensively gift-wrapped hour of tedium, ruined by a pretentious, cliché-ridden ("Fame comes to many but immortality is a luxury afforded very few," etc.) script by Kenneth Tynan. Why is it that when writers cannot come to the point, make an interesting statement, create a uniform pattern of ideas that flow in a simple direction, or be amusing, they always quote Shakespeare?

March 29, 1968

Christine Jorgensen, the original Girl in the Freudian Slip, made one of his-her rare appearances on ABC's new Dick Cavett *This Morning* show this week and the result was unexpectedly delightful. Cavett is fast becoming one of the most enormously likable interviewers on TV because he knows which questions to ask, when to ask them, and when to shut up. He is much better at it than any of the nighttime egomaniacs because he appears genuinely interested in other people instead of racking up ratings, and he doesn't seem afraid to let his guests know they sometimes know more than he does. With Christine, he provided an interesting and entertaining show in spite of a ticklish subject and an awkward start. "I don't know whether to shake hands or what," he fumbled. But La Jorgensen was ready for him. "We could try some of that OR WHAT," snapped Denmark's most popular creation since Hamlet, adding quickly, "I didn't mean to throw you a curve." "You didn't used to have any curves to throw," quipped Cavett on the up-take. It was like a brisk game of ping-pong. Neither one outsmarted the other.

Miss Jorgensen brushed away some of the cobwebs and answered some startingly frank questions. Examples: The only reason her transfiguration was so publicized was because it came at a time when the *Daily News* needed a new hit scandal to replace the Mickey Jelke trial. Three surgical procedures were performed on him-her; now the whole thing can be done in one transsexual package kit. She can marry at any time, but is now engaged in a brouhaha with the government over the question of whether the "sex" blank on birth certificates is legal as anything more than a document of identification. ("Birth certificates do not establish your sex—they put on it whatever they think you are at the time of birth. You can change." Amen.) She still gets all her government Armed Forces insurance in the name George Jorgensen because her lawyer says, "For heaven's sake, don't get the Veterans Administration upset—they're confused enough as it is." Interesting personal sidelight: there is only one sister in her family, so the Jorgensen family name will now die when she does.

She showed slides of herself as the GI George in 1946, after her first operation, and after a year of hormone treatments; delivered a sermon on what's wrong with America's sexually frustrated youth ("The old myth that you have to be a cigar-smoking truck driver type to prove your masculinity is happily disappearing"); and make a plea for better understanding of the thirty thousand known transsexuals in America today who are afraid to have the operations because of publicity. "There are many I meet and don't even know it." "Don't look at me," grinned Cavett. "I know who and what I am." Said he-she, "Do you?" Cavett took it like a good sport.

Miss Jorgensen was a real lady, which I suppose is the best compliment I can pay. She appeared to be brainy, honest, literate, with a warm sense of humor. At one point she even gave a brilliant layman's lecture on the differences between homosexuality, transvestitism (99 percent of which, I was astonished to learn, is heterosexual), and transsexuality, where one is born with an underdeveloped psyche, biochemistry, genetic structure and sexual apparatus of the opposite sex. Cavett couldn't resist one last pun on the sexual organ bit. "I'm not sure I grasp that."

In *Myra Breckinridge*, Gore Vidal says "the relationship between consumer and advertiser is the last demonstration of *necessary* love in the West, and its principal form of expression is the television commercial." I wonder what Dick Cavett's early-morning consumers thought when, after interviewing Christine Jorgensen, he broke for a Niagara Starch commercial called "The First Drag Race for Women."

Don't miss *Jesse Owens Returns To Berlin.* Painstakingly produced, written and directed by Bud Greenspan, this is one sports special that transcends the label and becomes a moving and profound human document. Jesse Owens, in case you've forgotten, is the son of an Alabama tenant farmer who became one of the world's greatest athletes, bringing fame, honor, and pride to America in 1936 when he won four gold medals at the Berlin Olympics. More important, he at the same time practically single-handedly destroyed Hitler's mad Nazi myth of Aryan superiority by beating all the other racers and winning the love and respect of even the German athletes. Recorded by hundreds of cameras, the event is recreated here with added footage of Owens today, at 55, returning to the scene of his former triumphs in a divided Berlin. Hitler is gone and Owens is still around, to prove the point even better.

The show features wonderful atmosphere of the pomp and monstrous circumstance of marching swastikas as the young Negro athlete with stars and stripes on his track uniform waits on the sidelines without fanfare.

Best shots: the American team passing in review and tipping their hats instead of giving the customary Nazi salute and Hitler fuming as Owens swept all the honors for America. (He later refused to shake the Negro's hand.) The moment when the American flag goes up and the band plays "The Star Spangled Banner" is so thrilling it sends ice water down the old cervix.

Today, with all the black athletes boycotting the 1968 Olympics, Owens's story has added significance. The friendly field of healthy competition is the one place where bigotry doesn't count. Facing Hitler and winning fairly proved more than today's insane black power leaders will ever prove. According to Owens, athletes should hang their political and social prejudices on the line, go to the Olympics and show the world what the brotherhood of man is really all about. Wonderful man, wonderful show.

April 5, 1968

Dull television weeks produce dull television columns, and this had to be one of the most disastrous weeks in the history of the medium. I think what we had was a failure to communicate. Pet Clark did a special that was anything but special, a man played a broom on *The Dick Cavett Show* and elsewhere the dial was full of reruns of old shows that were all terrible in the first place. You know it had to be boring when the most exciting event was President Johnson's televised decision to leave politics to the politicians and head for the hills of Possum Pie Land. It was the only performance of the week that deserved an Emmy.

David Susskind momentarily relieved the tedium with a Sunday night show on the silly and pathetic lives of male models, in which the pungent observation was made that Jockey short models make more money than General Westmoreland does commanding the forces in Vietnam. Four ripe Revlon-bronzed faces from glossy magazines sat on the panel—three vanilla ice creams and one tutti frutti—expounding on the skin game. All of them admitted making $50 an hour posing in a $200 suit was a better way to compensate for having nothing better to do in life than driving a cab or slinging beans. "I want to be an actor, but the problem with modeling is that nobody takes me seriously," said one, getting in a plug for any agents who might be watching. "Maybe that's because you assume an acute narcissism," flashed David, obviously amused by being surrounded by so much peacock vanity.

One model admitted self-conscious eroticism in the TV cigarette commercials. "When you're smoking, you don't think about smoking, you think something lewd and lascivious." (Maybe that explains why most of the cigarette commercials are so unbearable.) They all had different opinions on what a model's hardest job is. One said it was the ability to withstand pain, like being tied to things with your hands behind your back. (He didn't tell where you had to go to catch his work. Shucks.) Another said it was getting thrown by a horse in cowboy commercials. A third admitted the hardest job was changing clothes in Central Park without getting arrested for indecent exposure. Oh, it makes you wonder how they get up in the morning.

After reading Cleveland Amory's enthusiastic review in last week's *TV Guide*, I was anxious to catch *Rowan and Martin's Laugh-In*, NBC's new Monday night comedy show. Unfortunately, I did catch it and although if sanity prevails I will never see it again, I must admit it does seem like the best reason I can think of for spending Monday night out at the movies. People pour water all over each other and rip each other's clothes off, men drop their pants at every opportunity, and a hideously unfeminine assortment of women who look like prostitutes and B-girls sing songs and tell glaringly unfunny jokes about sex. These sour little vignettes are pasted together with Silly Putty right out of *Hellzapoppin*, consisting of ludicrous sight gags (the eyes on a girl's bikini bra suddenly wink), knock-knock jokes that went out of style in high school, prepubic name jokes ("If Shirley Temple Black married Tyrone Power, her name would be Shirley Black Power"), and one-line urps so old they are hairy: "One fly to the other fly: Hey buddy, your man's showing." "Boris says the elections in South Vietnam were so successful LBJ is thinking of running THERE." "I went to the movies last night and had to move three times before anyone bothered me." Between cream pies and naked men taking showers under girls with watering cans, news flashes dart across the bottom of the screen in Times Square fashion: "Sophia Loren Injured by Accordion." "It's a boy for the Laurence Harveys." There was one lonely grin when Ruth Buzzi, a Flaming Thirties type who looks like the second lead in an old Preston Sturges movie, stood on a penthouse roof singing "Oh, I'm falling . . ." and fell off the roof. Otherwise, it was Pukesville all the way home.

This hysterical excuse for comedy looks like it was dreamed up by hacks who had frontal lobotomies performed in 1935. The skits are right out of old *Collier's* cartoons and are performed by fools who seem perfectly content to do anything for money. Most of it is in rotten, smutty bad taste and some of it is a great deal worse than that. The only gags on this show are the sounds of the audience being sick to its stomach.

The worst thing about *The Danny Thomas Hour* is Danny Thomas, who narrates his dramas by reading badly written bridges between scenes. But I was optimistically willing to watch anything that followed *Rowan and Martin's Laugh-In* just to relieve the bad taste. Monday night Thomas introduced a slick little fiction about big-time New York journalism and a female press agent who wages war against the slimy columnist of a scandal sheet who blackmails clients with sordid secrets from Gestapo files hidden in the wall.

It was a silly show, but like I said, anything was better than *Rowan and Martin's Laugh-In*. And some of it was funnier too, like Michael Rennie's line, "He's the blackmailing boil on the nose of the free American press," and Thomas's annoying interruptions at tense moments to say things like "Well, Stacey McCall has just lost another client, now she may even lose her own life." Like a Bernard Geis novel, the show also provided a lot of fun trying to figure out who everyone was. Was Barry Sullivan Walter Winchell or Dorothy Kilgallen? Was Michael Rennie Ed Sullivan? And what about Carolyn Jones (very good, by the way), the brave New York press agent who valiantly fights injustice? Was she really Betty Lee Hunt?

For some strange reason, ABC felt the urge to repeat the Mia Farrow *Johnny Belinda*. Several Mia defenders have pointed out to me that this was her finest performance. They were absolutely right. She didn't say one word during the entire show.

Hollywood

April 12, 1968

The only difference between watching television in Hollywood and New York is that you watch it more in Hollywood because there's nothing else to do. This week the Academy Awards got all the attention, but there were a few other things going on.

Like a nauseating parade of gutless "specials" that were singularly and collectively pointless, humorless, and uninspired:

(1) The genius of Michel Legrand, conducting an orchestra that sounded like three hundred graduates from the Paris Conservatoire, in lethal front-line combat with the Electric Prunes almost saved Dick Van Dyke's second CBS special. But not quite. A heavy hand conducted the comedy routines, which kept getting in the way. Five writers were listed for the hackneyed revue sketches. I hope they have paid-up unemployment insurance.

(2) Rural R.F.D. route shut-ins and cable subscribers who watch television between capsule culture clipped with pinking shears from the *Reader's Digest* doubtlessly had a grand old time on the Wayne Newton special on ABC, but it was hell on more eclectic tastes. Called *One More Time*, its gimmick was to bring back people from the old-age home of pop recording stars to revive petrified hit records of the past, providing at the same time a chance for rubber-faced Wayne Newton to mess them all up again. The show did more than revive old songs. It also revived memories of algebra books, juke boxes, sock hops in the gymnasium after basketball practice, and nectar sodas after Esther Williams movies with that whatever-happened-to girl from down the block. But depressingly enough, it also reminded me of how hideously awful those songs were in the first place and bringing back gallumphing old war horses like Frankie Laine and seedy Johnnie Ray or toneless bellowers like Kay Starr and Louis Jordan (remember the Tympany Five?) only made things worse. Even the camp value of such a period horror was sadly minimized by the revolting appearance every third chorus by the star of the show, Wayne Newton, a pie-faced choirboy soprano who looks like a preadolescent parking lot attendant with the gout.

(3) ABC's Ernie Kovacs special provided one last look at scenes

clipped from old Ernie Kovacs specials directed, produced, dreamed up, and written by Ernie Kovacs. If you were not an Ernie Kovacs fan to begin with, you were automatically in trouble. If you were a 50/50 borderline Ernie Kovacs observer (like me) you were probably alternately bored and amused. I was both. The Nairobi Trio and the omnipresent somnambula of Kovacs as Percy Dovetails, man nebbish, left me colder than ever but I did enjoy certain flashes of cleverness he used to have, like setting stage props to music. As a legacy, I guess Ernie Kovacs has left behind a startling blend of the routine, the ridiculous, and the lyrical. Strange man, half-interesting hour.

(4) Alan King's special on NBC was merely vulgar, witless, and dull (as usual) and obviously meant to be seen while chewing bubble gum. More spoofs, blackout skits, and satires than Malibu has mussels. Gurus, Japanese karjitsu, TV, Medicare, the Oscars, the Ku Klux Klan, and Britishers were the targets and the viewers were the victims. The more I see of television variety specials, the more I agree with James Agee, who once wrote, "Vaudeville is dead. I wish to God someone would bury it."

April 19, 1968

Funny how times are always catching up with each other. In 1953, when *The Robe* was unleashed on an unsuspecting public, Hollywood was trying to get even with television for keeping people out of the movie houses to watch wonderful programs like *Studio One* or *Philco Playhouse* or *The United States Steel Hour*. Now television is no longer wonderful and just to prove it, the networks are cluttering up the dials with all kinds of B movies. Ironically, it's the movies that are gaining from the backlash.

The Robe, for example, may have been one of the worst movies ever made, but no matter how bad it was, it was worse on television. Maybe Hollywood knew what it was doing all along. The faulty color processing on this hammy epic was not preserved, so the specially introduced DeLuxe Color ended up on the home screen looking like the sepia tone in an old Hopalong Cassidy western. And Cinemascope, the now-outdated but then specially invented screen process people lined up at the box office to watch unravel before their astonished eyes in 1953, chopped up the picture so much by the time it was sifted through the boob tube that actor's heads and arms were severed and panoramic scenes in vineyards and palaces resulted in closeups of rocks and chairs with the people on both ends missing.

As for *The Robe*, what can be said of a movie in which Jean Simmons refers to Christ's Crucifixion clothes on the cross by saying, "Come on, Marcellus Gallio, are you going to let this Robe come between our love?" Half Virginia Hills passion play, half Joe Levine–Steve Reeves spectacular, this is the kind of phony biblical opus in which you know immediately the good guys from the bad guys because the good guys hear heavenly choirs conducted by Alfred Newman and the bad guys are all personal friends of Caligula.

It's hard to know where to place the blame: 20th Century-Fox, for not burning the negative; or television, where so much cheap junk already crowds the air nobody is likely to notice. Either way, *The Robe* was a special Easter Sunday insult from ABC. Let's hope it doesn't get to be an annual tradition.

Speaking of cheap junk, NBC just had to rerun *Movin' with Nancy*, billed as the "full-hour musical spectacular that won Nancy Sinatra the coveted Hollywood Star of Tomorrow award." Bull. Hollywood's casting couches must have busted their springs, because this show was so god-awful it boggles the imagination. I don't mind a singer being bad if she's bad with style. Nancy Sinatra has hair like mildewed moss and there is so much mascara circling her eyes she looks like she's going to break out any second and warn everybody about Dunsinane. Money she's got. Style she ain't. On *Movin' with Nancy*, she was nothing but a hash-slinger slumming it up in an Andy Warhol movie. And no matter how hard she tries to showcase her voice, no matter how many top musicians she hires, no matter how many different types of songs she adds to her repertoire, or how much money she shells out to her arrangers, her palsied voice comes no closer to resembling real singing than milk from a coconut comes to resembling milk from a Jersey cow. And yet she survives, a girl with absolutely no conceivable talent recognizable to the human eye or ear, while girls who can perform circles around her drop by the wayside. Why? The only two reasons I can think of are (1) nepotism and (2) bad taste.

First her father's record company has poured a small fortune into promoting and publicizing her boots off. (Don't brush aside too hastily the importance of the Sinatra name, bankroll, and influence.) Although she possesses none of her Dad's musical knowledge or talent (incredible that she could have grown up around it with none of it rubbing off), it's a sorry fact we're all going to have to face that she has never had to struggle. (When you struggle, you learn and develop, and Nancy Sinatra has never had time for that.) And finally, after having her stuffed down their throats with every Sunday newspaper supplement and every morning cup of coffee and in every drive to the office or the P.T.A. on the car radio (disc jockeys being the worst perpetrators of junk music in the world), the public seems to have decided the hell with it. Just listen. It's better than flipping the dial and you can wear yourself out searching for something better.

And so, dear fellow sufferers, we're stuck with something implacable, immovable, and here to stay called Nancy Sinatra. And if there is anything more excruciatingly unendurable than listening to her records, it's watching her on television. In her hands, songs become weapons. "Jackson," which she sang with Lee Hazelwood, is a chunky, good-natured song. She reached a plateau of hillbilly nasality on this song that didn't have any trouble matching her ability, although I fear it must have seemed insulting to genuine hillbillies to hear their music hacksawed to death by a swinger from PJ's on the Sunset Strip who seems about as much at home in spurs as a tortilla in Alaska. Whoever wrongly advised her, however, to attempt a complicated and vocally difficult song like "Who Will Buy?" should have his charge account canceled in Vegas. In fact, everyone connected with this disaster should sue, including the very mysterious "very close relative" who all but butchered "Younger Than Springtime." But then again, I guess the strain of working with so miniscule a talent on so bland a project as *Movin' with Nancy* was enough to ruin anybody's reputation. Even Frank sounded like an amateur.

The third *Jacques Cousteau Underwater Special* on ABC was an educational and entertaining delight. This time the Calypso ship journeyed to Europa, an uninhabitable stone island two hundred miles off the coast of Madagascar in the Indian Ocean, where the great green sea turtles, older in lineage than dinosaurs, guide themselves each year through centuries of marvelous instinctive memories to mate and lay their eggs. Year after year they swim thousands of miles to this hideous eyesore, do the dance of love, form a line, come ashore at dawn, build their holes in the sand, lay piles of eggs that remain in the sand for sixty days, then leave the baby turtles to crawl back to the ocean alone, trying to escape the murderous angular frigate birds that prey on them like vultures. By the end of the show, I had spent so much time in the strange turtle world they were like lovable, clumsy friends and it was even more moving to see Cousteau's crew trying to save the lives of the mother turtles who, exhausted from giving labor, often blunder into roots where, unable to crawl backward, they bake in the sun and are eaten alive by hermit crabs. Damnedest thing you ever saw, and I hope you did.

April 26, 1968

The Oscars may have been a fiasco, but the Tony Awards show on NBC proved that Hollywood has no monopoly on turning extravaganzas into bile. Broadway can't stage 'em much better. Producer Alexander Cohen is a man of taste and talent, but the success of last year's stylish Tony show must have gone to his head. This year he tried to stage a circus and ended up with a freak sideshow. Proving, of course, that a stage crammed full of fabulous stars is not enough to make the theater anything more than a word in search of a definition. Cohen had the stage and some of the biggest stars in the world and he still blew it.

To me, the Tonys always represented the hardest wall in the theater to scale, the biggest goal in the theater to reach, the greatest height in the theater to achieve. This year they lost their importance and lost their value. Tonys were tossed around like Crackerjacks to flop shows, mediocre talents, and worse, to people who have nothing whatsoever to do with the theater. In addition, the Tony show was poorly written, clumsily thrown together and too long. Peter Ustinov looked apoplectic and kept apologizing for the whole affair. Angela Lansbury was supposed to be the evening's hostess and although she looked sunny and dazzling and as good enough to eat as a chilled lemon sherbet on a hot summer day as she explained how the Tonys are meaningful awards and not just a popularity contest (have at thee, Oscar!), we kept seeing more of Jack Benny than Angela Lansbury. WHY? I like Jack Benny, but what does he have to do with the theater?

Then the first award (set design) went to *Rosencrantz and Guildenstern*, a show with a bare stage. OOPS. Things were already off to a bad start.

Then Onna White's sensational Greek dances in *Illya Darling* lost out in the choreography awards to Gower Champion's balloons. "I don't know how to break this news to Clive Barnes," said Champion. Neither do I, especially since the award was followed by two numbers from his show which were awful enough to keep people out of the Broadway theater for the next ten years. Robert Goulet, the most Italian-sounding French Canadian I've ever heard, sang "The Happy Time," followed by all three stars of the show hitting enough flats on "A Certain Girl" to set my teeth on edge. (Strange choices to show from a show whose only show-stopper —"Without Me"—was nowhere to be seen.)

None of Ustinov's feeble attempts to explain the "special" Tony to Audrey Hepburn made any sense. She looked ravishing and spoke eloquently (misreading the cue cards a few times) but any way you look at it a Tony award to Audrey Hepburn for deserting the theater for more money in Hollywood is still preposterous. If you're going to start giving Tonys to all the movie stars who once appeared on Broadway at the beginnings of their careers, you might as well give out three thousand automatic Tonys next week and get it over with. It looked like nothing more than a sickly excuse to inject some big-time glamour into the show and get a bigger rating by bringing on names the great unwashed public could identify, since most of the theater names nominated this year were total unknowns to anyone west of Trenton. And if anyone has an eye on ratings, it's Alex Cohen, who knows the value of keeping a sponsor like Eastern Airlines happy. I can spot politics when I see politics in action.

Equally unexplainable was Gregory Peck's appearance, Marlene Dietrich's Tony for consenting to grace Broadway with her one-woman show after cursing and avoiding it for twenty years, Maurice Chevalier's sentimental Tony for passing his eightieth birthday, David Merrick's Tony (for doing what?), and a Tony to the brilliant APA Repertory Company, which is denied eligibility in the awards by rule. (This in itself shows how foolish the whole megilla is, and I loved Helen Hayes for reminding everybody of the fact in a ladylike way.) I don't know why the Tonys even bother to have rules at all, since they were all broken. Replacements are not eligible, yet a Tony was presented to Pearl Bailey, a replacement. Ridiculous! Off-Broadway shows are not allowed to win Tonys, yet the best musical of the year (*Your Own Thing*) was presented off-Broadway while the Best Musical award went to *Hallelujah Baby!*, a flop disaster that isn't even running anymore. Insulting!

This brings up the subject of musicals, a category so ludicrous in a year in which not one respectable musical opened on Broadway it should have been eliminated. "Broadway just somehow has the knack," said Miss Lansbury. Whoever forced her to say that line should have been run out of town on a fence. The musical numbers on the show were so bad they were laughable and so obviously embarrassingly second-rate, Cohen had to prevail upon shows from other years to provide decent enough entertainment to get everybody through the night without being laughed out of the theater. Everybody kept talking about *Hallelujah Baby!* as though it still existed. Then the Best Musical Actress award (which, within all realms of sanity, should have gone to Melina Mercouri for providing the stage with its only single musical performance of any major importance last season) went to not only one but two women in flops that already closed months ago. How do you explain that? And while you're at it, Alex, how do you explain the fact that both Mike Nichols and Tom Stoppard had already prepared acceptance speeches filmed in Europe for their awards? This made the whole business of the sealed, protected envelopes a joke. Not even the Oscars would sink low enough to hoke up chicanery that blatant. Sandy Dennis provided the most honest moment of the evening when she nearly choked of embarrassment admitting that Nichols was not there, but had already accepted his Best Director award in Rome. (Switch to a video tape of Nichols gloating over his Tony.) It seems the Golden Globes aren't the only awards that should be investigated.

No provisions were made for winners who didn't show up, leaving presenters like Anne Jackson and Shirley Booth to ad-lib their way out of embarrassing predicaments with egg on their faces. It was shocking that Cohen had not warned them ahead of time, since the winners didn't seem to be a secret. (Don't forget two winners had just been shown accepting on film.) Stars were introduced merely for the purpose of introducing other stars, who in turn introduced more stars. (Get those glamour names in there, fellows, don't forget Big Brother at the ad agency is watching.)

And the most unfortunate guests of the night were the poor wretches who were unlucky enough to get stuck onstage with Groucho Marx. Marx's appearance alone was a monument to amateurish rudeness and arrogant bad taste. Acceptance speeches are very big moments for people who win, and fools should not be allowed onstage to make fun of them. Groucho was insulting, ridiculous, and damnably unfunny and had no business being there. If Alexander Cohen ever throws an outrageous fake like that into the Tony awards again, I promise to be there personally to picket the theater. But then again, if he continues to allow the Groucho Marxes of the world to demean, cheapen, and muck up the Tonys any more than the depths to which they sank this year, the day will soon come when they won't be held in a theater at all. They'll be held at the Lambs Club.

May 3, 1968

Either I'm growing mellow, or the producers of stale TV musicals have been reading this column, because the past two weeks have seen a happy improvement in the quality of year-end entertainment specials. Recipe for curing what's wrong with TV specials: get Frank Sinatra, Ella Fitzgerald, and Antonio Carlos Jobim, give them an hour to wail their noses off, and get out of the way.

A Man and His Music gets my vote as the best musical hour of the year and NBC made up for boring everybody half to death with Nancy Sinatra's icky special by repeating it and, consequently, reminding us all how good TV can be when the pros take over from the hacks. Sinatra sang a hauntingly beautiful "Ol Man River" (a song I always snobbishly thought only William Warfield could sing) and revealed more truth about himself than any of his movies have ever shown: the lines in the face, the fatigue that goes with being a swinger who is too old to be a swinger, hitting the notes on their round little noggins like croquet balls.

The camera work (slow, bluesy effects superimposing head shots over body shots of Ella singing "Body and Soul") added mood and dimension to her singing, bringing back camera styles reminiscent of the much-lamented great Bobby Troup *Stars of Jazz* show. (Please, somebody, bring it back.) The byplay and casual conversation were sometimes scratchy (Ella should never talk), but when Ella and Frank sang "Goin' Out of My Head" together, magic happened.

The best was yet to come: Ella, scatting her way to Heaven on "Stompin' at the Savoy" and Sinatra sitting in an easy chair, smoking his sad cigarette and swinging Bossa Nova gingerly with the dazzling guitar clusters of Jobim wrapping his voice in a hammock of stars. Sinatra has never been in better voice or better company. No ring-a-ding-ding here. No dirty jokes from Sammy or Joey or Dino in the background to break up the concentration. Just sheer, beautiful, gutsy singing, hitting his audience over the head with his heart. It was the perfect formula for combining good taste with commercial marketability in packaging an entertainer for television, and I wish NBC would show it once a week.

Andy Williams's NBC special, *The H. Andrew Williams Kaleidoscope Co.*, wasn't bad either. Andy has been a square so long, he really tried to get with the times at last and the result was a tasty hour that showed how photographically and musically imaginative TV can be with brains behind the cameras instead of behind the desks. Like a kaleidoscope, the show kept visually changing patterns of sound and song like fun house mirrors, splitting into two and three images at one time while a backdrop of sliding panels like colored fabrics from Betsy Johnson dresses created a carnival of optical effects.

The Raelettes were there, swaying hips, flying hands and all. Ray Charles was a dynamo, making even a twelve-inch TV screen rock with emotion like it was opening night at the Copacabana. Simon and Garfunkel provided a tender and moving montage of old age, using action film and still photographs set to beautiful music from their new *Bookends* album. Draped in a diaphanous gown on a strange Guggenheim Museum-type stool, Mama Cass displayed all of her glorious lard in its solo TV debut, singing a very confusing song about a man in paisley drip dry suits who sweeps his floor with a melancholy broom. And any show would be worth watching just for a glimpse of Burt Bacharach conducting his own music. He swings. He jumps. He socks imaginary tennis balls. He seems always on the verge of sprouting helicopter wings.

Even the commercials were great. What looked like one hundred housewives crawled out of holes in the ground and escaped from a barbed-wire concentration camp to head straight for a finger-lickin' Kentucky fried chicken stand, and that beautiful, frightfully brainy Phyllis Kirk (too talented and bright to waste on commercials) took a cookie cutter, cut a hole right out of her kitchen carpet, and repaired it right before my eyes. By dawg. I don't know how many new Viking kitchen carpets she sold to housewives, but I'm convinced Phyllis Kirk could sell electric heaters in the Sahara Desert. She sure sold me.

I also enjoyed *Hallelujah Leslie!* on ABC, more for Leslie Uggams's passionate singing than anything else. The show itself was a thunderbolt of music, without those insulting comic skits that never come off, yet the attempt to give everything a "theme" often resulted in a strange mixture of misguided staging and curiously unmotivated settings for songs (Leslie in gold lamé on top of what looked like a United Nations Conference table singing "Goldfinger" to organ music). But there was a flash of choreographic brilliance to one wonderful rock segment that blended music and industrial power with a very sensual arrangement of "Groovy" sung to the sound of engines, hammers, saws, and pick axes.

Leslie sang "My Man" to the tune of "A Man and a Woman." Robert Morse clowned around in drag in a tomato-red muu-muu looking like Elsa Lanchester in *The Bride of Frankenstein*. Noel Harrison sang off-key and had the animation of a cadaver. A leather-jacketed Hell's Angels ballet troupe cracked tire chains and whips to "What the World Needs Now is Love." People sang in crystal balls and revolved to psychedelic strobe lights. And Leslie looked yummy. On the Tony Awards show everybody kept talking about how awful she looked and I must admit that seven-foot-high mass of tight fuzzy curls did make her resemble one of the guards at Buckingham Palace. But on her own special, she wore all the right wigs and lit up the screen every time she appeared, which, fortunately, was often.

After my recent mention of Hollywood columnist Rona Barrett, several people have pointed out to me that she is really a very nice lady underneath those untrimmed false eyelashes. I'm sure she is, but her news broadcasts on ABC are still wildly funny. One night last week I had barely recovered from her announcement that "Garbo went to the Factory and enjoyed the graffiti on the wall of the men's room" when Rona flashed a scoop: "Friends, Anna Maria Alberghetti is not dead, it's Anna Maria Mussolini!" You gotta admit it keep things jumping on the 11 o'clock news.

May 10, 1968

Gawd Bless Amurrka!" scowled LBJ, and they were off and running. Irving Berlin, music's token to apple pie and United States war bonds, was eighty years old, and Ed Sullivan knocked the history of Sunday night out of whack by coming on thirty minutes early to throw a ninety-minute party. Out of the woodwork came Fred Waring, whose Pennsylvanians slugged out Emma Lazarus's poem "Give Me Your Tired, Your Poor" between arty camera shots of the Statue of Liberty. The little immigrant from Mulberry Street had quite a night listening to nearly forty of his songs bounced, swung, grooved, danced, crooned, shing-a-linged, and all but mutilated by everyone from Bing Crosby to Diana Ross and the Supremes. Like most Ed Sullivan shows, it lacked style, precision, and glamour, but unlike most Ed Sullivan shows, it was entertaining. Ed mispronounced several names, technicians walked accidentally across the screen, and although we were saved from elephants, jugglers, and sadistic puppets, there was one curiously out-of-place vaudeville team called Morecambe and Wise, which should remain England's problem, not ours. Robert Goulet murdered three Berlin songs—"The Song is Ended," "All By Myself," and "All Alone"—with no help from anybody. Goulet is a marvelous performer onstage, within the context of a role, but standing center stage with a hand mike belting out love songs, he might as well be doing "The Star Spangled Banner" in the middle of Madison Square Garden.

All was not lost, however: Ethel Merman did an *Annie Get Your Gun* medley with enough energy to get the first rocket to Jupiter. Berlin himself was shown in an old Warner Brothers film clip singing "Oh How I Hate to Get Up in the Morning." Wonderful nostalgic moments from old Berlin movies showed Fred Astaire and Ginger Rogers dancing "Cheek to Cheek," Dennis Morgan doing a big furry Busby Berkeley number from *The Great Ziegfeld*, Bing Crosby singing "Blue Skies" to Joan Caulfield, and Judy Garland, looking like a strawberry sundae, walking down Fifth Avenue in *Easter Parade*. They were all better than the live talent. Harry James played dance music on a petrified trumpet (it's just not the same since he's not married to Betty Grable anymore) and Peter Gennaro stopped the show with a dazzling precision dance drill to "This Is the Army." At the end of the show, a cake with eighty candles came out on wheels and everybody in my living room placed bets that Kate Smith would pop out as a secret surprise guest and sing "God Bless America." She didn't. I guess it would be hard to keep Kate Smith a secret.

There's a hot pilot floating around ABC these days and everyone who has seen it is very excited. It has something to do with a new plan to jazz up the news and give NBC's Huntley-Brinkley and CBS's Walter Cronkite competition. The pilot covers everything from riots to nude male modeling to an interview with Dustin Hoffman. The object is to insert immediacy, theatricality, and back-of-the-book magazine features into ABC's regular news coverage, taking advantage of what the medium can do that newspapers cannot. In addition to regular news and political coverage, ABC plans to use guest columnists like Jimmy Breslin and Irv Kupcinet to line up pieces on everything from fashions to personality profiles. With ABC White House correspondent Frank Reynolds as anchor man, the campaign to rehaul the ABC evening news goes into effect May 27 on all ABC affiliates across the country who elect to carry it.

As for the Republican and Democratic nominating conventions, ABC has signed Gore Vidal and William F. Buckley, Jr., as special commentators to deliver ninety-minute summaries during the three-ring circuses. ("We expect some disagreement between them," says ABC news president Elmer Lower.) I'll say. It may be chaotic, but it won't be dull. And it all sounds like a great idea for getting viewers who never watch the news back in front of their TV dials this summer. Who knows? They might even learn something.

I finally caught up with CBS's new private eye show, *Mannix*. Like Gypsy's strippers, I thought all TV series had to have a gimmick to separate them from each other and give them some kind of identity. Not *Mannix*. This one copies everything from old Sam Spade radio plots to the movie hipness of *Harper* to TV's *Peter Gunn*. Instead of an organization called Interpol, *Mannix* features a new agency called Interact. Otherwise, it's the same old warmed-over yesterday's mashed potatoes. Not the least upsetting thing about *Mannix* is Mannix himself, played by Mike Connors, a prepackaged instant-defrost Italian caballero from the Polo Lounge of the Beverly Hills Hotel with the class of a chianti cork and the style of a store window dummy at Robert Hall.

May 17, 1968

Gripe all you want to about the sorry state of television, but when CBS comes up with something like *Secrets*, the ninety-minute play by Pulitzer Prize-winning playright Tad Mosel which brightened the tube Wednesday night and made up for several months of quality-barren tears in the

Cyclops eye, it's time to send up flares. *Secrets* was moving, illuminating, sensitive, cinnamon-flavored television drama, acted with intimate brilliance, produced with style and care by Martin (*Playhouse 90*) Manulis, and directed with consummate skill and an economic eye for infinite detail by Paul Bogart. It was one of the best ninety minutes I've ever spent in front of my living-room screen and I feel sorry for anyone who missed it.

Secrets was about secrets. What they do to people. What they are. Who has them. Who should find out. What happens when they do. It was about a lot more than that, too, but the message was strong and pungent and hit the heart just under the left ventricle. There was Arthur Hill, giving the performance of his career, as Bryan ("Bry") Gray, a successful certified public accountant who, at first glance, looks ordinary and predictable. Yellow broadcloth button-down shirts and hound's tooth suits from Bloomingdale's, office at 10, work through lunch, Metrecal between phone calls, drink at 6, second drink at 6:30 to get him through dinner, in bed early. There was the wonderful wife, a Barbara Bel Geddes type (played by Barbara Bel Geddes), slightly butchy with the years, good stock, cares about people, attends psychology seminars to keep involved, talks a lot about "this day and age," and watches Walter Cronkite for riot reports. And there was the sensitive bloomlike daughter, terribly chic and current, long stringy hair, slightly Leftish navy blue boutique dresses, very hip talk, searching for whatever it is out there past Radcliffe. One day mister-slightly-square-*New York Times* gets called for jury duty on a case involving an actress who has attempted to murder her homosexual son. Great shots of procedures in jury rooms and judge's chambers. It's all very exciting to the widow upstairs (played delicately priggishly by Katherine Bard, who never seems to get good parts anymore unless she works for her husband Martin Manulis, who produced *Secrets*—which, as it turns out, is one time I'm all for nepotism). It's all very exciting to everybody, it seems, except Bry. When he hears the name of the defendant—"Janet Ferguson"—he refuses to serve and gets himself disqualified from jury duty for private reasons that he insists will influence his ability to arrive at a fair and impartial verdict as a juror.

In the face of family and community curiosity, "What do you know about Bry?" becomes the key question. People who never noticed him before begin to suspect all sort of things. The wife, to whom he has been married for twenty-one years, who laments her daughter's boyfriend's name Warren because "you can't make a nickname out of it," and can't get to sleep at night until everybody's home, says, "I know him, I know my Bry."

But does anyone ever know anyone else? Bry won't give his reasons for refusing to serve on the jury. "Every once in awhile," he says, "just every once in awhile, there's something that must be private." Not good enough. "I didn't know that," says the wife. "I don't remember that part of the marriage ceremony." Curiosity begins to kill the cat. "There's a difference between privacy and secrecy," wails the wife, now building into a nagging frenzy, "privacy is when you shut the door while you dress. Secrecy is simply not being honest." Reputations are destroyed. To Bry's father, he was always a good boy. To his Army buddy and business partner (Barry Nelson, who revealed a flair for sensitive, analytical dramatic acting I never dreamed he had in him) he's a silent movie, a clam. After prying prattle over sherry, the wife's classroom textbook psychology breaks down the friend in a confusing, tearful admission of love for his wartime buddy. The statement could mean anything, but a lifetime friendship has been smashed. Secrets have revealed truths on the other side of the mirror that send people deeper into their patchwork quilt of guilt and suspicion. The wife begins to suspect homosexuality. The widow upstairs, to whom Bry is the nicest tenant in the building because he tips his hat, begins to suspect almost everything.

In time the secret comes out. Once, during World War II, Bry met an actress named Janet Ferguson and spent a ten-day furlough with her in a West Side walkup. Every day for ten days they went to a movie in which she had a bit part. That's all. Forgot the name of the movie, forgot the girl. When he finally meets the Janet Ferguson of the case, she is cheap, sleazy, a con-artist. (Played within a hair's-circumference of carnal, sideshow perfection by the multi-faceted, multi-talented Eileen Heckart, whose boundless energies, characterizations, and rainbow colors as an actress simply cannot be described by words alone: two scenes and she had me eating out of her Detchema-splashed palm.)

As it turns out, she's the wrong Janet Ferguson, but it's not important. What is important is the question raised by Tad Mosel's seemingly direct and simple but inwardly complex script: If a woman loves her husband, how much does she have a right to know? Isn't it curious how people always use the word "interested" as an excuse for checking up on each other? And, finally, the painful truth that people can live in one room together for years and be so many miles apart, so many years apart. A marriage license does not mean a title of ownership.

Finally, the wife is driven by hurt and pain into the hotel across the street from her apartment building to find out for herself what privacy means. What she learns is that she doesn't know anything, because you have nothing to be private about if there is nobody to share your privacy with. Otherwise, the word privacy simply means loneliness. She comes home, defeated, crying, and there is a simple but poignant reconciliation scene. Things will never be the same. The upstairs neighbor isn't speaking to them at all. The daughter has broken up with her boyfriend. Bry's buddy has left the firm on an unscheduled holiday, close to a nervous breakdown of self-doubt about his own masculinity. The sanctuary of marriage has become an open sore. Yet, somehow, things go on. "I'll never ask again, I promise," says Miss Bel Geddes. "And I promise if you do ask, I'll tell you," answers Mr. Hill. "Come to bed now. Everybody's home."

In the gentle beauty of its performances and the uncluttered sensibility of Tad Mosel's writing (he's still the best writer television ever produced, which proves how much the medium needs to forget all the hokum and chicanery it has spawned and get back to its roots), *Secrets* was compelling, suspenseful, and intelligent fare for people who still care where the medium is going. I applaud *CBS Playhouse* for making this kind of adult viewing possible in the face of all the commercial trash around it, and I salute General Telephone & Electronics for pouring money and support into turning out good taste with no commercial breaks to spoil the mood and bore everyone to death. Artistry is something seldom encountered on television. *Secrets* defined the word.

May 31, 1968

The best thing about *The Mothers-in-Law* is that it has its own built-in Red Cross kit. This is perhaps what separates it from *He and She,* a soppy cartoon bubble of a series on which the prognosis has already been announced negative and the patient has been left to bleed to death. Nobody expects television comedy to be anything more than lunatic slobber, but at least most shows should aim for attractive, funny, personable leading players to get them over the hurdles. On the balmiest day, *I Love Lucy, I Married Joan, Favorite Husband, Meet Millie,* and countless others could rely on the creative instincts of their leading players to pull the show (and the weary viewers) through. *He and She* has no such magical formula. Paula Prentiss, Dick Benjamin, and Jack Cassidy are not untalented, but they don't carry magic around in their thumbs for instant resuscitation, either. Their show needed adrenalin and they didn't deliver. It's been canceled.

The Mothers-In-Law, on the other hand, will survive. At least into the arms of next season. And I, for one, don't find the news too hard to take. Every time these mothers are in trouble because of one of their scripts (which, if my calculations are in any way accurate, is about 10 minutes after 8:30 E.S.T., every Sunday night) somebody pulls the emergency cord and the show's two resident nurses, Kaye Ballard and Eve Arden, get out their Band-Aids.

Last Sunday the dialogue was boring and straight-faced as ever, but Eve Arden did an instant Dietrich imitation on the back of a dining room chair and when things *really* sagged in the cellar direction (as they are wont to do often on this series), Kaye Ballard—who, in the zoo I live in, is considered by many to be the funniest woman ever captured alive by civilized man—played a flute and sang a rock song about a plumber à la Mama Cass, then threw her legs out of joint, extended her pinky in a petrified position and said, "Petah, Petah, give me the lettah!" "That's marvelous," said Eve. "Who was it?" panted Kayzie. "Doris Day!" Well, of course it's awful, but so is everything else that calls itself "domestic situation comedy" (a television term that actually allows everyone to talk in comic book balloons and get away with it). At least with these two nuts ad-libbing and improvising with a good solid background of two quick lefts to the funnybone behind them, the show *looks* a lot better than it really is. As long as lunatics with style keep bandaging its cuts and bruises, *The Mothers-In-Law* could run forever. Together, Arden and Ballard make NBC a painless place to be on Sunday nights.

Speaking of comedy, *The Carol Burnett Show* has, in my opinion, been the only consistently high-quality-level weekly variety show this year. Carol has enormous quantities of good taste and she is one of the few performers who showers the tube with it. This week she fractured me with a ravenously hyperthyroid skit by Kenny Solms and Gail Parent (talented, talented—they wrote the Johnson Wedding album with Fannie Flagg and the Miss America sketch in the current *New Faces* on Broadway) that satirized *The Dating Game*. The sight of Carol, a dreary spinster with thick glasses and hair in a bun who is terrified of men, her juices unleashed by the passionate horniness of the *Dating Game* show, leaning against the wall, her skirt falling below her thighs, climbing, panting, screeching, "Lemme at him, that's the one I want, that voice, lemme at him . . ." The mere thought of it now makes me chuckle.

Every week there is something unexpected and rather breathless to look for. There is a consistency of intelligence and wit on her show seldom encountered on the tube, and few of her attempts fail, mainly because she is one of the very few performers who brings to her work a wonderful vulnerability. When she falls on her nose, the bruise shows. You want her to get up and try all over again. Fortunately, she seldom has to, because she and her producer-husband Joe Hamilton have surrounded their show with people who know where it's at.

Until now, the only thing wrong with Carol has been too much talent and no way to channel it. There are as many sides to her ability as there are petals on a peony, yet none of them has ever been harnessed long enough to give the world a chance to know the lady behind the clown makeup better. She is probably the most genuinely funny comic in the great tradition of comics who make you laugh from the heart instead of the larynx since Lucille Ball rose to stardom in the Forties. She can out-belt Merman and over at Carnegie Hall word has it (from the stagehands who worked her concert with Julie Andrews there) that she can hold notes longer than anyone since Caruso. She can act with the pathos of all the children in the world who ever wanted to be somebody (I don't think I'll ever forget that ragamuffin usherette from the mezzanine at Loew's standing outside the MGM gates giving a tiny little Leo roar as she bottled up the desperation to be a "moom-pitcha star" in *Fade Out-Fade In,* a show which did its part to ruin her on Broadway). All of these qualities have sallied forth on Carol's weekly show, along with a new aspect of the Burnett personality: her ability to get inside a song and make it smile warmly.

For those not-yet-converted Burnett watchers who still think of her as a loud-mouthed soubrette with a buckboard bounce and too many teeth, *The Carol Burnett Show* provides a shiny opportunity to see an extraordinarily funny lady shine in ways never before exposed to the general public, subsidizing the practically bereft world of television comedy with some class for a change. For unabashed, hysterical Carol Burnett fans who don't need convincing (like me), it's simply rain from heaven in a season of drought.

June 7, 1968

With the summer terror coming in, television is turning its sights on the minorities who are always shouting they never get equal billing. If you got through the glop without skipping over to the crosswords, you probably noticed Jack Gould last Sunday in the *New York Times* pitching for a confrontation between Stokely Carmichael and the widow of the Rev. Dr. Martin Luther King, Jr., moderated by "Harry Belafonte, the singer." All over the dials, the networks are revamping their program schedules to include nonpartisan biracial news coverage. (Partially resulting, no doubt, from the enormous black eye recently given to the industry by President Johnson's National Advisory Committee on Civil Disorders, which reported to the federal government that the white television press is distrusted and held in contempt by blacks and the world offered to Negroes is predominantly white on television.)

So to shine up the old image, television is getting down to the nitty-gritty. Last Sunday in New York, an interesting new series debuted on the local ABC affiliate, Channel 7. *Like It Is* is the name and it promises lively reportage in representing the problems and solutions to them that concern the world in general and the million and a quarter Negroes and eight hundred thousand Puerto Ricans who form "The Other Society" of New York City in particular. The show is piloted by Robert Hooks and commentator Gil Noble. Each week they promise to go out into the streets, the alleys, and the garbage dumps to drag in stories that will possibly educate white Americans who still know nothing about anything outside their own immediate peer group.

On the first show, the stories were clumsy but well-meaning, and occasionally even entertainingly good journalism. There was a feature on Jackie McLean, the alto jazz saxophonist, blowing hot jazz into the purple night down at Slug's on the Lower East Side, then going home to a nearby housing project where he holds open house for neighborhood kids who want to learn music. It was interesting because it didn't gloss over or slick up a phony piece on some super-sexy Negro hero-image who lives in seven rooms with lots of rubber plants near Lincoln Center. This was a flesh-and-blood for-real Negro with problems. He can't make a living doing the thing he loves most and living in a natty housing development. But the smile on McLean's face was worth the back room at

Goody's as he worked at his counseling job with street urchins, teaching them how to beat drums and blow horns. It was a well-balanced feature: jazz is dying because it's black music, highly technical, very complex, and thousands of talented jazz musicians are walking the streets unable to work because they refuse to compromise their ideals and play rock junk. So, while some Negroes lose their jazz roots because of the trash-music takeover, others find ways to compensate, like refertilizing Negro youth with the love and technical knowhow of peace through music. Keeps 'em off the streets, too.

There was an East Harlem story about the combined efforts on East 97th Street to clean up a ghetto. Called "The Thing in the Spring," the cleanup campaign got so infectious the private citizens staged a pig-roast with music and every nationality pitched in. Instead of running from the ugliness, they came to beautify it. On the very block in which a woman was shot to death last summer in the riots, toddlers and matrons and nurses in white starchy uniforms and fat Poles and skinny Chinese boys and militant Negro teen-agers all worked side by side, carrying pails and paintbrushes and brooms, making beauty not war. Neighbors mixed their own concrete, planted shrubs, flowers, grass, and trees, and created a park on East 103d Street in one of New York's worst slums. One of the basements with thirty years of garbage was turned from a trash heap into a music center for neighborhood kids. By contrast, another street between Park and Madison was shown, still a jumble of rats, disease, and danger. Incredible! And only because the neighbors on this particular block didn't care enough to want the very best. This is where the children of the slums play their games and live out their childhoods and, unfortunately, learn about the kind of life that molds their minds for later years.

The most interesting feature on the show involved the pitfalls awaiting Negro models. Helena Brooks Nash, who runs an all-Negro modeling agency, brought along two perfectly gorgeous Negro girls and one very handsome all-American Negro boy and they were great. They named names and labeled prejudiced manufacturers of commercial brand products. They look superb, yet the only market open to them is *Ebony*. "Why can't we get into *Vogue* and *Harper's Bazaar*?" they demanded. Why indeed. They put the blame on the toothpaste ads ("Maclean's won't hire girls with black skin!"), beauty ads ("We use rinses on our hair to highlight, but Clairol only hires blondes!"), and prejudiced booking agents. They can't do voiceovers and they seldom get Grade A commercials on television unless they are used as token Negroes in the background during a crowd scene. They are top models, they deserve to hit the top. Yet where a white girl gets $30–$80,000 a year, Negro models have to settle for $5–$10,000 as a top salary. I wanted to hear more, but Hooks hushed them up (maybe they were getting phone calls from Maclean's and Clairol) and switched to a very unfortunate segment involving Billy Daniels (yes, he's alive and well and living in Beulah Land) who plugged a revolting song called "Maybe God Is Black." Revolting because it was ugly and badly written and smacked of commercial hard-sell. "Maybe in that great beyond, God may be a Heavenly blonde . . ." Must have been written by a gag writer for the *Laugh-In*. It had about that much class.

If *Like It Is* sticks to its guns and avoids flashy guests with hit records, it may have something. The models looked pretty disgusted after being cut off before their story was over and I don't blame them. That wasn't telling it like it is. Future weeks promise LeRoi Jones, a look at Negro culture, and a trip to the inside of the peanut butter jar down at Resurrection City in Washington. Stay tuned.

Elsewhere, Diahann Carroll is readying her fall series about a real, honest-to-pete widowed registered nurse raising a small son and having healthy, normal love interests with all sorts of healthy, normal men. (Maybe even white?) Negro actor Otis Young will be a post-Civil War ex-slave turned bounty hunter in *The Outcasts* on ABC. Don Marshall will be the Negro hero of a science fiction series about a land of giant anthropoids called *Land of the Giants* (what else?) on ABC. Clarence Williams, III, will be the third member of a hippie undercover police team on *The Mod Squad* on ABC, CBS will air seven *Of Black America* documentaries beginning July 2 and ABC will do six hour specials about every aspect of black vs. white relationships. Looks like a provocative time ahead, both in living color and compatible black and white. I hope.

June 14, 1968

Like hot lunches for orphans, field trips should be prescribed for critics. Most theater critics know absolutely nothing about the stage (as the current state of drama criticism aptly proves), and few movie critics have ever even worked as extras. Television criticism requires the least amount of intelligence and experience because the medium itself, like a gigantic amateur bank night at the local picture show, produces the least amount of intelligence at the hands of people who often appear to be totally inexperienced themselves. Still, I wanted a bit of experience in the medium just to see up close on a major network show if things were as chaotic, undisciplined and silly backstage as they appear on camera. I picked the Johnny Carson *Tonight* show, a near-fatal mistake to begin with since it has always been my personal conviction that Carson is the most overrated amateur since Evelyn and Her Magic Violin. As it turned out, I was right.

It took six months to get on. This show is so picky you almost have to show your birth certificate. Exceptions are made, of course, for really hot items like murderers and Tiny Tim, but if you want THEM and they don't want YOU, forget it.

A host of baffled bystanders called "talent coordinators" constantly stand by to confuse the guest and each other. One talent coordinator gets excited, interviews the guest for a couple of hours, then rushes into Carson Conference Meetings with a handful of notes, only to get shot down in the meeting by the other talent coordinators or Carson himself, whose list of prejudices against would-be guests runs to Catalina and back. ("Check Johnny first," is a key phrase backstage.)

Sometimes guests get right up to the starting gate before their race is canceled. Actress Carol White was interviewed for an afternoon once, then told she could be on the show if she went home and memorized the lyrics to three Cockney songs. When she got to the studio that night, she discovered she had been canceled at the last minute by New Orleans District Attorney Jim Garrison (a hot Carson "special").

I got canceled once a week for six months. Finally, I was accepted because I had a book to peddle. This meant another hour interview, because the one thing Carson cannot do is interview anyone cold. He simply doesn't care that much about people to find out about them himself. His talent coordinators do that.

Mysterious phone calls. "Mr. X will not be doing your interview; it will be handled by Miss Y." Ten minutes later the phone rings again. "Disregard the previous call, Mr. Reed. Mr. X can fit you in. Will you come to NBC at 1:10 P.M.?" Not one or two; by 1:10. You figure it out.

After all the interviews (the only thing you don't need is a blood test), I was told to be there at 6 P.M. (You only THINK it's on late at night. While you're watching in bed, Johnny—if he's smart—either watches the competition on the other channels or the late movie, which is almost always more entertaining.)

On my show, the other guests were a Midwestern school teacher, a cotton-candy headed starlet whose only claim to fame was being held (not long enough) over a panther pit on *Tarzan*, and James Garner. Everyone sat in barber chairs in a little pea-soup green room that smelled like dirty sweatsocks, while James Garner sang very loudly, "Everybody, wants my body, sometime . . ." and a tough lady who chewed bubble gum slapped enough makeup on our faces to qualify for a Busby Berkley production number.

(Note to secretary: send Johnny a bill for $42 for rubbing pancake and greasepaint into the collar of my brand new white crepe Palachio shirt.)

By 6:30, James Garner is being very show biz. "Sock it to me, sock it to me," he keeps roaring to several people who would like to, slapping everyone between the shoulder blades the way he always does in Doris Day movies that close in three days in drive-ins.

"Sign this, please," says a cold-voiced, ashen-faced man with a fountain pen. You sign something that says Johnny Carson isn't responsible if you get sued. Then you get sent to the "Green Room" where everyone sits with knees touching in a tiny airless space like the inside of a boxcar on its way to Auschwitz. The empty-headed starlet giggles, and James Garner says, "Sock it to me," as Johnny in that warm, lovable glow, which has made him famous, peers into the smoky room and says, "We gonna do this thing again tonight?"

Yes, we are. The orchestra beats it eight to the bar and we're on! The school teacher talks about integration. Watch that rating, boys. Carson gets rid of her fast with two tickets to the Latin Quarter. Then he attempts to play with a repulsive little Russian roulette toy that hits you in the face with a piece of meringue pie if you dial the toy to the wrong number. Naturally, the pie hits him in the face and everyone dies laughing. It endears him to his public to show he's a good sport, see. (Of course, nobody mentions the fact that if you buy the toy you have to make a new pie everytime you use it.)

The show drags on. The first thing you notice is how miserable everyone backstage seems. It takes more than a warm puppy to make happiness abound at the Carson show. Johnny is well known for his sudden temper, his cool aloofness, and his low tolerance level for guests who do not interest him.

Garner spends twenty-five minutes telling a boring story about two race car drivers who hit a bull on the highway. Terror reigns backstage. Johnny isn't smiling. Carson proves, as I watch, my original theory that he is a lousy interviewer. He gets absolutely nothing out of Garner OR the empty-headed starlet, who makes the startling remark that "All the milk in Paris is bad, that's why all Frenchmen are short." If people could see how Carson's backstage staff frowns at guests like these behind his back, maybe some of those undeserved ratings would drop.

The Big Moment arrives. Carson fingers my book. "It's the first time I've seen this book," he says. "That's some title—*Do You Sleep in the Nude?*" (after all that interviewing, he had never even heard of the book—do you begin to get the picture of how well organized this most famous of all nighttime TV shows really is?), to which the starlet replies: "Oh, yes I DO—I thought you'd never ask." Somehow, I manage to get on stage after my big intro was demolished, hating myself the whole time for being there at all. On camera, under lights hot enough to fry a chicken, the most annoying thing about Carson is his unwillingness to swing, to trust himself or his guests. Unlike Dick Cavett, Mike Douglas, or Merv Griffin, who are all much better interviewers, Carson gauges everything by the size of the laugh and the response to the electronic applause meters. He never looks at you; he's too busy (1) watching the audience to see if they are responding and (2) searching the face of his producer for reassurance. It is so nerve-wracking the guest soon distrusts himself and searches the audience to see if he's going over. It breaks up the concentration and makes everyone look as nervous and scratchy as a novitiate nun in Bermuda shorts.

I was surrounded by hostility. James Garner, who obviously never reads anything, kept asking: "What do you write?" and then insisted, "I never give interviews," even though I know no single editor who has ever asked him for one. Carson, unable to ask anything that did not relate in some personal way to his own ego, turned the tables on his researchers' long preshow interviews, by ignoring their notes and asking directly: "Interview me now." Somehow the whole gruesome affair was suddenly over. I had been scheduled in the last ten minutes of the show, called the "Writer's slot." By this time, most people have gone to bed. I guess Carson addicts don't read books.

The show finishes in time for the visiting electric toothbrush salesmen from Osage and Okmulgee to grab a bite at Whelan's Drug Store before getting back to the Hotel Taft. While they file solemnly toward the elevators, Carson vanishes. Nobody looks at anybody else. Certainly nobody ventures an opinion about the show before hearing what the boss man's reaction is. Real friendly place. I was left with a ruined white crepe Edwardian shirt, a violent stare from James Garner, and a very clear picture of how godawful the Carson show really is. Now I no longer need to worry about my critical opinion. I know this is television at its most derivative, unoriginal, uninspired, unimaginative worst. I was there. And like all the other masochists who have so little self-respect that they will submit to looking foolish on this sorry excuse for professional television just to promote themselves or sell a product, I deserved what I got. People who watch it do too, but the agony of home viewing has one distinct advantage over being there: you can turn the damn thing off.

Hollywood
June 21, 1968

With typical hysteria, Lotus Land over-reacted. In the wake of Senator Robert F. Kennedy's appalling murder, the fashionable new nonviolence trend has left Hollywood awash in a tidal wave of confusion this week. From the Polo Lounge to Malibu, LBJ's Violence Commission is clearly the biggest problem on everyone's face since Schwab's ran out of Bain de Soleil.

Jack Valenti howled in typical schoolboy fashion. Washington threatened government control. Movies and television shows were canceled. CBS whizzed its senior programming vice-president Mike Dann to the West Coast to red pencil all violence on upcoming shows, while CBS president Frank Stanton sent a crisp wire to Washington complaining that nothing has proved so far that the nation's violence is related to the fictional violence portrayed on television.

Nobody got any direct answers out of anybody else, but Hollywood's curiously sudden spark of suspicious patriotism was already beginning to smell like rotten fish. Obscure producers and directors nobody ever heard of began taking eye-catching full-page ads in *The Hollywood Reporter* and daily *Variety* like down-and-outers do to attract attention, announcing their willingness to relieve the industry of crime and mayhem with good clean work. To most observers, it all began to sound like phony publicity. (One trade ran the headline "Hollywood Rushes to Aid Government Ban on Violence" next to another headline announcing "*Boston Strangler* Set for Christmas Release!"

Get Smart, *Gunsmoke*, and a new show called *The Name of the Game* have ordered complete reappraisals of all scripts. *It Takes a Thief* threw out two upcoming episodes involving assassinations and—get this—CBS's new western *Lancer* even edited out one ambush and one shooting. Local stations were canceling all the old Bogart-Cagney movies. Newspapers were dropping comic strips like "Little Orphan Annie," and "Dick Tracy," which were American institutions long before anybody in Washington ever turned on their television sets to see what was happening out there in the real world beyond Capitol Hill.

Even the poor *Flying Nun* was in trouble. One of her shows was canceled. In it she was supposed to fly upon a mob planning a wipeout in a secret meeting. Imagine that!

OK, let's get down to where it's at. I'm as opposed to excessive violence as anyone else. I hate guns and I'm pushing for tighter gun control legislation. Hunters be damned; I don't think anyone should be allowed to kill a rabbit. I agree that television and movies showing violence for the sake of violence should be wiped out. And I have crusaded tirelessly for a reevaluation of network kiddie cartoons in which the demented minds of sadistically perverted screen writers are allowed to flood the nursery set with depravity and sex.

But get smart people, this whole "What's wrong with us, what are we doing?" attitude infecting Hollywood is turning into an ultra-dramatic McCarthy witchhunt that is striking blindly in every direction and promoting the glorification of personal reputations along the way. I'm not going to get upset about trade ads denouncing violence when they are signed by Shelley Winters, for chrissake! Miss Winters didn't seem too upset about violence when she eagerly pitched in to promote *Wild in the Streets*, one of the crummiest, most tasteless blood-lettings in recent screen history.

And I really got a laugh when old-time cowboy Rex Allen, whose name hasn't been mentioned by anybody in Hollywood for the last ten years, announced dramatically in *Newsweek* that he would never wear his six-shooters again, "because Westerns give the wrong image of the role of guns in American life." The movie Western is a part of American history depicting an age when guns were necessary for self-survival, and they always did (and still do) have no more effect on contemporary society than a glass of water has on the rain-parched Bori-Bori crater. Such outbursts only give the has-beens and never-weres a chance to make big publicity plays for public attention.

Jack Valenti's proposal of a voluntary rating system to mark certain films off-limits to children and Washington's hints of government control of the mass media are threats to journalism and could easily cause an artistic setback that could ruin the communications industry.

What are we going to do, suppress *Macbeth* the way the military junta has supressed the great tragedies in Greece?

Are we going to deny the Bible to our children because Cain slew Abel?

Hollywood is merely using the assassination of Bobby for another of its eternal coverups.

What TV needs to worry about is not violence but better and more creative programming. Instead of taking guns out of *Get Smart,* it would seem a much better move to just rid the air of clutter like *Get Smart* altogether and surface some intelligent programs to which people can relate. The roots of what ails television and films today have nothing to do with idiotic cowboys dropping their sixguns and nobody is going to solve the problem of alienated, decentralized social misfits like Sirhan Sirhan and Lee Harvey Oswald by cutting scripts in which the Flying Nun meets her first Mafia member.

I abhor violence for the sake of titillation, but I'd hate to see important American films like *In Cold Blood* and *The Boston Strangler* go down the drain just to massage bogus guilt complexes. Hollywood should produce more scripts that try to get to the heart of the human condition instead of covering it up, delve into the motivations behind the erupting sores of society that can fester and erupt in a Lee Harvey Oswald, not turn the screens of the world into nectar and ambrosia and an eternal Utopian never-ending Mother's Day. "Let's Curtail Violence," say all the Emperor's New Clothes people.

OK, I'll go along with that. But in Hollywood, where they go around beating their breasts saying, "I have sinned," and jumping on Jack Valenti's bandwagon, they're all screaming at Warren Beatty as though *Bonnie and Clyde* were responsible for the whole thing. When you need a scapegoat, it's so very easy to blame it all on TV and movies.

Not all the heads however, lost their cool last week in the wake of storm. Pamela Hansford Johnson, wife of C. P. Snow and the reigning literary lioness of London, has a point: "You Americans—here you are the greatest power on earth and what do you do? Give yourself a phony guilt complex. Rome at the height of Rome and Great Britain at the height of Great Britain would never have been caught dead apologizing for anything. Yet you Americans go around saying to the world how terrible you are—yet you go on doing all the terrible things to the rest of the world that great powers always do."

And Dick Zanuck, the bright, young studio head, of 20th Century-Fox, who is one of the industry spokesman flying to the White House next week to lunch with LBJ, says, "The invitation insinuated it would be a get-acquainted lunch, but I suppose it will be a lecture. I don't like violence, but I also think Hollywood is over reacting out of emotion instead of clear logic. Going overboard like this could breed more trouble than we have now. Movies must reflect the times, and these are violent times. If you're doing a war film, there's gonna be violence. It's merely a question of degree. At least in the movies we shoot with blanks, while the rest of the world is using real bullets."

It's all gotten way out of hand and turned into a gust of very bad news for the west. Violence cannot be eliminated by taking Hopalong Cassidy and "Little Orphan Annie" with her pancake eyes away from the American public any more than you can cure cancer by refusing to recognize the fact that it exists. The whole thing is beginning to sound like a terminal case of "mea culpa, mea culpa!" If Hollywood isn't careful, it will be goodbye art. Welcome home Shirley Temple.

Hollywood

June 28, 1968

"It'll be a long time before this town sees anything like this again," said George Cukor, who has watched them all come and go and ought to know.

And all around him the people cheered and clapped until their hands were red. Angela Lansbury came home to the town that never knew what to do with her and rubbed their noses in it.

No question about it: Tuesday night's opening of *Mame* at the Dorothy Chandler Pavilion in the Los Angeles Music Center was the event of the year in Hollywood. People in sleeping bags camped out in the streets, hoping for a chance to buy a last-minute ticket. Seats didn't exist. The big stars couldn't get in. Everyone from the Gregory Pecks to the Vincente Minnellis was clamoring for tickets, which were going for the black market price of $250 apiece. All for Angela. "We wanted this for her from the very beginning," said playwright Jerome Lawrence, who with Robert E. Lee co-authored *Mame* for Lansbury. "It all began right here at the Santa Ynez Inn in Malibu, and throughout the New York run we always dreamed of the day when Angela could come back in triumph."

That's a good word for it. But it almost never happened at all. Fryer & Carr, the producers of *Mame*, originally planned to make a deal giving Caesar's Palace in Las Vegas an exclusive on the show west of Denver. The authors had to threaten a lawsuit to bring it to Hollywood. Now they stand to make more than $2 million on the Lansbury name in Hollywood alone—at $9.50 a seat in a house that grosses $116,000 a week for a sold out ten weeks. You figure it out.

A week before it opened, there was more trouble. The actors' strike threatened to close the show in San Francisco. But there was such love backstage at *Mame* that through it all even the striking actors stood by their star. And vice versa. While Broadway stars were harumphing around putting down their choruses and while Mary Martin took off to an unlisted phone number in Palm Springs, Angela was carrying signs in the picket line in the Bay City. "She didn't have to do that," said one of the dancers in *Mame*. "She was one of us, and it was love that made us fight to get the show to Los Angeles. We could have gone home, but we knew how much it meant to her."

High in her penthouse overlooking the bridges and the yachts in the San Francisco Bay last week, Angela said: "Some of these kids were stranded out here on fifteen dollars per diem. They all agreed to come out to California for my sake in the first place. This show is like a family. When one eats, we all eat." So she opened up her apartment and fed them steaks and eggs and bacon and coffee made in a battered pot that she carries around in her luggage. And the love did not go unnoticed. Hippies threw flowers at her in the streets. At the No Name Bar in Sausalito, the bartender made rounds of Ramos gin fizzes in a blender and served them to an unpretentious star in blue jeans and her entourage. At the Gilded Cage, San Francisco's leading drag show, they even mounted an entire production number in which a female impersonator did a tribute to Lansbury to standing ovations. (You have to admit that's a special kind of recognition—when the drag queens dig you, you've arrived.)

But looming ahead was still L. A., a town where nobody goes anywhere except to screenings of their own pictures. "Angela Comes Home," announced the *Los Angeles Times*, and columnists were taking bets on whether Lansbury would get the movie—a fate still undecided. Unlike most directors, who never care what happens to their shows after they leave Broadway, Gene Saks flew out from New York to revise the show.

They didn't get the scenery moved and hung until Monday afternoon. The stage was too big (the Dorothy Chandler seats 3,243 people, which is a big change from the Winter Garden's 1,479 seat capacity). The entire show had to be rethought and re-evaluated. The cast worked without a break up to the Monday night preview. Fighting a sore throat on the day of the opening, Angela tried to rest in her home on the Malibu cliffs, taking time out to supervise her daughter Dede's dress for the opening and playing den mother to her children's surfer friends.

Backstage, they were moving enough flowers in to dress Forest Lawn for Easter. Jerry Herman paced nervously. "It's a little late to wish you luck," someone said. To which Herman replied, "Everything else was bad enough but this is Angie's night. I should never come to these things—the composer in tears—it's embarrassing."

They filed into the pavilion, a gigantic theater the size of a small gymnasium with wood paneled walls and a curtain with a metallic gold sunburst. Things got off to a bad start. The acoustics were bad. The mikes reverberated with feedback. The sound system was overamplified. The sets looked lost on that cavernous stage. But suddenly, she was there—blowing that trumpet and shimmering down the stairs in backless lemon spangles—and you could hear the ovation out in beautiful downtown Burbank. The show was better than ever. It looked brand new. The timing was perfect. Angela sang with a voice glorious and sunny and good enough to make hit records. The cast gave her everything, and she gave it back in spades—a singing, swinging Bernhardt, making every nuance count right down to the last eyelash. To still do that, after 2½ years of the same role, is a remarkable accomplishment and the audience let her know it. They stood and they screamed and they whistled their bravos, and one elderly gentleman sitting next to me—head of the makeup department at MGM for twenty-three years—said gently, "I saw 'em all come and go, from Garbo on down, and she's the only one of those girls who deserves this. It's so wonderful when it happens to a good person."

Backstage, in the rear of the greasepaint, Dick Van Dyke wiped the perspiration from his forehead in disbelief and Carol Channing stood with myopic tears running from her alarm-clock eyes. "I've never seen anything like it in my life!" she said. "It was the mikes," said Angela modestly. "Listen, I played here in *Dolly*, the mikes aren't so hot. It wasn't the mikes," said Channing, and everyone smiled with enough electricity to light Wilshire Boulevard on a Saturday night.

The audience stood outside the theater waiting for the 24-carat star who used to be what's-her-name. They may have worn cloth coats and carnation corsages, but one thing set them apart from the bored ultra-jaded audiences in New York—they were all smiling. They crowded around her and touched her like a garland with their hands outstretched. "I've never felt so wonderful, or so surrounded by love," she said, glowing. Then she climbed into her car with her family and friends and drove off down the freeway, clutching her roses.

And backstage, in the middle of the balloons and champagne and the 24 pound candy trees and the baskets of flowers, one telegram hung crisply from her dressing room mirror, signed by George Cukor, the director at MGM, who more than twenty years ago guided a frightened teenager fresh off the boat from London in the role of Nancy in *Gaslight*, the movie that won her an Oscar nomination and started it all. On it was typed a simple opening night message: "DEAR MISS LANSBURY: WE ARE LOOKING FOR A YOUNG WOMAN TO PLAY NANCY OLIVER, A VERY PRETTY SLIGHTLY IMPERTINENT HOUSE MAID. ANY SUGGESTIONS?" There weren't any.

Hollywood

July 12, 1968

Mini are here, and the tiny screening room in the Beverly Hills Hotel could hardly hold all the excitement. I'm always knocking television for its rotten programming, but if the networks are smart they'll pick up on this novel idea for a projected series that could revolutionize the medium and provide entertainment and information at the same time.

Dreamed up by Pat McDermott and Page Buckey, two of the brighter ex-public relations brains on the West Coast scene, *Mini* are short twenty-six-minute films that insiders in the business are getting very excited about. They have not been shown to the general public yet, but if the screening I attended in the Beverly Hills Hotel is any indication, *Mini* should be turning everybody on from Scarsdale to Santa Barbara before you can say Jack Gould.

"*Mini* think young, dance fast, and swing high; color it groovy, but with something to say," says the press release. OK. Roll it.

This *Mini* was called *The New Cinema.* It was like the *Laugh-In* in high gear. Tempoed to run downhill for the full twenty-six minutes right up to the finish line. No fad. No fill. Cranked way up. There was Peter Fonda speaking for a new generation of young moviemakers with hand-held 16-mm. cameras, saying, "Change was the dirtiest word the establishment knew. Now WE'RE the establishment and security is OUR dirty word." Everybody used to know what movies were—they became predictable. Now they're everybody's bag.

There's Andy Warhol, full of pimples and sores chewing gum in a disgusting closeup while Evil Viva says the trouble with all those boys in prep schools is that they talk about sex without getting any—take them out at night and get them some sex.

There's Francis Coppola rapping Warner Brothers, followed by Dame Edith Evans surrounded by a collage of beautiful camera angles of blossoming sunflowers, saying, "It's all quite different now. We had strong discipline in those days." Followed by Roman Polanski knocking it all: "The old people who represented Puritanism are dying off slowly." Followed by Dame Edith again, saying, "Don't you think you'd better just take me away?" Cut to Peter Fonda again telling it like it is: "McLuhan is right. The printed word is out. It took twenty or thirty years to read it all. By that time all the words had changed."

Cut to a series of magnificently photographed shots of what the New Cinema is all about: *Time* magazine covers. God is Dead. Anne Heywood's Lesbian masturbation scene from *The Fox.* Forty-second street marquees. Violence, sex. Hell's Angels. Polanski setting up angles with Mia Farrow in *Rosemary's Baby.* Suddenly the screen splits into three frames. A man kicks a dead body into a swimming pool in one frame, while Dame Edith Evans says, "The standards have all been lowered," in a second frame, and Francis Coppola, one of the most exciting young filmmakers to come out of Hollywood in years, says, "I don't think there's anything you can't put on film," in a third frame.

The New Cinema. It's as new as the times, as fresh as the young filmmakers who are grabbing it all with home-movie cameras and go-to-hell attitudes. It provides stars who don't live like stars or look like stars. The Gables and Coopers turn into heroes like Dustin Hoffman who can now afford to say, "I didn't really wanna do *The Graduate*." It can deify someone like a Warhol, who, when asked by an idealistic young interviewer what he'd do if a studio suddenly gave him two million dollars says, "I'd spend $2,000 and keep the rest." "He'd build another church for his muh-thuh," squeals Viva.

Lushly photographed and directed by Gary Young, *Mini* tells it true with both sides listening in. You can either side with Dame Edith or take a slow drag and put it all down with Hank's bad boy Peter. But you get it all in 26 minutes not 60 or 90 minutes of extraneous sludge expounded by discussion groups sitting around a long table in an overhauled warehouse on East 67th Street, and you get it from two personable, attractive young guys who act as weekly moderators for *Mini*. Terry Garin is a Greek god who wants to be a novelist and Paul Winfield is an Actor's Studio Negro who stirs the paste-pot and keeps the glue going between them. Together, they fit into what I call the tele-vérité style of *Mini*, able at a minute's notice to ride Yamahas with Peter Fonda or rap with the Warhol gang at The Factory or do a graceful dignified sit-down interview with Dame Edith Evans in the Rose Garden of the Beverly Hills Hotel.

As a team they are like a Route 66 Huntley and Brinkley. Plans include *Minis* on homosexuality, heart transplant, and even a Cafe La Mama style play with all the female parts played by Tiny Tim.

It's a magazine concept similar to what all the networks are aiming at in their revised fall news divisions, only cheaper. A single *Mini* can be brought in for $55,000, which puts the series in a comparable financial class with trash like the *Dating Game*. Shows like this, created by young people with something to say, furnish an opportunity for the networks to jazz up their programming at a nominal cost.

Still, the networks have so far been noncommittal. In Los Angeles, a town so square that LeRoi Jones's *The Toilet* could only be advertised in the *Los Angeles Times* as *The T——T*, NBC refused to buy the show unless Viva's prep-school sex education scene is changed.

According to the producers, the network has, however, OK'd the insertion (at the point where Viva says the word "sex") of the single shot from *Who's Afraid of Virginia Woolf?* where Elizabeth Taylor yells "Shit!" It's a question of control. If you work inside the network walls, creative channels must be compromised. *Mini* is an outside-the-walls kind of show created for people who think for themselves by outside-the-walls swingers. If you listen to the creeps in the network continuity departments, television will always be an enormous garbage disposal.

The only alternative seems to be for sponsors to get so interested in a series they'll take it away from the networks and syndicate it themselves. This is the direction in which television seems to be heading.

It is a decision the producers of *Mini* must now make. It's a tough spot for them to be in and I wish them luck. Television needs creative, fresh approaches to old worn-out formulas. I hope everybody gets to see *Mini* sooner or later. *Mini* are where it am.

Hollywood
July 19, 1968

To the thousands of tourists who descend upon Lotus Land each summer like the locusts in *The Good Earth*, the next best thing to being a moom-pitcha star is seeing one. They seldom do, unless they bribe the doorman at The Factory. But at $3.50 a head, they can get pretty close, thanks to the Universal studio tour. "The public not only has the right to see what goes on behind the scenes, but we've learned it's to the studio's advantage to show it," says one Universal spokesman. She's right. The tour has become a big business, paying off in huge yearly profits, and has promoted more than one Universal fiasco in terms of publicity and word-of-mouth back home in front of the TV set in Kankakee. And it's a darned good show.

They file in in their Bermuda shorts and their Woolworth bracelets and their Honolulu shirts toting Brownies and Swingers, ready to fire on the first big game that looks like a celebrity. They march behind the guards like Khyber Rifles past movie posters of Johnny Mack Brown as the *Man from Montana* and the Andrews Sisters in *Moonlight in Havana* while loudspeakers blare demo records from *Thoroughly Modern Millie*. On my tour I sat next to a man from Boulder, Colorado, who informed me, "We got burned over at Fox. Three bucks a head and all they show you is the *Peyton Place* sets and you gotta walk all the way." "Honey," said his wife, "that was because everythin' was closed. They wuz makin' some movie with that girl Barbra Strindberg." On the other side, I was squeezed in next to a bosomy blonde with a beehive hairdo and bluejeans from Dry Prong, Louisiana, who was so excited about her trip to Hollywood she even got vaccinated. "In three days I see the Wax Museum where they got real artists to make Marilyn Monroe and Frankenstein look real true to life, and the Chinese deer farm and Knott's Berry Farm. I'm gettin' a scrapbook."

We climbed aboard a pink and white fringed tram parked under a papier-mâché castle from an old Piper Laurie movie and we were off. Our tour guide was Sandy, an all-American Lee Remick type bristling with personality and Ivory soap in white loafers, white stockings, a white wash-and-wear ruffled blouse and a pumpkin orange culotte suit. "No smoking," she said sweetly, "we had a bad fire a year ago and it nearly destroyed an old Rock Hudson set." "What levee is that?" asked a tousled youth from Booneville, Mississippi, as the tram climbed a hill overlooking the Hollywood Freeway. First stop was the men's wardrobe department, a great quonset hut with walk-in closets marked *Creature from the Black Lagoon, McHale's Navy*, etc. "We age the costumes every morning and for war movies we even rub in blood made out of glycerine, dirt, ammonia and rubbing alcohol," said Sandy. "Aaaaah," sighed the tourists. There were costumes for Nazis, Mongols, Chinese emperors, Tong terrorists, Mau-Maus, Bagdad sultans and five hundred hippie outfits from a new Clint Eastwood movie that looked like you'd get Anthrax if you touched them. The last thing we saw was ten sewing machines going full blast and an elderly Negro with a GE steam iron.

"Every star has his own dressing room for the duration of his stay with us," smiled Sandy. "There's John Wayne's room—don't knock on *his* door—and here is Edith Head's." "Who's Edith Head? What movie was she in?" asked the beehive blonde, rubbing her vaccination. Edith had parasol-yellow doors and plastic rubber plants outside. Past rows of Bentleys and Silver Clouds, we came to the only dressing room on the lot open to visitors: a Model Home exhibit supposedly once used by Lana Turner. "She loves red and white and charcoal gray and antiques, so we designed it just for her. We really do try and please our stars. Unfortunately, she hasn't been here in some time." It looked like a window at Castro Convertible—purple Austrian draperies, bright red carpets, quill pens, a Louis Quinze sofa in patent leather, plastic roses and feather flowers in vases on which the rub-on-kit gold leaf was peeling. This was obviously the REAL *Imitation of Life*, in a style that could only be described as Early Grand Rapids.

Outside, Sandy suddenly pointed. "Look quick everybody, if you want to see a real celebrity. Edith Head is standing on her porch!" "Aaaaah," sighed the tourists, and the Brownie snappers went off like machine guns. Sandy turned to me: "These people are so desperate they want to see anybody. Tell them you're Robert Wagner and they'll follow you around all day."

Next: a real sound stage, with concrete walls five inches thick and a door weighing five tons. A baseball diamond with trees made of Hydrocal treated with calcium chloride and sprayed with green paint, rocks of foam rubber and a real sand pit. "It's less expensive than going to a real park in L. A.," said Sandy. "Also there's less danger of getting mugged." No attempt was made to gloss everything with sugar. We saw snow made from rock salt for ice-cream freezers ("Cornflakes make too much noise"), an 1850 bunkhouse from *The Virginian* with fake Winchesters on the wall, and a town with six streets that can be used for any country ("When you see Ben Gazzara traveling through foreign cities you think he's there, but all we do is change the languages on the buildings"). We learned why there are no ceilings on TV. ("Any time I see ceilings, I ain't watchin' no TV," drawled a bald Texan in a Stetson hat.) Then Sandy flipped a switch on a wall behind John Wayne's office window and a miniature freeway system squeaked along with little metal cars on a treadmill.

On to the *Sweet Charity* set. "Did anyone see the play?" asked Sandy cheerfully. Nobody had, but for thirty thousand dollars they expected perfection out of something called the Pompeii Club. "Humph," said a small child, who kicked the edge of a marble column and knocked a hole in it. The tourists watched themselves on fifteen thousand dollar crab dollies with videotape cartridges attached and strolled past a cheetah cage on white chiffon ropes with a suspended head that looked suspiciously like Elsie the Borden Cow. They were led through a street filled with Fiberglas cars ("We put midgets next to them and shoot them from a distance and make you think it's a bigger street than it is") and into a prop warehouse full of paper cannons and plaster of Paris antiques being aged with dirt and gold paint. "Smile real pretty now, because we have hidden cameras behind the walls—we're looking for stars of the future!" joked Sandy, and the tourists began taking pictures of each other. We saw slave cabins from *Uncle Tom's Cabin*, taxicabs, London buses and a South of the Border Mexican set standing right next to a gladiator school from *Spartacus*. On to Medicine Bow, Wyoming, the Idle Hour Pool Hall, Falmouth Castle, the lake from *Father Goose* with big water pumps making waves (the deepest part is six feet—and *you* thought Gary Grant was going to drown!), the native village from *The Ugly American*, McHale's ocean, Tyrone Power's riverboat from *Mississippi Gambler*, the prison from *Judgment at Nuremberg*, Checkpoint Charlie on the Berlin Wall.

Four hundred and twenty acres of land with its own mayor (Don

Knotts), its own sheriff (Andy Griffith), and a daily task force of six thousand Californians to keep it going—the largest movie studio in the world and it all started out as a chicken farm. Such is the glory of Hollywood. We stood in a primeval forest and through the wilderness we could look down on the San Fernando Valley and the Camelot castle over at Warner Brothers in Burbank, and, beyond that, the San Gabriel Mountains. Descending the trail like pink lizards, the tour trams angled past airplanes and Japanese pagodas and stagecoaches and even the fort from *Wagon Train*. "Only one out of every ten logs is wood," said Sandy, "the Indians have to aim arrows at the real ones, otherwise they bounce off the rubber logs and injure the extras." The tourists ate it up like strawberries. The only thing they didn't see was a movie star. "The stars hate the tour trains," confided Sandy. "James Drury closes his set every time we come down the hill. Ben Gazzara was awful. He tried to get the tour guides fired all the time."

The tour takes several hours. After it's over, you can stick around and see a stunt-man show or shake hands with Dracula. "The tourists love it," concluded Sandy, waving goodbye. "Tell them the horses are foam rubber or the swimming pools are made out of blue wax paper and they'll believe ANYTHING!" But like most things in Hollywood, the illusion is brief. Two minutes later, you're back on the Hollywood Freeway, where the smog does not come out of a machine and the accidents are real.

Hollywood
July 26, 1968

"Sit down!" yelled Bill Cosby, the Negro Mark Twain, and the scholarship section up in the top of the peanut galleries yelled right back. Then the ocean of humanity settled down with its hot dogs dripping. A thick haze of pot smoke settled in so quickly you could see it making purple clouds in the glow of the spotlights, curling in the air on its way to the Hollywood hills. An American flag waved precariously above the stage. Potted palms rustled in the breeze. People sipped hot coffee in paper cups and huddled under blankets for warmth in the frosty California night as Hollywood's biggest entertainment event of the year took place in the Hollywood Bowl, a gigantic clam shell with a thyroid condition. More than eighteen thousand people were there to raise money for Dr. Martin Luther King's fight in the Poor People's Campaign and see some of the biggest stars in show business do their things.

There were people as far back as the eye could see—so many that Cosby was threatening to pass out 8x10 glossies that move. "Some of you are so far back you're getting a delayed broadcast," he yelled. A plane flew across the starry sky and drowned him out. But Cosby is a great ad-libber. "On its way to Cuba," he winked to those of us down front. "You can tell when a plane is on its way to Cuba—they start putting subtitles on the movies." It was an easy-going California kind of evening. People chewed on chicken drumsticks and took flash photos of James Garner and Michael Crawford and Anouk Aimée and Abbe Lane and George Chakiris and anybody they could see through their binoculars.

The Tijuana Brass opened in darkness. Then through the rustles of applause up in the top of the sky, we could see the spotlight in the sea of heads revealing Herb Alpert making an ultra-dramatic entrance down through the thousands of people, all screaming and whistling as he sang, "This guy's in love with you," in a white ice cream suit.

It was one of the most exciting entrances I've ever seen, building in his move toward the stage through box seats and pot smoke as the music rose to a crescendo of flattened-fifths. The rest of the act, with its staccato timing, its Las Vegas style bandstand exuberance, and its overdose of collegiate hully-chee, could only be described as anticlimactic. (I've got news for the Tijuana Brass—you don't yell "OLE!" at the end of a Greek dance, even if Rona Barrett is clapping along.) Most of it was strictly for the box-lunch crowd.

More demanding tastes had to wait until 10:30, when Harry Belafonte turned everybody on with almost an hour of electricity. Thinking back to the old college frat house days, the Belafonte magic all comes back. But it's so easy these days to forget what a great entertainer Belafonte is—until you are once again confronted with it all. He moved like a panther, sang like his lungs were greased with maple syrup, and channeled a powerhouse of energy and animal magnetism into enough voltage to run Hoover Dam on a Saturday night. He even got in a few digs. "I been tellin' 'em in Hollywood for years there's more of us than Sidney Poitier."

Belafonte scatted with the brass section, danced with Bill Cosby, did Cupid leaps, pirouettes, and lizard lunges, and made every vowel count. Belafonte led the audience in his famous "Jamaican Farewell" singalong, and when the ladies in the audience sang "I'm going to see a girl in Kingston Town," he yelled, "No, no, ladies sing Boy here—I know you're stuck with Reagan but don't let him do *that* to you!" Then he introduced the Rev. Dr. Ralph Abernathy, Dr. Martin Luther King's successor, and leader of the Poor People's Campaign, and the entire sellout crowd stood and applauded with respect and dignity.

As an added treat, he closed by bringing on the Dolores Hall Gospel Singers who made Aretha Franklin's screaming look pale by comparison. With Belafonte in tow, they knocked the Bowl off its hinges and had eighteen thousand people eating out of the palms of their hands.

"Streisand's probably the only one alive who could follow an act like that," said the man next to me, and she did. The star spot of the evening had been saved for her, but by the time she came on it was already clear who had put the night in his pocket. Some of the Belafonte fans were making loud exits, but the schnozz came through loud and clear. Something hideous had happened to the microphones that distorted her voice on most of her high notes. She wore a cadaverous gown of draped green chiffon (Streisand should never wear green) with peacock feathers on the sleeves that made her look the size of Sophie Tucker. ("I'm not pregnant," she tried to explain, obviously embarrassed by her own appearance.) But her voice was thrilling and it was cradled in a ceiling of stars. None of the monstrous things you always hear about her seemed to matter. The audience bought it and she wrapped the whole thing up around midnight in the shortest but most eagerly awaited spot in the show.

They grossed more than $140,000, which, according to Abernathy, will go largely toward erecting a Poor People's Embassy in Washington. It was Hollywood's way of saying "We Care," and as a cause of the heart, it was a night people won't soon forget. I know I won't.

Baker, Oregon

August 2, 1968

As soon as we climbed out of the helicopter, we heard the music. "Hand me down that can of beans . . ." roared the goldminers. "Make them sound like the Red Army Chorus," said Alan Jay Lerner. And up on the hill 250 extras jumped and leaped and fell in a ton of mud.

At a fork in the East Eagle Creek, near 9,000-foot Boulder Peak in the

Wallowa-Whitman National Forest, Hollywood has come to make a $14 million super-extravangaza movie musical of *Paint Your Wagon*. The setting is one of the greatest natural fir and pine forests in America, yet the trees on the set are from Hollywood, the horses are brought in from a place in Nevada that teaches horses to act, the water oxen are from New England, the bear who plays a role in the wrestling scene is from Honolulu, the cows are from Texas, and the set designer is from Australia. The first things you see when you climb out of the mini-chopper are the towns. Two Gold Rush mining camps have been built by one of the biggest construction companies in the world at a cost of $2.5 million. One is called Tent City, complete with gold mines. The other is No Name City, which is Tent City seven months later (after the intermission)—a total town built on wires and pulleys, like an Erector set. The saloons, the churches, the whorehouses, everything does tricks. The roofs fly off, the ceilings cave in, and everything blows up and sinks into the river in a big climactic scene like Sodom and Gomorrah. In case they miss the shots (God forbid!), the buildings all snap back into place for a retake.

The entire location has to be seen to be believed, and it was all designed by John Truscott, who won some Oscars for *Camelot*. Not bad for a thirty-year-old Australian, but what does he know about the California Gold Rush? "We had gold in Australia, too," he grins, knee-deep in mud. Senator Wayne Morse thinks the whole thing is so impressive he's legislating to preserve the location for an Oregon tourist attraction after the movie people leave.

Not everyone is delirious, however. Nearly 600 people are here, living 47 miles from the set in a remote country ranch community called Baker (Pop. 9,986). It used to be a stage coach center during the Gold Rush. Now it is surrounded by ghost towns and porcupines, which keep giving all the Teamster's Union drivers flat tires on the dirt roads leading into the mountain trails. Baker has no recommendable restaurants and the actors always climb into their cars after washing off the mud and cow dung at the end of a hard day's shooting and say, "La Grenouille" to the drivers. Then they meet at the A&W Root Beer Stand for taco burgers.

The best food in town is at Josh and Nedda Logan's house. (The Logans were smart enough to bring along all their servants.) Or at Jean Seberg's, where her Spanish maid from Majorca makes great gazpacho. Clint Eastwood rides a motorcycle and lives on a ranch, where he rises at dawn to slop his own hogs. Lee Marvin simply opens another can of beer.

Jean Seberg had dust poisoning when she arrived, but now she's falling into the country routine like Linus with a new blanket. "The first week I would have packed my suitcases if anyone had invited me to a cookout," she says cheerfully. "Now I'm going to a barbecue my neighbor, Mrs. Johnson, is giving next week. I'm part of the local scene."

In the film she breastfeeds a baby on screen, rides horses, and sings a new song written for her by Alan Jay Lerner and André Previn. She wears Ungaros to the grocery store and the locals park in the driveway of her rented green house to see who comes and goes.

"I called my folks in Iowa and invited them to come and fish and I told my mother she wouldn't even have to get used to the place. It's just like Marshalltown."

Most of the extras love the location because they don't have to shave. Dirt and long hair and no deodorant are the order of the day. Shortly after the company arrived, 150 hippies showed up in the nearby woods passing out goldenrod and living on berries. Logan has hired most of them for the movie and Jean has become their Mother Superior. They take baths in her house and she bakes cakes for their weddings. Next week two hippies will be married under a waterfall and Jean, Lee Marvin, and Clint Eastwood will all be in the ceremony while the wedding march is played by Nitty Gritty Dirt Band. Along with some of the other crew members, the Nitty Grittys have moved out to the woods near the set in a trailer. They eat in the commissary, set up like picnic tables, and fish, ride horses, and swim in the icy streams of melted snow. "It's a long way from the Sunset Strip," says the Number One Nitty Gritty, "but they pay us the same money for a room in town and we've seen enough of that town to last the rest of our lives."

The temperature is thirty-five degrees tonight. Josh Logan stalks through the slime in baggy blue jeans, cowboy boots, a polo coat, and a New York hat. "I don't know what the hell I'm doing here," he said, "all these extras, all these unions to contend with. You're afraid to give anybody an extra line to say or the budget goes up $10,000. You have to organize all these horses, all these cows, all these people, get the shot during Magic Hour, while the sky is light enough to silhouette the nature you've come to photograph. I'm living each day to the next. I can't wait to get back to civilization."

Ten men haul in more mud and throw it all over the extras. Nedda Logan turns to Alan Jay Lerner: "Why, oh why couldn't we have gone to Arrowhead? Or even Lake Tahoe?"

"It's got to be difficult," quips Lerner, clutching the finished script for

Coco on his way to a private Lear jet which will fly him back to Los Angeles for conferences with Katharine Hepburn. "If it's not difficult it's not worth doing."

And you think musicals are easy to make. Spiders crawl across the ground. Jean Seberg sits near an oil lamp, playing poker with a full-blood Sioux Indian named Eddie Little Sky, a former member of the Green Berets, and a hunchback Chinese named Peanuts. Karen Lerner announces she's just driven over a pine stump and knocked a hole in the oil pan of a new Continental. Word arrives that one of the helicopters has gone down in the mountains and the crew had to walk to a farmhouse to phone for a mechanic. "Never a dull moment," says Jean Seberg, who is a long way from her fashionable house on the Rue du Bac in Paris, and even farther away from Truffaut and Godard.

On the way down the gorge, a porcupine galumphs across our path in the road like a lopsided old man. "Hand me down that can of beans . . ." roars the Red Army chorus through the virgin wilderness, and the mikes bounce the music up to the snow-capped peaks above the pines. And up on the rise, for the forty-fifth take, like witches in the moonlight, they're still jumping in the mud.

August 9, 1968

Some notes on the Republican Convention.

What it looked like, from the armchair, was the Emmy Awards of politics. What it actually was, from any view, is still to be determined. And throughout the whole boring, clumsy, chaotic fiasco one thought kept reoccurring: one of these jokers could actually be the next President!

The TV newsmen put on their own private show, and although all of the networks covered the whole carnival like Amateur Night in Punkin Crick, the sophistication of the newscasters provided the only stimulus in a crescendo of tedium. Monday's speeches by John Wayne and Barry Goldwater were hideous enough, but they in no way prepared anyone who wasn't already asleep for the thunderous banality of the sideshow that showed up on Tuesday.

Senator Everett Dirksen has got to be kidding. His pompous, blubbery, ultra-dramatic introduction of the party platform (which was deadly enough in its own right) was the biggest gag in the convention. He reminded me of radio's old-time comic strip character, Senator Claghorn, leading everyone in a repeat of the Pledge of Allegiance like Sunday school kids and quoting Lincoln and Oliver Cromwell while everyone on the floor fell asleep. The platform itself was standard campaign verbiage—banal, bland, neutral, and meaningless, and so general anyone from Mao Tse-tung to Doris Day could run on it. CBS did the best job of covering this part of the convention. While NBC showed Dirksen rattling on like an old-time religion, fire-and-brimstone country evangelist, the CBS cameras ignored the whole thing and concentrated on an interesting plank-by-plank platform breakdown with some acerbic side comments by Roger Mudd.

Where was the youthful virility that sparked the Kennedy campaigns? The Republicans bellowed and ranted about "Youth will be served," borrowing heavily on the "Camelot" theory, yet does anyone remember a youthful and invigorating Republican administration? Instead the GOP grab bag looked like a sack full of losers, rats who didn't give up the sinking ship early enough and are now standing on their tails to stay above water. Where was the drama? By the second day things were already so dull the most controversial question anyone asked was "Will Nixon win on the first ballot?" Where was the conflict? Even Ronald Reagan's "open candidacy" announcement was no surprise—he was available before he ever left the old Virginia Mayo movies at Warner Brothers.

The networks tried to cover it as faithfully as possible, but most of the commentators were so caustic and cynical they looked like they had the gout. Without saying a word, they did a brilliant job of pictorially editorializing the boredom of the event by simply showing the faces of the GOP delegates on the floor.

NBC's "total gavel-to-gavel coverage" was a crashing bore, like reading the *Congressional Record* word for word. Not even his red, white, and blue-striped tie hid Chet Huntley's apoplexy from the color cameras. Both NBC and CBS ignored the podium speakers at times, which was OK with me. Most of the delegates were ignoring them too. During the reading of the platform, several of the delegates were sound asleep in NBC's cruel closeups. Others read newspapers during the speeches, walked around, and had social visits with their friends.

Utter chaos reigned at CBS: Mikes went dead; commentators forgot people's names; interviews were cut off in mid-sentence. Even Tony Martin, who sang a couple of songs for the delegates, was ignored by the two networks "covering" the convention. The final insult came when Walter Cronkite referred to him as "Tony Bennett."

ABC ignored the whole thing and carried its regularly scheduled programs, reserving ninety minutes a night for a special late news windup. It was a clever idea, and saved us all from having to sit through the anesthesia of the endless caucuses, endless discussions of rural support versus urban support, endless bragging from the candidates on how well off they were on votes, endless miscalculations on the tallies, and endless interviews with delegates who had nothing on their minds but where the next barbecue was being held. ABC covered it like a magazine, with surprisingly informative and interesting backstage features, such as the photographic closeup on Nixon's secret communications system outside Convention Hall. CBS and NBC must have got wind of ABC's feature reports, because they started dropping a goldmine of trivia, such as Cronkite's evaluation of the cost of the convention balloons, and Huntley-Brinkley's earth-shattering announcement that 48 elephants had been stolen from the 110 inlaid squares in the Convention Hall carpeting.

Elsewhere on the networks, everybody was in there slugging. NBC's *Today Show* covered the convention with cleverness and individuality. Barbara Walters tried desperately to interview Pat Nixon and Happy Rockefeller, but they were both so terrified of cameras, she couldn't get near them. She did get to Nancy Reagan, who is probably the only Republican wife who photographs well. Nancy showed up looking lovelier than her subject matter, which was her husband: "I'm his greatest fan. I don't think there's anything in the world he can't do. No, he hasn't become more conservative. We found an old interview he gave with Hedda Hopper and he still has the same opinions now." On ABC, Dick Cavett added a wonderful light touch to the whole thing by assigning Bob and Ray to do some hilarious spoofing of both the convention and the way it was covered. They produced film reports that turned out to be three minutes of test patterns and made sudden flashes: "There is absolutely no truth to the rumors that the Mothers March for Stassen will take place tonight, or that several delegates have been stunned by Portuguese Men of War."

But the sorriest disappointment of the whole convention was ABC's eagerly awaited unveiling of the editorials of Gore Vidal and William F. Buckley, Jr. They turned out to be somebody's idea of a sick joke. Instead of using their wit and intelligence to enlighten viewers and cut through a soupy haze of GOP confusion, they sadly turned their venom on each other and ended up looking like *The Boys in the Band* impersonating two Ken dolls in heat. They spent most of their time quibbling over one of Rockefeller's ads, linking Reagan to the John Birch Society, verbally bitching each other over their own political convictions, and calling each other, "My dear."

"Vidal is nothing but a producer of perverted Hollywood prose," snapped Buckley, looking unhealthy and a bit perverted himself.

Vidal called Buckley "the Marie Antoinette of the right wing," and after one of Buckley's particularly schizoid defenses of Nixon policy on the war in Vietnam, during which he rolled his eyes with a lot of short, squeaky jerks of the head, Vidal retorted "I'm sorry Bill, I wasn't listening."

Round and round they went, like tigers turning to butter, but I never saw them make one point or get one fact straight. Maybe they were just putting each other on and having a grand old campy time, but like the rest of the lurid activities on the dial, I had an uneasy feeling it was all actually happening for real.

Ho hum, in the midst of all the affluence and luxury in Miami Beach, the sudden flourish of embarrassing excitement when Rev. Ralph Abernathy appeared leading sixty freedom-singing members of the Poor People's March and a team of mules through the lobby of the Fontainebleau Hotel was almost a welcome relief, but it didn't last long. The cameras quickly switched to a jolly Rockefeller boat waving confetti-colored balloons out in the surf. "There's no underestimating the suicidal tendencies of the Republican party," somebody remarked during the dreary week-long fun and games. Thanks to television, they proved their point.

August 16, 1968

When I first arrived in New York, penniless and friendless, I used to wander down to the Television Network Preview Theatre on Sixth Avenue. Later it moved into the old Toho movie house across from the Booth Theater on West 45th Street, and I went there, too. I went because it was free and I was always promised "exciting new television entertainment never before shown." I could also play critic as I sat with the tourists from Kansas City and the old-maid secretaries from Flushing and voted with an applause meter for my favorite television pilots. The whole thing was a promotion gimmick to sell vacuum cleaners and dental floss, but it was something to do at the time. And it's all coming back this summer.

It's too late to get any juice out of old television shows everyone's already seen and too early to unveil the iron-clad secrets behind the new fall programming schedules, so, striking out in desperation, the television networks have been reduced to showing old pilots for unused series that didn't sell. It's still a gimmick, because it's a cheap way to waste prime time on cornball stock footage that has already been paid for. "Premiere," the Monday night garbage disposal on CBS, came up with a 30-minute doozie this week. This thumbs-down series pilot was called *Out of the Blue*, and in it, John McMartin (whom I rather liked) played a stock Hollywood professor who gets invaded one night by four space creatures from a planet called Kurzon.

One of the "creatures" is Shirley Jones, who doesn't know anything. Like she doesn't even know what a bra or a panty girdle is until McMartin shows her a mail-order catalog. She's here to "study" this planet, see, and McMartin doesn't mind studying her a bit. Reciprocal intergalaxy trade. Then they all go to a party in Malibu, where nobody will believe they are from outer space. Then the professor goes to school and says, "It can't be true; I'm dreaming." Then he goes home and Shirley Jones is still there. The end. And you thought *My Mother the Car* was bad. If you've missed it, don't worry. Pack a box supper and catch it at the Television Network Preview Theatre this fall. They're still giving away free dental floss.

It's Happening, ABC's summer daytime lunatic revue, isn't happening at all. It just lies there in a watery cesspool of stupidity and no-talent. Still, people like Hubert Humphrey, who wouldn't be caught dead in such surroundings at saner times, are desperate enough for attention to allow themselves to be "interviewed" (I use the term loosely) by a beatle-wigged social question mark called Mark Lindsay, while teen-age social question marks with acne and bleached hair shout questions from the audience. Rock and roll wails deafeningly in the background. Professor Irwin Corey sometimes drops by to do five minutes of preadolescent pratfalls. Advice is passed out to teen-age psychos about everything from petting (Do psychedelic teen-agers actually still pet?) to mononucleosis. And on Tuesday a doctor, who looked like a friendly undertaker, delivered a monologue on chronically infected eardrums and soft-palate nasal defects caused by adenoid masses just before the whole thing broke for a commercial in which right before my very eyes a woman cleaned her bathroom bowl. Definitely a show for sick stomachs, and if you don't have one, *It's Happening* guarantees to provide one quick.

Of Black America was a distinguished CBS news special about slavery that provided both pain and enlightenment on the subject. Collected graphics and writings of various slaves in bondage illustrated the history of the Negro people and shed a profound light on what has made the Negro what he is today. Most shocking was the way the show related master-slave relationships in Nat Turner's day to the jet-age slavery of now. If for nothing else, the hour would have been complete just watching the opinions and attitudes of the descendants of plantation owners. Massa's not in the cold, cold ground after all. He's alive and well and living in Scarsdale.

People who don't watch Dick Cavett just aren't with it. In the aftermath of the GOP convention, Gloria Steinem, who wrote the brilliant *New York Magazine* piece, "Trying to Love Eugene," showed up on the Dick Cavett show Monday with some pungent remarks about Senator Eugene McCarthy. One fact with which I sadly agree: before the New Hampshire primary, when a lot of us were early McCarthy boosters, we hadn't yet been exposed to the man behind the image in all his infinite dullness.

Then we switched our loyalties to Bobby Kennedy. Now there seems to be no other visible choice. So, like most of us who selfishly like to think we have the true answer, Miss Steinem is trying to work for him again. "He's our minimum for survival," she said, and I think she's right. It's just too bad we have to settle for minimums.

On the same show, Paul Walter, Jr., the twenty-one-year-old delegate from Ohio who seconded the nomination of Harold Stassen and rocked the convention by closing with, "Thank you for your inattention," turned out to be an intelligent, articulate young man who came right out and opened a new window. The GOP convention to which he was a delegate so disgusted him, he says, that he is now switching allegiances to McCarthy. One more man for the team. Young Walter is also the first person on TV who has come right out and emphasized the only accomplishment of the Republican convention—showing an urgent need for the establishment of individual primaries in every state. Conventions are nonsense and they boost men to political power without giving the public a chance to be heard. If the fiasco in Miami proved anything at all, it proved they should be abolished. Quote of the week: "I think they should call their ticket Nixon-Agnew-Gesundheit!" Concurred Miss Steinem, "It sounds like a disease." And Cavett passed the cream and sugar.

Chicago

August 30, 1968

It was a sore full of pus, an eyesore, a blight on humanity, and it festered and erupted in Chicago, in an atmosphere of barbed wire and bayonets.

It seemed inevitable that the donkeys unleashed on the Windy City would be a little unruly, but it seems doubtful that anyone could in any way have been prepared for the mad-dog insanity that took place.

Democracy? That's a laugh. This was Fascism, and it was horrifying enough to make me stare in disbelief that it could possibly happen in America. It gave Nixon the chance of his life to win the election, and God knows what the Russians will do with the atrocities.

McCarthy predicted last week on NBC that the convention would be a "trial by ordeal," and he was right. There were unhappy Democrats, disgruntled Democrats, pompous Democrats, all colliding politically on practically everything, from Vietnam to loyalty oaths. While the band played "Just a Love Nest Cozy and Warm" the crowd swarmed and pushed and shoved and shook its fists and glared hotly at each other.

Mrs. Hilda Stokley of East Harlem accused Senator McCarthy of being a liar and using Julian Bond's Georgia delegation for his own personal gain. The papers kept yelling that the forces of Democracy were eroding. In all the chaos and confusion, the New York delegation got lost and nobody could find them.

On Tuesday night I stayed up until 3 A.M. while hours were wasted on foolishness such as caucuses, during which delegations would fight awhile, poll themselves, and tally their votes on issues that had already been previously decided by majority rule. There was no sense of parliamentary procedure anywhere on the dial.

On CBS, everybody got punchy. Harry Reasoner announced, "As if we need it, Anita Bryant is coming back for another musical interlude." To which Walter Cronkite asked: "Is she as pretty down on the podium as she is up here in the anchor booth?" "Well, I don't know what she looks like up there in the anchor booth," replied Reasoner, wiping his forehead.

The country's going to pot and Walter Cronkite and Harry Reasoner are discussing Anita Bryant's physical attributes, which, I might add, far outnumbered her vocal accomplishments.

On NBC, things weren't much better. Chet Huntley got so rattled he even introduced his fellow newsmen as CBS correspondents.

Lester Maddox looked more than ever before like Henry Hawk, standing in an empty room announcing to CBS that he was still a candidate. On Wednesday Paul Newman, a delegate from Connecticut, delivered a moving tribute to the late Adlai Stevenson along with Dore Schary and Ralph Bellamy. And another Connecticut delegate, playwright Arthur Miller, announced, "This is the most exciting and meaningless event I've ever attended," which may be the funniest thing he ever said. Singer Andy Williams, a delegate from Los Angeles, showed up two days late for everything, in a crew-neck sweater and a bow tie, to express dissatisfaction with the whole convention.

But the boil was just beginning to erupt. There was still Mayor Daley of Chicago, who got the Biggest Ass of the Convention Award by bringing bagpipes and fiendishly welcoming delegates to his Fascist police state without any reference to the tear gas bombs that were exploding near their hotel rooms or the cab strike or the transit strike or the telephone strike, which all but made their presence impossible. No mention either of Chicago's blue-helmeted cops jumping on the hippies and the college kids, breaking their arms and dragging them off in bloody heaps because they were protesting the slaughter of 25,000 American boys in Vietnam. It was like watching an uprising of the Nazi Gestapo.

The police assaulted twenty-one reporters and cameramen covering the convention, and everyone from *Newsweek* to Chicago's own *Daily News* was demanding meetings with the head of the Chicago police department. By the second day, there were 29 people in the hospital and 67 people in jail.

Inside the International Amphitheatre, things were no better. One security guard slugged CBS correspondent Dan Rather right before the eyes of millions of horrified viewers in a bawdy roughhouse attempt to shield the public from rightful information. It was hardly one of the best displays of Democracy I've ever seen. In fact, the Democrats made a mockery of the word.

Heads of delegations begged their delegates to stay as they walked disgustedly out of the convention. Truckloads of "Hubert Humphrey for President" demonstration garbage littered the Amphitheatre, but the McCarthy banners were barred from the convention floor. Legitimate delegates were beaten and dragged and stomped and carried bodily from the floor because their credentials were not around their necks like branded cattle, and when he tried to cover one such bloody incident at the hands of the Chicago storm troopers, CBS correspondent Mike Wallace got stomped and pushed along the floor with blood streaming down his head.

One thing that can be said of the revolting affair: it captured the raw nerves of this sick, demented country, while the GOP fiasco in Miami reflected nothing more than the width of a yawn. One thing that cannot be condoned: the use of Chicago in the first place. It's an ugly, hostile cesspool that only added fuel to the sewer of flames already plaguing the American system. I hope the people of Chicago are as ashamed of their police as the rest of the world is. And as for Mayor Daley, I'd say he has a lot of explaining to do.

All over the dial, the damage results came in on Mayor Daley. Roger Mudd on CBS called him "the arch enemy of his party." Walter Cronkite wanted to pack up everything and get the hell out of the sewer called Chicago. Eric Sevareid called it "the most disgraceful event in the history of political conventions." Mike Wallace was mauled and arrested. The program manager of one of the CBS evening news programs tried to aid a CBS cameraman who had been stomped on and wasn't even allowed to call an ambulance.

Speeches were made before millions of viewers trying to explain the police state atmosphere under which the convention was struggling to take place while Mayor Daley's henchmen were shown on camera laughing and clapping each other on the backs like locker-room buddies. Every time the delegates tried to move that the convention be adjourned and relocated in another city where fascism did not reign, the chair gaveled them down and treated them like dogs.

Film clips were shown through Walter Cronkite's anger, of an innocent Chicago woman trying to pick up some college kids in her car to save them from bayonets, only to have her car surrounded by machine guns and tear gas. By Wednesday night, 150 people had been brutally beaten at the hands of the Chicago police, many of them wearing white arm bands.

The question is: What do we do about it? Do we sit back and take it? The

Democratic party has lived up to its ass symbol. It has proved through massive ferocity, brutality, and atrocity that conventions do not reflect the citizens of America. It has suggested that the convention system cannot exist in a modern democracy. It has so alienated the Negroes that they will undoubtedly pull away and form a fourth party. And it has proved that it cannot run a convention, so how can it run another four-year war-mongering administration?

Finally, through the hysteria and the horror and the hate, Humphrey got his medal. But his medal looks dirty and tarnished. He has absolutely nothing to be proud of. We are stuck with the same boring, pompous, creepy-crawlies who are bound and determined to lead us into a poisonous future with the same kind of muddle we've had for the past four years.

"I'm not voting!" was the cry around the country last week, and now that the asses in Chicago have had their way, it's gonna get louder in November.

September 6, 1968

Reporting on the Democratic Convention, that Hitlerized version of Ringling Brothers, took up so much space last week there was no room left to discuss Lauren Bacall's fall fashion preview of the Paris collections on CBS.

As far as I'm concerned, the best fashion show ever recorded on film is still the Audrey Hepburn–Fred Astaire–Suzy Parker–Richard Avedon–Kay Thompson cornucopia in *Funny Face.* But CBS's report from Paris was the best example of how to photograph the world of fashion I've yet to see in the television medium (a medium that needs all the fashion it can get) and much of its success was due to the stunning presence of Betty Bacall herself. Curious as a Burmese cat and sleek as an ocelot on its way to Maximilian's, Betty did for Paris what Taylor did for London, Sophia did for Rome, and Melina did for Greece. She looked better than I've ever seen her look (very much à la *Designing Woman*, which is still the chicest movie she ever made in her Hollywood days) and she was a good reporter, too. She watched 1,000 editors, 800 buyers, and 300 models descend on the City of Light for eight days to view 35 collections. She lunched in a floating restaurant on the Seine with Marc Bohan, took the audience behind the scenes of the Dior maison where hemlines must surely be sewn with threads of solid gold, danced barefoot with Ungaro, walked through the woods with Yves St. Laurent, and waltzed slow motion in a silver checkerboard miniskirt with five young men in Cardin suits on her way to a male fashion show. She exposed the couturiers as men instead of walking calla lilies (Cardin admitted he had a $22 million gross last year and "a big turnover in friends") and made pungent side comments on everything she saw ("Fashion people live on gossip, nervous energy, espresso, and pep pills").

Milton Greene's camera work was refreshing and beautiful and almost too good for television. It all got a little too icky with all that mugging and hugging with Ungaro, and for this male viewer the whole show could have been cut by about twenty minutes with no expense to its dignity. But it showed fashion for the first time the way it should be utilized on television and it turned Lauren Bacall into the most breathtaking reporter these tired eyes have ever seen on the journalism scene. If only she had covered the fiasco in Chicago, the rest of the television week might not have been such a total eyesore!

"*I Dream of Jeannie* will not be presented tonight so we can present the following special program," said the announcer on NBC Wednesday night. Music to my ears even during the fall and winter television season when I'm not desperate, so thinking something might enliven the end-of-summer blues, I stuck around. Nothing much. Just half an hour of hokum propaganda from George Wallace at a mind-boggling prime time expense to his campaign for President. Between outbursts like "When I'm your President, I'm gonna take every Communist out of every defense plant in Texas," and narrative hoopla like "Why has George Wallace's popularity leaped? Because he's not afraid to speak out; he doesn't let the polls stop him," signs flashed on and off announcing the post office box in Montgomery, Alabama, where Americans who want to invest in a share of the future could send contributions. He's on the ballot in many states in the Union and he's filing law suits in others, so like it or not, he seems to be a Very Big Presence on the political scene. And occasionally, among the "y'all votes" and the "glad to see y'alls" and the "y'all come agains" he makes a statement:

On Vietnam: "We need some eyeball-to-eyeball talk with our allies. We've gotta tell them we're in trouble and you better help us or pay back some of the money you owe us." On law and order: "We're gonna have law and order in the streets of Washington if I have to put the National Guard every 5 feet apart wearing guns."

On the race problem: "I have never in my life made a statement against any race, creed, or nationality. In 1966 my wife received more Negro support than any other candidate."

On education: "I want to return control of the public school systems to the local boards so not one dime of your tax money going to Washington will be spent on busing your children any place you don't want them to go."

On the press: "*Time* and *Newsweek* are made for people who can't think, *Life* is made for people who can't read, and the *Saturday Evening Post* is made for people who can't read OR think. Don't believe anything in the *New York Times*. Don't forget when Castro took over Cuba he didn't fool us down in Alabama one bit, but the *New York Times* called him the George Washington of Cuba."

Finally, after an announcement that even a $5 contribution would help buy 200 bumper stickers for your car, Wallace closed with one of his vote-getting crowd-pleasers about the New York counterfeiters who accidentally printed some $18 bills. The bills were so pretty they didn't want to throw them away, so they decided to go down and pass them off on some of those ignorant Alabama hillbillies. They came to an old grizzled Alabama mountaineer store that looked like a good place to pass off the first one and asked the old grizzled Alabama mountaineer: "Can you give us change for an $18 bill?" Without batting an eye, the old grizzled Alabama mountaineer said, "Sure can. You want three sixes or two nines?"

It's Wallace's way of uniting the little unwashed masses of hard-working everyday people who are fed up with Humphrey and Nixon and getting them to vote for his independent party ticket in November. There must be a better way to do it, but neither Humphrey nor Nixon has discovered the key. According to the latest polls, Wallace is outsmarting both of them. And television sits and waits. There's enough prime time for everybody. All it costs is the taxpayer's money.

Summer television has been so desperate it has even resorted to talent contests. Mercifully, NBC's *Showcase '68* went off the Air Tuesday night in a burst of suicidal glory with all the winners throughout the summer turning up to compete for a ten thousand dollar prize in the middle of all the cotton candy and cattle dung at the Ohio State Fair. Most of the "talent" smelled as rotten as the atmosphere, but there was one amazingly talented, unbelievably young jazz group called the Craig Hundley Trio that swung some hair-raising jazz. Three geniuses who looked like real teen-agers instead of prehistoric cave men and played brilliant jazz instead of rock-psych-out-hip-protest-clatter you can dance to. Three judges who looked like dropouts from the Golden Door's all-male Jogging for Collapsed Lungs Week in Escondido gave the thousand bucks to something in Halloween costumes called Sly and the Family Stone, who gurgled and screamed their way through a torture chamber of dissonance that sounded like paraplegic Munchkins smashing garbage can lids together at 78 r.p.m. If you were unlucky enough, bored enough, or desperate enough you already know *Showcase '68* was sponsored by Bufferin. It may be the smartest move Bufferin ever made, because at the end of the hour I have serious doubts that there was a single viewer who didn't need one.

September 13, 1968

When the flamboyantly vulgar Mike Todd died on November 22, 1958, he was hard at work on a mind-boggling new movie process called Smellovision, which would enable the audience to smell everything on the screen. Be thankful for small favors. The process never got to television, so everybody was spared a whiff of *Around the World of Mike Todd*, which he had nothing to do with, which was shown last Sunday night on ABC, and which smelled bad enough the way it was.

The funniest spot on the show was an old film clip showing Todd and Elizabeth Taylor arriving at the 1956 Oscars hot on the heels of Debbie Reynolds and Eddie Fisher. After that, it was downhill all the way, and it looked suspiciously like a well-timed publicity gimmick to get a bit of new mileage out of the re-release of *Around the World in 80 Days*. Todd was an expert con-man who made a success out of bringing a certain kind of trash to the kind of public that clamored for it, but this "special" never got to the point of what he was all about.

"I'm Orson Welles," said Orson Welles, as though there was some doubt, "and Mike Todd was the most colorful of all showmen." There is still some doubt about that too, although in 60 minutes there were some fairly colorful facts to back up the assumption. He lost a million dollars twice before he was twenty-one. He had his first hit in 1939, when he produced an act in which a girl had her panties burned off onstage. With a $240,000 payroll and less than half of that in the bank, he went out and bought a diamond for Liz Taylor ("It was 29 and 7/8 carats because Mike said 30 carats would be vulgar," flickered Liz). It wasn't a very good example of why we're all supposed to love a heel. Nor was Art Buchwald's story of how Todd tried to gyp him out of $700 once by skipping town. But everybody smiled a lot, like they loved the guy.

Then there was Gypsy Rose Lee, bragging about Todd's meat-and-potatoes World's Fair shows that were low on class and high on nudity. ("My picture was even bigger than Stalin's," cooed Gypsy.) "He told Cole Porter how to write songs and even tried to tell me how to sing 'em," belted Ethel Merman. "He was the greatest hustler this town's ever seen," said Toots Shor, as though it was a commendation. Meanwhile he gambled heavily and lost not only thousands of dollars on the races but a whole race track, while his marriages all crumbled. (It would have been a lot more revealing to have had Joan Blondell, another ex-Mrs. Todd, talking about him than a lot of drinking cronies.)

About 20 minutes were actually devoted to this kind of flackery and the rest of the show was spent showing old film clips from *Around the World in 80 Days*, in which most of the names promised as guests appeared within the context of their actual roles. More interesting were the films of the colossal disaster Todd held at Madison Square Garden (remember?) when 18,000 people pushed and shoved and sweated and stole everything in sight while elegant women beat up kids over hamburgers and waiters hoarded champagne, watered it down, and sold it for $10 a bottle. Like most obituaries on film, it showed more about the people who "remember" than it did about the subject. Every time you heard the Mike Todd voice it was Martin Balsam talking. Were there no tapes of the original Mike Todd voice? And what of Mike Todd the man inside the clown suit? Was he always a circus? According to Elizabeth Taylor, the day after one of her famous divorces (to Michael Wilding, I believe) she was sitting in an office at MGM sipping a Coke(!!) when Todd "charged in like a bull, dragged me down the hall nearly breaking my arm, and said he had to marry me. I just looked at him the way a rabbit looks at a mongoose (!!) and thought 'He's out of his mind! He's stark-raving mad!'"

Was Mike Todd out of his mind? Was he really stark-raving mad? I'm sure I couldn't tell you on the basis of this cheap excuse for a television profile. The flamboyance was real, but the genius remains purely imaginary.

The wondrous Patricia Routledge, whose exposure to American audiences has to date been limited to a hazardous success of slow-witted American theatrical disasters far beneath her vast abilities, turned up on New York's Channel 13 Tuesday night in the first of a series of four one-hour dramas based on the life of Queen Victoria, and the pleasure derived from her characterization of the young queen at the beginning of her reign was the stuff great theatrical memories are made of. Miss Routledge was innocent and wise, with the rapturous voice of a starling at daybreak and the range of a battalion of ladies twice her age. The next three hours in future weeks will undoubtedly show her trials with Disraeli, her marriage to Albert, and her growing old with ginger on her tongue. In all her moods, Miss Routledge is, on the tiny cramped screen, the same kind of actress she is in the flesh—dependably superb.

I don't know why David Susskind is so unpopular. He continues to produce some of the best quality drama on television at a time in the medium's life-span when drama is a dirty word. And, if one can find enough compassion to forgive him for an occasional lapse of taste like *Laura*, his productions usually work on the mini-screen as though they were full-scale Broadway plays. *From Chekhov, with Love* was an hour of champagne Wednesday night on CBS. Nigel Davenport was dusty as an old antique in his sputtering impersonation of Maxim Gorky, but John Gielgud rolled out those sub-cellar R's with great relish as Chekhov himself, and the ladies in the cast—Peggy Ashcroft, Dorothy Tutin, and Wendy Hiller—were breathtaking to watch. Rarely does television get a chance to show such monumental acting in the course of ninety minutes and this was ninety minutes of the best television I've seen in a long, long time. Personally, I loathe tableau-style entertainments and after a few initial painted backdrops and cutout figures, tedium was a constant threat to Jonathan (*Beyond the Fringe*) Miller's thoughtful script. Any attempt to recreate Chekhov needs the tools of Chekhov, from mossy beards to stifling, three-ton velvet draperies. But the acting was so brilliant all imbalance was perfected instantly through the sheer magic and power of performers who could make parasols out of dust-mops by mere insinuation. It was an obvious gamble for CBS to devote ninety minutes of prime time to a play about Chekhov that didn't star Joey Bishop. Everyone connected with this production is to be applauded. Bravo, CBS. Bravo, David.

Two instalments of the new syndicated *Donald O'Connor Show* are, admittedly, no basis for a verdict, but from the looks of things I'd say it's going to have to shape up or, regrettably, ship out. I say regrettably because, as a devoted, dyed-in-the-wool *Singin' in the Rain* fan (we must be universal as well as legion—the last time I was in Paris I was awakened at 3 A.M. by French mippy-boppers dancing down the Rue de l'Université singing old Donald O'Connor numbers), I know MGM's ageless Peter Pan is capable of bigger and brighter things. Syndicated variety shows have tiny budgets, so I don't expect a Vincente Minnelli production number. But watching Debbie Reynolds do her petrified Zsa Zsa routine is hardly my idea of a revolutionary breakthrough in late-night television. Doing a funny take-off on *The Graduate* with the riotous Joyce Jameson and talented Carolyn Jones, and hoofing it with Ruby Keeler sparked up the second show a bit, but there's work to do. I'm not giving up. And even the way it looks now, it's a lot more fun to watch than the *Tonight Show*. But then, isn't everything?

September 20, 1968

Only the numbers keep changing. A year and three months after Barbra Streisand's "happening" in Central Park in the summer of 1967, the number of people who were there gets bigger all the time. When the event took place, the crowd was reported to check in at 100,000. Monsanto's expensive two-page trade ads for last Sunday's hour special on CBS claimed 128,000. *TV Guide* says 130,000. Give or take a few thousand sweating bodies, Barbra is a great talent, but before her awesome drawing power goes to the wrong people's heads, it might be well worth remembering that it was a hot, muggy night, when the steaming populace of New York was looking for any excuse known to man to get out in the streets and cool off, and, more important it was absolutely FREE. I'm surprised they didn't float over into Jersey City.

Fortunately, Barbra was worth it. The only sour note was a perfectly godawful dress designed by Irene Sharaff (I suspect foul play—Miss Sharaff is usually a genius) that looked like a cut-up parachute dyed in RIT. Otherwise, careful editing and a night on which Barbra was in excellent voice made her "happening" a triumph. Her material was tasty, her

Lower Second Avenue Kook City image was held to a minimum of ad-libbing, and the television audience (there they go again—Columbia Records, who recorded the sound track, claims twenty million viewers; Barbra's sponsor claims twenty-five million) saw only the best of the evening.

Highlights: some beautiful helicopter shots of New York after dark, Barbra doing a delightful reprise of one of her earliest underground hits "I'm in Love With Harold Mingert," a lovely arrangement of "Silent Night," and Barbra cradling the mob in the palm of her hand with two hair-raisingly magnificent new songs—"New Love Is Like a New Born Child" and "Natural Sounds." Thrilling.

What the audience at home didn't see (because of CBS's careful editing) were closeups of all the pimple-faced brats who had slept on the ground for two nights straight to see their idol, a swirling mob of hysterical humanity swarming, shoving, screaming, pushing, sitting in their gefilte fish and hot dog mustard, throwing Dixie Cups and beer cans at the cops, and littering Central Park with so many tons of greasy garbage it took a week and a half to clean it up and return all the found babies to all the lost mothers.

Television's stubborn insistence on outdating itself has never seemed more flagrant than in the new Saturday morning Archie Andrews kiddie show on CBS. When I was a kid, Saturday mornings meant sleeping late, raking leaves, and listening to the anthropology of my youth on the radio through the eyes of Archie, Reggie, Jughead, Betty, and Veronica. When I was seventeen, I was a man of the world. I proved it by throwing away two hundred Archie comic books with a throb in my throat. We may have been corny in the Fifties, but we knew where we were at.

Well, the gang at Riverdale High is back—animated, noisy, and Saturday mornings on CBS—and *nobody* seems to know where *anyone's* at. No Mod clothes for this gang. They still wear saddle oxfords and plaid skirts and—God, what will the swinging little sadists who call themselves today's children think?—they still say "Gee Whiz!" In Saturday's debut segment, there was a brief stab at a plot line when the gang got involved raising money to bring some entertainment to Riverdale High. Then there was a vain attempt to update things by having *my* Veronica stand at a piano while Jughead's dog Hot Dog (a new character) thumped his tail and everybody did a dance called the "Bubble Gum" to a forgettable rock song called "Bang-Shang-A-Lang." Oh wow! The excitement wouldn't stop.

The only thing wrong with this show is it comes about fifteen years too late. It's probably a lot healthier for kids than all the vampires and Lesbian warriors from outer space on the other Saturday morning kiddie shows, but just as unreal. This gang is as antiquated as Fritzi Ritz in wedgies.

So far, television's new season hasn't produced much in the way of originality, so NBC has added a Monday night movie (this week: *Madame X*), bringing the total number of network-movie nights to seven. Translation: there are now seven nights a week you can watch something old and terrible instead of something new and terrible. *Madame X*, quite fantastically, is not yet three years old, although it looked embalmed. The reasons why people have laughed and cried through this gluttonous camp five different times since 1916 are best left to accredited sado-masochists. I merely laughed. Lana Turner, in this fifth mummified remake, is forced to abandon her baby by her venomous mother-in-law (played by Constance Bennett, who looked more like Lana Turner's daughter) and years later, after plummeting to the depths in Mexico, being found half-dead in the snow by a dashing concert pianist and committing murder on the side, is defended in court by a lawyer who turns out to be her own son who doesn't know she is his own mother. Nobody but Ross Hunter has the nerve to make movies like this any more, but I'm kind of glad he does. Otherwise, whatever would we do for comedy? As Pauline Kael so aptly described it: "It's not even imitation of life; it's just imitation of movies." And they cried all the way to the bank.

Julia is the kind of show talented people with taste and sensitivity sit around at cocktail parties and wish television would produce. It took Hal Kanter to do it. Mr. Kanter, I'm a fan. *Julia* is a poignant, moving, sophisticated, human show which drops the phony laugh tracks and attaches its antenna to the human heart. It isn't funny ha-ha; it's for real.

On the first show Tuesday night on NBC, Diahann Carroll turned out to be the first Negro I've ever seen on television who is not a symbol of anything. She's just a beautiful, hard-working, intelligent, everyday kind of lady. I wish she lived next door to me. (P.S. She has also turned into a perfectly marvelous actress—warm, uncomplicated, natural and as true as a vitamin pill.) No sock it to me judge. No female Bill Cosby. Just a lady I'd like to be lucky enough to know. She is a registered nurse with the finest references and the highest qualifications who just happens to be black. She lives in a nice apartment on a nice street. Her husband has been killed in Vietnam and she has a child to raise, played with charm and un-self-conscious élan by Marc Copage, one of the most adorable kid actors I've seen on TV or anywhere else in a long, long time.

That's about it. No big-deal racial explosions, no pretentious social isometrics, no kitchen-sink Harlem psychiatry. Just life, the way it is lived with humor and class every day of the world by millions of other sane, well-adjusted people who also happen through no fault of their own to be black. Not that race is never mentioned. Julia is no Jeanne Crain in *Pinky*, passing for white. She has her problems. On the first show, she doesn't happen to be what her prospective employer has in mind. "Am I too old or too young?" she asks wearily with a pinch of sardonic wit flashing across her face. Later, a doctor from the clinic that has just refused to hire her, calls her up and offers her the job. Sample dialogue:

> Julia: "Has anybody told you?"
> Doctor: "Told me what?"
> Julia: "I'm colored."
> Doctor: "What color are you?"
> Julia: "I'm a Negro."
> Doctor: "Well, have you always been a Negro, or are you just trying to be fashionable? Be here at 9:00, and try to look pretty. I'm so tired of ugly nurses. I married one."

I fail to see anything wrong with dialogue like that, although there will undoubtedly be Negroes who object on general principle. Nor do I see anything wrong with the scene in which Corey, Julia's son, is told by his new little white friend, Earl J. Waggedorn, "You know what?" "What?" "Your mother's colored." "I'm colored, too!" "You are? Oh, boy!" Then they collapse in a bundle of sofa pillows and a new adventure begins. Anyone who thinks that is a phony scene knows absolutely nothing about the very special world of children.

I like the way *Julia* allows its characters to get acquainted with their new audience slowly, like new neighbors who don't want to intrude too fast or get too pushy. I like the way it refuses to acknowledge the old formula of making flashy introductions and hammering home tiresome dogma. I like the way Hal Kanter has fashioned his script and directed his players so that each scene takes its time. I like the actors (after all the drunks and SOB's Lloyd Nolan has been playing for years, it's especially nice to see him once again as a real person; I hope his role as Julia's boss gets better exposure in future episodes). Unless future instalments let me down, television seems to at last have a show with real blood in its veins instead of synthetic cellulose. Just call me prejudiced. I'm in love with *Julia.*

September 27, 1968

Like the flu, a new season of television is upon us and there's nothing much anyone can do about it, except maybe boycott the sponsors. There are teen-age cops, Jolly Green Giants, Bugs Bunny cartoons, sex-starved ghosts, Negro cowboys, a mouse who comes over on the *Mayflower*, enough series about unmarried parents with brats to raise to turn your stomach dark green, and so many old movies you need a box lunch and a change of clean underwear to sit through them all. Some samples:

The Doris Day Show (CBS). CBS has been very uncooperative this year, guarding Doris Day from the critics like she was the Transvaal Diamond and Murf the Surf was in town. Now that the first show of the series has been unleashed on an unsuspecting public, I can certainly understand why. Doris is a widow who gives up smelly old New York to raise her dead husband's two sons out on the farm with a retarded fieldhand and a Grandpa who looks like Lon Chaney in *The Wolf Man.* On the first show, Doris got to sing "Que Sera, Sera" three times (once in the shower while her kids were stealing her wallet) and everyone was always kissing each other on top of the head. Doris is an enormously natural and personable performer, but she's neither old nor ugly, so why, I'd like to ask, must all of her closeups be shot with so many filters over the camera lens that she looks like she's being photographed through Vaseline? Everything about this show is so icky-poo sweet and jim dandy confectionery you might know the sponsor would be Duncan Hines cake mix. At the end of the first segment, Doris closed her eyes and made a wish. I bet I know what it was . . .

Adam-12 (NBC). That grand old-timer, the embittered cop (played by Martin Milner, who looks neither grand nor old) who has just lost his partner on the precinct beat to a crook's bullet, is so bitter he's down on everything until a handsome brave new cop (Kent McCord) pops in full of passion and guts. Hoopla! The boys turn into the Batman and Robin of the Drag-net set. *Adam-12*, by the way, is the code number of the boys' patrol car. Now, what's a nice car like that doing on a lousy show like this?

The Ghost and Mrs. Muir (NBC). As pretty and talented as Hope Lange is, and as much as I've led the fight for years for more important roles for this highly underrated actress, she is hopelessly awash in a tidal wave of clichés on this silly ectoplasmic soap opera. A widow with two brats to raise (she and Doris Day should get together and save some dough on sitters), Mrs. Muir, while constantly reminding everybody within fifty miles that she has practically no money, buys a castle straight out of an old Bluebeard the Pirate movie. The castle is haunted, naturally, by a cantankerous bearded Lothario, an old salt of the sea who hates the idea of a woman living in his house. Mrs. Muir thinks nothing at all of living with a ghost, but she becomes downright exasperated when he refuses to materialize and blows chimney soot in her eyes to boot. "If there's one thing I can't stand, it's a cowardly ghost," says Mrs. Muir, stamping her foot. And if there's one thing I can't stand, it's *The Ghost and Mrs. Muir*.

(P.S. She also has a wooly, cuddly dog named Scuffy who licks everybody in the face a lot, as wooly, cuddly dogs are wont to do. This dog is not to be confused with Lord Nelson, the wooly, cuddly dog who licks everybody in the face a lot on *The Doris Day Show*. They are two different characters. Oh, yes. Mrs. Muir's house is called Gull Cottage. The only thing that moves are the gulls, who had absolutely no trouble whatsoever walking away with the first show. The way things are going on this show, something tells me they'll be looking for work elsewhere in about thirteen weeks.)

Land of the Giants (ABC). In some future year, one of those 2001 space flights to London goes awry and after being attacked by a kitten the size of a five-story house, several smart-aleck passengers who say bitchy things like "I love it—it'll never replace in-flight movies," and "What do we do for an encore?" land on an unidentified planet stocked with papier-mâché trees, enough elephant-sized rubber plants to fill the jungle exhibit at Disneyland, and a population of humorless giants who act like auditions for a ptomaine commercial.

On the first show, which looked like it was written in thirty minutes over a pastrami sandwich at the Stage Delicatessen, such stock characters as The Exceptional Child with The Wooly, Cuddly Dog (every new series has one), The Wisecracking Redhead, The Malibu Surfer Pilot, The Pretty Stewardess, The Negro Co-Pilot and The Man with the Mysterious Suitcase Filled with Unexplained Money found themselves imprisoned in test tubes by such stock villains as The Evil Scientist and The Evil Scientist's Gale Sondergaard-Like Lab Assistant. Future episodes promise such horrors as monstrous rats, tarantulas, and assorted other terrors bigger than a breadbox. "I'm afraid Flight 612 to London will be delayed," said the Malibu pilot caustically. It sounded like a threat to me.

Here's Lucy (CBS). The incompetent redheaded fruitcake is back with a new format, this time as a widow with two kids to raise. The only thing that saves this treacle is the absence of the family's wooly, cuddly dog. He may show up later. Lucy's new character is called Lucille Carter, who works for her brother-in-law (played by old Lucy regular Gale Gordon) in an employment agency. This gives Lucy the opportunity to meet lots of different zanies on each show and bring in different situations. Other regulars are Lucy's real-life children, Lucie, Jr., and Desi, Jr. Neither of them can act, but it doesn't seem to matter because this show is so terrible you wouldn't know it if they could. Sample witty line: When Lucie, Jr., gets laryngitis from surfing and botches her singing job at a private party, Mom says: "Does Mahalia Jackson go surfing before she sings?" I Love Lucy, but these scripts have got to get better . . .

Mayberry R.F.D. (CBS). Andy Griffith got tired of weekly TV, so they got rid of him by marrying him off. They got rid of Don Knotts by sending him on the honeymoon too. And they got rid of Ronnie Howard by sending him on a camping trip. Everyone else is still down in North Carolina and folksy as Granny's patchwork quilt, but without all the cornballs, this series looks much more charming. On the first show, Frances Bavier made great use of her three thousand assorted Aunt Somebody roles by milking the hell out of a scene in which she tried to steal eggs from under a reluctant hen on her first day on a farm. Ken Berry is an attractive and ingratiating performer as Sam Jones, a widower with a son to raise (zilch!) and everything's jake. I may be crazy, but I liked the unpretentiousness of this one.

MORE NEXT WEEK.

October 4, 1968

The Outcasts (ABC). Take one uppity ex-slave and one pompous, embittered, sullen, tough-talking, grim-jawed ex-slave owner and throw them together as bounty hunters for no explainable reason except that interracial themes are "in" this season, and you almost have a pretty good idea of how hopeless *The Outcasts* is. I say almost, because *The Outcasts* is even worse than it sounds. Abrasive is hardly the word for their relationship. They fight, snarl, beat each other to a bloody pulp as often as ABC's sensitivity to violence and bloodshed will allow, say clever things to each other like "You do have a natural advantage in the dark, boy—unless you happen to smile" and "That's mighty white of you—as the sayin' goes," and, according to one press release, "propagate a bond of respectful bigotry." Whatever that means. Don Murray must be desperate to lend his considerable talents to this dreary post-Civil War *Defiant Ones*. A deadly dull shoot-'em-up is no less deadly dull just because one of the critters doing the shooting is black. The first show involved a cavalry captain stealing silver on its way to be deposited in the U.S. Mint to pay for a trip to Paris. "Anyplace so I don't have to look at another saddle or another can of beans." I was with him all the way.

That's Life (ABC). A Broadway musical every Tuesday night that at least tries to be fresh and original. The format is the musical revue; the thin plotline traces the love life of a typical all-American boy-meets-girl team with different shows devoted to The Meeting, The Courtship, The Wedding, The Honeymoon, The New Baby, etc. What separates this hour of fluff from all the others is its use of the stage—each show takes place in a real proscenium theater with a live audience instead of canned laughs, with bloopers, missed cues, and fluffed lines left in to give the effect of the long-lost days of live TV. Be grateful for small favors.

Robert Morse, as the boy, looks like a cuddly panda and the show makes good use of his quivering, palpitating little Pogo voice on new songs and old standards. He also does the Gene Kelly bit on an occasional dance number and has a wacky way with a kooky line. E. J. Peaker makes a pretty, perky debut as the girl. All told, a pleasant way to kill an hour.

The Don Rickles Show (ABC). The only thing more obnoxious than a rude, insulting, arrogant bore is a rude, insulting, arrogant bore who goes around apologizing for it. Rickles used to be funny, but he seems to have become such an egomaniac that he has now fallen into the Carson-Bishop pit and I don't think he has the talent or the versatility to crawl back out again. The format of this silly imposter masquerading as a comedy show is unthinkably mechanical, but I was less annoyed by Rickles's boorishness than by his continual insistence that he's really vile but nice. Then he attempted to prove it with thirty minutes of seventh-grade humor during which he broke up constantly at his own paralyzed one-liners, insulted his announcer and orchestra plus a fat man in the audience ("Isn't this fun?" he pleaded), attacked a female German vocalist by saying, "I guess Daddy during the war was a ski instructor?" and displayed some stultifying examples of how to get dead silence from an audience. Sample: Pat McCormick, Rickles's weekly fall guy, literally fell down. Rickles jabbed, "I wish you welts all over your body; I hope you roll over and get a harpoon in your navel!" Oh sure, real comic genius here, folks. Just what television needs. Personally, I consider this the one show of the new season on which the commercial breaks will be more eagerly awaited than what goes on in-between.

Lancer (CBS). Eugene O'Neill in spurs. The father-son relationship between a phony cattle baron called Murdoch Lancer (some poor slob must have slaved over a hot Beverly Hills swimming pool for a day and a half to dream that one up) and his two cretin sons (one is a dandyish fop, the other is what the press agents call a "cynical gun-fighter" and a bandit to boot) is pretentious and desperate. But what this series does have is some handsomely photographed scenery and some well-paced action sequences good enough to grace a John Ford movie. Hatred boiled over in the first show when the father (crippled by a sniper's bullet, yet) summoned his sons (who didn't remember him, alas) to help him fight off evil marauders. Everybody hated everybody else for a good forty minutes, but by the end of the hour things were already getting tepid.

The Mod Squad (ABC). Three young punks three steps from jail get hired by the fuzz to pose as teen-age drug addicts, high school teachers, and all sorts of misfits to break up teen-age crime. Already the show promises more mod than squad and already it's in trouble. If you're as bored with the dirty toenail set as I am, you won't find much of interest here. Still, I enjoyed the energy and versatility of the show's three young stars. Clarence Williams III, Peggy Lipton (a luscious hippie-type in straw hair and leather minis), and Michael Cole (a tousled-hair motorcycle type with James Dean pretensions). If they save the idea from going under the knife before the final prognosis is pronounced negative, this series could have strong potential in the action genre.

Here Come the Brides (ABC). More yawns than girls, but here they come, new mates for the sex-starved Li'l Abners who inhabit a logging camp in 1870. Although they pretend to be pure of body and soul, most of the girls on this show look more like prostitutes than the virginal flowers they're supposed to play. None of them can act, but then neither can any of the men on the show. The whole thing was much more fun (and a lot less indigestible) when it was *Seven Brides for Seven Brothers* back in the heyday of MGM musicals. Rehashed and reduced to the twenty-one inch screen, the whole thing leaves me unthawably ice-cold.

The Ugliest Girl in Town (ABC). A funny idea that threatens to wear itself out fast unless more effective first aid is applied than the debut indicated. Peter Kastner, a fuzzy-wuzzy of a boy, with ears like cantaloupes, jaws like powder puffs, and a split between his teeth big enough to drive a Mack truck through, plays a Hollywood office boy who follows a dolly to swinging London disguised as a female model, and turns Carnaby Street on. Trouble is, Peter Kastner in drag looks like a dumpy Catskill boys' camp misfit with bad teeth and myopic eyes who flunks canoe and ends up as Brünnhilde in the end-of-summer operetta. Even the kind of London that could produce a Twiggy or fall for a Penelope Tree wouldn't be taken in by this. Kastner sounds like Tiny Tim. And as for the send-up haute couture he wears, I've seen better drag on French poodles.

The Outsider (NBC) is a tough private eye show in which Darren McGavin does the Mike Hammer bit once too often in a poverty-belt take-off on the Paul Newman movie *Harper*. *The Good Guys* (CBS) is an egg laid already fried in which Bob Denver, who seems to make a career out of tastelessness, plays an unmarried cab driver who is a loser because he always invents things like low-calorie aspirin. Nothing good ever happens on *The Outsider* and nothing whatsoever happens on *The Good Guys*. Neither comment is meant as a recommendation.

October 18, 1968

Television commits suicide with alarming frequency these days, and the new season is further proof. Word has just reached me that one of the best shows on television, and I DO mean *The Dick Cavett Show,* is in serious danger of being canceled by ABC. I'm not really surprised. Creative programming is the term they throw around like jelly beans at the networks, but shouldn't this also include scheduling the right show in the right time slot? Dick Cavett has always been on weekday mornings from 10:30 to 12, in a lousy time slot when the only people at home are housewives and mothers of preschool children who would much rather tune in to game shows on NBC or old reruns of *Beverly Hillbillies* and *Andy Griffith* on CBS to keep the little monsters quiet and pacified. This kind of audience would rather soak up a little mediocrity than stimulate early-morning brain cells. Cavett has too much wit, intelligence, and good clean boy-next-door charm to survive in such a cutthroat medium, but if there is any justice left in television (and frankly I doubt it) he will get a regular nighttime spot, where he can stimulate rather than fight for his life in the ratings. I'd like to see ABC put him on opposite Johnny Carson and get rid of Joey Bishop altogether. Then we'd have a true test of where audience intelligence (if there is such a thing) lies.

Similarly, ABC has a good new show on its hands that doesn't seem to be catching on. It's called *That's Life* and it would be a perfect show to have dinner with in a 7:30–8:30 time slot. So where does it end up? In a 10–11 slot on Tuesday nights when everyone is tuned to the NBC Tuesday night movie that begins at 9 following the wonderful *Julia.* (*Julia,* by the way, seems to be catching on, which is one positive sign in the chaos.) Result: a repulsive, blood-and-dirty-toenails epic called *The Mod Squad* gets the 7:30–8:30 spot so we can all watch teen-agers taking dope and getting shot at during the dinner hour and *That's Life,* which is good, clean, bright entertainment with a strong sense of style, fights for its life in the idiotic battle of the ratings. Years from now, some bewildered studio executive will undoubtedly say, "Well, we tried to bring back some of the semblance of live musical variety and Broadway caliber entertainment we used to have on live TV in a show called *That's Life* and we tried giving the public good taste and intelligence in a talk-show format with Dick Cavett, but they didn't catch on. The public doesn't want class, it wants garbage." As sure as the sun will rise tomorrow, you can expect that kind of head-scratching statement. But don't wonder why good television seldom exists anymore. Sometimes the men who run the networks are their own worst enemies. And yours.

The Bob Hope Comedy Special Monday night on NBC was so stale it might as well have been a rerun of an old Colgate Comedy Hour from 1950. But it's tedium was more than erased by the Mitzi Gaynor special which followed. *Mitzi* was ambrosia in a season of mildewed bread.

Funny, what happens to Hollywood stars. Sometimes they become so trapped in mediocrity they distort their careers to such an alarming degree that the public forgets how basically genuine their talent is. The fresh scrubbed-nose wonder of the early Doris Day has all but been obliterated in the memory by the quagmire of cheapjack silliness her career has become, so that all that talent and freshness and delicious appeal I used to applaud in her early days at Warner Brothers have all but been forgotten by a public with a short memory. Doris Day has turned into a joke. The talent and energy and class are still there, but she prefers to keep them hidden under forty pounds of spray net.

The same thing happened to Mitzi Gaynor. She turned out one hideous 20th Century-Fox musical after another, succumbing to the press agentry that she would become another Betty Grable if she was just exposed long enough and to enough people. The plan backfired. The projects she appeared in were so rotten the public's attention span wore out. But Mitzi was smart (or maybe she has advisers who were smarter). She held out for the right project that would provide the right memory stimulus, and in her Monday night NBC special all was forgiven.

Mitzi! was like sodium pentathol. I started counting backward and before you could say Alice Faye it all came back. First of all, there must be some truth to women looking better when they lose their baby fat, because Mitzi looks fantastic. Her skits were brilliant, concise, and potato-chip crisp, and provided her with a steamer trunk of fresh impersonations. She was a Minnie Pearl lady sighing over George Hamilton on a television studio tour. She was a sophisticated chanteuse doing a sleek rendition of "Love Is Blue." Then she missiled her way into a lightning sketch about pet peeves in which she demonstrated the kind of women who annoy her. She was a country club organizer type who met her girl friend for lunch and turned a simple party into a black tie affair with forty guests. She was a teen-age babysitter who gives away the plot of the movie her employers are going to see. Then she was one of those talky women planning the next day's menu in bed while her husband is dozing off to sleep. ("Now darling, what do you want, some nice turkey?" "Z-z-z, ham . . ." "Let's see, H-A-M-ham." Pause. "But I thought you liked my stew." "Z-z-z-oh yes, stew." "But darling, I've already written down ham!") Etc. Until I was rolling in front of the set with laughter.

We saw the voluptuous Mitzi, doing a smashing big-band jazz arrangement of a Peter Gennaro dance number called "Pretty for Me" with magical Hi-Los-type voices wailing jazz in the background. We saw beautiful photography, filtering down through orange sunspots in the sky, as Mitzi, totally without makeup or glamour, turned into a bored little kid in tennis shoes and a baseball cap walking across a deserted playground on the first day of school and wrapping her stubby arms around a private tree. It was a beautiful study of loneliness at the age when children can be crueler than politicians, and it showed a new, wistful, windswept side of Mitzi I had never seen before. She is a magnificant actress. So good, in fact, that she reminded me of Julie Harris discovering "the we of me" in *The Member of the Wedding*. (I know it's hard to believe, but you should have seen it. The girl is sensational.)

The late-movie sketch she reserved for last was first-rate stuff, with Mitzi doing *Reader's Digest* condensations of three very familiar leading ladies. She was Roz Russell, the tough lady exec, quoting magazine subscriptions, signing corporation mergers, and firing personnel in three languages in pillbox hats, football shoulder pads, hair nets, and Lois Lane shoulder-strap bags. She was Doris Day, being chased from bed to bed by Rock Hudson in Courrèges boots circa 1961, delivering each line in a new coiffure and a new fashion design, ending up in a wedding gown as the final lights went out. Interspersed with all the hilarity were shots of Phil Harris as one of those red-faced, smiling used-car salesmen. With each commercial break, he got madder and madder so that by the time Mitzi danced her way down an ivory staircase in a Busby Berkeley fog of technicolor smoke in what looked like three tons of peach chiffon (I think she was supposed to be spoofing Rita Hayworth, but she looked more like Elaine Stewart in *The Bad and the Beautiful*), the used-car salesman was yelling belligerently at the viewers, who hadn't bought any cars. "You ungrateful, bleary-eyed zombies, home watchin' all those crummy movies while I'm sellin' all these . . . I wouldn't buy one of those lemons if it had wheels on it . . ."

Written with cleverness, inventiveness, and rollicking wit by Ann Elder and Larry Hovis (a regular on the Rowan and Martin *Laugh-In*), it was one of the best hours I've ever spent in front of the tube. Mitzi Gaynor is obviously one of the colossal talents of our age—a lady of supersonic good taste, startling versatility, and mind-boggling beauty. Is it clear that I love her?

October 25, 1968

Hemingway's Spain was a bore, and I'm sorry about that, because I didn't want it to be. But television specials that are beautiful to look at can sometimes be like perfectly sculptured people who are beautiful to look at—total washouts when they open their mouths. The idea was to photograph the country Hemingway loved and wrote about in a documentary style, retracing the steps of his characters through their own words. There were the voices of Rod Steiger and Jason Robards, droning on like bored actors performing at a lectern in a concert hall, reading passages from *For Whom the Bell Tolls* while the color cameras recorded the steps of Robert Jordan's journey through the Spanish Civil War. There was the mist on the highway, the pines and the yellow fields of grain, the delicate green mountain slopes with crests of white snow on their aging bald heads, the bracken in the meadows, ripe and lusty and poetic. "On this bank Pilar the gypsy remembers how it was," read the narrator. Then Estelle Parsons, a bad choice for Pilar, read another section of the book while the camera showed empty streets and empty meadows. Imagine an Actors' Studio method actress reading a Spanish gypsy and you have a pretty good idea what she sounded like. I could understand only about every third word.

Death in the Afternoon traced Papa's drive from Malaga to Madrid through the wine country. You saw the restaurant where he ordered asparagus. You saw the bull ring at Ronda and the plaza de toros in Madrid, with the romantic pink hotels and the cool inland breezes along the way. Then you watched Antonio Ordonez, now almost forty but still one of Spain's greatest matador-heros, preparing for the ring, praying to the madonna, sweating from nervousness, hiding the nerves and the fear behind all the pompous show business in the ring, hamming it up for the tourists like he was Muhammad Ali. There were beautiful slow motion stuff on Ordonez in pink and gold and an inkling of the Spanish philosphy and the whole fatalistic attitude of the Spaniards that we're all born to die so the slaughter of a bull is not, to them, the worst thing that can happen. They lost me right there, and by the time the blood and the cruelty and the stupidity of it all had gone this far, producer Lester Cooper made sure we saw it all. The kill was a ghastly and inhuman sight. The Spanish love death and so did Hemingway. It showed in his work.

Then the show switched to some passages from *The Sun Also Rises*, which he wrote in 1926 about all of his restless friends who left Paris and went to Spain to drink and make love and talk and see the bulls. There were more home movies, everything from brown cathedrals and misty cloudless hills to the early morning madness that seeps into Pamplona before the running of the bulls. The cameras contrasted the Mardi Gras atmosphere of people getting stomped and gored by vicious bulls with the serenity of people sitting in the cafes after it is all over sipping grappa and watching the boats on the marina in the setting sun. It was beautiful to watch but like Jake Barnes and Lady Brett it all became stupefyingly dull when nothing ever happened. This, I think, is where the trouble was. Hemingway's descriptive passages were the weakest points of his work. He excelled in his ethical code, in the psychology of the human being exposed in all of his vulnerability, not in writing Fitzpatrick travelogues. One solid hour of descriptive narration with no action and no plot became a lushly photographed bore. And a bore is a bore is a bore.

The Sophia Loren special Wednesday night on ABC was a delightful hour well-spent with one of the world's great charmers. You never learn much from these hour-long publicity stunts masquerading as profiles, but this one was at least distracting. "Isn't television marvelous," I kept saying aloud, as the cameras showed me through the gates of the Villa Ponti, a 2,000-year-old hideaway twenty miles outside Rome near the catacombs on the old Via Appia. And there, in a bedroom that looked like a leftover set from *La Dolce Vita*, was the mia-est mama of them all, discussing her meetings with world leaders, saying things like "How much can a man who can cause the next atomic war care about your next movie?" Speaking out with her big hands, pointing with her Italian mozzarella fingers, she toured the slums of Naples where she was born illegitimately, told about being called a toothpick as a child because she was so ugly even her relatives could scarcely look her in the eyes. She reminisced about the war years ("We starved six days, on the seventh we ate") and pointed with pride to the toy wagon in her kitchen which is the only thing her real father ever gave her. (He didn't even give her a name—the "Loren" came years later when a press agent changed the "T" in Marta Toren's name to "L".) There was also a glint of real roots to the box office queen as she showed the green and gold wallpaper she won in her first beauty contest. It was her grandfather's prize possession and she has never had it removed from the halls of his house.

Interspersed with the glamour of a movie siren showing off Dior fashions, which is all these things usually amount to, were shots of a poverty-stricken childhood when she sat through *Blood and Sand* twelve times watching Tyrone Power make love to Linda Darnell, early poses for romance magazines with dialogue coming out of her mouth in an Italian balloon, comic book style. There were also shots of her playing one of the thousands of extras in *Quo Vadis* (she was one of the slaves fanning Deborah Kerr), and a remarkable series of film clips tracing her rise from peasant to aristocrat through her cheap Walgreen's period (remember the Sophia Loren cheap period, all bosoms and peasant blouses and hoop earrings?) right up to the magnificent super Romeo Salta special she is today.

What I liked most about the hour was the way it refused to gloss over the ugliness. Miss Loren discussed frankly her romance with Carlo Ponti, the years of frustration that have been caused by the Italian marriage laws and her feelings of failure as a woman because she cannot bear children. There were lovely shots of her playing with her younger sister's baby as she announced she would gladly renounce stardom for the life of a mother. But meanwhile the life of one of the most adored, expensive, and sought-after creatures in the world doesn't seem so tough to play, and Sophia Loren plays it well, fighting the killing pace, driven through work and a blazing ambition to overcome the hideous past, losing the real girl in the parts she plays. Only in the parts are there happy endings.

It was an ingratiating visit, beautifully filmed and edited and obviously written by someone who fell in love with the subject. And what a subject: her nose is too big, her mouth is too big, she has the composites of all the wrong things, but put them all together and—pow!! All the natural mistakes of beauty fall together to create a magnificent accident. I can hardly wait for the rerun.

Latest word on *The Dick Cavett Show*: rest easy. The most sophisticated, intelligent, versatile, attractive, and entertaining talk show on television will not be canceled until Dec. 27. That means Dick won't get fired until two days after Christmas. Sort of revives your faith in human nature, doesn't it?

November 1, 1968

Where did they all go, those bigger-than-life superstars of the golden age of movies? Ask any movie buff (like me) and he'll agree. Television just doesn't produce stars like the old-timers. They carried around their own lightning. They were the American Dream and the whole world dreamed of being just like them. Glamour? It's become a joke. Today we're stuck with creeps like Mia Farrow, who looks like a wet wharf rat, says dirty four-letter words to prove she's not retarded, and gets thrown out of the Edwardian Room because she's wearing dirty sandals and a bedspread. On television, there isn't one twenty-one-inch star who is in the same league with Katharine Hepburn or Clark Gable or Bogart or Bette Davis. And don't forget Joan Crawford, who turned psychiatric wards into acting classes for posterity to watch and played the classic hootchy-kootchy dancer who became the governor's wife in endless Warner Brothers epics with the passion of a mother alligator eating her young. In recent years, she's become a phony Pepsi-Cola salesman and it's been embarrassing. Dispensing platitudes and Pepsi. The miscasting has been glaringly obvious.

Well, Crawford's back and the CBS soap opera *The Secret Storm* has got her. All week CBS repeated the corny announcement, which sounded like one of the lines from the sudser itself: "Christina Crawford, who plays the role of Joan Kane, has been temporarily hospitalized. However, we are pleased to announce that today and until her recovery, her role will be played by her mother—Miss Joan Crawford!" And there she was, playing a tough broad in her twenties (I wouldn't have believed it unless I had seen it with my own eyes, which I most assuredly did) with the old *Mildred Pierce* bounce and bite, chewing her way through the worst dialogue since Francis the Mule learned to talk. I took notes. So help me, it went like this: "That's right Archie, ya got some nerve. You know the law's after ya? You got the gall to stand there and ask me for a hundred bucks. Have you gone NUTS?? Why does everything hafta happen to me? You're against me—the whole world's against me—NOW GET OUTTA HERE!!"

On the show I saw, she was full of the old fight, slapping men in the face, throwing them out of her pad, slamming doors in their faces, pushing people around, smoking what looked like fourteen cigarettes in less than half an hour, and finally breaking down into a most unladylike screaming, hysterical fit. She was awful. She was delicious. And oh God, what a pro. She lit up the afternoon mini-screen like it hasn't been lit up in years. I don't wish her daughter any ill will, but I hope she takes a nice rest before returning to *The Secret Storm*. Long enough to keep feeding Crawford fans Crawford and more Crawford. Doing her thing beats peddling Pepsi-Cola any day.

I'm all for Hollywood movies in prime time, but the network flicks this season just keep getting worse. Where are the great films? Television is buying up the trash nobody ever wanted to see in the first place and filling the evening hours with the junk so fast that it's becoming a pleasure once again to go out to the movies. The best movies are still the ones being shown on the late shows or on the independent stations. I hardly need to re-sell the point to anyone who suffered through *Suddenly Last Summer* a few Sundays ago or made it through fifteen minutes of such garbage as *The Nutty Professor*, *A Man Could Get Killed* or *The Glass Bottom Boat*. But the worst, it seems, is coming at you like a kick in the head next Wednesday night on ABC. Anyone tasteless or desperate enough to watch *John Goldfarb, Please Come Home* will certainly watch anything, and this is what they'll get for their time-wasting:

A frigid reporter (Shirley MacLaine), a top-secret U-2 pilot who can't fly a plane, a group of British prostitutes (one is called "Mandy," which shows how progressive the thinking is in this draff) who continually burst into the Frug at the oddest moments, and a contingent of Washington diplomats with the collective cranial capacity of a three-year-old moron (the State Department should sue) are trapped in a technicolor harem in a mythical country called Fawzia. The Jewish U-2 pilot, called "Wrong Way Goldfarb," sets out to spy on Russia, lands in the harem by mistake, calls himself "Lawrence," floats around the desert like a poor man's Peter O'Toole, ends up teaching football to a group of sadistic whirling dervishes.

While a blaring soundtrack grinds out monotonous rock music sung by Jaye P. Morgan, monogrammed locomotives plunge through the bedrooms at suggestive intervals carrying purple rabbits, poodles in hair ribbons and chimpanzees playing hand organs. Half-nude belly dancers are chased and pinched by the diplomats, who crow clichés like, "What are you doing after the orgy, my little Balkan ginger box?" Instead of traditional custard pies, everybody throws stuffed mongoose, and finally the entire Notre Dame football team gets into the act in a grisly game replete with exploding footballs, goats squirting milk in the eyes of the Fighting Irish, and a bevy of musical Arabs making forward passes on charging camels. In a finale that has to be seen to be believed (I'm not suggesting you watch it—it really happens!) Miss MacLaine beats both teams single-handed as she is catapulted over the goal line by an erupting oil well.

When it's not nauseatingly silly, this sorry excuse for using up television's valuable time is downright filthy. As MacLaine goes to bed with the pilot to escape being raped by the sultan, whom she thought was impotent, she yells, "I thought you said he was at half-mast!" There's enough unhealthy sex, enough nudity, enough musical beds, and enough smutty jokes to keep *Goldfarb* a topic of conversation around the locker rooms for the next two weeks.

Peter Ustinov is the double-talking, sex maniac sultan, playing him like a ludicrous Jet Set Buddha. Plowing through twenty-six orange and chartreuse sets atop a jet-propelled golf cart, and screaming and flying about like a demented, turbaned, homosexual swami, he gives the most embarrassing performance I've seen since Ann Sothern played a Model-T Ford with a broken carburetor. Shirley MacLaine is simply terrible, but I don't blame her. Edith Head draped her in hideous panties and bras that look like Halloween costumes and she has to take a bubble bath with a seal. The dubious credit of writing this mess goes to someone who calls himself William Peter Blatty, who has provided dialogue like, "How do I hate thee—let me count the ways," and, "Garlic is a girl's best sin." He should get out of town fast.

Shirley MacLaine strikes me as a smart girl. There must have been something she could have done to protect her career by buying up the print of this monstrosity before television got its grubby hands on it and exploited it for sponsor money. The networks need not cry poor mouth any longer about the inevitability of pay TV. By showing low-class smut like *John Goldfarb, Please Come Home* they are giving the advent of pay TV the biggest endorsement that is physically possible. It stinks, and if it gets a big Wednesday night rating next week (which wouldn't surprise me in the least, TV audiences being what they are these days), the people who watched it deserve to live with the smell.

November 8, 1968

Campaign '68 finally found its way to television. Tuesday night's election coverage was so routine that most of the people at the presidential party I attended spent more time talking about what kind of wine the catering service put into the lamb curry than they did in front of the television set. Most of the action was on ABC. I couldn't understand anything that went on at the Nixon headquarters in the Waldorf, thanks to some perfectly dreadful girl reporter who couldn't pronounce anyone's name right or even read her own notes, but at one point I distinctly heard her mention that some celebrity named "Julie Allyson" was sitting at a table with a red tablecloth. I assume she's the one who used to make movies with Dan Johnson, but I wouldn't swear to it. Otherwise, most of the wit belonged to Gore Vidal and William F. Buckley, who were back by popular demand. Vidal did say one really funny thing when he expressed gratitude for the year's discovery of Spiro Agnew, "a household word, who only last week pleasured us again with the immortal statement—'The U.S. is the greatest country in the nation.' "

But the most exciting part of the television coverage came Monday night, when the Harris and Gallup people were still so wishy-washy that the candidates grew desperate in the last minutes before the decision at dawn and turned to the tube for final appeals. The weasel-like attacks and the stump campaigning was all over and the three desperate men were beginning to look like beggars with tin cups and space age Jesus Christs all rolled into one. George Wallace couldn't find a network, so between strained choruses of "America the Beautiful" he took a more direct approach, addressing the audience on film wherever he could buy the time: "You KNOW we are going to win tomorrow," he announced. Then he bragged on Curtis LeMay (who must be standing in line at the unemployment bureau this morning) for "whipping the Nazis," blamed the press for trying to badmouth his campaign, and accused both the Republicans and Democrats of anarchy, violence in the streets, inflation, wasting the taxpayer's money, and building up Communist morale. So what else is new?

Hubert Humphrey, meanwhile, had discovered the entertainment value of TV. While Jimmy Durante was introducing him on film as "Herbert Humphrey" on NBC, the man himself, with Senator Edmund Muskie at his side, was "live from Hollywood" on ABC. "The President," said Danny Thomas, referring confidently to the Vice-President, "says let's go to work, so when the President speaks, we jump." From all over America people phoned in questions at the rate of 130,000 calls an hour while people like Frank Sinatra, Sonny and Cher, Cary Grant, Bill Cosby, and one of the Smothers Brothers (I can never tell one from the other) did the jumping as telephone operators.

The questions were lulus, varying in range from "How do your policies differ from socialism?" to "Can you give me a good reason for voting for the same platform I've had to put up with for the last four years?" One joker put Muskie on the spot by asking him his views on legalizing abortion and birth control. "It's not a federal responsibility," coughed HHH. Sen. Eugene McCarthy phoned in and got the biggest applause of the night. "You did the sweating, now we're doing the sweating, Gene," said HHH. There were a lot of assaults on Nixon ("The man who is going to be President has to have contact with everybody; they have to feel he cares —Nixon doesn't know much about young people—he hasn't appeared in the ghettos or on street corners—he doesn't have a past record of peace—he hasn't opened his heart or his mind," blah blah blah) and Paul Newman made several jibes at Agnew ("We keep getting reports that Nixon is all alone on his telethon, being fed questions by one person instead of talking to anyone who calls in—if he's not ashamed to have Agnew in the White House with him, why is he too ashamed to have him in the same television studio?") I'd like to have had an answer to that one myself.

What I didn't like about the Humphrey telethon was the way it all smacked of party loyalty. I realize movie stars feel obligated to get involved and speak up for their beliefs and perhaps, in some way, influence their fans to vote for their political choices at this crucial time in American history, but their presence really doesn't mean anything and Humphrey's telethon would have seemed more sincere without them. I was also amused by the number of celebrities on the show whom I had met and talked with last summer in Hollywood. They all hated Humphrey's guts before McCarthy's brief glory petered out. Now they've switched. Party loyalty, not belief in the man.

Then Ted Kennedy appeared on film reviving memories of the much more exciting 1960 election and playing on the emotions by praising Humphrey's "compassion and love for America." But that too was party talk and I didn't believe a word of it. He'd say the same thing about Lassie if he were running on the Democratic ticket. As for Humphrey and Muskie, they were loaded with statistics and figures as long as your arm, but I've never heard so much political double talk in my whole life.

Over on NBC, Nixon ditched the show business and answered questions culled from calls. Paul Newman's accusation was correct. He didn't talk directly to the callers. But the formal proved more effective because it allowed Nixon to answer more questions and eliminate unnecessary time-wasting repeats from bored viewers who were not paying attention. (If I heard Humphrey answer the question about lowering the voting age to eighteen once, I heard him answer it ten times.) Nixon was surprisingly honest, direct, and intelligent. He didn't beat around the bush with a lot of phony double talk and he spoke in terms everyone could understand without dragging in a lot of boring statistics to avoid getting into a controversy through a statement of personal opinion. I thought he was very impressive.

He threw a lot of cold water on Johnson's bombing pause and even announced that hundreds of supplies were now being moved down the Ho Chi Minh trail in Laos, that our men were being stacked up on casualty lists even during the bomb pause, and that our planes were helpless to aid them. This sent Humphrey into a furor: "Nixon is just trying to frighten the American people. It's an irresponsible act. We need to give our President support and encouragement now, not spread fear through misinformation." (A few minutes after both telethons were over, Nixon's announcement was made official on the late news reports.)

Nixon also surprised everyone by promising not to raise taxes, agreeing to hire both Negroes and Catholics in his administration, and discussing everything in personal terms from narcotics to the Tennessee Valley Authority. He agreed to communicate with the public on a regular live TV telephone show if elected. Finally, he cleared up the continuous Humphrey accusations that he had refused to debate him face to face on TV. According to Nixon, he agreed, even urged a debate, but Congress failed to pass the necessary bill making a two-man debate possible without including Wallace. Congress also failed the year Johnson was supposed to debate Goldwater. The two votes that kept the bill from passing belonged to—guess who? That's right, Senators Humphrey and Muskie. (At least, that's what Nixon said.)

Well, it was an interesting pre-election eve. Nobody said anything policy-wise we haven't been hearing promised by every candidate who ever came down the pike, but they were in there pitching, and television did a marvelous job of exposing their ideas, movie stars or no movie stars. I don't want anyone to think I'm defending Nixon at Humphrey's expense, because it should be no secret to anyone who followed my television convention coverage that I am not fond of either candidate. To me, this election year has been like choosing oleo over rancid butter simply because there was nothing fresh from the dairy in the house. And on both telethons the most interesting question of the night before the election was put to both candidates: "Why do you want to be President?" Neither of them had an answer.

November 15, 1968

I love Julie Harris. She is probably one of the few women in the world who could ever read *The New Leader* aloud and not bore me into unconsciousness. But I am beginning to wonder if she isn't being guided by the wrong people. Obviously she will try anything once. On the *Kraft Music Hall* Wednesday night she came frightfully close to destroying herself in an hour of mindless trash about comedy (I use the term loosely) in the year 2001. That's right, the Julie Harris of *The Lark* and *The Member of the Wedding* and *I Am a Camera*, playing an outer-space Rona Barrett, delivering gossip thirty-three years from now with a straight face: "Tiny Tim and Phyllis Diller are calling it quits. Their twelve children will be donated to the Smithsonian Institution." (Yeah, that's what I thought, too.)

Then she was an intergalactic momma married to Steve Allen (already I was too upset to look) whose teeny-bopper daughter brought home a controversial social problem when she announced her engagement to a robot. The robot was named Sheldon and he was a fashion model for Popular Mechanics. "He's malfunctioning!" yells the daughter. "Not on my rug!" says Julie Harris of *The Lark* and *The Member of the Wedding* and *I Am A Camera*. (Yeah, that's what I thought, too.)

Later she hailed a space taxi driven by Shelley Berman. "I'm in a hurry to get home—I'll pay double." "Where ya live? Jupiter? Saturn?" "No, Brooklyn." "Are you kiddin'? I don't go outta my way for NOBODY!!" (Yeah, that's what I thought, too.)

To top it all off, she sang the difficult Kurt Weill-Maxwell Anderson "Lost in the Stars" and sounded like Florence Foster Jenkins. I brushed away a tear of shame. First it was *Rawhide*, then *Gunsmoke*, then *Tarzan*. Now straight man for a bunch of comics. It hurts to see talent so mutilated.

C'mon, Julie, get back on Broadway, where you belong, and cut out all the nonsense. You're embarrassing all the people who still care about the real Julie Harris, and I'd like to think we are legion.

60 Minutes, the new CBS Tuesday night newsmagazine of the air, is a great idea executed with only a minimum of success and skill. This week anchorman Mike Wallace conducted a rather confused and ultimately pointless interview with Richard Nixon, during which the president-elect confessed he didn't care what his critics thought of him and equated his drive to succeed in politics with someone who is infected with the flu. None of which eased my mind one bit about his forthcoming four years in the White House. This headline spot on the show was followed by news features on the people of Prague, an interesting and informative dissection of the character of Charles de Gaulle by the publisher of *L'Express*, a rather humorous but equally pointless and absurdly childish look at Joe Namath by Dick Schaap, and, finally a chilling portrait of James Earl Ray's defense attorney, Percy Foreman, about as repulsive a character as anything I've seen outside the pages of Erskine Caldwell. Chewing his cud and charming the jurors with philosophy right out of the Farmer's Almanac, Texas-drawling Percy has defended people accused of heinous crimes in seven hundred cases, with a record of only fifty convictions and one execution. We were treated to actual shots of Percy in court, psychoanalyzing a juror, cross-examining a witness, and sweet-talking the court with enough movie courtroom sincerity to turn milk to clabber. "Percy," said one spectator, "tries everyone but his own client." (Which, it seems to me, makes him something like an enemy of the State.)

The Joe Namath segment was a disaster diluted by comic effects, such as a Sinatra record of "Nice 'n' Easy" played over the sound track and the sound of a cash register ringing every time Namath hit the ball. But the thing I really hate about *60 Minutes* is the capsule conversation at the end of each feature. Two simpletons in silhouette speak in what the show calls "Digressions." Sample, after the de Gaulle feature: "What do you think Americans think of de Gaulle?" "I think they'd like to tell him to go to hell." "Isn't that a bit strong?" "Yes, but it doesn't matter; he won't go where they tell him anyway." "Thank you." "Thank YOU." It's written by Andrew Rooney and it's horrible.

The Sense of Wonder (ABC) was a beautifully photographed seeing eye into the world of Rachel Carson, narrated by Helen Hayes. It was a special that asked the question: How can we preserve the earth unless we learn to care about it, and how can we care unless we learn to develop our sense of wonder?

To make us care, Miss Hayes told us to use our ears, eyes, nostrils, and fingertips. A patch of moss became a jungle. Doodlebugs through a magnifying glass became spotted leopards prowling that jungle. "Man has lost his capacity to foresee and forestall—he will end up destroying the earth," she quoted Albert Schweitzer as saying. Then she taught us how to see the things around us. Like Rachel Carson, the marine biologist-writer who died in 1964 after creating a hurricane of controversy with *Silent Spring*, the joy, excitement and mystery we found in the trees, skies, and water became an antidote against boredom and disenchantment. There was peace and contentment watching the shore crowd the surf while tiny occupants crawled among the rocks and into the gloom of the sea caves. Life lives even in solid rock, existing minutely as Lilliputian beings in a grain of sand. Simple snails with Chinese coolie hats crawled over mussels anchored to rocks by natural silk threads spun in their feet. Sand crabs endured the surf by burrowing down beneath the sand to escape it. There were wonderful closeups of petrified fields of barnacles defeating the threat of being washed away or crushed by the sea, imprisoned there forever opening their doors to stick out feathered tongues from the submerged rock waiting for the sea to bring their food. The quiet saga of the barnacle, like all the other wonders of our world, is there for the eye to see if we only have the curiosity to look.

There was a section on birds, from the early morning risers to the rhythmic night chanters, as the chorus picked up tempo and volume. There were insects, singing in a throbbing, swelling backyard symphony. Miss Hayes turned the hunt into a happy game, searching them out by flashlight, following the sounds of the individual instruments, then locating the players to see what they look like. The point, I think, was a pitch to conserve our natural resources, but I don't see anything wrong with that. Americans have the least respect for their streams and their fields and their lakes and their wildlife of any nation on earth and no time for waking up can be soon enough. Without being disgustingly June Haverish about the whole thing, Miss Hayes tried to teach a lesson: that even if we live in cities, there are wonderful things we can still ponder. The mystery of a growing seed planted in the potted earth of a kitchen window. The natural wonder of rain falling from about the skyscrapers. The migration of birds and changing of the seasons, which can be observed even in the middle of Central Park. The whispers and voices in the wind, even if it is heard around the corner of your apartment building. I loved the show. I only hope some of the hopeless slobs who never see anything around them but the ends of their noses learned something.

November 22, 1968

Works of consummate skill and beauty occur so very seldom in television that when they do I feel duty-bound to infect a potential audience with taste for such things with some of my own enthusiasm before it's too late. Therefore, I'm going out on a limb this week, recommending something that hasn't been shown yet. In television, where almost everything imaginable is governed by fear, stupidity, and insecurity, recommending or reviewing events (even favorably) before they happen is a cardinal sin punishable by banishment from network screening rooms. Frankly, I can think of worse tortures. And Truman Capote's *The Thanksgiving Visitor* is something so heart-warmingly special I'm afraid if I don't encourage you to see it in advance, you'll miss it. So whatever you are doing Thanksgiving night, I'd like to urge you to tune the set to ABC for one of the most uniquely moving hours you are likely to spend this year.

There isn't much of a plot, but it doesn't matter. *The Thanksgiving Visitor* is a tone poem, a memory piece about growing up in the South and what it was like to be Truman Capote as a child. It is a shimmering collage of sense memories and word pictures, pieced together in a quiet, hearthside kind of story and orchestrated through lovely writing, camera work, cutting, sound, and acting to show all the rapture and passion of a lonely and isolated country childhood spent in the stern protective clasp of relatives too old and in too much of a hurry to appreciate the world of children. Geraldine Page is back as the elderly and slightly dotty Miss Sook Faulk, Mr. Capote's favorite cousin from his earlier short story (and preceding TV special) *A Christmas Memory*. Then there's Uncle B and Sister Alice and Odd Henderson and Miz Mary Wheelright, a one-hundred-year-old crone who makes the best cold banana pudding in Alabama and plans to bury the secret of her recipe when she dies. There's the scissors grinder and Perk McCloud and all the other wonderful characters from Monroe County—simple, old-fashioned, patchwork quilt farm stock, poetic and windswept, but wise beyond their station.

I love this kind of writing and I know these characters, probably because my own childhood allows me to identify with them strongly. Growing up myself in isolated back-roads hamlets in the agrarian South, many of the nostalgic scenes from Mr. Capote's story come through as loud and clear and strong as the unforgettable memory of the first time I ever smelled gingerbread baking. It is this sense of poetic realism, glued together with an incredible eye for authentic detail, that makes *The Thanksgiving Visitor* a particularly heartening hour of happiness and joy. Mr. Capote obviously has an elephantine memory, for his floating island of the mind is chock full of dainty and endearing remembrances. Like the way it felt to be a skinny kid relentlessly pursued by the local bully, a red-haired ruffian with freckles who pinned him to the cold November ground on his way to the Saturday afternoon picture show and stole his dime. And when you see the dime, look closely—it's a real dime, from the Depression years. When Buddy (the name Mr. Capote gives himself) returns home from the encounter to the aging Miss Sook, the entire feeling changes with the scene. The cold, frosty freeze-in-the-throat from running with tears in his eyes in the outdoor wind blurs with the cozy feel of heat from the fire, the odor of cinnamon and nutmeg on the shelf, and the smells from the kitchen oilcloth (every Southern kitchen had oilcloth on the table). "One of these days we gonna sell my papa's cameo and we gonna get on a bus for New Orleans and never come back," says Miss Sook, and you are right there in their world with them.

Every sense of timing and rhythm and personal detail has been used with the dedication of a Buddhist priest in Frank Perry's direction to preserve the delicious intimacy of Mr. Capote's narrative. The actors are allowed to *think* right before our eyes. (When Miss Page pulls the turkey wishbone, she pulls little pieces of meat from the bone as she contemplates her wish. It's a moment out of time, but it adds years of intimacy to our knowledge of who she is when she hasn't actually told us much of anything in terms of explanatory self-description.) Scenes are allowed to take their time in developing their own course of action. With a bare minimum of dialogue, characters reveal themselves as total beings better than I've seen in the crowded hysteria of nine out of ten television hours. The boy Buddy lies in bed under the quilts cutting out Greta Garbo pictures and playing Rook on a feverish day home from school. Geraldine Page stares at a cobweb. They become people we all know (or should have). Later, in a marvelous moment during which the child refuses to kill the turkey for the Thanksgiving table, the first childhood curiosity about whether animals went to animal heaven comes flooding into the mind's eye in a rare ray of vision.

Frank Perry has directed these scenes with an economy of personal emotion, yet he has made them somehow triumphantly and universally moving.

The actors are good enough, when combined with the beautifully controlled camerawork of Joseph Brun, the lovely but softly gray-muted Southern farmland technicolor and the deeply knowledgeable settings by Gene Callahan, to make the hair stand on end. Many of the actors are amateurs, but their work is more florid and natural than most professionals I've seen daily on the tube. Michael Kearney as Buddy is an incredibly vivid child actor who played the young James Agee in the motion picture, *All the Way Home*, and continues to display perceptive and compassionate strength for an actor so young in years. Geraldine Page recreates the Sook character with heart-piercing warmth and skill, lending her indescribable genius to making the piece all but unimprovable (I wonder only about the effectiveness of Mr. Capote's customarily irritating and occasionally even maddening nasality in doing the narration Eleanor Perry has written for him.) Miss Page is so amazingly *old*—a sensitive, shy fern-like lady in her sixties, a recluse who wanders out beyond the county boundaries only in her own daydreams, a child-lady who gets her energy from the smiles of flowers and small children, who wears flour-sack aprons and coarse peasant stockings. Munching raisins and cooking 5 A.M. Sunday morning flapjacks. Trying to read a thermometer with bad eyesight. Smelling lemon wax. Groaning slightly when she moves her hardening bones from a deep sleep. Laughing at pictures of Fu Manchu. Preparing the table with the boy and talking about the eighty-year-old patched linen when she should really be encouraging him to play baseball. Stalking with the child through the chrysanthemums as though they were lions and only the biggest ones would do to kill for the Thanksgiving table.

Finally, the day is here. Relatives arrive, from lumber camps in loblolly forests to isolated country hamlets—bringing sweet potato casseroles and sugared almonds. Ancient cousins twice removed bringing ambrosia in Depression Fords right out of *Bonnie and Clyde*. And through all the excitement, the small but infinitely important friendship of the old woman and the small boy tests the depth of its capacity for trust when the "Thanksgiving visitor"—the town bully, who shows up to the child's chagrin—brings the dinner table to a moment of truth.

Fortunately, Mr. Capote still seems to be able to turn out prose that bears no relation to the Mr. Capote who throws parties after publishing his own guest lists in the *New York Times* and wastes time writing detective stories for Lee Radziwill to appear in. *The Thanksgiving Visitor* possesses the basic ingredients of true reason—the ability to recognize oneself, and others, as human beings in their ultimate reponsibility to each other. It cannot possibly be the work of a phony, although there will undoubtedly be people who dislike the show—the kind of people who also hate cocker spaniels, daisies, and butterflies. They will call it corny and sentimental, without recognizing everything about it to be of a quality several octaves above and beyond the level of almost everything else on television. Fortunately, I've never been on more than very brisk speaking terms with people who are afraid to cry. If luck holds, I never will be.

November 29, 1968

Notes on TV: Bad actors appear with annoying frequency on television. It's the only medium in which everything else looks so bad that bad actors seem more talented than they really are. Consequently, it's the only medium in which bad actors work steadily. Hugh O'Brian is not a bad actor; he just gets treated like one. Ever since I saw him in Samuel Taylor's play *First Love* I've been convinced that Hugh O'Brian was an actor of much vaster abilities than people (critics mostly) gave him credit for being. Bad movies and cowpoke roles in trashy TV westerns almost destroyed my faith. But sure enough, he turned up on Hallmark Hall of Fame last week in a play called *A Punt, A Pass and A Prayer*, and showed how much more depth he has as a human being and as a misused performer capable of good work than most of the hacks who write for him.

The play, about a pro football player too old to play but too stubborn to face the fact that he is washed up, was almost as boring, sophomoric, old-hat, and pretentious as its title. It was all I could do to stay awake. It was ninety minutes of tedious football talk about competition and good-old-days locker room jazz and comebacks and responsibility and failure that seemed more like three hours. But through it all, Hugh O'Brian gave a masterful, moving, many-faceted performance as that sad and defeated sports-world prototype—the has-been who doesn't know when to throw in the towel. I don't know why he doesn't get better scripts. Just unlucky, I guess.

Heidi was a two-hour overdose of Weltschmerz about which I now remember almost nothing except some nice shots of the Alps; a strong resistance to Jennifer Edwards, a ten-year-old child with a face as emotionless as a bowl of melted candle wax; a very great waste of some very big names like Jean Simmons and Maximilian Schell, who seemed to have no better clues to what they were doing there than I did; some cruel closeups of Michael Redgrave looking like John Huston's idea of what Moses looks like; and a desperate attempt to make everyone cry by showing a crippled child crawling up a steep and deserted mountaintop after falling out of an untended wheelchair. Actually one thing does stick in the memory. As the child began her scorpion ascent up the mountain, with a great wailing and gnashing of the teeth, NBC suddenly announced the football scores across the bottom of the screen. They didn't seem to care much more about the histrionics of childhood folklore than I did, but it was the cleverest way I've seen in ages for a network to get the audience's attention back.

Poor Olympic champion Peggy Fleming didn't seem to have a very good time on her Sunday night "special" on NBC, and frankly I don't blame her. Even old Sonja Henie movies knew when to get their girl off the ice before she made a fool of herself. But Peggy worked her skates off, moving through a ridiculous "Lara" number on an MGM sound stage, a discotheque, the hideously phony *Camelot* sets at Warners in Burbank, and sharing the Inglewood Forum with the Los Angeles Kings hockey team. Spanky and Our Gang, a super-dippy group with almost unequaled class and musicianly good taste, thawed things out momentarily on two groovy numbers, but Miss Fleming was as luckless as a snowball in hell with a guest like Richard Harris. I've never seen anyone yet who knew what to do with him, so Miss Fleming needn't feel too bad about falling on her face. Harris makes everything around him turn to bile. He can't sing. He can't act. He seems ill-prepared to "guest" on a variety special, since his very peculiar abilities do not include variety of any kind. He has the sense of humor of a hogshead cheese and the physical attractiveness of an unwashed corpse. I dare not say more, except to wish Peggy Fleming better luck next time, preferably in a vehicle that doesn't leave everyone ice cold.

The Chairman of the Board, on the other hand, worked hard on his Monday night CBS special, and once again made everything look as effortless as eating boysenberry pie. *Francis Albert Sinatra Does His Thing* didn't even need a title. The show spoke for itself. Sinatra was smart enough to ignore the current no-talent fads like the Richard Harrises of the world and stick to accomplished professionals. Diahann Carroll is no Ella, but she curled the whiskers on "His Is the Only Music That Makes Me Dance."

The Fifth Dimension, one of the most exciting with-it groups the so-called "new music" has produced, had the great good taste to perform the sophisticated, stylistically complicated Laura Nyro song "Stoned Soul Picnic." And Sinatra even demonstrated his own plugged-in knowledge of where the good new music is going by doing another of the fantastically brilliant Laura Nyro's songs, "Sweet Blindness." There were old standards, swinging big band up-tunes, spiritual songs, nothing but music, music, music . . . and sixty minutes of beautiful taste. I like the Sinatra specials because they demonstrate, in addition to great sounds, the economy with which an hour variety show can operate to produce superior entertainment. No overkill, oversell, or boring stand-up comics. Just hard work, few tricks and big talents doing what they do best. And what big talents do best is not sit around idly watching other lesser talents do it in a second-rate fashion. And that is what most misguided variety specials are all about. *Francis Albert Sinatra Does His Thing* may not have needed the title, but once it settled for one, at least it had the good sense to live up to it.

December 13, 1968

The Christmas season is upon us already and so far television has responded not with festive splendor but with assorted side dishes of fruits and nuts. *Pinocchio* was maybe the worst thing I've ever seen on the Hallmark Hall of Fame. Ernest Kinoy's dialogue was lower than anything ever presented at the Baptist Training Union Christmas pageant ("I'll always need you, Blue Fairy"; "Oh no, Pinocchio, real people just need each other"). The songs by Walter Marks were abominable, but Peter Noone (of Herman's Hermits) couldn't sing them anyway. With his nose puttied on and his face rouged and eyes painted to look like a marionette, he was Grimmer than a fairy tale. Burl Ives was mixed up in all of this mawkish saccharine. The bushy beard didn't help hide his embarrassment.

"In your heart there beats a drummer/that's your own sweet song he is playing," they sang and sang and sang, while the commercials for Hallmark candles looked more expensive than the show itself. If the blatant sucrose of kiddie night at the YMCA is Hallmark's idea of a Christmas present, I'll just wait for Halloween, thank you very much.

The *Peanuts* Christmas show turned up again on CBS for what seems like the umpteenth year. It gets worse each time, but at least these are comic strip cutouts making fools of themselves and not real live people attempting to stoop condescendingly to the level of child psychology. Kids are much brighter than these shows give them credit for being. Now what I'd really like to see is Tiny Tim playing Pinocchio and Burl Ives playing the Great Pumpkin. Then we'd have something.

The Supremes came crashing through the mire with a throbbing, pulsating, passionate hour of the wildest music this side of paradise Monday night on NBC. With their zappy new wigs every two minutes and their way out, jungle movie costumes designed by Michael Travis to look like gigantic hip-gyrating electric spider webs, they are the Patti, Maxine, and Laverne of Harlem. The Cotton Club is gone, but Diana Ross is here, with her tapping, swinging, swaying, undulating, hydroelectric-voltage-voiced Amazonians and if there is to be any record of history in the 1960's, the Motown sound of the Supremes is certain to be a major part of it. It was a musical special of such intense pleasure it must have been illegal.

The Road to Gettysburg (ABC) was a compelling and impressively assembled documentary that recreated a specific feeling of a specific time in American history by attempting to explore more than an event, but extended its focus to the psychological chasm which led up to and included the event itself. Through stills and excellent moving photography, the beautiful script by John Secondari followed the Civil War through its path of desecration, utilizing letters, diaries, and other accounts of the battles in a style similar to *Letters from Stalingrad.*

The Monday night special avoided clichés and shed light on many interesting and unpublicized sidelights of the war: the problems with arsenals, the confusion over uniforms, the insufficient medical knowledge (doctors thought the dysentery that took the lives of thousands was caused by bad air!), the chronicle of the sixty thousand Negroes who died in ranks—perhaps the only ones who knew what they were fighting for in the most insane mass slaughter this country has ever known. Innocents and children, annihilated to the tune of fifty-one thousand in Gettysburg alone—a holocaust neither side had planned. They ate corn meant for the horses just to stay alive. The troops were fed green apples and both sides survived on a sense of humor.

Secondari must have spent years accumulating the words of the soldiers, letters, newspaper clippings, library materials, art work, and sketches drawn by soldiers at Gettysburg to unfold the story. The work paid off in one of the most interesting and visually dramatic programs of the season. David Carradine, as the voice of Johnny Rebel, and Kevin McCarthy, as the voice of the Yankees, did brilliant jobs of voiceover. William Hartigan's photography far surpassed that of the typical television news special and John Hughes correlated the massive footage and edited it in such a way that not a moment seemed superfluous. It was one documentary that deserves to be repeated.

December 20, 1968

Beauty and the Beast (ABC) featured the San Francisco Ballet in a richly encrusted holiday gem narrated by Hayley Mills. Lynda Meyer, dancing the role of Beauty, Robert Gladstein as the Beast, and David Anderson as the Prince proved the great dancers of the world are not all in New York and Moscow, but the commercials broke in all the wrong places and interrupted some of their best moments onstage (i.e., at the moment the beast sheds his hair and turns once again into a white prince, their most delicate movements of the evening were cut in half to squeeze in a commercial). Hayley Mills's voice was full of childlike innocence ("Suddenly the beast was dying, and her heart went out to him . . .") but I couldn't help imagining her saying the words between puffs of cigar smoke. I didn't see it on a color set, so I'm not qualified to comment on the sets and costumes. More than any other art form, however, it seems to me that ballet on television must depend, for its enjoyment, on the quality of the reception and the richness of its color. Without these elements, the pleasure is negligible. Black and white ballet is like *Dumbo* restaged by the Communist party. No bubble-up.

New York Night (NBC) was an interesting but hardly unusual hour of disconnected impressions attempting to get some local color across to people who have never spent a night in New York. It began in an arch and heavily derivative way—slow motion film of people boarding subway trains and walking through St. Patrick's Cathedral to the tune of somber cello music.

Then it switched to blurred camera gimmicks with a mood change in tempo, leaping into wild bass and drum rhythms with voices like the Swingle Singers be-bopping jazz behind quick shots of Friday's, the *Hair* marquee, Maxwell's Plum, Noah's Ark, the singles scene in the East 60s. There was a sense of why singles gather like electric zombies, not wanting to be alone, boring each other silly with dilettante dialogue because they need to rub against something else that is alive in order to register some tangible proof of their own existence. Interesting flow of quotes over the noise and smoke: "I love your gold buttons"—"Sit down, will'ya, before somebody gets your seat"—"Boy, are you missing out"—"You won't believe this, but when Cary Grant comes to town, he uses my room."

Then Craig Claiborne called La Côte Basque one of the most beautiful restaurants in the world (!!) and took the viewer on a fascinating tour of dining-out that practically amounted to a religious experience, from the fantastic ballet-like Arnold Wesker show back in the kitchen to the brisk, desperate, snob activity around the serving trays, with a side discourse on how to prepare snow eggs. The best part of his cook's tour, however, was a trip down to the West Boondocks, a soul food joint downtown in a jazz setting of black-eyed peas, mustard greens, and sweet potato pie.

Car accidents. Go-go and navels at the Metropole. A party atop a big double bed in the middle of Times Square that looked staged for the camera (I can't believe anyone would really be stupid or boring enough to spend an evening in a bed in Times Square with natural abandon unless they were trying to get their names in the paper), featuring the creepiest instant-pop collection of would-be society gatecrashers ever assembled. Ratner's at midnight, where life and death are indistinguishable after the first spoonful (if you've ever eaten there, you know what I mean; if you haven't, miss it and stay well). Jean Shepard in the Village, looking at the hippies. (The hippies! Another joke, you folks from out of town, since most of them stand around looking like little Keene drawings from Deep Sewage, Nebraska.) Shepard is a comfortable Glenn Ford-slippers-pipe-cardigan-Al Capp-reader type, who seemed as cowed by all the slime as I am every time I go south of Eighth Street. ("If old Abe Lincoln walked through here in his old costume, with his beard and his hat, I'll bet nobody would even notice," mused Shepard, yuk, yuk.) Followed by a trip to Long John Nebel's late-night radio show high above Rockefeller Center, where he talked on the air to assorted nuts telephoning in their vices and freak-outs while the part of the city that is still sane enough after just trying to live here tried to sleep.

Trouble with any show that tries to explain the New York scene is that there is no New York scene. If you watch enough shows that intimidate you into going out and trying everything instead of staying home and suffering the fate of becoming a square, you'll just be disappointed and still square anyway. There are a million scenes. "The" scene is whatever street lamp you happen to be standing under. And anyway . . . E. B. White said it all much better a long time ago, before television even thought of it at all.

Judy Garland gave everyone her Christmas present early this year by appearing twice in one week on the electric screen. When Judy appears anywhere, the world holds its breath with fear and dread, but the lady herself usually sees herself through the mire with her unfailing sense of humor. *The Dick Cavett Show* was an unmitigated disaster. She showed up looking as if she had been demolished by a garbage truck. They are still talking backstage at the Cavett fracas about the way she behaved and the way she looked (they worked with her for three hours and she finally ended up wearing one of the talent coordinator's dresses, but it didn't help much).

And I still can't get over the way she sounded. But she warbled a few loathsome choruses of some alleged song called "The Jap-Jap-Jappys" (I think she made it up on the spot) and in a voice that sounded remarkably like Betty Hutton's at the time she had the well-publicized corns on her vocal chords removed she turned to Cavett and asked, "How does it feel to be a legend?" It broke everybody up and there was no place to go from there, so Cavett just let her talk. She got in some good ones.

On Bob Hope ("When he has nothing else to do around the house, he goes away and wherever he goes suddenly there's a war where there never was a war before"); on coffee breaks ("I stretch mine out with Juicy Fruit"), and on her many spectacular comebacks ("I'm the queen of the comebacks"). Finally Cavett asked her, "What do you do when unknown songwriters send you tunes to sing?" Snapped Judy: "The first thing you do is remember to send them back, or they'll sue the dickens out of you."

Later, she turned up on the Johnny Carson Open Mouth and by some miraculous bit of alchemy, she looked wonderful. The makeup was beautiful and the hair was beautiful and the voice sounded almost like a voice as she sang a lovely Christmas ballad called "Stay with Me Till after the Holidays." Both shows were taped at the same time of the evening, so there was no reason why she should have been better prepared for one than she was for the other. But perhaps seeing herself on the earlier Cavett fiasco was a bit like Ray Milland seeing the bat come out of the wall in *The Lost*

Weekend. At any rate, she was a different lady on the Carson show. Too bad, because in typical Carson fashion, he got absolutely nothing out of her and the interview portion of the show was such a ludicrous waste of everybody's time that Judy and her flaming audience might as well have stayed home under the Christmas tree.

Immediately after her introduction, Carson broke for one of his ten thousand boring commercials. Then there was an interminable discussion of sugar plums and snowflakes during which everyone ate an alleged sugar plum. Then he turned to Judy for the big interview:

"Somebody said you were upset." "People always say that, that I'm always upset." "Are you always upset?" "Only as often as you are."

Then Carson pulled the same old petrified ego crap: "You interview me. I've never been interviewed on the show. Ask me anything." It all sounded too suffocatingly familiar for words. But the audience, which looked as though it had just been released en masse from Bellevue in time for at-home Christmas therapy, screamed its forced, embarrassing bravos over absolutely nothing at all. But Judy was, as always, a real, funny, and unsolvable riddle.

So I can see why they clap, in much the same way families clap each holiday season when the oldest star for the top of the tree is brought out of the dusty box for the 10,000th time. It's worn, it's been chewed on by countless generations of babies, its light doesn't work and its glow is dimmed, but it brings back memories and it's good to have around. So is Judy.

And I hope your Christmas deserves applause, too.

December 27, 1968

It was quite a week. Hong Kong flu broke out aboard the Apollo 8, Julie Nixon got married, Shirley Booth made a rare appearance on TV playing a mother victimized by a murderous gang of smugglers (on Christmas Eve, yet). And all over the dial, there were more flying nuns, singing priests, drunken Santa Clauses, tacky miracles, and talking Christmas trees than you could shake off with a stick. Never being the last to leap aboard every commercial money-making bandwagon that comes along, season or otherwise, TV milked the hell out of Christmas and robbed it of whatever dignity it has left in an interminable gumpot of specials, most of them long on popcorn balls and short on intelligence, wit, sophistication, or interest.

On Saturday on CBS New York's Prince Street Players presented another dreary rendition of *Pinocchio* only one or two sub-cellar steps above the Hallmark version I had to suffer through a few weeks ago. This one at least had an actor (John Jay) who made something halfway believable out of the title role. Nothing to shout about.

Later in the same day, Channel 5 presented an even drearier concoction featuring conductor Ray Conniff, alleged comic Alan Young, and some wooden-headed dum-dums called the Pixiekin Puppets in songs, games, and, in the will-wonders-never-cease department, a film excursion to Santa Claus' house. It was a trip all right.

Then on Saturday night there was plenty of television-to-decorate-the-tree-by. Jackie Gleason dreamed his way into a Christmas storybook fantasy where he met Art Carney as Old King Cole, Sheila MacRae as the Old Woman in the Shoe, and assorted other people old enough to know better. If that didn't turn your stomach bright green, you could hear Bing Crosby sing "White Christmas" either on NBC, where the movie of the same name (a really ghastly movie even for Paramount in the '50s, and that's saying a mouthful) popped and fizzled to a worn-out score by Irving Berlin, or on ABC where the whole Bingle Clan hosted the *Hollywood Palace* on a night to forget. (I quickly switched to a 1961 German horror flick called *The Strangler of Blackmoor Castle*, followed by Boris Karloff in *Corridors of Blood*, approximately four hours of unrelieved rapture that saved the week.)

On Sunday, the worst opera I have ever heard sung in English or any other language lasted for one solid hour on ABC. It was called *The Shephardes Playe*. It was accompanied by an orchestra filled with tambourines, and I hope I never hear of it again as long as I live.

On NBC, Carmen Dragon conducted the Glendale Symphony (now THERE's a real coup!) while an army of mechanical toys danced Tchaikovsky. I may never complain again about Truman Capote's voice after hearing James Mason slaughter tender selections from Mr. Capote's masterpiece of seasonal poetry, *A Christmas Memory*, on the Skitch Henderson Christmas variety hour. After Eli Wallach and Anne Jackson read kids' letters to God and Lillian Hayman sang a rocking gospel hymn and some revolting Santa Claus who looked like he was in his cups told a lot of revolting Santa Claus jokes, Mason took the lectern. Reading with cold disrespect like an IBM running out of current, he mispronounced and stumbled over half the words and threw away the rest of Mr. Capote's graceful prose in a snobby nasal British accent that allowed me to understand only one out of every three syllables. After wasting a lot of time and ruining the mood of the rural Alabama Christmas he was trying to establish by asking everyone in the studio what a "satsuma" was, he then sacrificed the poetry, the careful precision of Mr. Capote's words, the delicate feeling for human interrelationships in a holiday season of love and the tone of Christmas in the countryside—sacrificed it to coldness, indifference, bad preparation, and terrible interpretative reading. I hope Mr. Capote was nowhere within miles of a TV set.

As the week wore on into Christmas Day there was a Navy Christmas, an Air Force Christmas, a Salvation Army Christmas, more masses and cantatas than Excedrin tablets, and, believe it or not, a couple of items I could even sit through without needing one. Victor Borge's Bell Telephone special on NBC was an interesting peek at how children around the world celebrate the birth of Christ in their native songs and costumes. (It would have been worth tuning into this show just to watch the children being trained at the magnificent Ballet Folklorico de Mexico school.) *Christ Is Born* on ABC was a beautifully photographed documentary on the Nativity story first telecast in 1966, with nicely shot and edited footage of Jerusalem, the Sea of Galilee, and King Herod's stronghold, Masada, near the Dead Sea, and another brilliant script by John Secondari, who is turning out some fine work at ABC. (He also wrote the masterful *Road to Gettysburg* special I reviewed Dec. 13.)

Another happy delight was the CBS Christmas special *How the Grinch Stole Christmas*, the lovable Dr. Seuss story about the mythical country of Who-ville and the Scrooge-like Grinch who had green skin, red eyes, and a spiteful heart. The songs were tuneful and smart, and Boris Karloff's make-believe villainy a perfect wedding of misery, meanness, and mellifluous cheer. His marvelous vocal range has the effect of a musical instrument and hearing it run the scale in this most unusual children's story was a delicious and unexpected addition to the Christmas potpourri. Then there was a CBS rerun of the majestic Vladimir Horowitz Carnegie Hall recital, uninterrupted by stupid commercials and a welcome gift in any season.

Movie wise, it might as well have been April Fool's Day, with all the drek like *The Great Sioux Massacre, East of Sudan*, and *The House of the Seven Hawks*. Network movies were for the very desperate and the very tasteless. But the local channels in New York retaliated with a literal stampede of every movie you ever heard of (and some you never want to hear of again) about nuns and Christmas, as though the two operate as a team. There were the *Little Nuns*, Ingrid Bergman hamming it up in *Bells of St. Mary's*, Lili Palmer as a German nun smuggling Jewish children out of a concentration camp in *Conspiracy of Hearts*, Audrey Hepburn throwing in the towel in *The Nun's Story*, Loretta Young as a nun involved with a gangster (naughty Loretta!) in *Come to the Stable*—nuns, nuns, and more nuns. (One channel couldn't get any nun movies, so it just showed the Jean Seberg *St. Joan*—oh well, that was reason enough to pray.)

And for the really big laugh, there was Frank Sinatra as a scrawny little priest trying to hire a press agent for God in *Miracle of the Bells*, one of the most horrendous pseudo-religious treacles ever turned out of Hollywood. Not to mention *Christmas Eve, Christmas Holiday, Christmas in Connecticut, Christmas Inn*, and two or three versions of *A Christmas Carol*. And squeezed in among the prayerbooks unnoticed was a great Preston Sturges flick, *Remember the Night*, which is maybe the best Christmas card Hollywood ever sent. So all told, I guess there was a lot to be thankful for this Christmas on television. Mainly that it's all over until next year. Same time, same stations.

January 3, 1969

"It's as though a page of yo' life was comin' to an end," said Lady Bird Johnson last Friday night, and Howard K. Smith and the ABC cameras were there to make it official as she said goodbye. Like all the other First Ladies throughout history who never really asked to be anything special, the importance of her job made her the unofficial female leader of the world, whether we liked it or not. She came without really being invited, she had to stand by a man who was never popular to begin with, then watch him fall slowly and steadily out of favor even with the members of his own party. But her head was high, she never cried wolf, she was always a lady, and when history has its say, I think the world will be surprised to discover that Lady Bird made a much saner contribution to the preservation of a stronger, longer-lasting America than the more popular First Lady before her.

They made fun of her nose, they laughed at her funny Texas drawl, they drew bird pictures, they called her corny. But I wonder. While the rest of the country shook its head as the cities burned and the death tolls mounted, Lady Bird planted trees and made speeches about soil conservation and the preservation of America's natural scenic grandeur. Hoping that by making things more beautiful, maybe she could revive some respect for a nation that still had a few reasons left to be proud of itself. While the hypocrites and the trouble-makers marched on Washington with protests and bans and bombs and pamphlets of every description, Lady Bird was trying to give 2½ million children insurance against dropping out of society by initiating the Head Start program. Except for Eleanor Roosevelt, she was the most active First Lady in behalf of this country's needs the White House has ever had.

I was reminded of these things as I watched, with sympathy and admiration, while Mrs. Johnson reviewed with pride and modesty her years in the White House. She stood in the yellow oval room where John and Abigail Adams first entertained the heads of six world powers in 1801 and talked about it all. About the ringing phone at 4 A.M.—always urgent but never anything good—which she would always remember with terror as a symbol of the crazed and horrible times during which her husband's administration had the misfortune of taking place.

She shared moments of happiness, too, such as the day when the first Johnson grandchild had his official White House photo taken with one foot planted firmly in his birthday cake. She showed films of a county fair held on the south lawn of the White House, Lynda's wedding, the 1967 Christmas the family celebrated with their eyes on Vietnam, the official ceremonies held inside and outside the presidential mansion; she shared the secret nooks where she sought refuge in the midst of chaos, and displayed personal photographs never before shown of the First Family. She was candid, honest, unphony, and not afraid to share a joke. And she was quite moving when she summoned up the whole administration and her reason for standing by LBJ even when the hours looked darkest in a period of American history that could only be modestly described as turbulent: "The people choose their President, they didn't choose me. But only one person chooses the First Lady—and she must support him. He's all she's got."

One thing you could say about Lady Bird without fear of contradiction:

she wasn't just another pretty face. But in its maturity and understanding and crinkled country kindness, it's a face I feel we're all going to miss in the years ahead.

Briefly, but importantly, I'd like to mention two other appearances of ultimate joy that brightened the television week: Shirley Booth's heartbreaking Lola in the tender, dreary, realistically painful 1952 movie version of William Inge's *Come Back, Little Sheba.* It's the best thing NBC has shown this year in its otherwise boring lineup of terrible B flicks. And I hope you caught the rerun of Hal Holbrook's masterful *Mark Twain Tonight* (CBS) . . . the best impersonation of an old man by a young man I've ever witnessed. And last, a slight nod to NBC and *Roberto Rossellini's Sicily*, the Sunday night documentary, which was fine as long as it stuck to facts (Mafia dominance, wailing funerals, pervasive poverty) and awful when it started pretentiously romanticizing the place. Don't tell me about how beautiful Sicily is, fellows. I've been there. And I can still smell it.

January 10, 1969

The New Shows.

Male of the Species (NBC). I've been carrying the flag for better television drama as long as I can remember. I've even strained a few of my standards to the breaking point to be nice to what little drama there is left in these flea-bitten TV days, with the hope that good reviews might encourage the networks to schedule more quality programming. But I expect quality, not some dreary, pretentious excuse for quality like *Male of the Species*, which showed up last Friday night on NBC with an impressive cast from London. This was not theater. It wasn't even good warmed-over *Studio One.* It was just plain old reheated English trifle glopped about with dialogue more banal than custard sauce.

Welsh playwright Alun Owen, who also wrote the nonscreenplay for the Beatles' *A Hard Day's Night*, penned three short nonplays about disillusionment in a young girl's life, attempting (but failing) to show what rotten, nasty, good-for-nothing bastards men are. A young actress named Anna Calder-Marshall was absolutely first-rate as the girl through whose life the three lousy pigs who are supposed to represent all mankind trampled with their knickers down. First, there was her widowed father in Act One, written like a take-off on an early kitchen sink drama by John Osborne. He's a real louse, see, who drove her mother away years ago through his grisly affairs with tarts, then made up a story about how her mother was really a whore just so she'd lavish all her attention on him. He's a liar and definitely no gentleman and he was played brilliantly, believe it or not, by Sean Connery. The End.

In Act Two, the girl has turned into a warped young hag who unconditionally hates everything in pants. She has long since refused to ever speak to her father again (which saves Sean Connery from having to go back to the studio for overtime) and sets her sights on destroying an office Alfie (played with excessive doses of tedium by Michael Caine, naturally). I didn't pay much attention to this act because I couldn't understand much of anything Michael Caine said. Which was just as well, because what little I caught was the worst dialogue of the year. "Me love's sloppin' and spillin' all over the place wid the wait o' moi luv fer yew." Like that. I don't know what kind of language he was speaking, but you needed subtitles. Anyway, he found out she was making a fool of him by pretending not to know how to kiss a man, so he ended up jilting her. The End.

In Act Three, she finds true love with an older man—a crisp, precise, slightly womanly barrister, played by Paul Scofield with a quiet artistry that was both controlled and dazzling, which, of course, is the hardest kind of greatness to achieve. She gives her all to this pipe-smoking, dog-petting, fireplace, English manor house, cardigan sweater cliché—then he turns out to be married, cunning, lecherous, and given to making a habit of seducing girls and then walking out like a coward. Her heart is broken forever. The End—almost. For the American version, a special happy ending was inserted that will not be shown in the British version of the show—a silly, sophomoric epilogue archly narrated by none other than Sir Laurence Olivier (with great blotches of dried egg on his face) in which the girl finds happiness-ever-after in a Fitzpatrick travelogue sunset with the Alfie character from Act Two, who was the slimiest character of the three.

Except for Caine, who resembles a vagrant sloth and who is in desperate need of diction and elocution lessons, the actors were marvelous. They all worked for charity, with the proceeds going to rebuild an English home for aging actors. Their cause was just; their vehicle was absurd.

The First Tuesday (NBC) is the peacock network's answer to CBS's *60 Minutes*, only twice as long. It threatens to appear for two hours on the first Tuesday of every month. The first instalment was some kind of sick joke. There's the peculiar set that looks like a jail, in which Sandy Vanocur, the show's anchor man, stands with his arms pinned to his side like some kind of aluminum robot and shouts his lines like an actor trying to reach the second balcony. There is no expression in his voice and the effect is most appalling. The first show led off with a profile of Philip Blaiberg, the Capetown heart transplant survivor. Mr. Blaiberg was shown swimming, answering fan mail, discussing his sexual prowess, and dancing on New Year's Eve while a sound track played "Zing Went the Strings of My Heart." I began to laugh. Then Mr. Blaiberg, who, you may remember, received the transplant of a heart that belonged to a Negro man, was asked: "Most people say things like 'I mean it from the bottom of my heart' but you can't say that. I guess what I'm trying to ask is, do you feel there's a stranger in your midst?" It was beginning to look and sound like a satire.

The next segment was a really colossal waste of time about baton twirling that was like one of those terrible short subjects I used to have to sit through in the movies when I was a kid, waiting for the main feature. There were visits to such obscure shrines as the National Baton Twirling Association and the National Twirling Hall of Fame, followed by the most unbelievable interview I've ever seen with a pathetic eleven-year-old child who travels around the country on airplanes all alone, driven by her fanatic mother to smile and twirl, with this simple philosophy: "I like twirling because I want to win a lot and make my parents happy." Then she quite innocently told a horror story that sounded like an audition for the Grand Guignol: "I was chasing my brother, trying to hit him with my baton, and I fell through a plate of glass and cut my jugular vein open and they had to give me six-and-a-half pints of blood and all I could think of was 'Please let me live so I can go to Mississippi and win the championship.' " Followed by a closeup of a lifetime scar across her neck and the voice of an NBC announcer: "Despite her ruptured jugular, she almost achieved a fairy tale finish . . ." It had to be written by Jules Feiffer.

Next came a mind-blower. A visit with Charles Atlas at age seventy-six. What he looks like I can't tell you, but his stomach was sucked in so tight he could hardly talk, and even when he did the sound track drowned out his voice with the sound of drum rolls. I guess the point was how kicky we can all be at seventy-six if we exercise every day, but at the end of his interview (a riot, by the way, with quotes like "De way I got started, dis man followed me down da beach and said he was admirin' my body and said I was Apollo and Hercules all rolled inta one and after dat I let 'em use me for da arms, legs, and everything") a most drippy thing happened. A skinny weakling runs up to Charles Atlas on the beach and kicks sand in his face and he's too old to fight back. Without his knowledge, this staged scene allowed the show to make a mockery of his whole life and blow his whole theory to hell about teaching skinny weaklings how to defend themselves if someone kicks sand in their faces at the beach. (Remember the old ads on the backs of the comic books?) At about this point, *The First Tuesday* began to look like a mockery of American customs, mores, and traditions.

This was followed by a casual mention of the astronauts and Apollo 8, as though what they did wasn't really important, accompanied by a visual mockery of the space program (stills of the moon with bullets in its eyes, etc.) while a rock-and-roll record played "Everyone's Gone to the Moon." Pointless and humorless.

The best part of the show's two hours was a feature on Cuba, a look at Castro's new twenty-first century revolutionaries, with some fascinating but terrifying footage of American hippies, sick and demented draft dodgers, and Black Panthers who have defected to Cuba to be brainwashed into spreading Communist poison throughout the world. There was one interview with a pitiful twenty-six-year-old girl from Georgia who announced she would take guns and shoot any Americans, even her own family, if they tried to invade Cuba, and another interview with another loony American expatriate who is married to a Cuban, who teaches English, and who works long hours in the deadly hot sugar-cane fields to put money back into Castro's pocket. There was smuggled film from Radio Havana, dedicated to spewing Communist propaganda to Miami, and eerie talks with Cuban youths dedicated to guerrilla war, bloodshed, and violence.

But the saddest thing of all was the film on the new Cuban babies, taken from their parents and housed in government nurseries where they are fed political revolutionary propaganda from birth. Academic freedom has been replaced by armed militia, with young American exiles crying, "We are ready to give up our lives if necessary to liberate other countries from American imperialism." And yet, if it's so great, why do more than a thousand refugees flee Cuba each week seeking sanctuary in Miami? The show left little doubt that Cuba is one of the most pathetic, victimized little countries on the face of the earth, and I suppose, in a way, so much anti-American Communist manifesto coming from the mouths of Americans represents a kind of coming of age for TV. It would never have been shown during the McCarthy era.

The show closed out with a depressing portrait of poor, tormented Rita

Hayworth at the age of fifty, trying to live down the manufactured image of "Hollywood sex goddess" in a town that is like a series of booby hatches connected by freeways. Today she finds it hard to get work in Hollywood, where apparently it's Gilda or nothing. But unlike most of the has-been dames who had it all, she has a great sense of humor about not having it anymore. Vanocur: "Do you miss the attention?" Rita: "No, because I didn't like it when I had it." Vanocur getting into the really dum-dum questions: "How is a sex goddess manufactured?" Rita: "That's impossible to tell unless you have several hours." Vanocur: "I have." Rita, getting testy: "Well, I haven't."

After five marriages, she lives in an empty house with no friends ("In Hollywood," says Vanocur, "she's known as a loner—which is a nice way of saying she's pretty much alone") with a view ruined by Glenn Ford's TV antenna. She rarely goes out, but there was one shot of Bing Crosby asking her to play golf backstage at the San Francisco Film Festival, and another sad shot of the former sex queen driving alone through Beverly Hills while the soundtrack cleverly played Fred Astaire singing "You Were Never Lovelier." But Bing Crosby never showed up for golf and Glenn Ford, despite all his promises in *Gilda*, never moved his antenna.

The Cuba and Hayworth segments were pretty good examples of inspired television reporting. But the rest of the debut show on this new magazine-of-the-air was a disaster. *First Tuesday* needs to decide whether it is going to be a news special, or whether it is going to be a series of featurettes that scare the living daylights out of everybody through social satire. If it is going to be the former, it has to forget this first show ever happened and start all over again. If it is going to be the latter, it still has to forget this first show ever happened and start all over again. And whenever it decides what it is going to be, it should be it in half the time. Two hours is one hour too long.

January 17, 1969

Jean Claude Killy is a horse in midstream. Like most athletes, he's facing that difficult period after the ball is over and wondering, after winning three Olympic gold medals, how he can top it and what to do next. According to *Killy Le Champion*, a bogus "special" shown last Monday night on ABC, the answer is easy. Become a celebrity. Except for the first twenty minutes or so, during which there were some wonderful shots of Killy skiing, the show was a fashionable waste of time, cleverly edited to include enough shots of Killy doing enough different things to interest everybody. Like most specials that never sitck to the point, it was a bore—and frankly, it showed Killy off like a dilettante.

It started off on a biographical track. Killy outskiing his own instructors by the age of nine. Killy leaving school at fifteen and singlemindedly devoting himself to conquering the world on skis. Sort of an Abominable Snowman, you might say. Good footage of his 1966 world championship victory at Portillo, Chile, where he broke all records as the fastest downhill skier in history (80 m.p.h.). Then the portion of the show devoted to the 1968 Olympics in Grenoble did a fine job of capturing the Killy personality. There was Killy, jogging through the Alps like a skinny bear in a blue and red bunny suit, Killy playing with his best friend, a seven-year-old child from his village of Val d'Isère, Killy in various stages of moodiness, from the eve of the Olympics as he stared out of the window at a silent snowfall while his roommates strummed a guitar, to his pride in his own skill as he was pronounced the world's greatest skier, among the pomp and pageantry of the 10th Winter Olympics.

Then the letdown. "I was looking for something I could commit myself to—perhaps I would find it in Hollywood," someone got him to say for the soundtrack. Then the narration slurpily droned: "At Universal Studios, Killy wonders if he can become a part of this strange other world . . ." Duh! The rest of the show was pretty much like that. Phony and a little sad. Killy leaping over sand hills in a dune-buggy race. Killy shooting pool with James Garner, who wears more beads and jewelry in his own poolroom than he does on the *Tonight Show*. Killy learning to open a parachute as he jumps out of a plane. Killy surfing. Killy riding a motorcycle. Killy taking Barbara Hancock, whom he doesn't even know, to a movie premiere. Killy dancing with Jean Seberg at The Daisy and watching, embarrassed, while she tries on clothes at Rudi Gernreich's salon. Killy sitting in the middle of the desert listening to his friends, folk singers Buffy Ford and John Stewart, as they sing their latest recordings for Capitol Records. It was twenty minutes to the point and nearly an hour of padding. Maybe that's what his life is all about these days—padding. I don't like to think so. But I will give him credit for one thing: milking the hell out of those three gold medals.

With nothing but his medals and his smile (and some very smart personal management), he has a line of commercial ski products, he has been offered a part in a movie, he is bylining how-to-ski articles for several national magazines (with no writing experience whatsoever), he has just signed a three-year contract with the Chevrolet motor division of General Motors to serve as a spokesman for Chevrolet, and in addition to his ABC special he has another thirteen-week series each Sunday afternoon on CBS called *The Killy Style*, which, according to the press release from Killy's press agents, "involves not only skiing at the most famous resorts all over the world but Killy's way of life as an international celebrity."

OK. It's all a good job of exploitation for money. I just hate to see champions exploited as though they were Hollywood blondes. Back to the slopes, kiddo, before you become the French George Plimpton.

To Love a Child was an ABC special about adoption narrated with tenderness and depth by Maureen Stapleton and photographed in wonderful cinéma vérité style like the best kind of small documentary, similar to the sort of thing the Maysle Brothers are doing. It followed one couple through the adoption process—applications, interviews, questions, tears, waiting, meeting the baby for the first time, and off-the-cuff views of both the prospective parents and the adoption agency officials, so you got a total picture of what goes on behind the scenes—and paralleled their story with the pathetic plight of an unmarried, expectant mother and her fears for the future of the child she is giving up for adoption.

Actors with millions of dollars behind their careers and weeks of retakes could not have performed so majestically as the real people on this show. There was one scene, in which the mother is finally told she can have a child from the agency, that she and her husband have passed all the qualified tests. She breaks down and cries. She doesn't know, at this instant, whether she should reach for a Kleenex in the outstretched hand of the lady from the adoption agency or accept her husband's handkerchief. It is this heart-stopping moment of indecision, this kind of tiny emotional catharsis, which is so impossible to merely act—and which makes for much more throbbing drama than any script can provide, the kind of drama television needs more of.

Everybody talks about how rotten commercial television is, but a man named Charles Sopkin has written a wonderfully imaginative, hilarious, and highly recommended new book that proves it. It's called *Seven Glorious Days, Seven Fun-Filled Nights*, and it is published by Simon & Schuster.

It seems Mr. Sopkin, a much braver man than anyone I know, recently devoted himself to watching all six New York channels for a full week—from dawn (with Aline Saarinen and all those women with moustaches and garter belts) to Johnny Carson and the late, late shows. It's a very sick book, because anyone who flagpole-sits through 168 solid hours of Joey Bishop, Merv Griffin, Dick Cavett, Captain Kangaroo, Tarzan, The Smothers Brothers, the Beverly Hillbillies, Ed Sullivan, Pay Cards, Girl Talk, Supermarket Sweep, The Secret Storm, Mr. Terrific, Patti Page, Moms Mabley, Alan Burke, Birthday House, Totie Fields, and everything else, interspersed occasionally with the Adenauer funeral and a color visit to the Sistine Chapel, cannot possibly survive the experience a well man. Mr. Sopkin concludes that television is sicker than he is, a national disgrace, in fact "My frank opinion now is that there is *no* way to make television better. It is what it is." AMEN and God bless us, every one.

Women's Wear Daily

Movie Reviews

January 24, 1969

The general state of TV lately has been so genuinely rotten I've considered selling my set for second-hand junk. Bad idea. Trying to get even scrap metal prices for a TV set is like selling Maria Montez a mongoose. So I try to watch some of the new shows. First, a new soap opera called *Hidden Faces*. This show is so bad it makes even the vampires on *Dark Shadows* look good. In the episode I caught, the acting, direction, and camerawork were so poor you wonder how these people were ever allowed in the union. One couple was planning an engagement party and the young man beamed romantically, "Just wait until tonight, when I slip that finger on your hand!" Later another actor who looked like he had amnesia burst into a room shouting, "I rushed right over when I heard the news on the radiator!" Scout's honor.

Then I saw something on CBS called *The Queen and I*, about an over-aged ocean liner called the *Amsterdam Queen* which is in love with Billy De Wolfe, both of which should be sold for scrap along with the whole series; followed by a "special on ABC starring something equally unbelievable to the naked eye called Tom Jones—a stomach-churning, pelvis-tossing No-Talent sporting thirteen pounds of greasy Brillo on top of his head and wearing old discarded sequined and spangled Elvis Presley costumes that went out of style fifteen years ago. According to the press poop ABC is sending out about this enigma, Tom Jones (such originality! such daring!) "works his body as energetically and eloquently as his larynx. Tarzan is a shrinking violet by comparison. Elvis Presley's early contortions would seem like those of a gentle butterfly if seen side by side. In his full writhing agony of song"—and get this next part—"he looks as if he could eat the average pop group, complete with guitars, for breakfast." They actually pay people to write like that over at ABC. Scout's honor.

I don't suppose anything further need be said about Tom Jones (ABC's press department has already destroyed him with purpler prose than anything I could write) except that his extraordinarily repulsive act will be around each and every week on an ABC series called *This Is Tom Jones,* on which he promises to sing in the same style in which he does almost everything else—straight from the crotch.

No, television seems to be accomplishing only one thing these days. It's driving more and more people right straight into the comforting blackness of the nearest movie house. TV caters to the idiot level. The theater is expensive, pretentious, and boring. Movies is where all the action is. More people are going to movies, movies are bolder and bigger and livelier and more fun to look at than ever before. It's a medium that knows few limitations. And frankly, I'd rather sit through a bad movie than a bad play or a bad TV show. Audiences have become spoiled by too much palaver in front of the boob tube—they are ruder than ever and they talk more. But except for obvious trash like *Candy* and *Joanna,* they know how to be quiet when they're getting their money's worth.

They were attentive as owls, for example, in *The Stalking Moon.* I've seen horrible westerns in my day, but as well as I can remember *The Stalking Moon* is the first "horror western" ever made. It's *Psycho* in spurs, and being a horror movie fanatic for as long as I can remember, I loved it.

The plot is very simple. Gregory Peck is an Indian scout, circa 1881, named Sam Varner (no relation to the Varners in Faulkner) who is retiring after twenty years of Army service to live out his days in the quiet peace of a small ranch in New Mexico. On his last maneuver, he rounds up a group of Apaches who have escaped from government reservations and discovers in the howling pack of savages one frightened, speechless, tortured white woman clutching a small half-breed son. She has been a prisoner for ten years and now Peck represents her only lifeline to freedom. She follows him through the desert wasteland in a nervous terror, looking behind her for some sign of quiet menace. The audience never knows any more at any given moment than what it sees. The rest of the film follows this restless trio as they are viciously and insanely pursued by evil and death, in the form of a psychopathic mass murderer named Salvaje, who is the Apache father of the woman's child.

The beauty of the film lies in the enormous sensitivity with which Robert Mulligan has directed it. There is only a scattering of dialogue. The characters do not develop through talk, but through a sharing of the unseen terror waiting for them behind each rock, huddling together out of fright and the need for reassurance and understanding, like lost skiers huddling together for warmth on a deserted mountain trail in the middle of a blizzard. It is the way they come together, sharing life in silence, which makes the familiarity of their situation and the details of this kind of western transcend the obvious. In a sense, John Huston's *The Unforgiven* was also about white men awaiting an Indian massacre, but Mulligan's film is smaller, more personal, and therefore more isolated and terrifying. Also, the terror is never actually shown. Mulligan uses his camera like an animal—peering around corners, darting under branches, groping for shelter in a sandstorm. The camera, therefore, is the victim of whatever lies out there in the howling dark under the stalking moon. The terror is unseen, like the ghost in *The Haunting*, which makes the blood freeze even quicker in the veins. Each scene is blocked and paced until it rises to a crescendo of fried nerves, as the man, woman, and child are stalked by an evil that leaves a trail of blood in its shadowy path. Every dog, every man, every breathing thing that enters their lives is monstrously slaughtered in a bloodbath of unseen horror as the film stalks toward its shattering conclusion.

Gregory Peck works as well under Mulligan's watchful direction as he did in their earlier *To Kill a Mockingbird*. Eva Marie Saint is sheer magic to watch as she peels away the layers of the woman and rebuilds the entire character structure of a pathetic creature, sealed off from life, who must learn to speak, touch, use a fork, need a man, and cry without frozen horror all over again. Like Joanne Woodward, she is one of the best actresses in movies today. *The Stalking Moon* is really the only film she's made since *All Fall Down* that has used her properly, without taking her sensitivity for granted. Robert Forster, who went unnoticed as the peculiar soldier with a penchant for riding horses in the nude and stealing Elizabeth Taylor's panties in *Reflections in a Golden Eye*, adds depth and color to a small part as a half-breed whose friendship leads to his own self-destruction.

Charles Lang is one cinematographer who knows how to shoot the West like an anthropologist instead of a postcard manufacturer. Through his camera lens, the desert and mountain vistas of Nevada actually look like craters of the moon. Every frame is shot with economy and style—from the deserted stagecoach stop and primitive railroad tracks to the disemboweled towers of rock slicing the cobalt blue sky—adding authenticity and quiet grandeur to contrast the nightmare battle of good vs. evil at the core of the film. Everything about *The Stalking Moon* is excellent, adding up to one of the best horror films out of Hollywood in a long, long time.

It proves my point about movies vs. television. Just compare the care, talent, and uniqueness with which it energizes the tired old genre of western movies to any of the look-alike, sound-alike "quickie" shoot-em-ups on TV and you get a pretty good idea of the difference in quality between what is being accomplished in the two media. They both use cameras, but movies is where it's at, baby.

January 31, 1969

If I'm going to write a regular column about movies, I told myself last week, I'd better go out and see some. And so I have spent so much time in dark rooms in the past seven days that I have opened a charge account at Bausch & Lomb. Unfortunately, I'm not sure ruining my eyesight was worth it. I haven't much to report: *The Fixer* is a crashing bore. *The Brotherhood* has Boris Kaufman's usual genius for photographing scenes as though he was giving birth; otherwise, it's a pretty routine flick about the Mafia, with a stunning performance by Kirk Douglas. *Joanna*, *The Magus*, and *Candy* are too far beneath contempt to warrant even a passing comment.

The Sergeant is cheap, old-fashioned, sentimental trash about a latent homosexual who assumes command of a postwar American Army camp in France, takes a fancy to a blue-eyed blond G.I., and shoots himself through the head when his amorous advances are rejected with a clout on the jaw. It's an easy movie to read more serious meanings into, simply because Rod Steiger is so good as the sergeant that he evokes sympathy. Watching him, I was almost tempted to go along with the film's insistence that this kind of man might do this kind of thing. But the G.I. (John Phillip Law) is too dense to be believable and Dennis Murphy's screenplay is so naïve, so badly written, and, in the final analysis, so unconvincing, that I was forced to remind myself that yes, Virginia, movies have changed since the days of the Hays office, even though the people who made *The Sergeant* must not have been watching while they grew up. Homosexuals can get away with it now. They don't commit suicide anymore, especially with Freudian symbols like guns. *The Sergeant* is about as courageous, interesting, and up-to-date as sex in a granny gown.

The Decline and Fall of a Bird Watcher is really a funny idea, somewhat raggedly based on Evelyn Waugh's satirical novel *Decline and Fall*, which fell apart somewhere along the way. It concerns an innocent who gets involved with such corrupt symbols of the rich and eccentric British upperclass as a kidnapper, a wooden-legged bigamist, a schoolboy who gets shot in the foot, a cleric who gets his head sawed off and an affluent madam who poisoned her husband by putting ground glass in his Turkish coffee in order to freely pursue her hobby—selling girls into white slavery in Tangier. Trouble is, the film has no style (except for all the pink, purple, and Harlem-green Rolls Royces that keep popping up like Easter eggs, it could be set in any era), and Robin Phillips, the actor who plays the innocent, looks much too cocky and world-weary to ever be believable as a naïve second cousin to *Candy*. None of it ever comes off, although it does provide another opportunity to watch the fabulous Genevieve Page in action, and several really marvelous British character actors from the London stage—notably Colin Blakely, Felix Aylmer, Patrick Magee, Leo McKern, and Donald Wolfit—inject the whole disorganized affair with more polish and dignity than it deserves. Old pros have saved more than one misguided movie, and this is one misguided movie chock full of them that desperately needs saving.

Of all the films I've seen lately, I very much admired *The Stalking Moon*, which I wrote about last Friday, and *Greetings*, an impertinent, delicious little satire about draft dodgers and computer dating, directed by a twenty-eight-year-old filmmaker named Brian De Palma, who also had a hand in writing the script. De Palma's film has its flaws. He has not learned how to do very much with a camera; his film has very little structure (and what little there is owes its life to the worst of Godard); some of the improvised situations (at least they look improvised) tend to go on too long. But there is an enormous amount of raw vitality in *Greetings* of the sort I find sadly lacking in most Hollywood movies. There are wonderful performances by a cast of fresh and inventive young actors who aren't jaded enough yet to be inhibited. And few big budget movies contain as much wit and purpose.

The title of the film, as anyone who has ever received an induction notice from the draft board will quickly recognize, is the first word from Uncle Sam, the beginning of the end. One of the three Lotharios in the film gets his, and most of the action centers around the steps his two buddies take to get him rejected. First, he tries to get his leg busted by picking a fight with two spades on 125th Street. Then he goes through a training manual on how to turn instant fag (knit shirt, shave under the arms, limp wrist, lace bikini panties, a pair of socks in the fly). Finally they try to keep him awake for three days as they walk ledges, hop through the zoo, and relate exciting sex fantasies ("So there we are, see, all naked . . . and these two girls make me lie down, see, and they cover me from head to toe with whipped cream and then they start to lick it off . . ."). He gets drafted anyway, and here is where the sex computer enters the picture and gets in the way. The rest of the movie follows the three boys through their various pursuits and it's difficult to keep up with all the substructures. One boy becomes so paranoid he fills out the computer application ("Do you think I'm 'unusually attractive,' or just 'regularly attractive'?" "I don't know, man, *lie!*") and winds up in a pornographic movie. The second buddy devises a remarkable series of ingenious ways to seduce girls, ending up acting out his fantasies by stripping a Viet Cong sex kitten in the marshes while a news camera records the event for the folks back home. The third chum pursues clues in his private attempts to clear up the Kennedy assassination by drawing bullet holes on naked girls to enlist their aid (while seducing the poor darlings, of course) and ends up shot through the brain by a mysterious man he is trailing in one of the film's truly bizarre moments.

It doesn't always work, and it is done to a horrible rock score by the Children of Paradise, a group about which the less heard the better. But considering the fact that it was made for less than forty thousand dollars, this biting freakout of a movie becomes something of a small, uncut diamond in the rough. In its confrontation with the sickness and inertia gnawing at the hearts of youth today, *Greetings* takes deadly aim at Johnson, Vietnam, politics, fetishism, voyeurism, *Blow-Up*, the Warren Report, and the absurdity of life—which, for forty thousand dollars, is a lot for a little movie to do, and more than any Hollywood movie has ever done.

At the 34th Street East, where I saw the movie, they are also showing a charming, subtle, and wonderfully unpretentious short called *Going to Work in the Morning in Brooklyn*, which I highly recommend. It traces a young man's early morning ritual, from alarm clock to office, with humor and slyness and a deadly precision for detail. The funniest scene takes place in a men's room when, after washing his face to keep his sleepy eyes open, the hero gropes for the paper towel receptacle, spilling them all over the floor. He finally solves the problem of what to do with all the mess by dropping it out of the window and starting his own ticker tape parade. It's more a Valentine to New York than anything else, proving that even in the dreary humdrum sameness of city routine, there's excitement just around the corner. I predict very big things for the amiable comic who plays the young man. His name is Bill Fiore, and he slightly resembles a Pomeranian whose face has just been stroked in the wrong direction.

February 7, 1969

Somewhere, in some dark screening room, in some dark century not long ago, some person or thing (probably *Variety*, which seems to have cornered the market on words that never should have existed in the first place) invented the word "sleeper" to describe a movie with everything going against it that turns out to be much better than everyone ever expected. *Buona Sera, Mrs. Campbell* is just such a movie. I hesitate to list all the reasons why I had to be dragged unwillingly to see it, but some of them are (1) the title (Can you wait to be the first in line to see something called *Buona Sera, Mrs. Campbell?*); (2) the director (Melvin Frank, who used to make the "Road" pictures with Hope and Crosby and who also produced it, is not my idea of America's answer to Fellini); (3) the cast. I mean, this movie stars Gina Lollobrigida, and you lost me right there. It also stars Shelley Winters, and even if it *didn't* star Gina Lollobrigida you lost me *again* right there. Then it goes and backs them up with some fine male screen performers like—are you sitting down?—Peter Lawford, Phil Silvers, Telly Savalas, and Philippe Leroy. That ought to get them into the theaters out in Pelican Falls.

So. Prejudices out in the open where you can choose your weapons, the next thing I have to tell you is that if you let any of the horrors listed above keep you from seeing *Buona Sera, Mrs. Campbell*, you will miss one of the funniest, most deliciously acted, cleverly directed, and entertainingly well-scripted comedies out of Hollywood since *The Facts of Life*, which, come to think if it, was also a "sleeper" directed by Melvin Frank. Perhaps, then, it's Frank to whom credit is due for making a genuinely delightful movie full of very real people involved in very recognizable (and therefore even funnier) human situations. Even better, the people in Frank's movie are basically decent people who are perfectly capable of striking responsive chords in the kind of audience that is always writing letters to theater exhibitors and movie producers wondering whatever happened to Preston Sturges. Well, let's see if that audience really cares what happened to good, wholesome comedy without dirt and sex and smut. Let's see how many of them go to see *Buona Sera, Mrs. Campbell.*

The plot: one of those postwar 40s themes about the three army buddies who make it back to the Italian postcard village where they left Miss True Love behind to bear a child. Each buddy thinks the kid is his. But Mama, who has been milking each of her former G. I. Joes for Baby's college tuition all these years, is in an even worse dilemma: they are all descending upon her for a reunion of their old army unit in the town square and, naturally, each wants to see his progeny. Baby, meanwhile, is no baggy-eyed creature with a scarf around her head from an old Vittorio De Sica movie. She's a very hip minicutie who has very definite ideas of her own about living with a married man in Paris and who thinks each of the men coming to visit her Mom is a pal of her presumably dead papa's from his old battalion. To complicate things even further, the guys' wives decide to tag along at the last minute, providing problems of *their* own. It all sounds very complex and probably even a bit Hollywood-awful. But nothing I can say for *Buona Sera, Mrs. Campbell* will adequately prepare you for either the clichés—mistaken identities, chance meetings, narrow escapes, musical doors, and vulgar jokes—or how fresh and inventive they all seem under Frank's direction. It is witty, urbane, sophisticated fun and it is even very touching at times.

Gina Lollobrigida is miraculously adept at comedy timing, and something wonderful keeps happening to her figure and face. She is appealing and wise and warm and all the things Italian movie stars never are after they pass forty. I think, in this movie, I have seen her for the very first time. Phil Silvers and Shelley Winters, as fat, aging, suburban gargoyles with a brood of no-neck monsters, are the perfect choices for the roles they play (I've seen Miss Winters dining out on so much scenery in all the wrong dramatic roles for so long I actually forgot she could play comedy without slobbering). Telly Savalas is even endearing, which must be something of a screen "first," and Peter Lawford manages some fine moments, too. The movie was lushly photographed on location in Italy, (instead of on the back lot at Goldwyn); the script (co-authored by Mr. Frank) owes something to *The Miracle of Morgan's Creek*, but finds its own frantic energy through several bold slashes and even more subtle brushstrokes of the rare kind of comedy (deftly from the heart, instead of splashy in the face) I seldom see in this age of over-kill. None of it is ever pseudo-sick, in the style of the "new comedy" like *Candy*, nor is any of it moronically pseudo-"in," in the style of Richard Lester. It brings back good humor and good taste, rekindles my faith in mankind while allowing me to laugh at it at the same time, and gives several misunderstood and almost always badly used performers a chance to pick up the pieces and start all over again. For all these things, and for the opportunity it provides for audiences everywhere to discover that the best movies often come in the most unexpected surprise packages instead of in the more well-publicized tinsel, I applaud it vigorously.

I fell asleep three times in *Martyrs of Love*, the new Czech film by Jan Nemec. It tells three deadly dull stories that attempt, with the aid of a heavy-handed, clumping musical score and no dialogue, to explore the romantic fantasies of three daydreaming Czech teen-agers with the resulting quality of an amateur night in Prague. Up to now, I've been hard-pressed to come up with a logical reason for the Communist takeover of Czechoslovakia. Now I can see why they did it. To stop movies like *Martyrs of Love*. Stay away; and stay awake.

February 14, 1969

I'm not sure anyone who reads this column—or, for that matter, anyone who can even read at all—will want to know about John Wayne's new movie, *The Hellfighters*. But I feel duty-bound to tell you anyway, just so the next time somebody tells you they don't make movies like this anymore, you can tell them to drop dead.

This movie is so bad it almost defies description. The people who made it (the director is Andrew McLaglen, who was married to Veda Ann Borg) must have been living in some time tunnel somewhere for the past twenty years, because I haven't seen anything this corny since John Wayne made *Tycoon* back in 1948. Ah, yes. *Tycoon*. About which James Agee's entire notice read: "Several tons of dynamite are set off in this movie; none of it under the right people." Ditto *The Hellfighters*.

You've heard about kids who follow the surf? Well, this time Big Duke and Jim Hutton are emotionally underdeveloped children who follow fire engines. In fact, they even run this company, see, that allows them to go around putting out fires and gives them lots of opportunities to pick up girls with different accents on a variety of colorful movie sets. Big Duke has a wife and daughter who left him twenty years ago. The script says it was because they couldn't stand tramping around to all those dirty oil rigs while he puts out fires, but my guess is that they sneaked off one afternoon and saw *Tycoon* and just never came back. Anyway, when a derrick falls on Big Duke, Daughter flies in from her ski weekend at Jackson Hole and he gets to say special Big Duke lines like "The last time I saw you, you were in rompers." Like that. She turns out to be Katharine Ross, whose career seems to be disintegrating faster than you can say *The Graduate*. And fifteen minutes after she comes on, *she* gets to say "I'm a little uncertain about this," which gave the audience at the preview I attended the chance to applaud wildly.

She is pretty certain, however, about Jim Hutton, who is struggling amiably to be a new Jimmy Stewart without much success. They get hitched and buy out Big Duke's business and the scene switches to the Universal lot's Da Nang Hilton set, where the introductions run something like "Hello, Ahmal." "My son-in-law." "My daughter." "My pleasure." Duke doesn't care what anyone says as long as he's left alone to get rehitched himself to his former wife, back on the scene and disguised as Vera Miles, who always gets stuck in roles that hide her talent under a bushel basket.

But you guessed it. There's one more fire, this time down on the Universal lot's South American set. This is a multiple all-time fire engine chaser's triple-threat super-duper fire and, well, it's just too much for the kids to handle, being so exhausted from being newly married and all. So they call Big Duke ("We've been trying to reach you for days, but there's guerrilla activity in the hills") and the director tells Vera Miles to turn on her worried look. Vera wrinkles her brow and I don't have to tell anyone who has ever seen a Big Duke Wayne movie what happens next.

The Hellfighters is the kind of movie in which every closeup of a stick of dynamite is accompanied by a 365-piece orchestra, actors show surprise by coughing loudly into their coffee cups, and the boss's daughter who has never been near an oil well in her life drives right past the police barricades in an open convertible and cruises right up to an exploding poison gas mine with a look of positive delight. One minute Big Duke gets his lung punctured; the next time you see him his arm is in a sling. And by all means dig the Universal lot's Houston office set with all the miniature cars buzzing past the picture window on a treadmill at the rate of about four miles per hour. (I counted the same red station wagon seventeen times in one scene.) Even the clinches in this flick are so phony that every time one actor kisses another, it looks like two department store dummies falling on each other.

In the last scene, Vera Miles hops a helicopter to where the guerrilla action is and loves it. Just before the "The End" sign flashes across the Universal sky, Big Duke squeezes her and grins: "I think we oughta get her a tin hat."

How about a tin cup instead? One more movie like *The Hellfighters* and she'll need one.

Mayerling is a ghastly misfortune that proves, among other things: zither music is a crashing bore; Catherine Deneuve is the worst actress since Kim Novak and should never *ever* make another movie without subtitles; Omar Sharif should retire and become a professional bridge player, which is what he keeps telling everyone he wants to do anyway; Terence Young is a terrible director when it comes to shooting any scene with less than fifty people in it; James Mason should really stop taking roles just for the money and then boring everybody to death by walking through them in a trance; and movie companies should stop spending millions of dollars on fabulous costumes, gold palaces, hunting lodges, sumptuous chateaux, and thousands of extras, then saddle the trappings with the kind of script in which a valet enters each morning and says, "God be thanked for sparing His Highness another day to live."

There are, on the other hand, three good things about *Mayerling*—Genevieve Page, who plays a deliciously impish society procuress rather like an 1888 *Hello Dolly*; Ava Gardner, who, as Omar Sharif's sixty-year-old mother is totally miscast but beautiful and appealing and sad enough to almost save the movie; and a lavish ballroom sequence more than a little "borrowed" from Vincente Minnelli! But then almost everything about *Mayerling* seems borrowed from something. Like the morgue.

February 21, 1969

I'm sick of movies about youth, but I'm even sicker of movies about youth made by people who don't know anything about youth, and if you don't think that statement makes sense, go see Jacques Demy's new movie, *Model Shop*. Apparently Demy ran out of ideas after *The Young Girls of*

Rochefort, so he decided to come to America and make a real honest-to-pete Hollywood movie about a mixed-up drop-out waiting to be drafted. If this movie is all he knows and all he learned about America, he should have stayed home in Paris. He could have made a much better movie about American dropouts just by hanging out at Le Drugstore.

As the movie opens, Gary Lockwood (*2001*) and some really ridiculous peroxide blonde who speaks in such a monotone she sounds dubbed are getting out of bed in some very peculiar rundown house with pink, white, chrome yellow, and mint-green walls in the middle of a lot of strange oil wells. (I've lived in Los Angeles, but I *never* saw anything like *this*!) The blonde is like a young, strident Frances Langford playing the female half of "The Bickersons," which Demy probably doesn't know anything about. She is also ugly. Anyway, she berates him for being a shiftless bum ("I honestly don't think you're committed to anything!") and for awhile I thought I was back in *Joanna*. Then the finance company comes to take away the car and during the next half-hour or so, Demy's camera follows Lockwood through the traffic while he searches for a pal to borrow $100 from. A hairy, talentless rock group called Spirit makes a guest appearance saying things like "Hey man, everything's cool" and "What's happenin', baby?" They also get in some plugs for their new album. (People are always plugging things in Godard movies and Demy, not being original, well . . .)

I don't know what Demy promised Anouk Aimée to persuade her to be in this mess (maybe she can't read English and didn't know what the script was about) but suddenly she appears as a model named Lola, which could be construed to be the "Lola" of Demy's famous film *Lola* transported to California. (Aha! You're catching on!) For $12 you can take pornagraphic pictures of Lola ("What would you like? Boots or whip?") so Lockwood blows the rest of his car-payment loan and shoots away. They end up in bed in Lola's apartment, which has pink, white, chrome yellow, and mint-green walls, and which she shares with a spade chick who kisses her a lot. Both chicks are very broke, but they drive a gorgeous white 1968 Mercury convertible. Anyway, in bed the lovers say a lot of naïve things that prove that Anouk Aimée is not the only one who has no knowledge of English—Demy can't write it, either. "I don't know if it's the way your shoulder curves, or the line of your neck, but it's pure joy," says Lockwood. "You speak as if you were just discovering love, cheri," purrs Anouk. Like that. Lockwood puts his trousers on, dashes back to the house where the oil wells are still pumping, jilts the blonde, and makes plans to ditch the draft board and go AWOL with Lola. He picks up the phone and the spade chick roommate tells him Lola has already left. (They've got fast plane schedules in L. A.) "Left? Gone? You mean, for *France*?" The tears roll down his unshaven face. Outside, the men from the finance company are towing his car away. There is no "The End." Not even an arty "Fin." The screen just turns purple and you know it's over because the people around you start waking up.

The entire movie looks as though its entire budget was less than Lockwood's car payments. The interior shots are so amateurishly lit there are shadows behind windows, door facings, even the actors' heads. The sound is terrible; at times, the dialogue is drowned out by the sound of airplanes overhead. But I will say one thing for *Model Shop*—it's the kind of flick heavy on the French idea of American "realism." That means every time an actor makes a long-distance phone call he repeats the area code.

Accompanying *Model Shop* at the Cinema Rendezvous is a short subject by Jacques Demy's wife, Agnes Varda. While Demy was in Los Angeles playing around with his silly little dropout flick and wasting Columbia's money, his wife was up in San Francisco shooting her own tedious little bore about a long-lost uncle of hers who lives on a houseboat in Sausalito. Miss Varda obviously considered her uncle a wonderful subject for a film to be shown in commercial American movie houses, because he is one of the oldest living flower children in captivity, because he takes people on long sailboat rides that are fun to photograph and because he hates the Establishment and says shocking things about America. She was wrong. All she proves is that people—even French lady film directors—who shove their home movies down the throats of others should be arrested.

February 28, 1969

The Prime of Miss Jean Brodie is a magnificent achievement; a broad, lyrical, beautifully written exploitation of the life of a vain, ridiculous schoolteacher in Edinburgh in 1932 who held in her nervous, twitchy little hands the power to rule the lives of most of the young girls in her care.

"Give me a girl at an impressionable age," said Miss Brodie, "and she's mine for life." With those words, a kind of unexplainable literary magic happened; Miss Jean Brodie jumped off the pages of Muriel Spark's novel and became a legend. Vanessa Redgrave played her on the stage in London and Zoe Caldwell played her in New York. But in the rich, colorful, crisply adapted movie version Miss Brodie gains new dimensions, new heights of character development, new inspiration. And I think it is almost entirely because of an actress named Maggie Smith, for whom my admiration and awe are boundless.

Dedicated to her girls in the "prime" of her life, making them weep with tales of lovers slain on the battle green of Flanders, feeding them pâté de foie gras on the lawn while their classmates toil in the mess hall, spouting fascist propaganda about her romanticized Mussolini, or teaching them to walk with their heads held high "like Sybil Thorndyke," Maggie Smith has the face and the voice of a thousand-page novel. In one scene, I counted almost twenty changes in her mood, her attitude, her facial response. I don't think I've ever seen anything quite like her, and I doubt that I ever will again. She has made the most profound impression on me of any actress I've seen since Kim Stanley appeared in *The Goddess* some ten or twelve years ago.

Ronald Neame has directed the film economically—no gimmicks, fancy camera angles, or showing of the muscles, for which I am immensely grateful. With an actress of Miss Smith's fantastic range, you don't make up for any losses by dazzling the audience with visual cake icing. Miss Smith is an eight-course feast. She is very lucky to have wonderful, sensitively written scenes (Jay Presson Allen's script is one of the best I've come across in a long time). And the supporting cast is simply miraculous. (One of the troubles with the Broadway production was the supporting cast—right out of an acting class in some 54th Street loft.)

In the movie, there is, for example, the awesome Celia Johnson, in her first film in ten years, as the stern headmistress who is always trying to throw cold water on Miss Brodie's eccentric teaching methods. I was especially fond of the way she knocked the props out from under *La Traviata*. ("Nonsense! Violetta was a thoroughly silly woman with diseased lungs!") Robert Stephens, who is Maggie Smith's husband in real life, is brilliant as one of Miss Brodie's baleful lovers; Pamela Franklin is turning into one of the most skillful and many-faceted young actresses on the screen. Ted Moore, who photographed *A Man for All Seasons*, has captured the city of Edinburgh in all its gritty purple glory. Indeed the entire film seems bathed in heather—from the army blanket grays of Brodie's girls to her own conservative and sensible mauves, tans, and violets. Rod McKuen has contributed a score that is plaintive and romantic without being sentimental, and there are no words to gauge the relief I felt when there was no icky theme song at the end of the picture sung by Judy Collins or Glen Campbell.

I could with pleasure fill twenty times this space with a partial listing of all the specific achievements in this movie and I still wouldn't be able to express fully how much I enjoyed it. But one thing I'd like to make perfectly clear: Maggie Smith is the actress of the year, the freshest, most creative force to happen to movies in a very long time. At a time in the history of movies when the age of the freak is upon us, she has the power to revolutionize the whole system of stars and star-thinking. Every actress currently working in films should be required to see *The Prime of Miss Jean Brodie* ten times. (Well, with someone like Mia Farrow, maybe fifteen.) Watching Maggie Smith is a privilege that comes rapturously close to bliss.

Very Happy Alexander is a gentle, sunny little caprice about a happy, simple Frenchman whose shrewish wife works him in the fields like a galley slave, checking on him with car horns, bells, and a walkie-talkie radio. When she dies, he goes to bed for two months, sending his scruffy dog to buy groceries and make excuses to the neighbors. Opportunity knocks once more in the form of a sexy blonde. Should Alexander return to his former responsibilities a pillar of the community, or remain a happy moron? Not the most exciting or original or inspiring film I've ever seen; but there is charm here, a lovely chase sequence in which a powdered sugar looking wedding party rips through a field of ripe sunflowers, and some delightful work by Philippe Noiret in a style pleasantly derived from Jacques Tati.

March 7, 1969

Somebody should do something about Otto Preminger. Like, teach the man how to make movies.

I can't recall a single director in the history of movies who has turned out so many rotten pictures or been so continuously ridiculed by every critic with even the most rudimentary classroom knowledge of what films are all about. Yet Hollywood keeps giving him the money to grind them out like cheese sandwiches at Chock Full o' Nuts, and they get sorrier and soggier.

Just when I thought *Hurry Sundown* was the worst movie possible for any man to make without being run out of the industry on a rail, along comes an exercise in brainless gibberish called *Skidoo*. This movie is crummy even by Preminger standards. And that, baby, is a mouthful of crumbs.

This alleged "satire" tackles such really "hilarious" subjects as hippies, LSD, the teen-age drug scene, the Mafia, prisons, draft dodgers, and sex. Like most Preminger films, the emphasis is mainly on sex, with the weakest qualities—mental and physical—of each cast member exposed in the ugliest and most unflattering light.

Actors are insane to work for this man, but actors are also masochists. How else can you explain a scene (which has nothing to do with the rest of the film and consequently serves no other purpose except to make a fool out of a vulnerable performer) like the one in which Carol Channing strips down to her panties and bra and offers to have sex with Frankie Avalon?

How else do you explain the scene in which a revolting creature with no talent discernible to the naked eye who calls herself Donyale Luna and who looks like a concentration camp survivor, strips and rapes John Phillip Law, who looks equally ridiculous in one of Jeff Chandler's leftover wigs from his son-of-Cochise period at Universal? Or the scene in which the Orange County Ramblers (ever hear of them?) play football in the nude? Or the one in which Austin Pendleton, a new Preminger "discovery" who resembles a hairy pelican, takes his shirt off?

Like most Preminger epics, this one is also full of "cameo" performances. Preminger hires everyone he can get, then manages to pull their worst work out of them.

Groucho Marx as "God" is too embarrassing to go into. Rudi Gernreich's costumes should be burned. Nilsson's music sounds as if it was written and performed in a munitions factory.

The whole mess was written by someone named Doran William Cannon, whose idea of humorous dialogue runs something like this: "You are Mario Benedict? Better known as Eggs?" Remember that name. Doran William Cannon. Run from it if you ever see it again.

People belch a lot in *Skidoo*, but they don't laugh much. It all looks painfully like a comedy made by a man without a sense of humor. (I'm beginning to think Preminger is never funny anyway unless he's making a so-called "serious" movie. *Hurry Sundown* was much funnier than *Skidoo.*) And he seems anxious to prove that he isn't funny by failing to be cautious enough to even cover himself in his most humorless moments.

In the end, Jackie Gleason floats off into the sky in a garbage can. Is it a bird? Is it a plane? "No," says some minor character, "just a great big blob of nothing."

After suffering stone-faced through *Skidoo,* I don't need to tell you what gloriously insulting retorts a line like that gives the audience the opportunity to yell back at the screen.

In *Twisted Nerve,* the young Canadian actor Hywel Bennett plays a sexual psychopath hatchet murderer masquerading as a mentally retarded twenty-one-year-old. Hayley Mills innocently shelters him from a shoplifting rap, takes him home to Mummy's boarding house, and cuddles him like a baby brother. Mummy, not caring much for his mind and being typically English and all, gets the hots for his body when the lights go out and ends up in the woodshed ready to be packaged by the A&P.

There are some scary moments, but the sex scenes are dull (I'm getting weary of all these men's bare behinds), the hatchet-murder scenes are bloody and repulsive, the camera work gets carried away with itself and loses the story, and the basic premise is so absurd that the National Association for Retarded Children has forced the film to be preceded by a disclaimer.

Chromosome imbalance is an interesting subject but the misleading notion that a twisted ganglion, an extra gene, or a history of mongoloidism in a family structure can result in criminal behavior is just plain silly.

Good performances by Billie Whitelaw, Phillis Calvert, Frank Finlay, and especially Hayley Mills, who is turning into quite a stunning little actress.

A lot of doors keep opening and slamming in *The Big Bounce,* but nobody ever goes anywhere. It's the kind of movie in which every time the script comes to a dead end the actors take their clothes off to keep the audience from falling asleep, and even the one good fight scene ends up in a geranium patch with a discussion of how to stop a nosebleed.

Warners-Seven Arts spared no luxury in introducing Ryan O'Neal (of TV's *Peyton Place,* remember?) and his pretty wife Leigh Taylor-Young to the screen. The only thing they forgot was to give them people to play.

O'Neal is a fruit picker on "California's largest artichoke and cucumber ranch" and Miss Taylor-Young is the dim-witted, violence-loving mistress of a pickle manufacturer. If you think that's funny, wait until you hear their dialogue. Sample: "I wasn't trying to win any goddam war in the army; I was just trying to stay alive." "Did you make it?"

It's the kind of script in which every scene ends with a sly innuendo and every question is answered by another question. It's called stalling for time. "How did a girl like you get involved with a guy like that?" "Does it really matter?" "How old are you?" "How old do I have to be?" It's nerve-jangling just waiting around for somebody to do something that might resemble a plot development.

Finally Miss Taylor-Young gets a bellyful of all that smart talk. So she goes out and throws rocks through people's windows, has sex in their beds, steals things, eats toast and a bowl of grapes for breakfast, has three nude scenes, performs one felonious assault and one hit-and-run accident, single-handedly destroys one entire glass house on the Warners-Seven Arts lot, foams at the mouth in a marvelously uncontrolled mad scene obviously designed to turn Olivia de Havilland green with envy and riddles another character with an endless stream of bullets (I stopped counting after five).

The idea, I suppose, was to make a poor man's *Pretty Poison*. It doesn't work, because *The Big Bounce* is devoid of style, wit, or cleverness. Instead, it substitutes tough-chic tastlessness.

After he has had sex with his very naked leading lady on top of a tombstone in a deserted graveyard, O'Neal meets up with crusty old Van Heflin (who is fast turning into a replacement for the late, crusty old Charles Bickford, even to the point of looking like him). "You," says Heflin, leering like a dirty old beer-drinking voyeur, "look like the mouse that was just swallowed up by the pussy."

Ryan O'Neal and Leigh Taylor-Young look like people I'd much rather know personally than watch on the screen. They are very attractive and physical, they leap around on top of each other a lot like young guppies in heat, and for all I know, they might even have talent. But it will take a much better movie than *The Big Bounce* to prove it.

March 14, 1969

The German Wehrmacht Alpine Troops (I never even knew there was such a thing) are all holed up in a castle in the Bavarian Alps with a captured American general who happens to be a close personal friend of General

Eisenhower. Very Top Drawer. If he's not rescued, it could be the end of the second front in the war in Europe. Holy Frozen Toenails! This is a job for Richard Burton and Clint Eastwood!

And if you can stop being so serious and sophisticated while this bizarre Mutt and Jeff spy team maneuvers through Nazi-occupied territory with no papers or passports, spouting British and American accents without ever being suspected, you will have a wonderful time at *Where Eagles Dare.*

This is genuinely entertaining spy hokum with much more style than most spy movies, a plot with more twists than a scenic railway and chock full of equal doses of suspense, action, and well-timed anxiety. With the aid of beautiful, talented Mary Ure, Burton and Eastwood destroy ten fighter planes, wreck an entire airport, shoot out the control tower, steal a plane, and escape under machine-gun fire, dynamite a castle filled with thousands of Nazi SS men, scale walls, fall off roofs, sabotage cable cars suspended in mid-air over the Alps, and single-handedly knock off half the German army—and all they get is one slight flesh wound on Burton's hand, no bigger than a bite from Elizabeth Taylor.

Nobody in the movie seems to take all this corn any more seriously than the audience does. (At one point, Burton climbs the wall of the castle on a rope and Mary Ure says: "Why do you go on these insane missions? You're getting too old." I loved it.)

Where Eagles Dare has brilliant acting, good sound effects (during the cable-car explosion, you also hear the cables rattling in the Alpine wind long after the noise dies down), and beautiful photography (dig the aerial shots through the spokes of a parachute as it lands, carrying its cargo to the downy icy softness below). There isn't a single believable scene in it, yet in a week during which I agonized through *If*, *Three in the Attic*, *Stolen Kisses* and the vile and disgusting *I Am Curious (Yellow)*, there's something to be said for a movie—ANY movie—which holds the interest. *Where Eagles Dare* is exactly what it looks like—explosive, exciting, high-style, fast-paced *kitsch*—and it's damned good to have it around.

Stolen Kisses, the title of the new François Truffaut movie, comes from a sloppy, saccharine little *chanson* by Charles Trenet that unfortunately sets the mood for the whole sentimental treacle. Probably because I have so much respect for Truffaut, this latest disappointment seems harder to take than most of the other disappointments I've seen lately, like *If*, which is fast gaining one of the most overblown, overrated reputations of any movie since *The Graduate.*

When *The 400 Blows* came out in 1959, I was struck dumb with admiration for this then twenty-seven-year-old genius—for his use of photography, for the way in which he liberated film by pulling the audience into the screen and for the way he used documentary realism (how many times, I wonder, has one scene alone—the one where the child cute-hero, Antoine Doinel, is interviewed by the Establishment psychologist—been copied by other directors?) to insure a flow of life in its most natural (as opposed to theatrical) form.

I don't think I will ever forget the final shot in that film, ending the picture prematurely before its logical conclusion—the tortured child, unwanted by society, has taken on the adult world with increasing annoyance to it, thus justifying society's desire to be rid of him. Finally he is pushed to the edge of his freedom. Nothing remains between him and the ocean. His frightened, tough little eyes dart out to the sea, then back to the shore where society is crushing in on him. Truffaut's camera freezes into a still photograph. His problems become the audience's problems. There is simply no way to escape involvement.

It is one of the few times I feel the movies have brought me close to a true catharsis between life and art.

The critics jumped to all sorts of rabid conclusions, searching for answers to this baffling dilemma. Stanley Kauffmann, I remember, even suggested suicide, tabloid newspaper-style. Well, Antoine is back, for the third time, played by Jean-Pierre Léaud. In *Love at Twenty* he appeared briefly to enlist in the French army. In *Stolen Kisses* he just hangs around trying to go through the situations set up by Truffaut, but any resemblance to the desperate, sensitive Parisien-style Dead End Kid in *The 400 Blows* is purely accidental. The callous, unjust adults of his earlier world have turned into —well, charming, lovable, and thoroughly harmless eccentrics.

As *Stolen Kisses* opens, he is being discharged after spending most of his time in a military prison. Antoine is free to begin his apprenticeship in the art of living.

Sadly, Truffaut seems to have been so heavily influenced by *The Graduate* that his idea of "the art of living" is a kind of softheadedness that turns the agile young Léaud into a kind of St. Germain des Prés version of Dustin Hoffman.

Women slobber over him like bitches in heat, usually after ignoring him until his Sad Sack nebbishness touches them in some hidden area of the heart. He is fired from a job as hotel nightwatchman because he is made the innocent patsy in a detective's scheme to avenge a betrayed husband.

Working as an underground investigator stationed in a shoestore, he later finds himself the target of passion for the owner's wife (Delphine Seyrig, who plays Anne Bancroft to his Dustin Hoffman).

And in the end, he is sitting on a park bench with the sweet young thing who first avoided him, then fell in love with him because she found his left-footed bumbling buffoonery so "charmant." This is Claude Jade, who plays the Katharine Ross character. None of these people are ever anything more than caricatures; nothing they do or say is ever believable for more than a minute and a half.

The movie is very casual, but the very nature of its flabbiness, its good-natured onionhead informality, makes me more aware than ever of how hard it is trying. Worse, it is so repetitious, so full of reworked threads from old Truffaut movies: the flights of pigeons and the boy-vs.-city charisma (*The 400 Blows*); the use of motors and jalopies (*Jules and Jim*); the carefully arranged family TV-watching scene (*Love at Twenty*); the constant shots of people following each other up and down streets for no apparent reason at all except to waste footage and stretch the vignettes into a full-length film (*Soft Skin*).

Jean-Pierre Léaud is all butterfingers, which makes him charming in this new age that hates young people to have intelligence. But all the confusion apparent in his performance does not seem to come entirely from the role.

Truffaut seems to be asking him to portray the inner Truffaut according to whichever mood he had on each particular shooting day. He has Léaud displaying a passion for the Avenue Junot, where Truffaut's idol Jean Renoir lives in Paris. He takes him through the paces of his own private life (Truffaut also deserted the army and worked at all kinds of odd jobs). But Léaud seems ill-fitted to the part. His performances in movies like *Le Départ* have proved his maturity and I can no longer take this kind of fake innocence at face value, any more than I care to see Tony Perkins play the kind of gawking innocent he played in *Phaedra* again. Léaud is growing up as an actor (and, hopefully, as a person) while Truffaut, now thirty-seven, is digressing.

These nostalgic backward glances toward boyhood are getting dull. Especially in the scene with the older woman. With absolutely no preparation, she offers him coffee. He flees down the stairs, all knock-kneed and tongue-tied. She finds out his address and follows him to his garret. (Ah yes, they still live in garrets . . .) He huddles naked under the sheets while she delivers a four-minute monologue on the subject of worldliness.

She locks the door, drops the key into a vase, then walks toward the bed . . . The scene has everything but Simon and Garfunkel music.

Truffaut's quasi-autobiographies are turning melancholy, soft, and sentimental. *Stolen Kisses* drags its audience down into his own creamy satin-pillowed memory of lyrical innocence-gone-astray that quite frankly doesn't seem worth the bother. Only the French could feel all washed up at thirty-seven; if Truffaut makes any more movies like this one, I'm going to start believing him.

Stolen Kisses makes what's left of the New Wave seem distinctly Old Drizzle.

March 21, 1969

If I were Anthony Newley, I would have opened *Can Hieronymus Merkin Ever Forget Mercy Humppe and Find True Happiness?, etc., etc.* in Siberia during Christmas week and called it a day. Maybe that way nobody would ever have heard about it and Newley's reputation would have been saved. This way, I'm not sure he'll ever work again, and quite frankly, I'm not sure he deserves to.

It is always painful to watch someone you respect and admire make a fool of himself in public, but I don't think I've ever experienced anything quite so excruciating as watching the kind of moronic, sub-cretin Super Fool Newley makes of himself in this cheap, sewer-level, pornographic home movie.

This grimy, seedy, thoroughly embarrassing skin flick is totally lacking in class, humor, taste, or talent—which is a pretty sorry state of affairs right there, since I have always considered Newley a man of considerable class, humor, taste, and talent. Like the flowers in Pete Seeger's song, I just don't know where it's gone.

Apparently he once saw *8½* and never got over it, because this pretentious search for self-identity at the audience's expense smacks of that movie's basic intentions without any of its profundity, with a great many bits and pieces of the worst, most banal elements of *Candy*, *Lolita*, *Juliet of the Spirits*, *Stop the World—I Want to Get Off*, and *Candide* thrown in.

The movie begins on a deserted strip of very peculiar looking beach at Malta, as a puppet with a white flour face and a nose like a great maraschino cherry is trapped in the glare of a spotlight. (This, I think, represents innocence, but I wouldn't swear to it.) Like Geppetto's Pinocchio creation, this wooden dummy knows there is something out there besides woodpeckers.

The Devil shows up in the form of Milton Berle in Little Lord Fauntleroy pants, who introduces him to bare asses, big breasts, and other assorted natural wonders and gives Newley an opportunity to romp around naked with hundreds of girls who look like Bourbon Street strippers, then turn director and make a movie-within-a-movie as repentance for performing "the ritual murder of the female race."

Newley's own two small babies are forced to watch while he relives his rotten, ridiculous, wasted life and thereby purges his own dirty-minded, lecherous, locker-room ego.

Milton Berle drops in and out, saying lines like, "I wish somebody'd throw me a line in this picture," and George Jessel, who plays something called "The Presence," looks as though he has just been given three days to live.

Newley, who doesn't know enough about his own limitations to realize he still has a lot to learn about directing, has managed to make the whole mess look like a series of grainy Playboy layouts. The writing is so abominable that metaphors and similes erupt like boils in the Old Testament. People say things like, "I'm just a caraway seed on the rye bread of life" with straight faces, and images like "antelope turds" are conjured every few minutes to beg for laughs that never come.

The musical numbers range in style from old Betty Grable ("I've got a sky full of bluebirds . . .") to old London Palladium ("Lilacs bloomin' in Piccadilly Circus . . .") and Newley sings them like a nervous TV talk-show host who doesn't want his audience to discover his guests have talent.

He's still a fine singer, and I'd like to be able to say the same for his acting, but unfortunately he hasn't written very much of anything he or anyone else can act. So he forces his own two babies to sit still and watch while he sings to them a song called "What a Son of a Bitch I Am," tells a lot of raunchy jokes, performs cunnilingus on a naked girl underwater, and dances his way (out of step) through a revolting musical number stark naked.

That takes guts right there. The sight of Anthony Newley naked is enough to make you turn the other way, just praying you'll turn into a pillar of salt.

Finally, it must have appeared even to a man of Newley's fantastic ego that this whole crappy affair was falling apart, because he drags in his wife to titillate the men, hires his own friends to help him salvage his reputation (i.e., Tom Stern, Samantha Eggar's husband, as a producer), and drops a few "in" names just to win over the "in" Beverly Hills crowd. (As Berle slices open a chicken's neck and drips the blood all over a naked girl's breasts, he chants "Abelo Lastfogelo, Abelo Lastfogelo!" Nobody even grinned at the screening in New York. I guess they don't know Abe Lastfogel is Warren Beatty's agent at William Morris and Warren Beatty was Joan Collins' *amour* before she met Newley and . . . well, you know how feeble "in" jokes are. But they'll laugh at *anything* in Beverly Hills.)

Making one last, desperate move to get the waning (mostly snoring, by this time) audience's attention back, Newley has a disgusting old letch feed his own baby daughter an ice cream cone and then run his hand up her dress in a scene that should get some kind of award for the ultimate crest in stupendous bad taste.

By this point, I had given up on Newley, but what about Joan Collins? How could she allow her own children to be dragged through this filthy charade? As it turns out, this is one of the very few American movies ever made to receive an "X" rating. I don't think it deserves an "X." I think it deserves a very special encomium—like maybe an "I" rating. For "immature" audiences only.

If Anthony Newley doesn't get back to the serious nature of what his own incredible talent can do, if he doesn't cut out all the nonsense and stop boring everybody to death with all the breast-beating bravura about how big his own ego is, he's going to be very shocked to wake up some day and discover that nobody has been listening.

Pendulum is a routine little programmer that starts out pretending to explore a provocative subject (the rights of individuals from whom forced confessions have been obtained in criminal court cases) and ends up just another grim, hackneyed thriller about a cop (George Peppard) trying to track down the murderer of his own wife (Jean Seberg).

Seberg is totally wasted. Peppard, Richard Kiley, and a young actor named Robert Lyons, as a schizoid baby-faced killer, turn in strong performances. But it is the underrated Madeleine Sherwood, in a brilliantly-acted bit part, who momentarily brings the film to its feet.

I've seen creative performances in my day, but dig the scene in which Miss Sherwood, as a tramp with a hangover, tries to act like a mother for the first time in her life and only succeeds in driving her son up the wall at the breakfast table by picking seeds out of his orange juice while he is trying to drink it. It has nothing to do with anything the movie is supposed to be about, but it turns out to be the best scene in the picture. Which, I suppose, says something about where *Pendulum* is at.

March 28, 1969

Baby Love is sort of an updated, Chelsea psychiatrist's version of *Guest in the House*, with a rather dilapidated looking nymphet named Linda Hayden playing Anne Baxter. I missed all the critics' screenings of this one, so by the time I caught up with it in the theater, the scant audience I sat with was about equally divided between mod photographers with their Leicas clicking and dirty old men chuckling under the crunches of their Mounds bars. I suspect they were all pretty disillusioned for, although a lot goes on in *Baby Love*, nothing much happens.

I mean, there's this big suicide build-up with lots of steam rising from the bathtub and the cat tracking bloody paw-prints across the floor, but all you see is the reaction on the face of the person who discovers the body. An attempted rape scene builds suspensefully through gauzy leaves and along luscious limey riverbanks shot through a filter lens, but the tempo leads to nothing when a woman with a police dog happens by and the rapists scatter. A nubile young thing splashes like a porpoise in a bikini while a middle-aged man sweats his way through several heated pushups, but all he ever sees is a slight ripple of baby thigh.

Drums roll and strings sob while Baby Love sucks her thumb, daydreams about being seduced by Cassius Clay, and occasionally bares her breasts long enough to send the members of the household she is visiting stark-raving mad. Junior stares into space, Mom turns into a raving, panting Lesbian and Dad lights the wrong ends of his filter ciggies.

As a psychological thriller, it's pretty tame stuff. As polished filmmaking, not even its camera tricks (quick cut from Baby Love gobbling a strawberry tart to closeup of a sow in a pig pen) disguise the fact that it is pretty pedestrian stuff. And as the nymphet, Linda Hayden is not in very interesting physical condition for the part.

In *The Castle* Maximilian Schell is a land surveyor who is invited to a snowy, godforsaken land ruled an an ominous castle. He tries to rent a horse to take him there, but nobody will take his business. He wanders into a public washhouse where a woman nurses her baby on her breasts, and gets thrown out. No stranger can enter the castle without permission. Where can he get it? Only from the castle itself. For what seems like the next three days of moviegoing, he seeks this same permission—which, of course, never comes.

Feudalistic maids giggle at him. Looking for clues, he visits the mayor's office, a peculiar establishment in which the village records are kept in yellowed stacks of crumbling papers filled with rats that scurry and squeak across the floor when the files topple and fall through the air like paper airplanes. No luck.

During the rest of this interminable test of endurance, Schell becomes more and more downtrodden and sick as he shuffles unshaven and haggard through the endless stream of secretaries, record-keepers, position-recommenders, and permit-granters—both official and unofficial. "Don't be frustrated by the disappointments." "I know the obstacles seem insurmountable." "Discipline is the thing which gives the world a sense of balance." And on and on, while the music gets weirder and Schell goes madder and madder. Definitely a movie to tap your feet through.

The Franz Kafka story on which it is based made a definite point about the futility of man on an age of identification papers, documents, systems, bureaucracies, and red tape. The point would be made just as well (and twice as interesting) in half of this movie's running time. To make matters worse, the film suffers from faulty dubbing, low-key acting that looks like some Yugoslav amateur group, and an overdose of literary pretentiousness.

The sets look like a series of army latrines. The cast may be the least attractive group yet assembled on one movie screen. The women are cows, the children seem undernourished, and the men look like tubercular janitors. *The Castle* was never finished. Franz Kafka was still working on it when he died near Vienna in 1924. He must have bored himself to death.

The Illustrated Man is thoroughly expendable back-lot science fiction that manages to achieve the dubious distinction of turning the literary flair of Ray Bradbury into a B movie.

Rod Steiger is a hobo who meets up with a country boy (Robert Drivas) on the bank of a lake. His entire body is covered with tattoos and as he reveals each new "skin illustration" to the boy, a new science-fiction adventure unravels, either in a flashback or flash forward. The first subplot is based on Bradbury's fascinating short story, "The Veldt." Claire Bloom, as the mysterious lady tattoo artist who tantalizes Steiger into being "illustrated" before she will hit the sack with him, puts her hand inside his shirt and says she feels lions. Presto! Director Jack Smight (who has been watching too many old Howard Hawks movies on TV) cuts to an African tundra roamed by lions and vultures.

The tundra is imagined by their children, who can turn a knob on an electronic device and project themselves into any play world of their own desire. Labor laws have goofed everything up. People only work six months a year. The kids' parents are bored with all the free time, so they sit around drinking in their plastic bubble. "Make love to me." "Why?" "Maybe this time it will be different." Now this African tundra thing. They get sore at the kids, the kids feel they're being persecuted. Next morning, when space-age marriage counselor Drivas shows up, the parents have disappeared, but the lions on the tundra are chewing on some very new bones.

Sub-plot 2 is about four space men marooned on a rainy planet covered with giant rubbery cauliflowers. It is a kind of comment on man's survival by sheer brute force, but since they all die either a cowardly death or a violent death it remains a mere comment instead of becoming a statement.

Sub-plot 3 takes place shortly after a world conference which has announced the last night before the end of the world. Steiger (as a kind of Adam figure) and Claire Bloom (as a sexy Eve) wrestle with the problem of whether to kill off their children (the law) or take a chance (reason). Neither of these adventures is very interesting, although they are broken up by trips back to the country lake that (1) give Robert Drivas a chance to do a nude scene that has nothing whatsoever to do with the rest of the picture and (2) give Rod Steiger a chance to get in some hammy speeches about spiders and snakes and ticks and creepy crawlies that suck your blood, which also have nothing whatsoever to do with the rest of the picture.

It's not scary, it's not effective, it's not sexually titillating (although there are lots of suggestive bits about tattoo needles as instruments of sexual pain and pleasure). It's not even good science fiction. And until you witness with disbelieving eyes the awesome spectacle of Rod Steiger completely nude, covered with a zillion bugs and snakes and roses, you only *think* you've seen ugly.

April 4, 1969

There's a lot of absurd talk going around about *Goodbye, Columbus* being an anti-Semitic movie. I'm not surprised. They've been accusing Philip Roth of being an anti-Semitic writer for years. Trouble is, Roth knows his own people—knows and *cares* about them—better than most Jews know themselves. He is the most Jewish Jew in captivity today, and *Goodbye, Columbus* is the best thing he ever wrote. I think he wrote it before he learned how to masturbate.

The movie director Larry Peerce, who directed *One Potato, Two Potato,* has fashioned from it is the warmest, friendliest, funniest, most huggable film I've seen in a very long time. I plan to see it again and again until it becomes an old friend.

I'm not Jewish, so you can start accusing me of not knowing beans about the subject right now and get it over with. But I do know a good movie when I see one, even if it does come sprinkled with an obvious cliché like the Jewish wedding to end all Jewish weddings. The book's New Jersey country club locale has been changed to Westchester (another cliché), which I thought had already been done to a *bien cuit* charcoal blister in *The Swimmer.*

I see the point, though. Westchester is a much funnier place than New Jersey any day, and even though growing up in Philip Roth Land is something I know nothing about (it's another world from creole gumbo and the Louisiana bayous), I do know enough about Westchester to still get a bang out of the scene in which the aunt keeps taking the pot roast out of the oven and saying, "Don't put the wet towel on the furniture."

I've met all the people in *Goodbye, Columbus* before. They're real, all right. Real and delightful to know.

Arnold Schulman is the perfect writer to transpose Roth to the screen. In *Love with the Proper Stranger,* he once wrote an unforgettable scene in which Tom Bosley brought Natalie Wood home for dinner and she spent a riotous evening listening to his two yenta sisters. *Goodbye, Columbus* is filled with the same tough, precise little Jewish girls who speak in definite verb conjugations and end up going to Bennington.

Ali MacGraw, a magical new actress who looks constantly as though she has just washed her face with Dr. Laszlo's sea mud soap, is the perfect newcomer to portray Brenda, the embodiment of inverted snobbism so prevalent in girls who are born in the Bronx, then move to Westchester when their papas make good and end up playing tennis cautiously so the balls won't hit their $1,000 nose jobs.

Loping across a Westchester lawn in slow motion, she resembles a tall white egret walking on legs like elegant stilts. I think she is quite the most enchanting new actress I've seen on the screen since Joan Hackett.

In fact, the entire cast is flawless. Richard Benjamin, as a kind of bumbling collegiate sex maniac who spends most of his life taking cold showers, has the grace of an impertinent sloth in tennis sneaks. Jack Klugman, as Miss MacGraw's father, is every nouveau-riche business merchant-family man I've ever known—kind, trumpy, good, thoroughly decent, with the worst table manners since Stanley Kowalski. Nan Martin doesn't look or sound very Jewish as the girl's mother, but at least you won't be able to accuse her of being a cliché. (Watching her creaming her hands in bed with the *Johnny Carson Show* on is a mental picture I never want to forget.)

And perhaps the single most ingratiating actor in the entire film is the girl's kid brother—a lumbering young rhino named Michael Meyers. Meyers is a great big gum-chewing lummox who washes out his jock straps in the sink, shakes hands like he was pumping for oil, thrashes into a room like he was laying siege to a foreign country, and crashes into bed in his underwear every night to listen to Andre Kostelanetz records.

He is one of those miracles of casting, like Harold Russell in *The Best Years of Our Lives,* chosen because no acting is required other than living in front of a camera for a few days. (Russell, you may recall, did not need to wear a hook in his arm for the role of a handicapped war veteran; he already had one.)

If there is any doubt in anyone's mind about whether *Goodbye, Columbus* is true or not, let me hasten to add that Meyers is no actor at all. He's a college student from New Rochelle, and after the screening I attended, he stood up, taller than the fence around a missiles project, grinned boyishly and left painful creases in the palm of each hand he shook.

A small, bosomy lady with orange hair and a parched Miami tan then hugged him vigorously around the waist and said, "My little dum-dum." She was his mother and she could easily have stepped right down from the screen out of any one of a dozen scenes.

Without a good script, you can assemble the most brilliant actors in the world and their abilities will be wasted if they have nothing to work with. *Goodbye, Columbus* is fortunate enough to have a ripe, colorful script bursting with comic possibilities. There is a dinner table scene full of clumsy, class-structural self-consciousness that is a joy to watch. There is a funny scene at the 42d Street public library with a nervous librarian eating an egg and pepper sandwich.

There is the wildest Jewish wedding in the history of movies, blazing with a collage of carousel impressions—cigars and chopped chicken livers and two uncles in the carpet business named Manny and Max pacing the dance floor measuring their carpets, little girls dancing with each other and eating the bells off the cake, people who look like leftovers from a Grossinger's Passover party dancing to "Havah Nagilah" . . . of course it's vulgar. But it is also endearing and spirited and true.

Larry Peerce seems to have instilled so much confidence in all of his actors and all of his bit players and all of his extras that they go beyond the bounds of conventional role development. Instead of becoming extensions of the characters, the roles they play become extensions of the actors.

Peerce has also thrown in some terrible, wornout directorial clichés such as the techniques of slow-motion underwater swimming and two faces silhouetted against the sun. And frankly, I hope I never see another movie in which two young people fall in love while walking through an endless stream of quick cuts denoting the passing of summer, while a rock group wails a sound track theme song. I'm sorry he couldn't resist the temptation to be obvious and banal.

Still, my complaints are minor and grouchy and they have very little to do with the overwhelming impact this film has made on me as a whole. After the flow of stupid creeps in such brainless youth-identity-crisis movies as *Joanna*, *The Touchables*, *Three in the Attic*, *The Impossible Years*, *Model Shop*, *Wild in the Streets*, etc., etc., it's a refreshing and healthy change of pace to see college-age kids with sensitivity and intelligence and believable responses to life and sex the way it exists in reality instead of inside the rancid heads of perverted screenwriters. The people in *Goodbye, Columbus* look like real people, wear clothes that look like real clothes instead of Bleecker Street hock-shop rejects and say real words instead of profane, hopped-up jabberwocky.

Whether you're Jewish or not, I don't see how you can fail to recognize and respect the beauty and laughter and human insight present in Philip Roth's story and Peerce's direction and Schulman's script and in the breathtaking performance of this movie's startling, splendid cast. Together, out of what looks suspiciously like love, they have produced a film that is more than just a comedy about young Jewish people with different social backgrounds falling in love. They have painted a portrait of a civilization.

Some Jews will no doubt still be defensive and uptight and say *Goodbye, Columbus* doesn't tell it true. But, as one of my Jewish friends has pointed out to me, truth is not the question here. The problem is whether or not you can accept the difference between what is true and what is *unbearably true.*

April 11, 1969

Support Your Local Sheriff, which breezed into town with no advance warning this week, is a gentle, hilarious spoof of the Old West that comes as one of the major unheralded surprises of the movie season.

Unadorned with million-dollar costumes and unsupported by a cast of thousands, this delightful valentine to the land of buttons and bows proves that cowboy movie humor is ten times more interesting and fun to sit through than cowboy movie violence and bloodshed.

Every cliché you ever saw as a child, sitting through those interminable Wild Bill Elliott-Lynne Roberts serials, is here: the cool, mild-mannered, wavy-haired, WASPish sheriff who can polish off a band of renegade Indians or gun down a whole herd of horse thieves without missing a sip of his sarsaparilla; the richest girl in town; the richest girl in town's conniving father, and, of course, the meanest, orneriest gang of thugs, cut-throats, and good-fer-nuthin' critters in chaps and spurs since Belle Starr met up with the Dalton Gang. All these mavericks are prodded, primed, and patted gently through comic scenes of such epic put-on proportions that I, for one, never wanted things to reach the "The End" sign.

Burt Kennedy, who directed one of my favorite forgotten movies called *The Rounders*, is one of the few filmmakers working in Hollywood who can get more laughs out of sensitive, quiet comedy than a whole warehouse full of Jerry Lewis pies. As in *The Rounders*, he has here lined up a buckboard of rough-hewn old character actors like Walter Brennan, Jack Elam, Harry Morgan, Henry Jones, and Gene Evans, who seem to genuinely know how to play comedy without begging for favors. Just turn them loose in a technicolor town so detailed and realistic that smoke even curls out of the pot-bellied stoves, and they seem to know instinctively what to do, like dolphins in water.

James Garner, as the sheriff who never raises his voice, but runs marauders out of town instead by throwing rocks at them, proves to be a first-rate comic with a deft sense of rhythm for the comedy genre and almost an Actors Studio approach to naturalism.

Joan Hackett, as Prudy Perkins, a tomboy for whom accidents hang around waiting to happen, proves once and for all that she could probably even play a door facing and steal scenes from the rest of the room. One scene in particular, in which she tries to make biscuits while singing "Rock of Ages" with her bustle on fire, convinces me that she is an actress so filled with splendors both visual and esthetic that I wish to hell somebody would give her bigger parts to chew on.

Peter Stone has written a respectable enough script for the movie version of *Sweet Charity*, but you'd hardly know it. This noisy, clattering, annoyingly photographed disaster has so many things wrong with it, the script practically gets stomped to death. Bob Fosse, who directed and choreographed the same property on Broadway with the magic of his wife Gwen Verdon blinding everything in sight and covering up the deficiencies, has turned his movie directorial debut into something not entirely unlike the test flight of some nuclear rocket bound for Mars.

He has avoided all the MGM clichés, to be sure, but he has gone so hog-stomping wild with the camera, ramming all those new techniques (can it be that he has really just learned about the zoom lens?) down the audience's throat, that the result is much less entertaining than anything MGM turned out in the old Gene Kelly days.

Sweet Charity, with its lens jumping and its people turned into X-rays and its cameras swinging, looks like nine out of ten movies shot in the 1960s, only more boring. You are always aware of exactly where the camera is in every shot because it makes you so dizzy you have the spots in front of your eyes to prove it.

Nothing ever just happens naturally, or out of the birth of an unplanned moment. The audience is never allowed the luxury of discovering anything for itself. Almost every scene begins and ends with that annoying zoom lens rushing into and back out of the shot, like some slap-happy tourist who has just bought his first Polaroid to use on the Grand Canyon. The camera lens pans the sky and trees and buildings so fast it never takes time to focus on anything. (The "My Personal Property" number whirls across the New York skyline so quickly you need Dramamine just to get through it.)

Aside from the camera work, most of which was so stomach-churning I found myself looking *away* from the screen more often than *at* it, there are other problems. The story is much too slim to sustain a movie this long (only ten minutes under three hours), in spite of Peter Stone's funny lines. Giulietta Masina and Gwen Verdon, who both played the whore with the heart of gold in previous versions of the same story, got by on raw, human, gusty, heart-breaking ragamuffin genius.

Shirley MacLaine simply gets by on mannerisms. She's tacky and tough, and she has a way with a comic line, but she never got any sympathy from me. When she was jilted by John McMartin, the only man in her life who ever came close enough to smell the altar, I was with him all the way, because in the previous scene Miss MacLaine had made such a pig of herself in a badly directed series of unflattering closeups that only her unappealing qualities were accented, and none of the charm that should make the audience love Charity in spite of her cheapness.

Masina and Verdon were no ladies, but they were vulnerable. Their overwhelming virtues as delicate, frail human beings far surpassed their vulgarities as chippies. In Miss MacLaine's portrayal, there's nothing left but elbows and toenails and Woolworth perfume.

The choreography is wonderful, but it needs Verdon to dance it. It's also hard to see. If there's one thing I hate in a musical, it's a musical number shot in closeup with all the feet missing. Many of Cy Coleman's and Dorothy Fields' best songs have been cut from the original score. "Baby Dream Your Dream," "You Should See Yourself" and Charity's soliloquy which opened the show and established the character (with some of the cleverest lyrics ever written) are all deleted.

In their place, there is something called "It's a Nice Face" (not up to the usual Coleman-Fields standards), a new "Sweet Charity" theme (with an arrangement that is borrowed heavily from Burt Bacharach) and "My Personal Property," a swinging item that is almost destroyed by Shirley MacLaine and all those camera blurs in the movie but which sounds pretty much like a Tin Pan Alley classic when Bobby Short sings it over at the Carlyle these nights.

Most of the musical numbers are shot in such a deranged collection of frenetic camera styles that you never really get a chance to hear the songs. "I'm a Brass Band" is the most cinematic number; also the main one in which I really noticed the feet. "The Rhythm of Life" has energy, but looks thrown in for no serviceable reason except to jazz up the film with a guest appearance by Sammy Davis. "There's Gotta Be Somethin' Better Than This" shows off the brassy dancing of Chita Rivera and Paula Kelly on a New York rooftop, but looks like old warmed-over Jerome Robbins. The sets look like Las Vegas hotel lobbies.

In the final analysis, the spirit of Gwen Verdon hovers about like some unwelcome apparition, serving as a painful reminder of the stupidity of Hollywood casting directors who insist on casting roles with box office names instead of with the Broadway performers who originated them. It's too bad, because with all the self-conscious dazzle of Bob Fosse's artiness it is forced to survive, *Sweet Charity* needs blood in its veins, not ghosts in its wings.

April 18, 1969

Albert and David Maysles are two brothers who go around with movie cameras slung over their shoulders, photographing the insides of people's souls. They call it "direct cinema," and it is. Unlike the cinéma vérité antics of people like Godard, their movies do not capture people off-guard while their dogs are urinating on the sidewalk. They do not hide inside garbage cans or in baby carriages. They walk right into the minds and hearts and homes of their subjects and record their brain waves and their pulse beats and the molasses stains on their kitchen tablecloths.

In 1963 they produced their first full-blown work, a devastating and highly controversial profile of Joseph E. Levine. They followed this with a television documentary on the Beatles in America, a visit with Truman Capote, and *Meet Marlon Brando*, a highlight of the 1966 New York Film Festival.

As a body of work, the Maysles' films constitute some of the most exciting stuff being turned out in the present era of the movies; certainly they are likely to have a more profound and lasting effect on the kinds of movies young filmmakers will be making in the future than any of the flashier but more temporary showoffs.

Salesman, which opened Thursday at the 68th Street Playhouse, is the first film the Maysles have made for commercial release and by far the one with the most regard for detail, insight and cinematic edge. Without the use of actors, costumes, sets, or even a script, it is as dramatic and suspenseful as any human drama I've ever seen in any medium. It is total realism, with none of the contrivances of plot mechanics necessary to make fiction happen. This achievement alone makes the film worth seeing.

But *Salesman* is so much more important on so many other levels than it is possible to suggest in a mere review. That is why it is important to bring to it a keen knowledge (or at the very least, a *working* knowledge) of what the rest of the world is like Out There where they don't have ten channels on TV and nobody reads the *New York Times.* Only then is it possible to appreciate something of what *Salesman* is trying to show, to be touched by what it examines when it turns over all those rocks.

Salesman is about four Bible salesmen. It looks as simple and as natural as Granny in the kitchen making gingerbread. But it took five months to find the salesmen, six weeks of intensive filming, and fifteen months to edit. The fact that the film is so staggering in its impact is even more amazing when you stop and realize that it was made by a crew of two who designed and built their own camera equipment, which they carried into people's homes and cars unobtrusively. Result: a film ten times more fascinating than a lot of the big-budget hokum turned out by Hollywood and an experience that sticks in the memory.

"Sellin' Bibles is a good business. The money's out there and go out and get it," says the supervisor of the Bible Sales Convention. So the Maysles' cameras watch them do it, following the four salesmen through the bleak New England snow, down to the plastic phoniness of suburban Miami. And painting a picture, along the way, of a civilization Out There most of us in our smug, sophisticated New York cocoons are totally unaware of.

With his list of prospective Bible purchasers provided by local churches, the salesman they call "The Badger" drives around looking for house numbers in the dreary town of Opa Locka singing "If I Were A Rich Man" from *Fiddler on the Roof*, then muttering under his breath behind the wheel of his car, "If I was a rich man, I wouldn't be goin' on this shit list." Selling the word of God for dollars and cents. And the Maysles capture it all. Their movie is so full of natural, unplanned outbursts of comic vitality it is never dull for a single moment.

Aside from the salesmen, there is a vast supporting cast of real customers, proving the greatest performances have never been captured in any Hollywood movie. The best actors are all Out There in the Boondocks. "Suppose y'all kiddin' us," chides one beastly housewife, "who do we get in touch with? The FBI?" Buying the word of God for $49.95.

"I had a woman she said it gave her comfort just looking at the pictures—and she was a Ph.D."

"I'm cuttin' off the $3 service charge 'cause whether or not you bought it or not it was nice talkin' to you and that's not just the Irish blarney." "My husband was a Irishman."

"There are many people who know the Bible. There are many people who can quote from the Bible. But you're different. You know the *bizness!*"

"I wish you all the luck." "Well, thank you, I just hope I get around to reading it."

"We have three plans on it. Cash, c.o.d., and also they have a little Catholic honor plan. Which plan—which plan—would be best for you, A, B, or C?"

Little Willy Lomans. Tired, still hoping to make that retirement money some day and get the hell out. Talking their dreams away with a slug of beer in some crappy motel room. Listening to crummy music on their car radios before they have to get out on the steaming hot highway and fix a flat tire. Talking housewives into turning over their last five dollars (before their husbands come home) for a down payment on some tacky gilt-edged Du Pont fabricord plastic-and-nylon-bound Bible they don't need and don't even want. Staring at their customers in boredom and exhaustion, desperately hoping to make one last commission on the word of God from fat men in T-shirts and women in hair curlers listening to "The Boston Pops Plays The Beatles" on old stand-up Victrolas. Getting a thousand screen doors slammed in their faces and fighting off a thousand flies and eating a thousand watery hamburgers in a thousand look-alike road houses.

It's hard to believe, but you get to know the salesmen so well that by the time the Maysles cameras move in on the hick customers sucking on their thumbs and trying to make their decisions you end up actually rooting for the poor slobs yourself. The suspense becomes unbearable.

The real horror in *Salesman* is the way it peels back the scab and reveals an unwashed America that it is impossible to imagine, even while watching it happen on the screen. These people who live in trailer houses and read *True Confessions* and rock in their rocking chairs while watching the headlights pull into their driveways through the porch screen. Who are they? They are Bible readers, Sweet Buns, and they are Out There, in that one nation indivisible somewhere on the other side of the George Washington Bridge, waiting for us all.

Mailbag: Among a flood of other letters regarding my review two weeks ago of *Goodbye, Columbus*, all of which I appreciate, I would especially like to thank the eagle eye who reminds me that Richard Benjamin's aunt said, "Don't put the wet towel on the furniture" in the Bronx, not Westchester.

And, if she'll accept it, I'd like to send an apology to Mrs. Norman Meyers of New Rochelle, mother of Michael Meyers, the human giraffe who plays Ali MacGraw's hilarious kid brother in the picture. Referring to my description of a Jewish lady pointed out to me as Michael's real-life mother—a short, likable blonde with an orange peel Miami tan who hugged him around the waist and called him a "dum-dum" after the *Goodbye, Columbus* preview—Mrs. Meyers writes: "I am a tall woman in stature of 5 foot 10 inches, size 36 bra, brunette, a working woman who hasn't had a vacation for over five years. I am afraid that the publicity for which I should be delighted and say 'Thank you' has caused numerous calls from friends to find out if my husband and I were among the new divorce statistics, or if he had taken someone else to the preview. I have always been a brunette and even though Miss Clairol assists me now and then, I do feel you have misrepresented me all around."

April 25, 1969

Pier Paolo Pasolini has a crotch fetish. His movies are always shot from the crotch, into the crotch, around the crotch. All of which proves that Mr. Pasolini is a very smart man. When you make movies as horrendously pretentious as *Teorema* you need crotches. Or breasts. Or rear ends. Or *something!* Just to keep people from walking out.

The unfortunate thing about *Teorema,* aside from the fact that it is one of the silliest movies ever made, is that the crotches aren't enough. People are walking out anyway. I stayed, out of morbid curiosity, just to have some kind of permanent record that a movie this bad could actually exist. It's the kind of pseudo-atheist propaganda movie that makes molehills out of mountains.

Terence Stamp, appearing frightfully embarrassed by the entire proceedings, shows up out of nowhere one day to visit a wealthy industrialist and his family in Milan. Before the family can even say "Mi piace!" they are dropping their underwear all over the place like monkeys in heat and Stamp is crawling around through all their beds. The daughter (a peculiar young actress who seems retarded) leads him to her room to show him her photograph album, unbuttons her blouse, and *whammo!* The son peeks under Stamp's blanket to drool over his nude body and Stamp springs out of bed, into the other twin bed with the innocent lad, and *whammo!* The mother (Silvana Mangano, looking a bit like a plastic broccoli) drops her panties over the balcony, lies down on the floor in broad daylight for the young guest to stand over her and smile wryly, and *whammo!* The father, who seems to be dying of some unexplained disease, falls in love when the boy lifts his pajama legs over his head and holds them there in some kind of symbolic religio-sexual grip in the funniest, weirdest scene of all (no *whammo!*). Then the poor, bestial maid, who looks very much like the boy in *Closely Watched Trains*, gets hers. She's too low on the socialistic Italian totem pole to make the same bizarre advances as the rest of the uppercrust, so she just stares at Stamp's crotch while she's mowing the lawn, then stops the mower, races into the kitchen and shoves the gas pipe down her throat. He saves her, carries her to the bed, the old crone raises her skirt, and—you guessed it—*whammo!*

By now, the whole household is aroused, in more ways than one. The father wakes, walks around the grounds at dawn, peeps through his son's door, smiles as he watches Terence Stamp turn in his son's arms, then goes back to bed and attacks his wife. Between vignettes there are shots of shadows passing over the shifting sands. Interlaced with dozens of closeups of Stamp's crotch, a voice on the sound track quotes Jeremiah. When the actors aren't after each other, they read aloud from Tolstoy. What this movie needs is a little Mantovani.

One day Stamp leaves abruptly, his *fait accompli*, no doubt. The family goes mad. Up to this point, the movie has largely been mercifully silent, but suddenly everybody bursts into a dialogue like "You make me aware of my otherness!" (Scout's honor). The father looks painfully at Stamp and says, "You certainly have come here to destroy." (Several people laughed quite rudely at that one.) But Stamp vanishes in a cloud of mozzarella. Sis clenches her fists, turns blue, goes into a living coma, and has to be carted off on a stretcher. Mom becomes a nymphomaniac who picks up hustlers on the streets of Milan and fornicates with them in ditches (in full view of a symbolic church steeple, natch). Junior runs away from home, paints a canvas and then urinates on it. Dad turns into a pervert who haunt's men's rooms and takes his clothes off in the middle of a train station. And the maid—well, she's the simplest common denominator in Pasolini's Communistic social structure, so she runs away to a vacant lot where she eats weeds, her hair turns white, and she becomes a saint who cures children's boils and eventually levitates over the garbage dump.

Please do not send me three hundred letters explaining how Terence Stamp is really God or an angel or the Devil, or that Pasolini's film is a symbolic allegory. I've heard it all already, and nobody is going to convince me that *Teorema* is not a wildly hilarious comedy send-up of Antonioni. Although it is a simply terrible movie in every conceivable way, I must admit I found it fascinating in its total absurdity. The fact is, I laughed all the way through it. And while the laughs may have been decidedly unintentional, they at least kept me awake. Which is more than I can say for the people around me.

Space restrictions make it impossible to comment at length on *The Wanderer*, but it is a film of rare and extraordinary tenderness that I find impossible to praise highly enough. The warm heart of youthful idealism vs. the cold toes of adult reality is a theme I thought the movies had just about worn to an exhausted frazzle until I saw this magnificent Easter egg of beauty and gentle charm. Jean-Gabriel Albicocco, whose sensual otherworldliness turned *The Girl With The Golden Eyes* into an underground sensation a few years ago, has borrowed stylistically from Renoir here, but the way he sees provincial France at the turn of the century makes this the most breathtakingly photographed feast for the eye since *Elvira Madigan*. And if Brigitte Fossey isn't the most beautiful girl this side of the Jeu de Paumes, I'll turn in my "Gloria Steinem For President" button.

May 2, 1969

Great acting, Shaw used to say, occurs only when arrogance meets courage and sheer madness takes over. Watching Vanessa Redgrave crashing her way through the labyrinthian mud pie Karel Reisz has made of *The Loves of Isadora*, I'm inclined to agree. She simply does not know the meaning of the word fear. Perhaps it is that she does not know enough about real life to play real people. Or perhaps it is that she is so sure of her overpowering gifts that she doesn't care whether she makes a fool of herself or not. But the result is that she is always at her best when she plays mad, possessed, unconventional oddballs. While other actresses play-acting the same high-school Max Factor mannerisms of decadence, old age, and red-headed eccentricity would be laughed off the screen, Miss Redgrave merely towers over everything, clinging to her own raw nerve with bloodshot eyes. She is like a rhinoceros in heat in this film—stamping, thrashing, slobbering, foaming at the mouth, running at the nose and eyes, clawing and rooting and snorting her way through scene after scene that would be largely forgettable without her—and Heaven help the poor creatures who get trampled underfoot when they try to get in her way.

There is simply no point in discussing the film itself. It is formless, spasmodic, annoying, and much too long, even in its current cut version. Without Miss Redgrave, there would indeed be no film. With her brooding presence, however, the experience becomes fascinating to watch. Here she is, the only real hippie movie star of the 1960s, playing the world's first original flower child, quoting Nietzsche, dancing barefoot through dry leaves while her mad brother Raymond plays the flute, eating oysters and champagne ("The food of Aphrodite"), and living only one philosophy—"Beauty is truth, truth beauty; that is all we know on Earth, and all we need to know."

Isadora Duncan is depicted in this film and in Miss Redgrave's bizarre performance as a talentless, fraudulent lunatic, a silly, vain, undependable, and desperately tragic woman who canceled engagements without notice, holed up in garrets with starving artists while they painted her stark naked dancing through moonlight filtering across the floor, had babies by her lovers without marrying them, ran through icy waves pregnant, scandalizing society, dissipating and eventually destroying herself. Her children drowned in an accident, she married a Russian poet half her age and a great deal madder than she was who displayed a fondness for waving pistols at press conferences, and eventually ended up an ugly, wasted old broad writing her memoirs, despondent and penniless, in a shuttered house overlooking the sea. All these vignettes are accomplished through the use of decor and characterization more than through the use of a sensible screenplay, yet, unlike most movie biographies, I felt I knew something of the woman's likable peculiarities by the time the film reached that last inevitable and quite famous death scene, with Isadora being strangled by her own scarf caught in the spokes of her new lover's sports car. How easy it would have been to continue the narrative. But Reisz cleverly pans from the death car to the gloomy lights of the oceanside dance from which Isadora has just made her last glorious and theatrical exit. The tinny dance band plays "Bye Bye Blackbird" and the camera holds for a very long time on the constant lap of waves lit by an eerie moon. Life goes on; the world is her survivor.

Structurally, *Isadora* is a mess. There are dream sequences, annoying flashbacks, self-conscious intercutting, and a bit too much pointless hammer-and-sickle stuff for my taste. People wander in and out of the film without being identified or explained. Most of the dancing is terrible. Vanessa Redgrave looks patently ridiculous prancing about in all those Grecian togas, like a wood nymph gone berserk, but I'm told Isadora never could dance either, so maybe the joke is fraught with irony. Her American accent comes and goes. At best, she sounds exactly like Joanne Woodward (notice especially the laugh and watch the way she rolls her tongue across her upper lip as though she had just come to the set from a screening of *The Three Faces of Eve*). At worst, she sounds and acts like a midwestern librarian on her first trip to the Playboy Club.

Yet *Isadora* is, in the final analysis, remarkably visual. The physical design of the picture is magnificent. The sets are fantastic, from the cathedrals of Russia to Jason Robards's white cockatoo-infested swimming pool that looks like a Malayan temple. And there are scenes of pastoral splendor I will never forget, like the one in which she is dancing with her little *oiseaux blancs* across the kelly green lawn of a twelve-hundred-acre chateau, pregnant as a cow in a swanlike tunic, as her current lover arrives in a white convertible carrying baskets of strawberries. It's a very strange film, but madness can be memorable.

Anyone seriously concerned about the decline of the Hollywood comedy is well-advised to check up on *If It's Tuesday it Must Be Belgium*, over at Radio City Music Hall. This hilarious patchwork quilt of postcard views of wacky American tourists abroad is irresistible and winning, and Sandy Baron, as a poor schmuck who makes the fatal mistake of looking up Italian relatives in Venice, and Reva Rose, as a pregnant wife who gets on the wrong tour bus and misses the entire trip by heading in the opposite direction, are two of the very funny faces who make it so.

May 9, 1969

Death of a Gunfighter. Lena Horne, as anyone old enough to drink anything stronger than Perrier water already knows, seldom makes mistakes. This inept, boring, laughably cliché-ridden Western (which whinnied into town this week with a great deal of understandable secrecy) is the biggest lulu of her career.

The fact that Negroes no longer have to play mammies and butlers saying "Dinner is served" is a healthy sign, but taking roles just because they have no mention of racial identity in them doesn't prove a thing if the roles are vacuous and badly written. Not all the bad movie roles in the old days were written for blacks, you know. Ask Yvonne DeCarlo.

In this dreary soap opera in spurs, Lena Horne plays Yvonne DeCarlo (local madam who naturally is also the mistress of the town sheriff) to Richard Widmark's Rod Cameron (poor misunderstood lawman nobody likes). The whole town wants him dead because he represents the town conscience, see. Seems he knows what everyone was up to all those years while their wives were off making preserves at the Ladies Aid. Everybody tries to talk him into leaving peaceable-like, but whenever they mention retiring he ups and slaps them in the face. (The script never explains why he'd want to stay in the stupid town in the first place, but questions like that make you a smart-ass.)

The only person who likes him is this freckled sheriff-worshipper who talks like Holden Caulfield ("Sheriff, you know anything about sex? She's drivin' me right out of my stupid mind—right *out!*") and looks like Huck Finn with a face full of boils and acne scars. Widmark is obviously as repelled by this pest as I was, because he slaps him too.

Then this tough Mexican gets off a train and the music rises to a blistering crescendo as he swaggers through the streets touching his gunbelt. People flee. Windows fly shut. The audience braces for a shootout. The tough Mexican strides into the saloon. *Something* is about to happen to relieve the tedium, right? Wrong. He merely leans across the bar and sighs, "I need a drink!"

Shucks, it's only John Saxon, who plays this unexplainable walkon as though he has driven in from Malibu for the day and is anxious to get home before dark. Widmark slaps him in the face, too.

Outside of a certain segment of society I'd just as soon not discuss, I've never heard of so many men slapping each other in the face. The only person in the movie who doesn't get slapped is Lena Horne, who makes up for the embarrassment of being seen by her fans in such trivia by saying all of her lines as though she was singing "We're Having a Heat Wave."

The direction (by Don Siegel, who may not be a good director, but who is certainly a sensible one for taking his name off the credits for reasons he needn't explain) is chock full of interesting tidbits (i.e., every time a man dies, there is a closeup of a candle flame being extinguished). The town of Cottonwood Springs, where all the yawns take place, has a lovely aquamarine City Hall and a cheery matching citron yellow savings back. It's supposed to be the Old West, but it looks more like Knott's Berry Farm.

Hannibal Brooks is best described as a humorless, totally worthless Cook's Tour of World War Two in which Oliver Reed falls in love with a twelve-ton elephant, but I can think of no better description of their co-star, Michael J. Pollard, than that of my friend Paul Zimmerman of *Newsweek*, who insists he looks exactly like Dopey of the Seven Dwarfs.

May 16, 1969

Laughter in the Dark is a grim, hypnotic nightmare that Tony Richardson has fashioned from the sixth of Vladimir Nabokov's sixteen novels, and although it isn't what you might call a pleasant experience, I must admit I found it absorbing and fascinating. Rather like coming upon a murder in the middle of Fifth Avenue. You hate the sight of blood, but something holds you there, keeps you from crossing the street.

I long ago ceased to consider Nabokov anything less than one of the few genuine literary geniuses of the twentieth century, yet like all geniuses, he is difficult and often quite erratic. Tony Richardson has cut down on the baroque structure of his style, but nothing has been sacrificed in terms of quality or atmosphere. The result is a tidy, beautifully mounted suspense story about a wealthy and titled London art dealer (Nicol Williamson) who spends most of his life at auctions, goes home every night to a sumptuous, easy life with a wife who is passive and frigid, and slowly begins to retreat into a tortured daydream of sexual fantasy. He's no Babbitt, but he's no Lord Snowdon, either. He hangs around West End movie houses, picks up an usherette and slowly begins a descent, through his own stupidity, into a tunnel of degradation and madness.

Up to this point, it's a neatly updated twist on the old *Blue Angel* theme. But the chippie (Anna Karina) has carefully manicured plans of her own. She gets rid of the wife, moves vinyl furniture into the town house, and persuades Williamson to hire as a new assistant her old boyfriend, a sinister, murky type whom she passes off as a homosexual. This *ménage à trois* forms the basis for a second movie on the underlying themes of obsession and jealousy that is as sensual and exciting as anything I've seen on the screen in a long time. After Williamson is blinded in a crash, Karina takes him to rest in a secluded Spanish villa where, unknown to him, her lover soundlessly occupies the adjoining bedroom. The movie turns into a classic study of sado-masochism and cruelty, leading eventually to a game of blind man's bluff that ends in self-destruction and tragedy.

Richardson has filled the movie with beautiful, erotic touches. His sense of detail and rhythm and silence is a marvel to watch. He gets more than I ever thought possible out of the cold red velvet plushness of Sotheby's and the funeral hush of the Royal Film Theatre. Then, as the movie builds to heights of seething passion and brutality, he contrasts these cool settings with heat and sun and the parch-throated dryness of bodies constricting in the confined space of the deserted villa. The film is so real that I could almost feel the sunshine as it filtered across the naked backsides.

Richardson's impeccable waste-not-want-not direction is so good it almost makes me believe Nicol Williamson. I say "almost" because, although it is easy to see what a powerful actor he is, I find it difficult to accept him in roles that require him to assume the identities of men with class and station. He's a wonderful Jimmy Porter, but Nabokov is not John Osborne, and the sight of an Osborne hero in blue cardigan and gray wool Saville Row slacks, watering the hydrangeas in the conservatory and retorting, "Yes, quite" when a pompous relative says, "They're absolutely sopping—it really won't do, old boy," seems distinctly out of kelter. He looks and sounds more like a greengrocer who got in through the back door and, finding nobody home, decided to stay and try on the emperor's new clothes.

The Mad Room is *Ladies in Retirement* in mini-skirts. Horror film buff that I am, I've been known to travel anywhere from Newark drive-ins to the dark hells of 42d Street for a good scare, but I should have stayed in bed for this one. This mod remake of the 1941 thriller has the two homicidal old ladies changed to a couple of teenage squirts who, after being asked to hide the fact that they've been in an insane asylum for twelve years, say "I'll try—but that's sick!" (Child murderers are getting mighty uppity these days.) It's supposed to put terror in the heart, but with Shelley Winters yelling four-letter words at everyone in sight, Stella Stevens illustrating psychic disorder by rolling her eyes like Eddie Cantor, and an interracial love affair with a maid who looks, walks, and talks like a wind-up Prissy doll, all *The Mad Room* does is tickle the funnybone. The scariest pretend moment in the whole movie is supposed to occur when an animal dismembers a human hand, but this movie is so inept the dog turns out to be nothing more than just a lovable old leftover from the Disney Shaggy Dog School who wanders forlornly about the set with a ketchup-covered plastic hand from a department store dummy in its mouth like a week-old newspaper. It was the best laugh I had all week.

Les Gauloises Bleues is enough to scare the living daylights out of any movie critic who secretly yearns to write and direct movies some day instead of merely reviewing them. It is a debut film by Michel Cournot, former film critic for *Nouvel Observateur* and chief promoter of Claude Lelouch. Lelouch was apparently so grateful that he promised to produce Cournot's first movie if he ever got around to writing one. This is it, and although I slept through more than half of it, I saw enough people walking against slate-colored walls in white raincoats, enough shots of kids reading Babar books intercut with men hanging from nooses, enough nuns cutting the word "human" out of billboards, enough heavy-handed symbolism involving dough people being shoved into baker's ovens, enough scenes not so much written or acted or directed as "arranged," like abstract paintings (green vegetables on blue floors, yellow sunflowers groping past green walls), and enough formless, boring leftist political propaganda to convince me that Monsieur Cournot should get out of the business while he's still behind.

May 23, 1969

Of all the movies I've seen lately, there is almost nothing I can recommend without blushing. *Whatever Happened to Aunt Alice?* is a vile little bore interesting only because of the actresses who appear in it. Mildred Dunnock does her mousy old-maid Mildred Dunnock bit; Ruth Gordon proves what a pro she is even when she chews the scenery—even when the scenery is Arizona cactus—and Geraldine Page appears to have had a wonderful time playing all the things she remembered from old Bette Davis movies.

The plot is a silly thing about a widow who murders a succession of elderly housekeepers for their stock investments. It has some pretentious dialogue ("She's like crabgrass—never quelled but always cropping up secretly and victoriously in another spot") and good atmosphere (a squatty old house done in dark amber colors, lots of stone and Oriental rugs—perfect for Arizona). And it is always an experience just to watch Geraldine Page. I especially enjoyed the scene in which she eats bacon—chewing on it, digesting each fiber of it, breaking up each sentence between bites to savor its juices—and I don't think I've ever seen any actress react to the smell of another actress' perfume in quite the way in which it seems to make Miss Page's nose crinkle.

Still, the film disappoints. It has no style, no sense of direction, not even the vaguest kind of suspense inherent in a second-rate Alfred Hitchcock half-hour TV show. And the women are all shot in an annoying series of ghastly closeups that make them look like corpses that have just been prepared by a cosmetologist for an open casket viewing.

Number One is a curious mixture of football and soap opera. It's that old malarkey about the pro-star who is too old to cut the mustard and too hard-headed to send out for sandwiches. There's some great live-action stuff in the heat and passion and sweat of the actual game, but it's not a football documentary, it's more a psycho-drama about the men beneath the shoulder pads, and the lushes and leeches who hang on to the life of a winner on his way down. Charlton Heston is the loser, and if there is any doubt left in anyone's mind about his acting ability, *Number One* should erase it hastily and sufficiently. Tom Gries, the director who got the best performance of Heston's career out of him in *Will Penny*, is once again at the helm. He seems to inspire actors. Under his guidance, Heston takes on new dimensions as an actor; his pro-football star is all new pain and old wounds. A craggy, moss-covered grit covers that great stone façade. When he speaks, life comes out instead of words.

Gries has a fine eye for technical detail, too. There is a wonderful casualness of locker room talk and one breakfast briefing session with the team is so authentic that you almost forget you are watching a movie. He draws great strength from New Orleans as a backdrop for the inner conflict of the man himself, using its jazz and its wet pavement and the smell of stale beer and the look of rotting moss as contrasts to the flashiness of his declining stardom. *Number One* is not a great film, or even a very important one, but it's admirable, and some of the other people who help make it so are Jessica Walter, Bruce Dern, Bobby Troup, and a smokily sinister young actress named Diana Muldaur, who reminded me of an Al Capp drawing of Ella Raines.

Take the Money and Run, an alleged comedy written by, directed by, and starring Woody Allen, was filmed in San Francisco because, according to

Mr. Allen, "it's a nicer place to spend the summer than Cleveland." But obviously not necessarily a better place to make good movies. I've seen funnier ones come out of the American Legion Hall in Baton Rouge, Louisiana.

La Chamade is a worthless trifle by Françoise Sagan about adultery, which, translated, means of course a lot of French sports cars, a lot of accordion music, a lot of Yves St. Laurent fashions, and a *soupçon* of the kind of French technicolor that looks like the film has been buttered instead of processed. Critics must be allowed their prejudices. Catherine Deneuve is one of mine. She stirs in me about as much passion as a statue made of ice cream. As a rich Paris housewife who leaves her furs and jewels to live in a garret with a starving student, I didn't believe her for a minute. The trouble with movies like this is that today, when everybody is doing everything to everybody else right out in the open, movies about husbands and wives committing adultery seem awfully corny. I did enjoy one scene, though. On her way out the door to live in the garret, Miss Deneuve's maid Pauline says: "I made jam—the kind you like—take a jar." I liked old Pauline for that. The rest of the film, however, is strictly for ugly secretaries.

Alice's Restaurant is a formless, pointless, plotless piece of trash directed by Arthur Penn, who should know better, about that lost, no-where civilization of rock singers and folk creeps too simple-minded to know that all that "make love not war" talk means nothing if it isn't taken into the government and Madison Avenue and television and all the other places where sham and hate and pretentiousness are spawned. The silly, long-haired little drug addicts and bores in this movie merely drop a pile of garbage on a lovely pastoral Massachusetts town and then drop out. Arlo Guthrie, whose song "The Alice's Restaurant Massacree" inspired this mess, looks like Bea Lillie and has an annoying way of delivering all of his lines by putting his teeth firmly together and talking with his mouth fixed in a wide, closed smile, like a bad imitation of James Cagney. His best friend looks exactly like Kim Hunter in *Planet of the Apes*. The acting is uniformly nauseating and so is the picture. You don't have to actually eat in Alice's Restaurant to get ptomaine; just see the movie.

In *Staircase*, Rex Harrison is back and Richard Burton's got him. Rex is a depressing nit with lavender ties and varicose veins who faces a jail sentence for appearing in public in women's clothes, and Burton is a yellowing sow's ear with a case of *alopecia* and a "face like a Gibbon's bottom." The two aging homosexuals from Charles Dyer's play have been stripped of their dignity and their humanity in this reprehensible Stanley Donen movie. Burton and Harrison are dreadful and whenever they aren't screaming at each other, there are closeups of urine and excrement in the bed of Cathleen Nesbitt, as Burton's toothless old invalid hag of a mother. *Staircase* is a boring, humorless embarrassment. If you think you can't survive without seeing Harrison and Burton biting, bitching, slashing, and whacking away at each other like Mutt and Jeff in drag, think harder.

People Meet and Sweet Music Fills the Heart proves there's still something rotten in Denmark. I don't think I've ever seen a worse movie than this, but if I have, it pales in the memory by comparison.

There is nothing salvageable about this gigantic Danish tranquilizer—not one scene, not one performance, not one isolated moment worth sitting through. Everyone in it, everyone connected with it and everything about it is mind-bendingly incompetent, but it is Danish director-scenarist-editor-producer Henning Carlsen who must bear the wrath of all civilized people who get innocently trapped in any theater in the world in which this dreary pileup of ninety-four minutes of burnable footage is shown. He's the real villain.

Don't ask me what it's about. The official synopsis handed out at the press screening I attended hinted mystically that the film is "both real and unreal . . . a dream about reality . . . uses color tones to help distinguish truth from illusion . . . but which is which?" Obviously nobody connected with the picture knows, and I wouldn't think of becoming the first person in the world to care.

All I know is that Harriet Andersson, that excellent Swedish actress who seems to have temporarily taken leave of her senses, plays a dancer named Sofia who is on her way from Copenhagen to Rio (on a train, yet) in a white fright wig. ("Could anything be more erotic than a train?" announces a sign that flashes across the screen in silent-film style.)

Across the aisle sits a washed-out, milky-faced boy with white hair and black circles under his eyes who offers her a cigarette. ("Could anything be more erotic than a cigarette?" flashes another sign.) They end up having sex on a toilet seat.

The movie should have ended right there, but it plods on as their lives continue through the years. The boy marries his girl friend, but alas, she's a lesbian. Sofia becomes the mistress of an ugly actor who introduces her to a wealthy South American who turns out to be her mother's former husband. They murder the South American. She becomes a whore in a Rio brothel and discovers the madam (who looks like Helen Traubel) is her dead father's former mistress from the war. Her lover returns home and ends up in bed with Sofia's mother.

By this time, things are so ridiculously confusing the lines actually run like this: "You are Ramon Salvador's murderer!" "I am Sofia Peterson's mother!" I walked out at the point where Sofia's night club partner from the Rio brothel turned up on a Secaucus, New Jersey, fire engine.

Unfortunately, I stayed long enough to hear some of the dialogue. Otherwise, I would never have believed it: "My legs so ached to embrace him, it shook me up!" "I can't stay for another cup of coffee because my boy friend's expecting a juicy steak this evening"—cut to closeup of the girl's crotch—"and I've got a lovely piece of meat for him." "My soul is a rotten orange you can stick your finger into!" (That was the best of the lot, you'll have to admit.)

The whole thing is filmed in old Sepia Tone, like old Johnny Mack Brown cowboy serials. Everyone seems so desperate to cash in on some of the *I Am Curious* action they can't even walk out of a room without rubbing the marble nipples on the breasts of whatever statue they pass on the way to the door.

The idea is the world is a very small place after all and everyone is linked in some way to everyone else—an idea I find foolish to begin with. But this movie is so incomprehensible it also becomes ultimately boring. "Are you bored?" asks Miss Andersson at one point, taking off her bra. "Yes, we're being bored together," answers her lover. "This is *real* boredom." It sure is.

The kisses are boring, the camera work is boring, the things people say are boring, the people who say them are boring . . . as I said, I don't ever remember seeing a worse movie. I'd suggest dumping it in the East River, but I'm afraid it would poison the fish.

May 26, 1969

Midnight Cowboy is probably the most savage indictment against the City of New York ever captured on film. It is even more depressing and heartbreaking than movies like *On the Bowery* because instead of concentrating on one aspect of underground life it shows what can happen to young people who drift into town from saner places looking for—what?—Something better or more exciting or more liberal or more glamorous than back home?—and how the city beats them down.

It is an honest, infuriating, lacerating look at the coldness of the city and what people do to survive in it.

After seeing it, I can't imagine why anyone in his right mind would ever want to come here. Or, indeed, why any of us stay here at all.

I should mention that *Midnight Cowboy* is also a very funny movie. The free-swinging humor in Waldo Salt's screenplay and in wonderfully etched performances by Dustin Hoffman, Brenda Vaccarro, Sylvia Miles and others, keeps the whole thing from careening over the edge of sadness and becoming mawkish and dead-beat.

But most of the success of the film truly belongs to Jon Voight, who plays "one helluva stud" from Texas named Joe Buck with such coltish naïveté that he performs the miracle of keeping the audience in his pocket during the entire film. He is almost never off the screen, and when he is, it falls apart.

I wish I could describe the pleasure I derived from watching him travel through the country on a Greyhound Bus, all booted and spurred in his best Roy Rogers drag, with his transistor recording the pulse beat of the Bible Belt ("Jesus wants to know how many sent in five dollars for their home worship kits!"). When he arrives, unpacks his *Playboy* centerfolds and his Paul Newman *Hud* posters in the stark depravity of the Hotel Dixie and sets about conquering New York, something lurches in the heart for him. And when he is beaten and snubbed by the city, ending up as a male hustler in 42d Street movie houses out of loneliness and insecurity, you want to say, "Yeah, fellow, I know . . ." even if you don't.

There isn't a single isolated moment that Voight doesn't touch the heart and make the character appealing. Even when he does something brutal, like stuff the telephone down a customer's throat or force a scared kid who has just performed a sex act in a movie seat to hand over his watch, Voight makes you *care*. He is half-clod, half-poet, like a Wyoming saddle tramp playing Dorian Gray, and the effect of his power and sensitivity is scalding.

There are problems with the rest of the movie. It is much too long, the Texas flashbacks are confusing and shot through so many filters they are visually incomprehensible (Why did Joe's girl go mad? Did the gang of toughs rape them both, or just Joe? Why was she taken away in an ambulance? Why did he want to come to New York in the first place?) The psychedelic party scene with Viva and the Warhol creeps is endless, boring, pointless, and should be re-edited. Dustin Hoffman is supposed to have a bum leg, but his limp varies from scene to scene, at times giving the impression he is doing the Carioca.

But throughout, director John Schlesinger has made New York as much a character as anyone else. Beneath the gloss and the poodles urinating and the natives who have to stop and think which subway to take to get to the Statue of Liberty, there is the desperate panic and the hostility and the isolation of the human heart that happens in New York like no place on earth. Even the Accutron sign seems to tick away the time in lethal gasps.

The freaks in the subways and the lunatics in the late-night Automats, the breaking of locks on shoeshine kits and stealing from pregnant Puerto Rican women in laundromats, and the blood banks and the madness and filth—it all adds up to a collage of screaming, crawling, vomiting humanity that makes *Midnight Cowboy* a nasty but unforgettable screen experience.

The Home Movie as Porny Put-on

I can't imagine any serious critic giving more than, say, ten minutes of consideration to the films of Andy Warhol, but it has recently been brought to my shocked attention that there are enough fools Out There still willing to pay three bucks and sometimes more to see his peep shows that they are actually showing a profit. I think it's because the world is spoofing itself, sending itself up. Commerce is a dirty word, sex without orgasm is as much an everyday experience as watering the geraniums, enthusiasm has been slowly and agonizingly replaced by *ennui.*

It seems only right that freaks like Tiny Tim, Allen Ginsberg, and Andy Warhol should come into their own. They are the supreme send-ups, because they have nothing to lose. And when you come right down to it, what's the alternative? Hollywood has become so phony and corrupt that even the most amateurish, hackneyed Warhol film sometimes looks more realistic than the elephantine studio-sealed technicolor spoofs like *What's New, Pussycat?* and *John Goldfarb, Please Come Home*, or, more recently, *The Magus* and *Che!* and *Alice's Restaurant.*

Andy Warhol, like the rest of the underground cinema, is largely a Frankenstein created by publicity. Amateur journals like *Cahiers du Cinéma* and Jonas Mekas's *Film Culture* and the *Village Voice* and even, to some degree, *Newsweek*, which will do anything to make itself sound more *outré* than *Time*, have fed the Warhol spoofs of experimentation and pornography until they have reached that segment of the film public composed of college students and draft dodgers and homosexuals and social drop-outs who have, in turn, spread the word to the rest of the world. For a while, it was impossible to attend a fight or a horse race or even a political rally (not to mention a cocktail party) without the subject of Warhol popping up. Warhol pictures were the next rung on the ladder toward that ultimate obscenity—the self send-up.

Warhol is merely a joke now. He has contributed nothing of any real significance to the contemporary cinema. Oddly enough, in light of what has been happening in the movies lately, films like *I am Curious—Yellow* which, in my opinion, is worse than anything Andy ever turned out in his sleep—have made Warhol look rather like the Shirley Temple of the soiled-sheets and dirty-toenail set. We've graduated. Warhol was just a trend, a phase of our self-corruption. Like the Beatles, he has almost become respectable. Heavens to Betsy, Virginia, his latest film, *Blue Movie*, is even about a man doing it to a *woman!* (Although there is still some debate about whether that is an accurate description of Viva. I'm not quite certain.)

Warhol movies have become strangely ingratiating. All those pathetic bodies full of bruises and teeth bites, crawling about like inmates trying to get out of the pages of Dante before they go to press—they really are quite touching, because they make no statement, they make no point, they cannot be taken seriously. The films of Warhol lack beauty, expressiveness, meaning, relevance to anything but a certain group of social rejects who find in them, perhaps, temporary escapes from narcotics and folk music. For them, Warhol will always be the grand old man of camp. For the rest of us, his films have become, as Pauline Kael says, "time killers on the way to the grave."

Andy has been around for a long time (he's into his fading forties now). Ever since he stopped painting Brillo boxes and tomato soup cans, he has been turning out flicks. Nobody paid any more attention to them for a while than they would to anyone else's dirty home movies. But Andy was smart. (Anyone who could get Ethel Scull to commission him for a portrait, then take her to a photo booth on 42nd Street, snap a series of wallet-size Kodaks, blow them up on a frame and charge $25,000 and *get it*, has *got* to be smart.) He knew the only way to get people to pay attention was to make movies that were the ultimate insults to their intelligence. So he trained his camera on a man sleeping for eight hours with the sound track tuned to an all-night disc jockey show. Nobody I know ever sat through *Sleep*, but it was outrageous enough to get more newspaper space than any Kazan movie ever got.

Then Andy made his first major full-length flick, *The Chelsea Girls*, and the police actually let him show it in public. *Above* the ground. When a writer friend of mine went to interview him on the set (which turned out to be a cheap hotel room), Andy turned on his cameras for a demonstration of the Warhol skill, went in for a take, and realized about twenty minutes later he had forgotten to take the cover off the lens. That's how he makes movies, and *The Chelsea Girls* shows it.

Chelsea Girls is a 3½-hour cesspool of vulgarity and talentless confusion which is about as interesting as the inside of a toilet bowl. It is so amateurish that during intermission, when the sound track accidentally came back on from behind the closed curtains, the audience thought it was part of the movie. It is thoroughly useless as cinema, because it has no style, explores no horizons, invents no new forms and botches all the old ones. Worst of all —it is ugly to look at, stupefyingly dull, and technically unbearable. People drop mikes, the camera runs out of film and starts again, the lens is constantly out of focus (take a Dramamine before entering, because Andy has just now discovered the zoom lens, man, and *wow!*), and the few brave homosexuals, lesbians, and drug addicts Andy has persuaded to camp it up are so unable to sustain even the single thread of a scene that they often look right into the camera and break up.

What, you ask, does it show? Two screens split, with two images running simultaneously. The ugliest pock-marked transvestite I've ever seen sings songs from *Annie Get Your Gun*. An expressionless girl combs her hair for half an hour while an effeminate boy (I *think* it's a boy) washes a coffee pot. A big fat Lesbian gives herself a shot of dope in the behind, complaining "I haven't had sex since Genevieve got hepatitis." Four of the most disgustingly dirty homosexuals ever dragged from the gutters of Third Avenue and cornered in one room eat orange slices and roll around on top of each other in bed; finally, a second Lesbian pulls one of the boys' dirty jockey shorts off, exposing him. Another Lesbian beats up her girl friend and threatens to pull the nails off a fourth one. A hophead with a chain around his neck sips from a king-size Coke bottle and screams at the camera that he is the Pope. "Where is Heaven?" asks a greasy-haired Andy Warhol superstar, who arrives for Confession. "You figure it out, Mary, I'll give ya a road map."

These and a few other revolting rejects from sane society talk about masturbation, Ex-Lax, Maria Montez, LSD, and pubic hair over a soundtrack that is so bad it sounds like it's being phoned in from the next town. Which is exactly where you'll wish *you* are, if you are depraved enough to sit through more than twenty minutes of *The Chelsea Girls*.

This was followed by several very minor Warhol efforts—*My Hustler, Bike Boy*, and *Blow Job*, the latter being particularly memorable to me because I attended the "world premiere" at Columbia University.

By now, Warhol had come to be regarded as something of a cinematic Louis Ablafaya among the student radicals. The premiere drew an enthusiastic standing-room-only crowd; Warhol himself was in the audience and had promised to speak at the conclusion of the film. The audience sat attentively during the first few minutes of the film, which showed a boy's face. That's all. Just a face. But something was obviously *happening* down below, out of camera range. The audience got restless. The put-on was putting them down and they didn't like it. They finally began to yell things at the screen, most of them unprintable. Total chaos finally broke out when one voice (a girl's) screamed: "We came to see a blow job, and we stayed to get screwed!" Tomatoes and eggs were thrown at the screen; Warhol was whisked to safety through the raging, jeering, angry mob and rushed to a waiting car. So much for *Blow Job*. And so much for that honorary degree from Columbia.

A year ago, I was supposed to fly to Arizona to do a piece for *Esquire* about Andy making his first cowboy movie on the old John Wayne sets near Tucson. Andy works fast. By the time I got my tickets, the movie was already finished and the group had left town. The result is *Lonesome Cowboys*, in which Andy and his circus side-show of fag hags and homosexuals prove once more how dull, boring, ugly, and thoroughly talentless they all are by dressing up in cowboy drag and improvising a piece of humorless trash on horseback. Tourists wander in and out of background shots with their Brownie Hawkeyes. The soundtrack screams and sputters like a streetcar breaking down. Everything looks like it has been spliced together, but I can't be sure—splicing would be an innovation for Warhol.

Viva gets slapped around a lot, knocked down, thrown into mud puddles and generally humiliated beyond all endurance in a symbolic fag put-down of the female sex. The "cowboys" look like Hollywood Boulevard drag queens who just looted Teepee Town. They get stoned on pot, talk about getting their hair done and ride around on worn-out nags on their last legs before the glue factory. One stands by a hitching post doing ballet exercises so his thighs will hold six-guns better ("It builds up the buns!"). Occasionally they pull each other's pants down and roll around in the dirt, but mostly they just talk dirty, and incomprehensibly, and look like monsters from outer space. If you're the kind of perverted creep who digs this bit, stay out of *Lonesome Cowboys* and get yourself into the nearest Turkish bath. You'll get more for your money.

Blue Movie, Warhol's latest, is being billed as "a film about the Vietnam war and what we can do about it." Peculiarly enough, it devotes its piddling to the subject of heterosexual pornography, although its two stars are Viva, looking a bit more femine than usual, and Louis Waldon, one of the "cowboys" from *Lonesome Cowboys*—an aging, stubby little man who is not in particularly good physical shape for the assignment. They wrestle on the bed, engage in sexual intercourse shot from every conceivable angle but always in a series of monotonous tight and medium closeups, eat hamburgers, take a shower together, and talk, talk, *talk*, about Nixon, John Lindsay, cops, termites, and athlete's foot. All of which demonstrates, of course, what we can do about the Vietnam war.

I am still waiting for some kind of movie of some kind of lasting significance from the Factory of Andy Warhol. *Flesh* came closest, but Warhol had nothing to do with that except lend his name to its release. It featured the first naked Warhol superstar I've ever seen who could act (Joe Dallesandro) and dialogue so sharp it was a delight to hear. Paul Morrissey's direction was patchy and the camerawork was as terrible as you might expect from people who have spent most of their time at Warhol's side, but in the way in which it utilized people in their most arresting behavioral patterns, as stripped of pretense as babies on their mothers' breasts, and in the way it showed how film can be opened up to expand our way of thinking outside conventional film barriers, *Flesh* was a wildly funny and highly innovational movie. Yet to my knowledge, it has never been reviewed by a major critic, while such inferior Warhol tripe as *Chelsea Girls* has been all but deified by obscure critics who still get all their ideas from old Susan Sontag essays.

Perhaps Warhol's contribution to movies will some day find some kind of expression in the work of his disciples, like Paul Morrissey. But the work of Warhol himself is no different from the old college days when we used to train cameras on each other in Psychology 101 class. Except, of course, that Warhol gets paid to put us on. Matter of fact, for all their filth and degeneracy, the only shocking thing about these stag movies is that, for charging the public money to see them, Andy and his Super-jerks haven't been turned in to the Better Business Bureau.

Holiday

January 1969

The end of an old year, or the beginning of a new one, is that time on the calendar which seems designed especially to drive film critics bananas. Movie companies save up their costliest extravagances and release them in a flood of breast-beating, hoping to qualify the films they spent their biggest budgets on for the Academy Awards race. Then in January, after the Christmas refuse is swept away and all the crowds go home, the backlog of sleepers, low-budget art films, and studio question marks nobody was sure of are unleashed in a rip tide. It's called taking inventory, wiping the slate clean, balancing the books. It's that time of year for filling new prescriptions for glasses. Here then, to catch everybody up, some notes, offered gallantly from the darkness of year-end screening rooms:

Secret Ceremony. The disintegration of Elizabeth Taylor has been a very sad thing to stand by helplessly and watch, but something ghastly has happened over the course of her last four or five films. She has become a hideous parody of herself—a fat, sloppy, yelling, screeching banshee, turning awkwardly into a kind of American Magnani. The screen produces so few natural works of art that to see them untended and used with disrespect is rather like chewing gum in the Louvre. I have always reacted to her beauty and talent in much the same way as the late James Agee, who once remarked, after seeing *National Velvet*, that he was so blinded by her personal magnetism he hardly felt qualified to arrive at any sensible assessment of her work. Working from a new axiom that an artist who is his own worst enemy deserves no sympathy, I am no longer intimidated after flinching through *Secret Ceremony*.

This piece of garbage is so totally ridiculous that I can't imagine why anyone would want to be *in* it, much less pay to *see* it. It's a bizarre charade in which a retarded lunatic (Mia Farrow, naturally) picks up a sullen, cynical prostitute in a graveyard and pretends she is her mother.

With no explanation whatsoever, the whore plays along, and returns to a Gothic mansion where the child lives alone surrounded by several million dollars worth of deliciously weird antiques, including an amalgam of automatic birdcages in which a zoo of stuffed creatures wail their heads off when you flip an electric switch. "You always came back, except the last time, when the pain was bad and the wind knocked down the cherry tree," says Mia, rolling her zombie eyes and catching the drool with her tongue at a point just north of her overwrought Adam's apple.

Elizabeth Taylor has absolutely no idea what she's talking about and neither does anyone else, but she's not asking questions, because there's a mink coat in the closet. So they take baths together (an ill-advised scene, since Miss Taylor in the nude has come to resemble an enormous boiled turnip), sleep in the same bed and begin a peculiar series of Lesbian advances and rejections, also thrown in for no explainable reason except to juice up the ads for something that is really a fake. That's about all there is to the movie, except that Robert Mitchum (in the worst bit of miscasting since Doris Day played a pregnant housewife shot through the stomach by the Ku Klux Klan in *Storm Warning*) shows up with a hippie beard and invites some flap about whether or not he raped his own step-daughter. The game is up, after what seems like a marathon of tedium, when Miss Taylor rips Mia's doll from under her dress to prove she's not really pregnant. This makes Mia so mad she slashes her finger with a razor blade, swallows all the sleeping pills she can find, and dies, leaving Miss Taylor to stab Mitchum through the heart as he peers into the coffin.

There are many reasons why *Secret Ceremony* is a detestable film, but the chief annoyance to me was the way everybody went along with the silly shenanigans without asking a single sensible question. The first time Miss Taylor is approached by the child-lunatic she is sitting on a bus. It isn't a crowded bus. In fact, she is the only passenger. A Charles Addams apparition in a black hood sidles up to her, stares at her face with red werewolf eyes, and makes several noises from beyond the grave. Miss Taylor merely treats the scene as though she has a mild cold coming on. She seems, in her process of self-denigration, to have also lost the ability to act, something she used to be able to do quite well. The clumsy American acting styles of the three leads seem diametrically opposed to the cold, professional Irish Murdoch quality of Joseph Losey's direction, and several talented people in supporting roles (Pamela Brown and Peggy Ashcroft among them) are allowed to walk away with what little is left of the whole mess with easy aplomb. Mia Farrow, I am convinced, is incapable of playing anything but demented creeps. The simplest gestures, like opening doors and saying "Dinner is served," defeat her. And Joseph Losey, without the added benefit of his usual Harold Pinter screenplays to check his extravagances at the door, seems to have temporarily gone to seed as a director. What they've all tried to do is make a Gothic tale of role reversal, but all they've come up with is a masterpiece of confusion.

Barbarella. Glossy science fiction trash, which appears to be *2001: A Space Odyssey* seen through the eyes of Helen Gurley Brown and photographed by *Vogue*, and which never makes use of its opportunities, which is okay with me, since its opportunities are probably appreciated best by Harvard boys who sit around the *Crimson* office after school reading *The Story of O* aloud to each other. I have learned through experience not to expect much from the art nouveau direction of Roger Vadim anymore (although I remember with fondness *Blood and Roses*, his particularly endearing confection about jet-set vampires and, unmistakably, his best film), but I find his manipulation of Jane Fonda increasingly more indigestible with each successive film. In this smoker room version of an intergalactic *Candy*, she is required to do nothing more than coordinate a certain toss of her mane with a certain toss of her mammary glands. Miss Fonda, I am happy to report, is in excellent physical shape for the assignment.

The Fixer. A terrible misfortune, from start to finish, this monstrosity John Frankenheimer has made from Bernard Malamud's novel shows what can happen when an anti-Establishment director sets out to have his cake and eat it too, not realizing it was only, after all, a moldy bagel. In this interminable film, Alan Bates plays a Jew with a British accent thrown into a Russian prison for false reasons and tortured, whipped, humiliated, and stripped of his manhood for even more reasons too boring and complex to go into. Mr. Bates is too fat for the role and after two years of unrelieved brutality he is even fatter. I'd say something was wrong with the credulity of that kind of casting. Dirk Bogarde is a sympathetic lawyer who keeps coming back like a song as either an angel or a ghost, I was never sure which. The acting ranges from amateurish to downright embarrassing; the script—by Dalton Trumbo—reeks of preachy self-commitment but the cause gets fogged in by limpid pseudo-poetry bordering on shallow melodrama; the direction is humorless and sometimes even patently absurd; and although the entire company was taken to Budapest at a lot of expense, with a great deal of publicity, and under a great deal of duress, discomfort, and political apathy, there isn't one scene in it that couldn't have been shot on the MGM back lot in Culver City.

Frankenheimer has attempted to make *The Fixer* look more like literature than film; but there is such a gray winter morning look to it that it seems sapped of its vitality. There is no evidence of any reverence for character or background or atmosphere. Its theme—the right of any human being to try to defend or practice living even at the ultimate risk of martyrdom—should have been as simple to portray as an aspen tree in autumn. It shouldn't have been mucked about in a clash of egos, and it certainly doesn't need to hammer home its point with bloodshed, hysteria, and heartbreak. People have different ideas of how to fritter away their time. Sitting through 2½ hours of badly photographed sadness, violence, and ultimate tedium is not mine.

The Subject Was Roses. Pure soap opera, but directed with such cool beauty by Ulu Grosbard, written with such sincerity by Frank Gilroy, and performed with such an abundance of skill and reality by Patricia Neal, Frank Albertson, and Martin Sheen, that I could not feel one foot of the film was wasted. This story about a disillusioned Bronx family readjusting to their son's return from the Army is strictly vintage *Philco Playhouse* from the early Fifties, but it contains some of the best acting I've seen on film this year and its truths are so basic and honest I cannot imagine anyone being seriously offended by the tears it extracts. I found it to be just about the best thing America has turned out this season, with the exception of *Rachel, Rachel.*

Les Biches. Lesbianism and insanity on the rise in St. Tropez, not necessarily in that order.

The Charge of the Light Brigade. A sumptuous bore by Tony Richardson, beautifully photographed and archly acted by stuffy Britishers who perform as though they were posing for Brueghel paintings. Lovely icy winters and green watercolor springs, waltzing cotillions and animated effects by Richard Williams that look like they just stepped out of the pages of *Punch*. But after an hour and a half of watching Trevor Howard's Mt. Rushmore face sip moselle in the officer's mess and agonizing as Vanessa Redgrave and David Hemmings walked through pastoral mill ponds, I began to wish the whole bloody thing would amount to something more interesting. It did, finally. The endless shots of breaking in horses, the dozens of tiny formalities, petty jealousies, and pompous blitherings finally added up to Tony Richardson's view of what Her Majesty's forces were probably like during the Crimean War—a thousand years of precious lunatic protocol produced by the empty heads of lace-cuffed muttonheads. In the Battle of Sebastopol, war was a romantic adventure, where men in command traded insults and talked of babies and table linens, and where, in the heat of battle, there was always time for a picnic spread on the lookout point. It all adds up rather predictably—with a few horses being shot through the heads and an actual amputation shown onscreen—as a colossal waste of everyone's time, including mine.

The Lion in Winter. I've always been fascinated by the idea of taking history out of context, showing historical events and exposing the psyches of historical heroes, in contemporary translation easy enough for modern audiences to understand. Can the language of modern times, dissipated through years of erosion, rise to the occasion? Only, it seems, if someone with James Goldman's flair for composition and ear for dialogue is doing the writing. This adaptation of his Broadway play is a film for people who love the beauty of language and marvel at the poetry words can become when they are molded together by a real craftsman instead of a hack. The year is 1183, but the impact is now.

Katharine Hepburn is magnificent as Eleanor of Aquitaine, a role that finally rises to the level her extraordinary genius is prepared to meet, and although Peter O'Toole, as Henry II, foams at the mouth and rolls his eyes a lot—in short, doing the Peter O'Toole bit with a sidecar of annoying mannerisms—they are intriguingly paired in a film full of clanging doors, crowing cocks, and entrances heralded by trumpets and madrigals. I would recommend it highly if that were all I could say for it, and I could say a great deal more if I had the space.

The Boston Strangler. A stringy, hodge-podge about the killer-that-stalked-Boston, practically destroyed by pretentious camerawork, a self-conscious use of split screens stolen from Norman Jewison, and a desperate attempt on the part of Director Richard (*Dr. Dolittle*) Fleischer to keep the whole thing above the level of an ordinary whodunit that only succeeds in thwarting the movie's most exciting possibilities. Fleischer bungled his chance to make a movie as thrilling as the book by crowding the screen with so many slices of action that the involvement in each individual section of the action is minimized. Instead of that freeze in the throat I've often felt in a good mystery when a victim is about to get it, I got dizzy watching, simultaneously, on the same screen at one time, a vast network of telephone company operators checking their lines, girls getting obscene calls, the caller's lips moving while some cutter has been too chicken to let us hear the words, the strangler's footsteps climbing the stairs, the faces of onlookers in the street listening to a speech by the Boston police commissioner, and a series of *cinéma vérité* interviews with women. The play-by-play terror that overtakes a city, then a nation, is juxtaposed with government agency red-tape stupidity. Good old-fashioned melodrama turns into social comment. The choice could, in more capable hands, be an acceptable one, but Fleischer stretches his socio-psychological preaching to include such clichés as homosexuals in a gay bar, two corny Lesbians right out of the pages of Radclyffe Hall, and lunatic cops who mouthe lines right out of Mickey Spillane like "So what? Everybody's banging everbody—it's a horny world."

Henry Fonda plays former Massachusetts Assistant D.A. John Bottomly in a manner more boring than the paper he's written on. There is one hilarious scene of total absurdity in which he is interviewed by commentator Alex Dreier that has to be seen to be believed (it ends with Dreier saying, "And now, back to Strangler Headquarters . . ."). A lot of people walked out during that one, but the majority of the audience waited until Leora Dana, as Fonda's wife, comforted him in the middle of the night with, "Don't be too hard on yourself—I know I didn't marry Justice Oliver Wendell Holmes." You've got to admit they don't write dialogue like that any more.

Tony Curtis has moments as the killer, peeling away layers of psychiatric imbalance as he discovers his inner psyche by pantomiming the re-enactment of his crimes against a white wall in a series of closeups as his putty nose shakes, his hands quiver and close in on a nooselike grasp, his breath shortens, and his throat sobs while imaginary heads fall out of joint. It is a performance worth watching, but it comes after the film is half over, having already lost its audience through arty direction and terrible scriptwriting.

Shalako. Sean Connery, as an American Indian scout with a British accent, and Brigitte Bardot, as a French countess who helps him fight off warring Apaches, provide more laughs than anyone intended. I liked it, probably for all the wrong reasons, but mainly because I *do* know a good comedy when I see one.

I Love You, Alice B. Toklas. A depressing little comic-strip bubble more than completely deflated by the glaringly unfunny presence of Peter Sellers, who gave up all interest in discipline, style, structure, or well-written scripts about the same time Dinah Shore gave up selling Chevrolets.

Joanna and *The Touchables.* Here are two incomprehensible pop-art bores dedicated to the Andy Warhol principle that people will pay money to see *anything* if it assaults the senses and the intelligence with enough amorality and impudence to be passed off as "interesting." Neither film is distinguishable from the other; both are glorifications of those darling, misunderstood, dippy, with-it London teen-age clichés that decorate the pages of *Crawdaddy!*, dress in costumes that look like old discarded Mardi Gras jokes, and make sane human beings seem prehistoric as pterodactyls. Both films are awash with Disney cartoon technicolor, pretentious fashion-magazine photography and no evidence anywhere of anything resembling style, discipline, structure, wit, plot, or originality. *Joanna* involves an unbelievable looking dolly named Genevieve Waite, who talks like Little Lulu, parades around naked through most of the film with a body that looks like Peter Fonda's in *The Trip*, and talks a lot about "commitment" as she goes naïvely to bed with a Negro. It was directed by Michael Sarne, who, according to my program notes, "is 27, wears old American blue jeans, drives a convertible Rolls Royce and eats in the same Chinese restaurant every night." I am more than prepared to believe it.

The Touchables involves three imitation Georgy Girls (or was it four? It's hard to tell; they all look alike in these amateurish "swinging London" frappes) with a fondness for walkie-talkies, Chiquita banana posters, and making love to a wax dummy of Michael Caine stolen from Tussaud's. They dress up like nuns, kidnap a teen idol from a homosexual wrestling match, and take him to a glass bubble in the middle of an island for the purpose of fornicating until he drops dead from exhaustion. The plan doesn't work. He's a heartier lad than they had in mind, even though he looks more like a girl than any of them and displays a penchant for lemon dressing gowns, black bikinis, and flowing chiffon scarfs. So they shoot him through the head with a rifle while the sound track blares rock and roll and the boom-happy camera blurs everything into a wail of dissonance. I haven't [illegible] vaguest idea what any of it is supposed to mean, but somehow I [illegible] comfortable in the knowledge that I won't miss much if I never find [illegible] I hesitate to mention any of the people involved, since I doubt that [illegible]'ll ever hear of any of them again, but I don't mind telling you that both bits of mindless trash were made by 20th Century-Fox, which shows the depths to which some studios will sink to keep potential moviegoers safely at home in front of their television sets.

February 1969

The Magus is a pretty good example of how not to turn a book into a movie. Plays are easier to transform from one medium to another; they already have a built-in rhythm. But books are delicate things. They need guidance, if they are to play as well as they read. *The Magus* may not be the most misguided picture ever made (what with competition like *Hurry Sundown* and *The Legend of Lylah Clare* still fresh in the memory) but it's in there pitching.

John Fowles's eerily poetic novel was a quest for reality in a charade of illusions. As with life, several possible "meanings" could be read into the story of a schoolteacher involved with a modern magician and a kaleidoscope of women in varying degrees of ambiguity. Above all, it was gripping, puzzling, tantalizing, and ultimately readable. But good books seldom make good movies, and this one is pretty awful. Fowles wrote his own screenplay (a gargantuan mistake), including many of the things that physically happen in his convoluted plot, but leaving out all the resonance and mystery. And Guy Green was the worst possible choice for a director. A film like this, requiring the viewer to become so visually anesthesized against the illogic of what happens that he will go along with the alchemy without getting bored, demands a Fellini, someone who's half-mad to begin with. Mr. Green, whose only previous success was *A Patch of Blue*, works best with a kind of documentary realism, which, when applied to such voodoo as schizophrenia, visions of fire, talking computers, dream montages, tarot cards, people disappearing through rocks, and supernatural black magic, kills all the fun. The whole movie should be a maze of impressions in the mind, a never-ending nightmare—*not* a series of literal O. Henry-like twists. By reducing the illusion to comic strip proportions, the audience becomes re less, the movie becomes slipshod and superficial. It has somewhat the sa effect as watching a comedy directed by a man without a sense of humor *Fantasia* reassembled by the March of Time.

The rest of what Hollywood has done to *The Magus* is too disgraceful to go into, but I would like to suggest that the sadists who cast movies like this find ways of torturing the beautiful but vacuous Candice Bergen more merciful than convincing her she can play roles several light years beyond her range and ability. Miss Bergen has terrific hair, terrific skin, terrific eyes, a terrific smile, a terrific tan, and a super-terrific inability to demonstrate a single emotion on the screen that comes anywhere close to even the most rudimentary knowledge of what acting is all about. For the role of Lily (in the book she was twins, but I guess Miss Bergen had enough trouble with *one* character; it must have seemed easier to write out a character than hire a better actress) the film cries out for a Lilith, someone just weird and unbalanced enough in appearance to keep an audience guessing. Miss Bergen is just too apple pie. When she enters, to the sound of violins, pretending it is 1915, and says "It is very warm; is there any news from Flanders?" she's about as convincing as a high school thespian playing Anna Karenina.

She suffers, but not alone. Everyone else is miscast, too. Anna Karina, the gamin from the Godard pictures, is totally wasted in her first American movie as an airline stewardess who spouts clichés like "I don't love you—deep down, deep *deep* down in you, there's someone totally different—*that's* who I love!" Saying a line like that would be hard in any language, but working in English, she is at a distinct disadvantage (bringing to mind Ingrid Thulin's similarly disastrous Hollywood debut in *The Four Horsemen of the Apocalypse*) and either she has been photographed poorly or she has bad teeth. As the patriarch in whose Greek villa the mysteries unfold, Anthony Quinn wrestles with the huge task of being both magus and priest, martyr and judge, but he merely comes off looking like a clairvoyant Onassis.

The less said the better about Michael Caine's dreary, sloth-eyed, totally insincere work as the hero of the piece, but I would like to raise one question: Why is it that the men with the worst physiques in films continually appear in more than half the footage in each of their successive pictures wearing little more than a smile? Mr. Caine joins that dubiously select list of leading men—Laurence Harvey, Peter Sellers, and Alan Bates among them—who should insist on a write-in clause in each contract protecting them from taking *off* their clothes. Not that male nudity is likely to offend female moviegoers. Quite the contrary. But I can't imagine any female who prefers her movie's hero with a flat tire around his middle. Things are tough enough at home.

Whether you know it or not, if you were never lucky enough to see the dynamic Beryl Reid, either in London or on Broadway, brandish her brilliance over stunned audiences in Frank Marcus's play *The Killing of Sister George,* you have been a little poorer in life. But by one of those extraordinary movie miracles—as rare in these box office conscious days as purple velocipedes—Miss Reid has been allowed to recreate, literally preserve for posterity, her role in the movie. Someone up there in that great projection room in the sky has been looking over us all.

Miss Reid's colossal performance as the dethroned soap opera queen of the BBC who, in private life away from the mikes, just happens also to be a Lesbian, is not only the best piece of acting I've seen on film this year, but—risking the total alienation of that portion of the public that likes its critics with blood on their hands—I'd like to go even further. *The Killing of Sister George* is unimpeachably the best picture I've seen in quite some time.

It is also the *only* film about homosexuality I've ever seen that deals with the subject not as a problem or stigma, but as part of the natural order of things—with humor, dignity, sincerity, sobriety, honesty, and candor. Until now, movies and homosexuality have mixed like milk and vinegar. Seldom have homosexuals been allowed to survive (a gun in the mouth is the most obvious way for them to bid adieu and repent for their sins, although Sandy Dennis rather uniquely preferred to let a tree fall between her legs in *The Fox*) and even when they do, they end up either with a lifetime of remorse and guilt (*The Victim*) or discover, as in *Tea and Sympathy*, that it was all really only a ghastly mistake after all. They seldom have any fun (a homosexual laughing it up would, to Hollywood, be as incongruous as a British horror movie without an antique shop—as though nothing bizarre ever happens in, say, Regent's Park) and in some way they *always* pay.

Sister George puts a stop to all that. I don't mean to imply it is some kind of tawdry "dikes can be fun" burlesque. But it's no baggy-eyed *Therese and Isabelle*, either. George and her flatmate Childie are no Radclyffe Hall storybook clichés. The power of their story lies in its universality. Exchange any character in it with a member of the opposite sex and the truth of what the film has to say about life and the way we all live it on our own terms is equally pungent. Acting out their childish contritions and cruel little punishments, they dig brutally away at each other, doing terrible things to each other in the name of love. They reach out in desperation, their hands finding their way across a darkened room for reassurance. They drink too much. They shout too much. They get at each other's souls too much. They cry too much and they laugh too much, not always because things are funny, but sometimes because a laugh is the only reservation for the sanest seat in the house tomorrow. They don't kill themselves or want to get married or spend the rest of their lives in solitary confinement. The only way they "pay" is to know who they are. Then they go to bed with a hangover and start all over again the next day. Just like life.

Lukas Heller's script has opened up the play, expanded its potential, changed the action from radio to TV, taken it out to the London streets, backstage at the BBC, and into the smoky hell of Lesbian bars (one particularly vivid scene was actually filmed inside the notorious Gateways, a private Lesbian bar off King's Road where no cameras have ever been allowed before). The Lesbians in this scene are the real thing, amateurs whose work is more florid and natural than most professionals I've seen in nine out of ten ordinary Hollywood "gay bar" scenes (if you doubt me, compare them to the ridiculous extras in *The Boston Strangler*). One masturbation scene is likely to make a few little old ladies nastily uncomfortable, but the loss of a few Doris Day fans is a small price to pay for the liberation of the cinema from the archaic shackles that have restricted it from showing the passions of reality.

I have enormous respect for Director Robert Aldrich for resisting the Hollywood casting-couch temptation to cast box office "names" (how easy it would have been to team Bette Davis and Julie Christie) and for keeping his film clean and direct without distracting Richard Lester cuts and fades and pans. Aldrich has photographed *George* in a conventional way—closeup, medium shot, long shot, back to closeup—and it is a wise choice with material this meaty. Only one-dimensional scripts need camouflaging with flashy gimmicks. Visually, and in detail, and in nearly everything he does with people, I think it is his finest movie. A few people have complained to me that they feel the film is too long. It does move slowly, but even its occasional monotony is used to good advantage. Boredom is part of the Lesbian life, too. And I can't think of a single shot I'd sacrifice.

As for the actors, they are all but unimprovable. Susannah York, as the feminine, insecure, doll-playing Childie, has the petulant, flower-nibbling quality of a vagrant orphan. Coral Browne, a majestically creative and almost always badly used actress, gets her first good role in years in films, as the crusty, dignified lady from the BBC whose unpleasant duty it is to inform Sister George she is being killed off in the soap opera ("We're doing everything to show it's the lorry's fault"), while doing a little seduction job of her own with George's flatmate on the side. Miss Browne is a svelte, calculating, upper-class cobra, a kind of Jeanmaire with fangs.

Which brings me to the impossible task of attempting to give some indication of how good Beryl Reid is. She simply *is* George: funny as a top banana at the Palladium in her Oliver Hardy drag, puffing her cigar with hot, desperate, parched little breaths. When she sits in a chair, her bottom makes blunt little thuds through her pleated tweeds. Screaming out in helpless, defenseless humiliation, she is heartbreaking. Like most great comics, she never pushes the character into caricature. She is tough, mean, jealous, and selfish, but she never becomes sad, depressing or a truckdriver stereotype. And there is always the sense of humor that makes her a sympathetic character. ("Not all girls are raving bloody Lesbians, you know," yells Miss York at one point; "That," sighs Miss Reid in one of the great comic takes of the era, "is a misfortune I'm well aware of.") When she works for a laugh, she constructs and plays her line by cruelly controlled degrees, bringing the audience up the ladder to the top rung, then shaking it down with a collision of finely timed nuances. It's a lusty, brawling, brilliant performance. And between the heart of the giddy, proud, nasty little character she plays and the screen that reflects it, she establishes an interplay, a rapturous splendor, of the disciplined energy that is art.

March 1969

Trying to make a movie out of Chekhov is a job for masochists, which says something, I suppose, for Sidney Lumet, who has tried it with *The Sea Gull*. It's a slow, restless movie about boredom and the challenge, it seems to me, is to keep it from turning into the very thing it is about. Lumet is a good enough director to almost pull it off, but eventually his adoration of Chekhov (and what I feel basically is the built-in resistance in Chekhov's work to the film medium) gets the best of him. One should go away from Chekhov (if one must go at all) stuffed with shashlik. I left Mr. Lumet's film as though it were a Chinese dinner—it was temporarily satisfying, but it didn't stick to the ribs, and it wore off too soon.

"Hurry up, we're half asleep already," yawned Simone Signoret not ten minutes after the film began, and I was forced to take her literally. Lumet has not permitted his bored, disillusioned, selfish characters to become pitiable grotesques, the way they often do in British repertory, but he has not made them very Russian, either. Since they are played largely by British actors, they act more like English eccentrics than coarsened and insignificant Russian country gentry. The film is beautifully directed and photographed, in an abundance of vigorous fresh air and clean raw sunlight, but since Lumet shot his movie on location on a lake near Stockholm, the whole thing looks more like *Elvira Madigan* than the world of Chekhov.

Several critics have complained that the highly impressive cast doesn't seem to do much ensemble playing. With a wide range of acting styles extending from the very underground French toughness of Simone Signoret to the very American Actors' Studio method of Kathleen Widdoes, it is impossible to accuse the cast of a similarity in acting techniques. But I remember reading once an observation by someone—Peter Ustinov, I believe—that teamwork and Chekhov are, in acting terms, incompatible. I agree. And here is where Lumet has triumphed. He has used closeups to isolate his characters from each other and emphasize their deafness and blindness to the world outside their own suffocated, unfulfilled egos. The very theme is estrangement; every character is in love with someone else. A hand kiss is as far as anyone gets to another's soul. This is typified in one finely executed moment when Miss Signoret extends her hand to one admirer while being kissed on the cheek by another. An entire character analysis flashes across the faces of both suitors, but Miss Signoret doesn't even notice. The play is a sad symphony and Lumet has staged it in a mood of elegy, allowing the members of his elaborate cast to play their own solos, occasionally interrupting each other's monologues, but seldom listening to what anyone else is saying. The result (amazing, under the circumstances) is that nobody chews the scenery or steals the show from anyone else.

Miss Signoret tries. Her quiet, large face, with its prehensile lips and Gioconda smile, makes word pictures even when other actors are speaking. She has several lovely moments, especially one in which she lies in a hammock eating grapes in a great fluff of lemon chiffon, informing the others she is fond of them but they bore her silly. She is selfish, foul-tempered, shrewd, bitchy, and marvelous. She is also hopelessly miscast, but it hardly ever becomes noticeable.

I also liked Kathleen Widdoes, as the miserable, destroyed Masha, hopelessly in love with the wrong kind of man. Shrieking her lines in desperate, beak-like movements, later answering people curtly, half-throwing away her lines in a tired, unhappy exhaustion, she is the epitome of the girl of every age for whom life has been a supreme swindle. Miss Widdoes is a glowingly beautiful actress who seems to work well under Lumet's baton (she was Helena in his film *The Group*). In *The Sea Gull*, her Masha is played with more colors, subtleties, and shadings than I have ever seen it played before. She almost steals the picture.

It's the British actors who are all hopeless (except for Alfred Lynch, another vastly underrated actor, who squeezes several hundred more nuances out of the role of Miss Widdoes's unloved husband than it deserves). Where the Russians act with their lives, English actors act with their mellifluous voices. Stanislavski often made his actors act without *any* words, to be certain that their faces and bodies were doing their work as well. Surely David Warner, as Konstantin, is all voice and little else. He seems bloodless as a celery stalk and looks, with his pimples and hippie hair, like a rock and roll singer. Harry Andrews huffs and puffs a great deal as Miss Signoret's elderly brother who finally succumbs to old age and senility, but he infects the part with much the same intolerable mumbling and inaudibility that kept me from understanding him in another Lumet film, *The Hill.* He is a strong actor, but unintelligible. Eileen Herlie is wasted as Miss Widdoes's mother and Ronald Radd, as her husband, plays a bore boringly. To play a writer with no talent and no ambition who is irresistible to women, I could have thought of a more appealing physical type than the bland James Mason for the role of Trigorin. And I got a fit of yawns while Vanessa Redgrave, in one of her nostril-flaring closeups (painfully reminiscent of *Camelot*), was learning to be a woman scorned by too many clouts on the chin by life. She is the oldest eighteen-year-old Nina I've ever seen and most of her work in the role—sprinkled with more nail-biting, hair-pulling, throat-clutching mannerisms than most method actors ever dreamed of—looks annoyingly like an audition for the role of Isadora Duncan.

Finally, all that soul-searching, all that unrequited breast-beating, all that self-revelation of the insignificance of the individual, left me disturbed and unfulfilled. I went to see Chekhov, and I got Katherine Mansfield instead.

Also playing:

The Birthday Party. A good stage-to-screen transition by Harold Pinter, whose work is difficult to perform in either medium. I don't agree with Judith Crist, who thinks it "brings pure Pinter to film audiences for the first time in purely cinematic terms"; *The Servant* is a far superior film. Yet credit is due to director William Friedkin for holding an audience's interest with a movie taking place in only one room without resorting to the annoying use of flashbacks, and to the excellent performances of Robert Shaw, Patrick Magee (the Marquis de Sade in *Marat/Sade*), Sidney Tafler, and others, who make deceptive hum-drum externals throb with lurking terrors and the menaces hidden in the pauses of everyday conversation. Like most allegories, *The Birthday Party* is a difficult film to understand (I once read that Pinter originally intended it to have 249 meanings), yet it is unlikely to leave anyone cold.

Oliver! I cannot take *Oliver!* very seriously, either as sugarplum fantasy or as a tickle in the ribs of Charles Dickens, though I imagine were he here, he'd let out one helluva howl—of rage, not laughter. Still, it's harmless enough, and rather nice to look at. John Box, who designed *Lawrence of Arabia* and *Doctor Zhivago*, has literally reconstructed nineteenth-century London in a dazzling but realistic array of architectural splendor, with such an eye for detail you can almost smell the cabbage leaves and horse dung under the carriage wheels. The workhouse sets and the Cheapside docks are especially well-structured. Oswald Morris, whose photography turned Zeffirelli's *The Taming of the Shrew* into a Renaissance painting, has framed each shot with an eye for easing masses of people through his lens with ease and naturalness. Sir Carol Reed has filled the streets with high-stepping fishwives and clog-hopping bobbies, whirling vendors, and marching Queen's Guards, and so many dancing butchers whirling in white aprons that they resemble powdered sugar carousel horses. Shimmering green parks become ablaze with girls in bright pinafores and boys in baby-blue smocks, and Bloomsbury never beamed so glossily birthday-cake white.

There is so much distraction that it becomes easy to overlook the outrageous high-school thespian play scene-chewing of Ron Moody, the most Jewish Fagin this side of the Anderson Yiddish Theatre on lower Second Avenue, and difficult to detect the almost total lack of versatility behind the sky blue eyes of Mark Lester, as the most photogenic Oliver Twist I've ever seen. Lionel Bart's score is lumpy, tired, and not very good, but there is good work by Shani Wallis as a show-stopping Nancy, Jack Wild as an Artful Dodger good enough to make me forget Anthony Newley in the part, Oliver Reed as about as evil and vicious a villain as you could ever conjure from a cauldron, and a battered old curmudgeon of a dog named Bullseye, who steals the picture with the damnedest performance by anything with four legs I've seen on the screen since Flicka played a neurotic colt in love with Roddy McDowall.

Mayerling. It seems incredible that anyone living in the exotic turbulence of 1969 would spend several million dollars remaking something as corny and sentimental and old-fashioned as this dreary love-and-suicide saga of poor, doomed Prince Rudolf and seventeen-year-old Baroness Maria Vetsera, but

Terence Young seems to have a directorial flair for self-destruction. This treacle, set to temple-pounding Khachaturian music, is so corny it looks like it came out of a vault. Emperor Franz-Joseph (James Mason) peers sadly at Austrian dragoons fighting in the streets of Vienna: "So we've come to this." That lovable, misunderstood youth Crown Prince Rudolf, heir to the Hapsburg throne, worries about the insanity of his relative Ludwig, declines a rose, and desperately eyes his future: "I've tried politics, gambling —I'm not interested in young men—no, I'm afraid the prince must resign himself to boredom." Finally he meets true love, forbidden by the court. They embrace. "Oh, if only you were not a Hapsburg prince!" she says. All to the accompaniment of enough gold leaf to refurbish the Louvre, quaint ski lodges like Grandma Moses Christmas cards, cotillion balls, pheasant hunts, a ballroom waltz that is a direct steal from Vincente Minnelli's *Madame Bovary*, and enough zither music and shots of candlesticks photographed through lace to drive you stark-raving mad. The acting is so terrible you need subtitles, especially when Catherine Deneuve is on the screen. She's no Danielle Darrieux, who played the baroness in the 1936 film version with an incandescent glow. But then Omar Sharif, as Rudolf, is no Charles Boyer, either. The best thing about *Mayerling* is the brief appearance of Ava Gardner, who plays the sixty-year-old mother of Sharif with the kind of magic and mystery appropriate for the most illustrious woman in 1888. She resembles a bruised flower now, but she gives the only interesting performance in a film which, without her presence, would be stagnant as a swamp.

Candy. To merely call this repulsive, talentless little 42nd Street peep show the worst picture of the year would be philanthropic. Just call it the worst picture ever made.

April 1969

I must be getting old. I can remember a time when I loved musicals. I even sat through *Pagan Love Song* twice, just to see Esther Williams sing "Sea of the Moon" to Howard Keel. But the glamour has worn off. My tolerance level gets lower and lower each year. Perhaps this is the price one pays for the loss of innocence, but I don't think so. I think I'm getting tired of movie musicals because they just aren't fun any more. Either they look old and tired and down-in-the-lip (Streisand wails her way through a torch song at the end of *Funny Girl* and her fans all yell, but Ann Blyth already played the scene in *The Helen Morgan Story*, and, before that, Judy Garland in *A Star Is Born*) or they're boring and pretentious, like *Sweet Charity*, which is going around announcing itself as "the musical of the 70's." Whatever that is supposed to mean, don't believe it. *Sweet Charity* is the worst-photographed musical I've ever seen; aside from that, it's just plain awful.

Why? If anyone should know how to make a big, splashy, expensive musical, Bob Fosse is the man. He leaped and jitterbugged and boyishly grinned his way through lots of old MGM musicals like *Kiss Me Kate* and *Give a Girl a Break*, then fled to Broadway, married Gwen Verdon, and choreographed all of her greatest successes. Mr. Fosse knows his apples. He has no right to invest so much time and money in turning out a disaster, yet *Sweet Charity* is the kind of platinum clinker designed to send audiences flying in the opposite direction, toward the safety of their television sets. At least you can watch TV without becoming myopic.

I may be wrong, but it looks to me like Mr. Fosse is as tired of musicals as I am. So he has avoided all the old MGM sound stage clichés and hired a cameraman who, by treating his camera like a Gatling gun and ramming all the new gimmicks he just learned in the last Richard Lester movie down his audience's throat, has regrettably coined a few clichés of his own. The camera in this movie is so damned busy—moving around, zooming in and out of staircase bannisters, scaling up and down the sides of walls and able to leap tall buildings at a single bound—it's enough to send you right out of the theater to throw up. (The man to blame is Robert Surtees, who shot *The Graduate* and now seems drunk on his own perfume.)

In addition to the lousy camera work—so intolerable and blurry I found myself looking away from the screen more often than I was looking *at* it, just to avoid getting airsick—there are other problems. For one thing, the story itself, which has never been more than a lemon twist to begin with. As well as I remember, it began in 1952, when Fellini developed the role of a friendly, plucky little prostitute named Cabiria for his wife Giulietta Masina to play in a tiny scene in *The White Sheik*. She was so brilliant in it, that Fellini expanded the role into the memorable classic, *Nights of Cabiria*, in 1957. By the time Cabiria got to Broadway a few seasons ago, her name had been changed to Charity Hope Valentine, her producers had cleaned her up for the matinee ladies by making her a taxi dancer in a Broadway saloon (if only they knew!), and she was made immortal by the electrifying Gwen Verdon. She never amounted to anything more on paper than a cardboard cutout of a shabby broad who "runs her heart like a hotel, with guys checking in and out all the time." But in the hands of Masina and Verdon, two once-in-a-lifetime performers touched by a stroke of genius, the whore with a heart of gold became a legend.

In the hands of Shirley MacLaine, she's all silverplate. I like Miss MacLaine, but one thing is certain: she's not touched by a stroke of genius. She is not a great actress, she dances only adequately, and her singing voice is pleasant without any trace of power or presence. So to make up for all these deficits in a role that requires an encompassing knowledge of polished technique, Miss MacLaine knocks herself out in a series of movements all invented for Gwen Verdon. She knocks herself dead crawling into cars with her umbrella wide open, falling into lakes, crushing top hats between her knees, and folding her body into the inside of a tire. Suggestions of the fabulous Gwen Verdon are everywhere in her performance, in her kooky speech patterns, in her attempt at vocal characterization, in her walk, in her delivery of lines. Miss Verdon was even on the set trying to teach Miss MacLaine all of her old dance steps. But where Verdon brought tears to the eyes, MacLaine merely tests the endurance. She's all muscle and no heart. Frankly, I think she's too intelligent for the part. She's too on top of every situation, too feet on the ground, to be believable in the gullible dumb broad roles Betty Garrett and Vivien Blaine used to play She's tacky and tough, but just in case Mr. Fosse forgot to mention it to her, the role requires vulnerability.

The strangest thing about *Sweet Charity* is the way Fosse has become his own worst enemy. As a choreographer, he has designed dance movements that are innovational and clever, depending on a finely timed coordination of arms, torso, and hands with difficult staccato movements of the legs and feet. It's the kind of dancing Gwen Verdon does better than anyone else in the world. But Fosse has photographed his own dance numbers in such an annoying clutter of closeups that you seldom ever see the feet. He's thrown in one rooftop bit with Chita Rivera, Paula Kelly, and MacLaine that looks like a direct steal from *West Side Story*, and introduced Sammy Davis Jr. into a rock-gospel song that has energy but has nothing whatever to do with the movie. Then he tried to give the "Rich Man's Frug" number an aura of chic by turning the screen into different colors, but it all looks like a Las Vegas hotel lobby with people in pink and green wigs against phony marble statues, phony marble floors, and a flaming red backdrop. And finally, when it appears that he simply can't think of anything else to do, he exposes the negative and makes the whirling dancers look like moving X-rays.

One bright spot is John McMartin, as Charity's claustrophobic, Square City boyfriend. But in the final analysis, the ghost of Gwen Verdon hovers over everything about this clumsy, distracting, noisy excuse for entertainment. It's a shame, because *Sweet Charity* needs blood in its veins, not bats in its belfry.

The Hellfighters is the kind of movie in which John Wayne sets off several tons of dynamite to what sounds like the sound track of an old Vera Hruba Ralston movie, while his womenfolk all sit around in ugly hotel rooms with ugly paintings on the walls wearing ugly Edith Head dresses and looking bored. It seems pretty unbelievable to me that in this very advanced technological age a big Hollywood studio like Universal could still find an audience for a movie like *The Hellfighters*, but then this is the same studio that made Francis the Mule talk, so nothing should surprise me. They also tell me that some people still go to drive-in movies, where John Wayne pictures make a lot of money. That sounds logical. You can turn off the sound in drive-in movies.

Hell in the Pacific, a sober little duet about an American and a Japanese stranded on a deserted island during the war who must either join forces or die of starvation and loneliness, is really nothing much, I suppose, when you get right down to it. But John Boorman is one of the few really unique directors now working in films with a truly personal style. I love what he does, for example, with rain. And I was very impressed by the ease with which he builds tensions, then relaxes them in a tightly constricted space, using only two actors and an economically structured script. And, of course, it is always a pleasure to watch Toshiro Mifune in action.

Of all the pictures I've seen lately, I most enjoyed and most highly recommend *The Prime of Miss Jean Brodie*. Muriel Spark's novel about a vain, ridiculous, but powerfully influential Edinburgh schoolteacher in 1932 was a hit play in London with Vanessa Redgrave, a hit play in New York with Zoe Caldwell, and now a haunting, lyrical film with one of the most magnificent screen performances in the history of the medium by Maggie Smith. Words could never do justice to her work, to the skill and wit and sureness with which she nibbles and sips away the role of a passionate spinster driven to the brink of destruction by her own frustrations, but sitting there, staring incredulously, I found no need for words at all. Jay Presson Allen's screenplay is droll and poignant; Robert Stephens, Celia Johnson, Pamela Franklin, and a regiment of British theatrical royalty lend shrewd, touching, masterful support to their leading lady; Ronald Neame's direction is sturdy and quiet and perfectly within the meter of the film's established rhyme. But it is Maggie Smith who takes the film into the realm of immortality. Dedicated to her young charges in the prime of her life, she makes her impressionable subjects weep with tales of lovers fallen like autumn leaves on the battlefield in Flanders, feeds them pâté de foie gras *al fresco* while the others must saw their tough roast beef in the mess hall, spouts Fascist philosophy, and teaches them if they must eat sweets to at least cultivate a taste for the favorite sweet of the little Princess Margaret Rose.

Maggie Smith extends her forefinger to test the temperature, tilts her head like a tea cup on the edge of its saucer, and gently lifts her eyebrows in a masterpiece of character analysis most actresses twice her age take twenty years to master. Her face is a walking thousand-page novel. In her trust, dialogue becomes history. I have never seen anyone quite like her. In her subtlety, in her every nuance, in the way in which she can paralyze the screen by wrapping it in the timeless frozen space of a momentary smile, and in everything else she does, I must confess that I find her quite the most extraordinary actress to hit the screen since Kim Stanley in *The Goddess*. If critics could give Oscars, she would already have one from me.

May 1969

One of the very early lessons one learns about the movies is that great directors do not always make great movies. New films by four sacred cows—Luis Buñuel, Orson Welles, François Truffaut, and Jean-Luc Godard—are making the more selective rounds this month to prove the point. Of the four directors, Godard is my least favorite, yet his new one is the best of the lot. Buñuel never disappoints, Welles is showing signs of senility, and Truffaut has let me down with such a thud I'll get to him last.

After *Weekend,* I had serious doubts whether I'd ever sit through another Godard movie. Anyone who mistakes that phony, pretentious excuse for social comment as serious filmmaking is merely kidding himself. It was socially irresponsible, cinematically useless, politically simple-minded, and artistically banal. Worse, it was boring. But Godard just won't stay written off. *Pierrot le Fou* saves face. In all fairness, I must admit I first saw it in 1965 at the Venice Film Festival. It's not new. But it washes away the bad taste left by *Weekend* and it's a lot of fun.

Pierrot le Fou is a New Wave picnic, with Jean Paul Belmondo and Anna Karina as the ants. As a movie, it may not be much, but as a picnic . . . *formidable!* The plot? Nothing you should worry about. It is, after all, a Godard film. As such, it is filled with the usual Godard cynicisms about self-defeat and the destruction of the innocent in modern society; the Godard trickeries (while a TV set blares news of Vietnam, there is a closeup of the red "SS" portion of an American ESSO sign); and the Godard private jokes (Belmondo insults an American film director, who turns out to be Samuel Fuller). It is possible, as with all Godard films, to argue just whose movies and just which ideas from *Cahiers du Cinéma* have been borrowed to make up the whole. But one thing is certain—it would not be the *same* film without Belmondo.

It is *his* sandbox and Godard has allowed him to wallow audaciously in it in fruity, sun-ripened technicolor: Belmondo takes a bath *au naturel.* Belmondo does a Gene Kelly musical number on a deserted beach. Belmondo smashes a cake in a girl's face. Belmondo smokes a sad cigarette in bed, his head resting on a Picasso clown. Belmondo drives a Ford Galaxie convertible into the ocean. Belmondo faces center screen and reads Robert Browning to the audience with a parrot on his shoulder, Robinson Crusoe-style. Belmondo pours a drink on a naked woman at a naked cocktail party. Belmondo impersonates Michel Simon and Humphrey Bogart. Belmondo asks a garage attendant to "put a tiger in my tank." Belmondo spends the night with a girl only to wake up the next morning with a corpse. His audience cheers. He is once again the Belmondo his fans have come to expect—the innocent, tough little grease monkey in the wrinkled seersucker suit, the twentieth-century Harlequin saving the bad, rouge-cheeked Columbine from the gangsters with the walkie-talkies and driving the getaway car while the soundtrack grinds out music from old Republic "Boston Blackie" serials.

Godard has directed all of this movie buff *shtick* in the lemony sunshine south of St. Tropez with tongue planted firmly in cheek and valentines in his eyes. Anna Karina, Godard's ex-wife, who showed up quite badly in *The Magus* recently, deserves a special encomium: left alone and directed with affection, she is one of those rare combinations of lithe, passionate corruption and garden-party naïveté that come along once every few light years to ignite the screen. She has a frail toughness and eyes with a sad liquid brilliance. She is like a sexy lollipop.

As for Belmondo, he is one of the few men since Bogart who can really make both men and women *care*. If there is any such thing as pop art in the year 2000, Belmondo is certain to be its champion. A French Batman, he is a dream for movie masochists, and *Pierrot le Fou* is exquisitely styled, highly recommended torture.

The films of seventy-year-old Luis Buñuel have always seemed to me like big black sores, festering with sacrilegious pungency and erupting, eventually, with the core of some basic, hateful truth about the stupidity of man in a world of false idolatry. *Simon of the Desert*, like Buñuel's *Viridiana*, is shocking and restless, but it is also monstrously, wickedly funny in a way no American film has ever dared to be.

Buñuel takes his inspiration from Simon Stylites, the fifth-century monk who withdrew from the world to commune with God on top of a column in the middle of the desert. There he performs miracles that evoke the bad temper of a nasty, unappreciative lot, including a man whose hands, chopped off at the wrists, are restored; an inevitable, grieving mother; the Devil in the form of a temptress; some mad monks; and a dwarf goatherd—all representing superstition, mental blindness, ingratitude, evil, and worldly vice. Despite his prayers, the people just won't leave poor Simon alone. A jet-propelled coffin slides up through the desert sand by remote control and out pops a beautiful girl who bares her breasts into the camera, then suddenly changes into a wrinkled, stark naked old hag. Again, a hermaphrodite with beard, breasts, and a girl's voice brings Simon a baby lamb, in true New Testament style, then kicks it away. "Cut the crap," she shrieks, as Simon raises his head in prayer.

Finally it's simply too much, even for a fifth-century monk, and Simon is carried away by the hermaphrodite in a jet plane to Greenwich Village where, in the final shot, he (and the audience) is trapped in the center of ear-splitting trumpets, turtle-neck sweatered beatniks, and frugging nymphets in that modern-day equivalent to Hell on Earth: the discotheque.

The best thing about Simon, which was unveiled to a large ovation at both the Venice and New York film festivals, is that it is only forty-two minutes long, barely time for a Sunday school lesson. Time enough, however, for Buñuel to acidly sniff at religion, and expose us to seeds of vice and corruption spanning several centuries. The style is abrupt, the manner impolite. The effect is wildly, irreverantly, satanically memorable.

Orson Welles's *Immortal Story,* is also short. It runs sixty-three minutes, which, by my watch, is an hour too long. This screeching fiasco is supposed to be an Isak Dinesen tale about the wealthy Macao merchant who, having heard the one about the sailor and the elegant lady once too often, sets out to make it come true. Somewhere along the way, Isak Dinesen gives way to massive overdoses of Wellesian ego; nowhere along the way does anything of any interest happen. Welles seems unable to do anything these days unless he relates everything and everybody to his own selfish and tortured excessiveness. He belches, he mumbles, he upstages everyone, he chews on his tongue in monosyllabic gibberish. It's all very embarrassing. The film is photographed, quite curiously, in shades of putrid green. Like the insides of Greyhound buses.

François Truffaut's new film, *Stolen Kisses,* is a weak, watery little trifle, another of those tiresome "young dropout trying to get laid" movies I thought we were all well rid of. It is soft, sentimental, and tender, but the vigor and sting of Truffaut's earlier films is sadly missing. I'd almost prefer him cold and detached, as in *Fahrenheit 451,* to syrupy and sappy.

Remember the final shot of *The 400 Blows?* The tough little socially rejected adolescent named Antoine Doinel, pushed to the edge of his sanity, found himself on the shore, his eyes darting out to sea and back to land, where society was waiting. The camera froze into a still photograph and critics scurried to their psychology primers, searching for explanations. Stanley Kauffmann, I remember in particular, even went so far as to suggest that this final shot in Truffaut's quasi-autobiographical film reflected in the child's face a prediction of his own suicide. Well, rest easy. In *Stolen Kisses,* Doinel is back, and once again he is played by the charming young actor Jean-Pierre Léaud. Trouble is, Truffaut has turned him into a kind of Left Bank Dustin Hoffman. The desperation and the sensitivity have been replaced by a faddish stumblebum freakishness that actors like Hoffman have made fashionable. (There is simply no way of estimating the disastrous influence *The Graduate* has had on movies here and abroad.) We are suddenly asked to forget all about *The 400 Blows,* one of the greatest movies ever made, and invest new interest in the kind of nebbish Truffaut has turned it's tough young antihero into. I don't buy it. When will the movie directors of the world learn that people are simply not interested in the loss of anyone's virginity except their own?

Also playing:

You Don't Need Pajamas at Rosie's. Great title, but certainly the only great thing about this otherwise brainless bit of trivia about three American high school kids trying to get laid in Buffalo. The acting is right out of old *Ozzie and Harriet* ("Hi, David!" "Hi, Ricky!"); the direction is aimless and uninteresting, with ample time out for a bit of sightseeing at Niagara Falls ("Hey you guys—look! The Maid of the Mist!"); and the script is full of silly sight gags (dressed in a raincoat, one of the guys stands next to a tourist near the Falls and gets mistaken for his wife). Finally they meet up with Jacqueline Bisset, the stunning, delightful actress from *Bullit,* and mistake her for a prostitute. Summoning their masculinity, they hang around the Coke machine a lot "for quick energy" and inspect their teeth in the men's room mirror. Guess who gets the broad? Right. The sensitive, thoughtful one. ("Every young man must have his fill of conquests before he really loves," she says, touching him gently on the edge of the bed in a script manipulation more than a little reminiscent of the third-act curtain in *Tea and Sympathy.*) It's a terrible movie, but the kids are so cornily old-fashioned in their naïveté that, next to the perverted creeps in movies like *Three in the Attic*, they're almost refreshing. It's Disney with dirty jokes. (At press time, the word was out: the title had been changed to—get this for originality—*The First Time.* Now I can't even think of *one* good reason to see it.)

Support Your Local Sheriff. A cracker barrel of marvelous character actors (Henry Jones, Walter Brennan, Harry Morgan, Jack Elam, Kathleen Freeman) invest this lusty, roaring, brawling spoof of the old shoot-em-ups with more charm than mayhem. Without the use of gags or one-liners or flashy camera gimmicks, Director Burt Kennedy has produced a really delightful movie in which the comedy comes from within the context of keenly painted character portraits instead of pies in the face. Joan Hackett, as an accident-prone tomboy, is like Calamity Jane photographed by *Harper's Bazaar.*

I am Curious—Yellow. Wanna bet?

June 1969

Movies for children. There's a subject which, in recent months, has filled my mailbox with angry protests from disgruntled parents. Motion pictures, they accuse, are shirking a responsibility to the young. They are right, of course, but it all depends on what your definition of *young* really is. If young means immature, you are dead wrong. Hollywood studios (and the Disney people in particular) grind out flicks for the immature and unimaginative child with disturbing frequency. It's as though they are trying to unload one last shipment of hoola hoops before the only remaining bastion of under-twelve consumers finds out they're already out of style. (Kids are not so dumb; I have yet to meet a single child who actually enjoyed *Dr. Dolittle.*) If, on the other hand, *young* means joyous, innocent, still too inexperienced at the routine, the mundane, the *business* of life to be jaded by it, then movies can still be a rapturous thing. With summer coming on, children home from school, and family pictures breaking out around the country like a strawberry rash, it seems like a good time to examine the complaint.

An otter named Mij and a horse named Philip are the stars of two new films from England that may not quite compete with the financial grosses of the latest pornographic films from Sweden, but which I heartily recommend to anyone who prefers the beauty of animals to the paranoia of people. In *Ring of Bright Water* the ingratiating British actor, Bill Travers, plays a gentle, good-natured fellow at odds with mechanized society. After the usual establishment shots of IBM machines and files of code numbers (getting out of the way immediately the idea that the city is no place to live the good life), Mr. Travers discovers he has been computerized by his own computer. With the future robbed of all possibilities for surprise or change (what's to discover, when IBM computers of the world already know everything there is to know about us?), and generally dull as hell, he starts to worry. He becomes intrigued with an otter in a pet shop window who looks as caged and forlorn as he does, and after overhearing a plan to use his buddy in a circus act, he takes him home, where he discovers that otters are no better at fighting the London housing problem than sensitive young white collar workers (God knows how they'd survive in the New York fallout). After a series of almost too self-consciously cute assaults on Mr. Travers's flat, everything got so stagy that I was beginning to hate myself for even going to see a movie about an otter in the first place. But *Ring of Bright Water* really gets going when Mr. Travers purchases a dilapidated eighteenth-century cottage sagging into the sea on the Scottish coast. For anyone who has ever had any regard for beachcombing as a way of life, the movie is pure joy. The peaceful retreat offered by this pastoral Robert Burns landscape is a restful experience, with the surrounding fields, streams, and beaches becoming a symphony of muted backdrops against which the basic story unwinds. Jack Couffer, who directed some of the better Disney wildlife films (*The Incredible Journey, Legend of Lobo*), as well as a few of the sequences in *The Living Desert*, has added enough feeling for weather and light and space to make it more than just a routine kiddie programmer.

In addition to directing, he has co-authored the screenplay with Mr. Travers. As a team, their proper insertion of details in the lives of animals and a keen awareness of the peculiarities and problems of animals have given the creatures hilarious and very moving personalities. Most films about animals seem to think they can touch an audience by simply photographing their subjects in a series of natural movements. It's not enough. There has to be love.

Mr. Travers and his wife, Virginia McKenna, are two performers who obviously love animals as much as I do. They proved it by devoting several years to the making of *Born Free*, which was, in my estimation, a masterpiece of rare and human splendor, and they prove it again in *Ring of Bright Water*. Miss McKenna plays a village doctor who shares Mr. Travers's interest in and affection for animals and, of course, they fall in love. I didn't mind this sentimental touch, although I did find the characters pretty unbelievably naïve. (They never even kiss.)

The best scenes in the movie involve the animals and I cannot imagine a child of perception and gentility who will not be dazzled by the sight of a shark expedition in a small canoe, or the scene in which Mr. Travers tries to teach four earthbound baby geese how to fly. There is wonderful stuff of the same baby geese whose mother has been shot down by poachers, trained by instinct to follow anything that looks like a grownup mother goose, even if it's an otter. In the supporting cast, there are wonderfully scruffy dogs, vicious swans whose beaks can break an arm or pluck out an eye calmed by Miss McKenna's rapport and sympathy as she frees their baby cygnets from the brambles, and the most lovable assemblage of otters young and old ever viewed by man or beast. What very little story there is, is pretty forgettable. But *Ring of Bright Water* is one of the most enchanting works of natural wonder I've ever seen. I expect to see it again, for that matter.

I do not expect to see *Philip* again, but in spite of its obvious weaknesses, I rather enjoyed it while I was there. When I saw it, it was called *The White Colt*, a title that made very good sense at the time, since it was about a white colt. But movie studios have their own scatterbrained reasons for monkeying around with the titles of their films and attempts to analyze their self-destructive foolhardiness have been made in vain by wiser men than I. Perhaps *The White Colt* sounded too much like Steinbeck's *The Red Pony*. (Both films contain scenes with horses and birds, but the resemblance, I assure you, ends right there.) The film's name was changed to *Philip*, which is rather confusing, since the white colt as well as the leading character, a retarded child who cannot speak for some mysterious reason, are both named Philip and you never know whether the other people in the picture are calling the child or the horse.

There is very little dialogue in this picture, which helps, since the only time it really falls apart is when the human beings get in the way of the animals. You may also safely assume that with very little dialogue there is very little plot. What there is involves the raw-boned, good-but-dense parents (Sylvia Syms and Gordon Jackson) of a beautiful-but-dense child (played vacuously by Mark Lester, the blue-eyed, petulant dumpling from *Oliver!*) and the likable country gentry who inhabit the bleak and swollen moors of England. Almost all of them (except for John Mills, who, I am convinced, can play *anything*) are totally one-dimensional, especially the children, who stare blankly a good deal of the time and indulge in the simplest emotional reactions to life and nature.

The nature is much more interesting. There are some fine shots of the moors, heaving and bursting with life in the spring, and the animals are friendly and engaging, especially a raffish little falcon named Lady. The colt is a blue-eyed, flour-white stallion who looks drugged in a couple of scenes but who would probably do wonders for the role of Pegasus. When the horses and the birds are doing their thing, *Philip* has a bit of the power and excitement inherent in any good footage of wild and semiwild animals photographed in their natural ambiance. Unfortunately, they are not left alone very often. There is a lot of crying and gnashing of teeth and running away from home for no apparent reason, a pretentious theme song ("*The White Colt is waiting there to take you where your heart must go . . .*"), and entirely too much of that wild and rugged Heathcliff manipulation of young minds showing the boy leaping about through cold and foggy moors in slow motion, as though you just *know* he is going to grow up to be D. H. Lawrence.

Philip at times takes on the look of a *National Geographic* nature study. At other times, it more closely resembles one of those murkily lit British movies of the Forties with herds of wild horses lit by lightning in the fog of the moors while the London Philharmonic thrashed away in the background. Still, it's harmless enough as family entertainment, and some of it is even quite fascinating, which is more than I can say for most of the "G"-rated ("G" for garbage?) movies the kids are watching these days. And certainly several cuts above any of the so-called children's programs I've seen on television. And now *Philip* is being called *Run Silent, Run Free.* Figure that out.

I have no idea what the rating is on *Popi,* the new Alan Arkin picture, but I recommend it for children as well. There is one anxious moment in the film when Arkin, as a Puerto Rican widower faced with the problem of raising two small sons in the slum horrors of Harlem, sends the boys out to sea in a tottery skiff, hoping they will be picked up by the Coast Guard, mistaken for Cuban refugees, and relocated in a good home where they will taste the ambrosia of life. There's something rather rotten about the whole comic idea, and because the film is much too long, the joke wears thin long before its proper time. Like a hose with too many patches in it, comic passages stream through the second-rateness of it all, like water, without force or passion. Yet in its crude, blustering way, *Popi* says something about the invincibility of the human spirit, about what little boys mean to daddies, and vice versa. There are some sensible ideas at work here, executed with proper amounts of emotion, observation, and comic relief, which, hopefully, may stir more conscientious children to self-awareness. For those who just want a good yock, one shot of Arkin—as a busboy at the Hilton Ballroom pretending to yawn as an excuse to pop bits of leftover steak into his mouth from the plates of affluent New Yorkers—is distinctly first-class yockery. Pass the Worcestershire.

Smith! (with an exclamation point!) is the latest Disney opus, full of bright western sunsets, perky gingham skirts, good clean God-fearing folks who live on biscuits and strawberry jam and still go to Sunday school at the age of forty-five, and about as much depth as a nursery rhyme. Glenn Ford plays a Good Sam who befriends the local Indians to the recurring chagrin of his wife (Nancy Olson) and most of the local cops, a surly, bigoted lot whose running philosophy is "There are two ways you can get into trouble with Indians—if you try to hurt them or if you try to help them." But good, old lunkhearted Smith just can't resist when they call him "a big tree out in the grass when the sun is hot." Glenn Ford performs with a kind of club-footed aw-shucks naturalness and grace, but he is hopelessly adrift in a sea of corn.

The real story of the significant problems facing Indians who are treated like second-class citizens is an important one that the screen has never made anything but brief, squirmy little attempts to tell. *Smith!* doesn't even try. It is interesting only when an old heart-tugger named Chief Dan George, gnarled and windswept as a swampy cypress, is around to steal the picture. But the insulting thing about it is the caricature it paints of Indians as childlike, simple-minded creatures incapable of taking care of even their most basic needs. They are depicted as funny, dark-skinned children, buying Cadillacs and driving them into a lake, deserting their hay-mowing contracts to attend a local trial, and always trying to find an easy way to film-flam someone out of a fast buck. Somebody should teach Indians how to sue.

Hello Down There promises (*threatens* is a better word) to give children's movies a dirty name. I hesitate to even mention it, except to suggest that if you are interested in knowing which films to keep children *away* from, this one can top your list. Tiny minds with even the mildest curiosity will doubtlessly be bored to death in this interminable saga of life in an underwater house. Tony Randall, Janet Leigh, and the most unattractive cluster of teen-age morons this side of Dick Clark's swimming pool look like they are posing for models of inanimate plastic families who rotate on stages through the prefabricated homes in Westinghouse exhibits. Co-starring are two dolphins and Merv Griffin, all three of whom act as though they are going to be rewarded any second with a cold sardine.

July 1969

I have long suspected that all that is wrong with movies today does not stem from Hollywood alone, and considering with dread the long hours of dreary, trashy, pretentious footage from Europe I've been forced to sit through lately, I'm convinced that much of what is still sane and entertaining about filmmaking today is still coming from American films in general. American movies are easier to put down than European films because so many foreign films are so phony and deliberately incomprehensible that we tend to think about them longer to work out the confusions. American movies are easier to understand, we convince ourselves, therefore less important. Such quick analysis often leads audiences and critics (and I'm one of the guiltiest) to an easy put-down of American movies that is often unfair and unwarranted. Some of the criticism, I must admit, is justified; when you sit through about four hundred movies a year, as I do, you learn the hard way that only about one out of every five is worth the eye-strain. The rest is all yesterday's warmed over mashed potatoes. But when something extraordinary comes along, it deserves recognition. This summer American filmmakers have come up with three movies—*Last Summer, Winning,* and *True Grit*—which are so good, so entertaining, and so thoughtful they prove my point.

Last Summer is the best movie I've seen this year. I'd even go so far as to say it's the most intelligent film about young people ever made. The respect I've had for director Frank Perry and his writer-wife Eleanor has, for some time, been boundless. Their adaptations of Truman Capote's short stories on television and their work in films (*David and Lisa,* and to a somewhat lesser degree, *Ladybug, Ladybug* and *The Swimmer*) have raised the quality of the mediums several notches in the direction of the kind of sound artistic achievement that is foreign to them both, but nothing they have ever done quite prepared me for the emotional impact of *Last Summer.* When I left the screening, I was so shaken I walked around for hours with my hands in my pockets, deeply troubled and quite visibly moved. Without ever becoming mawkish or sentimental, the Perrys have presented a mature vision of the cruel and complicated world of children that stirs the mind and pierces the heart.

As *Last Summer* begins, Dan and Peter, two average Joe Teen-agers, are walking along a deserted strip of private beach on Fire Island. They come across a ravishing, with-it girl named Sandy, who has just rescued an injured sea gull. The three kids take the gull back to the girl's summer beach house and administer first aid. They remove a swallowed fish-hook and feed it bouillon, and through the easy ambiance of their teen lingo and the mutual isolation of their teen world, a friendship develops. These are real kids. They have nothing to do with the dirty, freaked-out, totally manufactured teen-age creeps who inhabit the American-International flicks. They are children of the affluent middle class, the kids in the *Seven-*

teen ads, radiant and sun-kissed, indulged in everything except the true values of what life is all about. This is the last summer of their childhood, on the dawn of that terrifying autumnal descent into the world of college and the draft and responsibility in a society that isn't half as glamorous as it seems in TV commercials.

As the summer drifts lyrically along, through the beer parties and the "major truth" games in the dunes, leisure turns to boredom, friendship turns to love. Beneath the sunny surface laughter, a subdevelopment emerges about the darker side of human nature, the primeval urge to destroy, and finally, the death of innocence. Beneath the wit, intelligence, and sensitivity with which these extraordinary youngsters express their attitudes toward the Establishment and explore the problems facing youth today, an intangible bond of sensuality builds among them. The whole experience is like a *ménage à trois* of the mind.

Their relationship changes with the entrance into their tightly knit world of an "outsider" named Rhoda—a pudgy, vulnerable, freckle-faced girl from Cleveland who writes poetry for the school paper and serves as the embodiment of everything "square" the others detest. The film becomes a parable of modern society. How secure we all are until faced with something we don't understand. To the others, Rhoda wears funny bathing suits, doesn't like the bitter taste of beer, and has too much of a social conscience. To Rhoda, the others are cruel, unfeeling, spoiled brats. Still, there is no agony more brutal than the emotional need to belong when you are not accepted. Rhoda clings to their companionship out of desperate loneliness. Like Frankie Addams in *The Member of the Wedding*, she is an "I" person searching for a "we." The tortuous path this curious trio takes her on in this last summer before the end of their innocence leads to tragedy and violence that I guarantee will not fail to shake every serious-minded person concerned about what is happening to the youth of this country.

Eleanor Perry has written the kind of screenplay one rarely encounters in today's movies—the kind in which not a single moment rings false or settles for being anything less than brilliant. Frank Perry has photographed it all with such an unusual regard for color and space and light that even the spume of the surf is like foam on top of a chocolate soda. Fire Island becomes a bridge between two worlds, a landscape out of time, only occasionally disrupted by the heart-stopping reality of Rhoda's intrusion.

Barbara Hershey, Richard Thomas, Bruce Davison, and Cathy Burns, the four young actors who play the leads, were unknown to me when I saw the film, but like a finely integrated chamber quartet, they pulled me into the smallness of their nestlike atmosphere with a conviction and spontaneity unequalled in my memory. Miss Burns, the young actress who plays the lonely, unwanted Rhoda, is especially awesome in her ability to touch the heart of an audience. The strength of her acting makes the absolute *realness* of Rhoda's tragedy so much more heartbreaking, compared to the childishness of the others. At one point, the children play the vicious truth game. One boy admits the worst thing he ever did was to make "Ritz cracker sandwiches out of snot and cream cheese" and give them to his cousin. These sophisticated kids, raised around homosexuals and alcoholic parents, fall down laughing. Miss Burns looks at them, unflinching. They force her to join the game and reveal a truth about herself. Frank Perry's camera moves in like a poisonous snake ready to strike, preventing her from moving, as she tells about the time, after her mother drowned, when she spat on her grave because she had no right to die so foolishly. It is a long, demanding scene, during which the camera stays in there, capturing every tear, every catch in the throat, every tick in the eye, until you know everything there is to know about this girl and what it's like to be alone and on the stand, testifying for your right to your own corner of the world. In the acting, and in the writing and camerawork and cutting and sound and direction, and in what it says about the world we live in, *Last Summer* is a work of art.

Until I saw *Winning*, I would have stared suspiciously at anyone who suggested that someday I would find myself rhapsodizing over a movie about stock car racing. Without the presence of Paul Newman and Joanne Woodward, it might still be pretty ordinary, like some dreary Frankie Avalon–Annette Funicello dragstrip romance; with the inventiveness of their contributions to it, *Winning* becomes a lesson in how to turn a simple idea into an artistic triumph.

There isn't much plot. Racing champ meets girl who works for Avis Rent A Car. Sex rears its ugly head. Wedding bells. Girl's teen-age son flips over his new dad. Girl gets bored and goes to bed with champ's best friend. The marriage breaks up and the son is torn between the two parents. Everyone discovers out of loneliness that success and silver cups and getting your picture in the paper doesn't mean a thing if you've nobody at home to share it with. Champ and his girl get back together and they all live happily ever after.

There is absolutely nothing extraordinary in any of this, yet I found it to be one of the most gripping movies I've seen this season. Unlike the Burtons, the Newmans are one husband-and-wife team who really work. From the way Miss Woodward phones her mother and promises not to leave the Avis people in the lurch to the way Mr. Newman clumsily meets his new son for the first time to the way they share a beer in a garden swing, it is a beautiful thing to watch the Newmans build even the most minor moments into throbbing portraits of character analysis. They do not re-enact vignettes from life so much as they act life itself.

In James Goldstone, they have found a director who seems to understand the way they work and who has given them ample space to move around in. Everything is so beautifully cut and edited that even the click of a phone is timed to coincide with the slam of a car door. Not one moment of the film is wasted. Goldstone knows how to take his time with a scene, so that the film is very European in its tempo. Yet in spite of its slowness and its naturalism and almost, in fact, *because* of it, *Winning* becomes, in a funny kind of way, a movie of unbearable suspense. Mr. Goldstone is a director who knows exactly what he's doing. Like John Boorman, who made a stunning debut a few years ago by turning an ordinary gangster melodrama called *Point Blank* into a film of pulsating tension, Goldstone knows how to take mundane subject matter and give it a unique feel, a look all its own. (Which should make him quite valuable if he plans to continue working in Hollywood.)

If for no other reason, see *Winning* for the racing footage. There is one spectacularly gorgeous collage of action in which the Indianapolis speedway comes to life in the dark pre-dawn hours of a rainy day that is breathtaking. From the quiet tom-tom throbs of car headlights in the fog, the build and heat and tempo rises as the sun breaks through and the track becomes a crowded Mardi Gras of cheerleaders and drum majorettes and marching Purdue University bands and cops and lost babies and Good Year helmets and balloons rising to the sky. And beneath the Valvoline signs and the monkey wrenches and the silver trophies there's the actual stuff of human drama.

Energy of this sort is all too seldom combined to make good entertainment, and movies as entertaining as *Winning* do not turn up every day. I cannot find words to recommend it more highly.

True Grit is the first time I have ever seen the movies use John Wayne intelligently. Even under oath, I can scarcely imagine anyone testifying to his ability as an actor, yet it seems to me he has a great deal of natural vinegar and practically no interest or talent in finding the right directors to distill it. In this vigorous, brawny version of Charles Portis's novel, Big Duke plays a smelly, fat, one-eyed drunk named Rooster Cogburn with such a wild display of skinned knees and good-natured ham that he comes close to stealing the picture. I don't mean to suggest he is at last getting a chance to play himself, but it looks like he is having more fun as a character actor, which, let's face it, is the direction in which his age is taking him.

There are other likable things in *True Grit*: sturdy, no-nonsense direction by Henry Hathaway; a script with a wonderful regard for details such as a boardinghouse that makes cowboys check their spurs before sitting down to chicken and dumplings (the table legs are scratched enough already); judges who eat peppermints in court to settle their stomachs before a hanging; dialogue like "I was raised Episcopal"/"I figured you for some kinda kneeler"; and beautiful, sensitive color photography by Lucien Ballard, who shot *Will Penny* and who knows how to capture the American west the way it really looks. (Notice especially the winter scenes, shot in natural snow on the western slopes of the Rocky Mountains.)

But most of the credit for making *True Grit* more than just a routine western programmer belongs to Kim Darby, one of the few young actresses in American movies today worth building a movie around. Miss Darby plays Mattie Ross, the curiously emotionless adolescent whose relentless quest for her father's killer forms the plot, with an uncanny vividness and eloquence that suggested to me Jo March rewritten by Zane Grey.

August 1969

Never, it seems, have so many young Americans been so critical of their country. The creeping dissatisfaction with the Establishment way of telling it like it *isn't* has erupted in the streets, in the classrooms, and in the courts. It seemed inevitable that it would eventually find its way into the movies; I can only express gratitude that it should be Peter Fonda who spent the time and energy in getting it there. Occasionally, his sounds like the only voice in the crowd that knows why it's protesting.

At times, *Easy Rider*—the new film Peter has produced with the aid of his friend Dennis Hopper (who directed, from a script co-authored by Peter and Terry Southern)—looks like a nature study filmed on an opium trip. There is a lot of amateurish horsing around ("You ever wanna be somebody else?"/"I'd like to be Porky Pig"), scenes that don't mean anything to anyone except the participants, direction and camerawork still searching for a definitive style—but before it's half-over, the whole thing begins to grow on you like a barnacle. I couldn't shake what I'd seen, even after I left the darkness of the screening room and hit the harsh reality of sidewalk sunlight. By taking up where Kerouac and Lawrence Lipton and all the Holy Barbarians left off, Fonda and Hopper have produced the definitive youth odyssey of the 1960s. *Easy Rider* is an excruciating look at where this country is today. It's about as horrifying an indictment of America as I've ever seen in any medium, and certainly a bold, courageous statement of life seldom matched in motion pictures.

Fonda and Hopper are two motorcyclists who hustle drugs across the border to rich hippie businessmen (a new cultural phenomenon, in case you haven't noticed, on a rapid rise in the good old U.S.A.) in order to pay for a trip from Los Angeles to the New Orleans Mardi Gras. Money from drugs enables them to be free and live their own life-style without compromising to society. The whole point of the movie, it seems to me, is to expose that American backbone called the "grass roots" along the way, and to tell it true about how America has gone to seed in the process. *Easy Rider* does all of this brilliantly, but it also exposes the sad, desperate nothingness of people who live on the wind. The two cyclists come across a group of mad, pathetic flower children, like a coven of witches, living in tents in the wilderness. I wasn't sure whether I was supposed to dig their way of life or not, but they all seemed like inmates from some prehistoric asylum to me.

The real power in the film lies not in the way it tries to glorify hippies but in the way it turns over the rocks of apple-pie America and reveals the slime inherent in human nature. "You name it, I'll throw rocks at 'em, sheriff," snarls one Southern bigot when the boys stop at a roadside cafe for a hamburger. "They look like refugees from a gorilla love-in," observes one country wit. A local dude they pick up on the way (magnificently played by a wonderful actor named Jack Nicholson) tells them, "Oh, they're not scared of you, they're scared of what you represent to them . . . freedom. It's real hard to be free when you're bought and sold on the marketplace. But don't ever tell anybody they ain't free, 'cause they gonna get real busy killin' and maimin' to prove they *are*."

After their friend is clubbed to death in his sleeping bag by local hoods, the two cyclists know their odyssey is almost over. They reach New Orleans, pick up two prostitutes, and the film plunges headlong into an elaborate acid trip that is much more interesting if you don't separate Peter Fonda from the character he plays (at one point, he puts his arms around a marble statue in the Rampart Street Cemetery that strongly resembles Henry Fonda and ad-libs several truth questions like "Why did you leave me when I was little?", etc.). Where is the American Dream? They hit the road again, but Fonda says, "We blew it." Minutes later, two Louisiana red-necks pull alongside in a pickup truck and blow their heads off. The film closes with a long shot of the motorcycles burning in a pillar of fire on the peaceful green highway.

The argument has been made that if the two leading characters had more stature as human beings you'd care more about them when their world is extinguished at the end of the film. I don't think that is the point. They are crude lunatics, but what kind of society would this be if survival and peace of mind and freedom were luxuries granted only to the beautiful and the sophisticated? The film's tragedy is that poets can't survive unless they get their hair cut.

I like the way *Easy Rider* successfully juxtaposes the scenery and the travelogue portions with the action and dialogue, showing the contrast between the poet's view of America (pastoral, green, at rest) with neurotic chaos as the cyclists get nearer to urbanization. I like the use of extras; even in the most natural films, local townspeople often seem arch and self-conscious next to the professional actors—not here. Nothing looks set-up. Nothing looks rehearsed. Peter Fonda and Dennis Hopper can be proud of a movie which, in all of its hysteria and venom, looks not so much photographed as actually lived, on the road, where the whole thing happens every day to people who refuse to run with the other horses. It's life, but it doesn't always end up in the movies.

Che! is a libelous fiction about Bolivian revolutionist Che Guevara in which several Cuban nationalists step to center screen and announce, "He who pays the piper calls the tune"; in which each plot sequence is introduced by a black-and-white fade-out with a narrator who addresses the audience with lines like "Everyone thinks Fidel Castro was a true military genius—don't you believe it—it was Che!—if you tell anyone I said so, I'll call you a liar!"; in which Jack Palance plays Castro like a comedy act on *The Ed Sullivan Show*; and in which Omar Sharif, as a Che Guevara who looks programmed by the CIA, plays the guerrilla leader as a cruel, hard, wheezing, asthmatic, brutal, unfeeling mass murderer, then turns to Castro and sighs, "I'm faced with enormous domestic problems!" To which Castro winks: "Che, sometimes I just don't understand you." The direction is by Richard Fleischer; the history by Aesop.

The April Fools has poor, bewildered Jack Lemmon roaming about New York in a paraffin daze because he has just met vapid, stone-faced Catherine Deneuve at a party the night before and both of them have decided instantly and without the slightest motivation to leave their respective mates and run away together. About fifteen minutes of plot and what seems like an eternity of padding, in a movie so phony it is difficult to believe it takes place in New York at all, but rather on some distant planet inhabited by children of paradise. This is the kind of screenwriter's New York where the guests at parties burst into fully orchestrated Burt Bacharach numbers and where everybody ends up for a night on the town at a discotheque where the maître d' is a midget, people sit around flaming bonfires while a jungle band plays early Martin Denny "Quiet Village" music that went out of style when I was a sophomore in college, you signal the waitresses by firing a pop gun at their derrieres, and the doorman says "Bwana wanna taxi?"

The only charming moments in the entire picture occur when Myrna Loy and Charles Boyer are on the screen, but their roles have been so ineptly written and so poorly edited that both of them become meaningless characters about whom nothing is ever revealed except that they live in a castle where they sleep all day and stay up all night watching Greta Garbo movies on television. It's disgraceful to see so much talent so disrespectfully taken advantage of, and even more depressing because it has been directed (if that's the word they're using this season for this kind of escapist drek) by Stuart Rosenberg, who did such a fashionable, controlled job with *Cool Hand Luke*. This time around, he has turned in what one critic calls "visual virtuosity as an end in itself" by attempting to hide the vacuous inertia of it all with a kaleidoscope of pop tunes, flossy photography, lush music, dialogue full of Thirties chic ("This is the most wonderful night of my life"; "You'd like Paris—it's so romantic!"), fancy camera angles, and distracting side-gimmicks like drunks and hookers and castrating wives, who wander in and out of the mire to pad the action.

The characters are all one-dimensional, like hawkers from a bad TV satire on New Haven railroad commuters. The talk is all stale. Jack Lemmon looks tired and angry, and the waxen animation of Catherine Deneuve, who should never *ever* appear in anything without subtitles, reminds me of a shiny new refrigerator that has just come unplugged from the wall.

Hard Contract is a flagrant example of the incredible, audacious depths to which some directors and writers will go to insult an audience's intelligence. It's that old Hollywood trick of making something look provocative and meaningful by filling a banal and pointless idea with a lot of confusing references to politics and parapsychology, disguising it with loaded, pretentious dialogue fraught with hidden meanings, and passing it off as art—just to make a rotten movie that isn't about much of anything at all look more important than it really is.

Basically, it's about a hired killer (James Coburn) on a mysterious mission to assassinate three Numero Unos along the picture postcard route in the playgrounds of the Jet Set. Enter sexy divorcee Lee Remick. He mistakes her for a prostitute, hires her for the night, falls in love, and learns the value of life and death, all in the course of one hour, forty-six minutes. How nice it would be if that were all. But in the heavy hands of S. Lee Pogostin, who not only wrote this trash but then had the colossal gall to direct it too, you don't even get a good hired-killer movie without everyone having some monumental sociological or psychological problem bigger than a breadbox and three times as boring.

Coburn can't make out unless he pays for sex. Lee Remick can't have an orgasm. Top all this off with a lot of dull talk about crime, murder, and the value of human life and a lot of heavy breathing, and you get the picture. The supporting cast all has problems, too: Lili Palmer, as a birdbrain tourist, carries around a burden of guilt because she's a rich, white Protestant. Patrick Magee begs punishment for being a former Nazi who sent thirty thousand gypsies to their deaths in the war. Burgess Meredith stands in front of Goya's "The Firing Squad" in Madrid's Prado museum and delivers a sermon about murder. Lee Remick, who should sue the cameraman for making her look twenty years older than she is, says assorted unbelievable lines like "Believe in me, for I am the Resurrection!" and rolls around on her hands and knees barking like a dog in a Tangier gutter. Sterling Hayden, as a retired killer, stands in a wheat field and spouts some kind of Mafia philosophy about how "Evil is a giant. Good is when evil takes a rest. Good is a rest period." At one point, Pogostin's script reaches untested heights of absurdity as two characters muse: "It's a miracle." "There's no such thing as a miracle." "I know, that's what makes it so miraculous." It all ends with Coburn dancing through a field of gypsies talking about the freedom and dignity of man while Lee Remick yells "More lies!" as the whole movie closes off in a daguerrotype frame, an old photographic trick Kazan used with a helicopter in *Wild River.*

Loaded dialogue cannot cover up a silly, empty movie; it can only momentarily stun and confuse an audience into forgetting about how vacant and boring the movie is. *Hard Contract* doesn't even have the sense to camouflage its pretentiousness with style or humor. It just lies there, like a hard lump in the esophagus; hash trying to pass itself off as *ratatouille.*

September 1969

Thank You All Very Much and *A Nice Girl Like Me* are both movies about unwed mothers—an abysmal subject that has always intrigued the British almost as much as the Marshall Plan, but which stirs in me about as much passion as the sight of a stillborn donkey. There's not much more I can say except to express concern that anyone but the most intensely deprived shut-in *True Confessions* reader would see enough meat in the subject to warrant further investigation. Still, here it is again, fresh from London with the bloom of technicolor smiling bravely through tears as though nobody had ever heard of *The L-Shaped Room.*

Thank You All Very Much shows Sandy Dennis as the daughter of the sort of proper British parents who never have time to discuss the facts of life, love, and the pill because they're too busy reading *The Economist* to glance up from their Cornish cream teas. In London doing graduate work, Sandy finds herself pregnant after a one-night encounter with a television journalist. This predicament arouses minor problems among her friends ("I suppose I'll have the baby"; "You *can't*—what about your thesis?"), but somehow a talented young director named Waris Hussein has found a way of fashioning it into a full-length film in which nothing much happens but which is nevertheless quite moving and satisfactory. The direction is superbly crisp and detailed; the acting of such a delicate and loving nature that instead of acting out roles, the actors seem to turn the characters they play into amplifications of their own personalities. Sandy Dennis has her detractors, but I find her mannered awkwardness poignant and impressive. And a young stage actor named Ian McKellan is obviously someone we'll be seeing a lot more of. As the journalist who gets Miss Dennis in the family way, he has the ingratiating look of a gerbil trying to pass an I.Q. test.

In *A Nice Girl Like Me,* Tweety Pie-voiced Barbara Ferris plays the daughter of a wealthy ambassador who dies, leaving her a house in London fully equipped with a craggy but loyal handyman (Harry Andrews) who doesn't take lightly to the fact that she is almost continually coming home pregnant by men whose names she can't remember. So, with typically British diplomacy, he marries her himself. That's about all there is to it, except some nice shots of dead leaves. Oh, yes. There *is* one almost-funny scene in which the girl's aunt, hastening to find her a husband to give all that progeny a legal name, supplies her with a boorish oaf who keeps trying to explain how he lost his glass eye in a swimming pool while one of the little fatherless brats keeps cudgeling him with Jello. W. C. Fields would have turned such a scene into a battered triumph. *A Nice Girl Like Me* pounds it into an unpersuasive yawn.

The Learning Tree is a warm, gentle remembrance of things past remarkable primarily because Gordon Parks is the man doing the remembering. Mr. Parks is a novelist, poet, composer and *Life* photo-journalist for whom my admiration knows no limits. He is also a Negro with the keenest sense of pride in both his life and his people it has ever been my good luck to witness. *The Learning Tree* is a portion of his autobiography, set in the same mid-1920's Kansas locale of William Inge's *Splendor in the Grass,* and revolving around events in the year of his mother's death. Structurally, the film is simple in its depiction of family life and the ways of young black teen-agers; cinematically, it is beautifully photographed by Burnett Guffey, who shot *Bonnie and Clyde.* But what I liked best about it is the way it lifts its head high, in both Mr. Parks's screenplay and direction, to show how alike people of all colors are in their search for a place in the sun. More than just telling a story, Mr. Parks has allowed us the rare privilege of seeing a way of life—from country barbecues to hymn-singing at the African Episcopal Church to riding out the assault on human dignity—no different from anyone else's in its honesty and integrity. All of which has led to a few assaults from that militant portion of Negro society for whom any black man not carrying a loaded revolver is an automatic Uncle Tom. That's all political hogwash. It's Mr. Parks's life story; he hasn't compromised in the telling of it simply because it's currently fashionable to be violently reactionary. The criticism has been made that the film is "old-fashioned." That label has never made much sense to me; it's like saying John O'Hara should write like Saul Bellow, or Truman Capote like Norman Mailer. The criticism has also been made that the film is sentimental. I agree that it is muted and idyllic in tone, but obviously he feels a soft, sentimental, happy nostalgia for his childhood. Why should this kind of nostalgia be a luxury reserved only for white writers?

The Learning Tree is a touching monument to the goodness of people at a time when most movies seem hell-bent on pandering to their baser instincts. I found it a positive expression of faith in the face of overwhelming obstacles, etched in strength, wisdom, and compassion. It is, in essence, an extension of the man Gordon Parks is today, a resolution of the kind of spirit that took him from the poverty of a Kansas farm to the heights of self-fulfillment. For all that, and for what it says about the American concept of the little man who gets ahead by saying *do* when everybody else says *don't*, I applaud Mr. Parks and his film with vigor. "It is worse to be irresolute than wrong," he says. With *The Learning Tree*, he is neither.

A Place for Lovers, stars Faye Dunaway and Marcello Mastroianni, in a luxuriously expensive example of Bette Davis-worship carried to impossible extremes. Twenty years ago, this gigantically silly story of a sad, valiant lady floating around the Italian Alps with a mink-eyelashed lover who doesn't know she's dying of a mystery disease might have been plausible on the radio accompanied by massive overdoses of organ music between Oxydol commercials, but in the harsh light of 1969, it's so corny all I could do while watching it was wonder why the hell she wasn't home in bed.

This heroine is so breathtakingly obtuse I had to read the film's publicity handout to learn "the casual elegance of her clothes is a clue to the fact that she is a fashion designer . . . despite her youth, there is a suggestion of fatigue in her face . . . she has been successful but she has not enjoyed life." She also sleeps in pearls and see-through Theodora Van Runkel nightgowns and is given to making cryptic remarks like "There are times in life when *nothing* is important and *everything* is important and the *simplest* things are the most *confusing*" to Ella Fitzgerald records. Then she sees Mastroianni on a TV screen, and according to the official MGM synopsis, "remembers that they had an odd brief encounter at an airport some time before. In a moment of overwhelming attraction, he had approached the girl and begged her to come away with him. She had replied that she was married and he had reluctantly departed, leaving her his card with his address in Italy and telephone number. Now he has driven all night to reach her; before the morning is over, they are lovers." Well, why not? The poor girl is dying, for Chrissake . . .

The pace is so draggy in this interminable soap opera that it takes just ten minutes under an hour to discover the heroine isn't feeling well. You know it because Mastroianni, who is required to do little more than roll his soulful cocker spaniel eyes until they fill with tears in the closeups, stares at the telephone in a glaze of waxen horror and says, "Morphine!" while slurpy strings die off in a slow, lethargic sigh in the distance. But no amount of plot trouble, pretentious dialogue, co-stars who are troubled by linguistics—or even driving headlong into a moving bus—seems to shake Faye Dunaway's chic deadpan. She plays the whole movie with pretty, composed boredom, like a frozen *sorbet à l'orange* that refuses to thaw. Vittorio DeSica is listed as the director, but frankly, *A Place for Lovers* looks not so much directed as merely whittled to death.

In *The Chairman*, a secret transmitter the size of an aspirin is implanted in Gregory Peck's mastoid gland. Not only that, but back in Washington there's a rather nasty rumor going around that there's a coil of explosive wire wrapped around the transmitter that can be set off whenever necessary to blow him up along with the entire Red Chinese Army. Although he plays the whole thing as though he is posing for a face-lift on Mt. Rushmore, he can't fool me. It's enough to give a man a terrible headache. I know it certainly gave *me* one.

Where's Jack? I'm sure I don't know; although I sat through this rumble-stumble Punch and Judy show about an hour longer than I should have, trying to find out. Half based on the life of eighteenth-century Robin Hood highwayman Jack Sheppard, half pseudo-preachy anti-Establishment propaganda about the courage of the individual vs. corrupt authority, it's the kind of thing Tommy Steele can do in his sleep. And does.

Three Into Two Won't Go. That old triangle again—lecherous Adam, frigid Eve, and the serpent dressed like Lolita—bent out of shape until it seems downright square. Judy Geeson, as the one-night stand, performs with such a bawdy, finger-licking frowsiness that she is oddly appealing, but Claire Bloom and Rod Steiger, as a humdrum, childless couple so bored with each other they are able to end their marriage without so much as a hang-nail grimace, sleepwalk through the entire film as though they have been novocained. Shortly after the film's completion, in their own off-screen marriage, they parted for real. Must've seen the rushes.

October 1969

Like last week's *New York Times*, the age of specialization has come and gone. Everyone is doing his own thing. Nobody is expected to live up to any particular image any more. Actresses, between pictures, are writing magazine articles on everything from Senator Eugene McCarthy to the Los Angeles roller derby. Critics, between reviews, are writing screenplays and producing pornographic off-Broadway musicals. Housewives, between mulligan stews, are ending up on the best-seller lists, and editors of literary periodicals, between red pencils, are playing the triangle with the New York Philharmonic. Well, why not? I think it's all very healthy and invigorating to see so many diverse and complicated people trying their hands at so many different things. And I am even happier now that I've seen a magnificent new movie called *Medium Cool*, directed by a cinematographer who got tired of shooting other people's pictures. It's a staggering and illuminating film that has hit me like a jolt of electro-shock therapy in a season of psychological placebos.

Haskell Wexler already knew how to make movies *look*. He has photographed lots of them. He even won an Oscar for *Who's Afraid of Virginia Woolf?* It wasn't enough. So he took his cameras to Chicago during the turbulent 1968 Democratic National Convention and wrote, directed, and produced his own film. He photographed Chicago inside its jails and its slums and its bedrooms. Then he took his cameras and shot the people there—and if you still think this country's not in trouble, I dare you to sit through the scene in *Medium Cool* actually filmed on a firing range for terrified female gun owners, or the one in which a white man gets trapped inside the apartment of a group of black militants, without squirming. Wexler got his fingers down hard on the pulse of this age and the results are recorded in *Medium Cool* for posterity.

Then he moved out into the streets and shot the blue shirts moving in on college students in Grant Park like a force of helmeted Nazi storm troopers. He shot the chants of kids with blood streaming out of their ears and eyes, yelling "Sieg heil!" at the cops while Mayor Daley moved into the convention hall to the tune of "Happy Days Are Here Again." He shot army tanks moving in on Red Cross nurses while women and children screamed "NBC, come back, stay with us!" and "The whole world is watching!" And out of it all came a great deal more than a document of hate. *Medium Cool* is no documentary, although in much of the investigative footage used in Washington, Wexler and his cast appear quite prominently. It is no *March of Time,* though Wexler did disguise his cameras with phony TV station call letters in order to get a sense of newsreel immediacy. It is the stuff of now, of what this country is up to and down on, exposed within the framework of motion picture technique—plot, dialogue, action, character development, atmosphere, mood, and tempo—like some extraordinary historical accident. And because it all works, it is one of the most powerful and moving human documents ever captured on film. In spite of its ridiculous "X" rating (yes, Granny, there's frontal nudity), I think the young people of the world should be required to see *Medium Cool* in schools, churches, and courtrooms. This is no phony, pretentious piece of throat-slashing slobber like Sam Peckinpah's *The Wild Bunch,* which goes around announcing good anti-violent intentions while exploiting and glorifying violence to the happy jingle of box-office coins. The blood that splashes on Wexler's camera lens is not glycerine. At one point, you can actually hear a voice screaming, "Look out, Haskell, it's real!" It's that miraculous circumstance seldom seen in American movies—the truth on film.

Against the backdrop of human drama being lived on the Chicago streets, there is a simple, contemporary story about the relationship between a television news cameraman and a young hillbilly woman from Appalachia, the widow of a coal miner killed in Vietnam, who is trying to eke out a living as a substitute teacher in the Chicago school system. I was quite moved by the way Wexler contrasted the girl's background (the pastoral simplicity of the Bible-thumping, religious-chanting mountain folk of West Virginia) with the hot, festering inferno of Chicago's urban violence to give a portrait of a human being lost within the shifting social rhythms of her own time. And the way he has written the role of the photographer raised several questions in my mind as to how much blame the press should share for glorifying the chaos and violence on today's front pages. "We cover news, we do not manufacture violence!" pleads the press in the film, yet when the photographer unravels a simple human-interest story of a Negro cabdriver who found ten thousand dollars in his cab, he is not allowed to tell it because it isn't controversial enough. "I got a convention coming up, plus I got a war and a nervous city!" yells his boss. And everywhere he turns, the cry goes up: "Let's get the guys with the cameras!" With forty-pound, twelve hundred dollar-lens cameras on their backs, the cameramen covering the news are like vulnerable children with power they don't know how to use—hated by the cops and hated by the people, with no place to hide from either.

Robert Forster, Verna Bloom, and especially a child named Harold Blankenship are such brilliant, natural actors you'd swear they were totally unaware of the camera—a not altogether impossible notion, since Mr. Wexler's camera is the secret weapon by which he exposes us all. He has come closer than any other American filmmaker in my memory to recording a supreme exposé of the psychotic, antisocial horror overtaking this nation and the people in it. In the final scene of *Medium Cool*, an automobile crashes into a tree and bursts into flame. Another car filled with apathetic joy-riders passes it by, its occupants recording the tragedy with handheld cameras. Perched on a camera lift nearby, Haskell Wexler himself is filming the tourists filming the flaming car with its dying corpses. Suddenly, as the audience shudders and cringes at the sight, Mr. Wexler turns his newsreel camera to center-screen and photographs the audience watching the movie in their comfortable armchairs. The entire film experience closes into the glossy blackness of the camera lens and there is no escape. We become part of the news, because whether it is a pleasant thought or not, we *are* the news. The effect of that realization is temporarily shattering; the consequences of what it means will last forever. At the end, *Medium Cool* is just beginning.

The Rain People is a kind of schizophrenic Fitzpatrick travelogue, shot from moving vehicles on an open highway, in which Shirley Knight plays a bored, neurotic, pregnant housewife who drives off one morning in the family station wagon and heads out across the United States in search of herself. On the road, she picks up a chunky, cheerful hitchhiker and convinces herself that if she can seduce him, perhaps it will at least be a new enough experience to revive a respect for what she left back home. Trouble is, he turns out to be a mentally retarded ex-football player with a metal plate in his head who so depends on her that she ends up with more emotional problems than she started out with. A pathetic relationship ensues, but the girl learns a new kind of responsibility to herself and to life after it is already too late.

It is a lyrical, tragic film that will undoubtedly disturb and provoke a great number of people who still think girls old enough to sign a marriage license should be equally mature enough to accept the commitment that goes along with it. They seldom are, of course; matter of fact, most of the young marrieds I know would make the late Brendan Behan seem tranquil as a store-window dummy.

Francis Coppola has managed to detail the hangups of young people in terms that are simultaneously bleak, beautiful, and realistic. Human drama is played out in roadside barbecue stands while people drink Dr. Peppers. A phone call on the Pennsylvania turnpike is actually made right there, with the soundtrack picking up car noises filtering in with the sounds of long distance. In the snow-cone drive-ins and the gas stations and the covered bridges, there is no suggestion of the booms and overhead lights and studio-sealed color that bathes out the reality of most Hollywood movies. And from his actors, Coppola extracts performances of quiet, poetic beauty: James Caan, as the football player, shuffles about in his little plaid shirt and his stadium jacket like a crew-cutted, lobotomized Joe Palooka; and Shirley Knight plays the troubled girl with awesome skill and the kind of tense, nervous passion usually reserved for but sadly lacking in the heroines of Victorian novels. Charlotte Brontë would have loved her.

Bob and Carol and Ted and Alice sounds like two 1945 radio soap operas running back to back. Don't let the title fool you. I'ts really a fascinating skinny-dip into the psychotic state of today's modern marriages, with particular emphasis on all the wife-swapping, head-shrinking, and free-thinking phenomena indigenous to modern marriage Beverly Hills-style. It's a story of modern swingers trying to get their thing together, told with vigor and crispness, directed by a young man named Paul Mazursky in a style that is a cross between Fellini and the Maysles Brothers, and acted with such a documentary-like honesty by Natalie Wood, Robert Culp, Dyan Cannon, and Elliott Gould that I often felt like I was intruding on their most private moments by peering through their most private keyholes. There is one fabulous trip to a nudist group-therapy camp in the San Gabriel Mountains (the kind of weekend spa where all the disturbed swingers in California are going these days, the way New Yorkers go to the Hamptons) that is one of the most involving sequences I've seen on film lately. Mazursky allows the camera to linger on his subjects in this and other scenes until they all but drop dead from humiliation before the scene changes.

I don't know whom to discredit for the uneven sections of the movie; in any other film, they might not seem so strident. But *Bob and Carol* is such a fine, personal statement that it becomes annoying when it begs for laughs with situations right out of Saturday night television comedy. At the precise moment when the two couples reach the moment of truth in a Las Vegas hotel room orgy that will finally test the bond of their friendship, the camera lingers much too long on Elliott Gould in the bathroom, preparing his toilet like a corny routine from some prehistoric night-club act by Pinky Lee. It's a desperate attempt to inject comic relief into a tense scene that doesn't need any comic relief. All it does is destroy the scene. Other sections of the film are formless and actionless, with an ending that has everyone in Las Vegas streaming symbolically out onto the Strip in twos, like stuffed animals on their way to some psychedelic Noah's Ark. The effect, like a pale imitation of *8½*, is so pretentious and silly it is embarrassing to watch.

Fortunately, the weak things about the picture are eclipsed by other moments of wit, intelligence, and insight. And even when things get clumsy and self-conscious, everything is redeemed by the vivid, throbbing sensitivity of Natalie Wood. A criminally underrated and often badly used actress, she is one of the few Hollywood-trained stars still working in films today who, with each successive role, seems to learn from the camera instead of trying to compete with it. In *Bob and Carol and Ted and Alice*, her portrait of a groovy upper-middle-class wife combines layers of humor, subtlety, and flowering beauty in a performance of hair-raising candor. She makes the screen bigger than it really is, which, after all, is what great movie acting has always been about. Unashamedly, I must confess I find her one of the wittiest and most hypnotic screen presences since Carole Lombard.

November 1969

The man who tries to make something of *The Madwoman of Chaillot* is, I fear, rather like the grownup who enters the retarded child in a Quiz Kids contest. Such men are too blinded by love to see the futility of the project. I can sympathize, but I must eventually side with the judges. The intentions are honorable; defeat is inevitable.

For all its wisdom and charm, *Madwoman* has never worked. It didn't work on Broadway, either as a play by Jean Giraudoux or later as a Jerry Herman musical vehicle for Angela Lansbury called *Dear World*, and it certainly does not work in this labored, confused, souped-up new movie version by Bryan Forbes. I suspected it was in trouble when John Huston left the film after shooting began and Forbes took over. Forbes works best in tightly constricted plot structures with realistic subject matter (*The L-Shaped Room*, *The Whisperers*). Working with the gossamer fantasy of *Madwoman*, he's up to his ears in quicksand and the film sinks right under him. At no time in this interminable film does he (or any of his actors, with the exception of Edith Evans) find the key to what makes Giraudoux tick. I have a feeling Forbes suspected this himself, because he has updated (a word that has always been an enemy to filmmaking) the plot by working in references to student riots and police brutality. The greed and corruption the Countess Aurelia fights in her lavendar chiffon hat from another era now includes nuclear science, the Communist threat, the stock market, and religious fanaticism. (There is one enormously heavy-handed scene in which she confuses an evil evangelist on matters Christian that seemed to me particularly bone-headed and obvious.) The victims of her moral crusade now include Wall Street brokers, computer magnates, prospectors, and business finance executives. There is still something likable and sweet about an old lady living in the sewer beneath the streets of Paris who one day comes into the sun and discovers the world is going to the dogs. In the original play, the bad guys wanted to drill for oil in the streets of Paris. The madwoman and her cronies found them guilty of a total lack of sensitivity, middle-class grossness. But the main trouble with the idea today, I feel, is that the world has changed so much since Giraudoux wrote his innocent little diatribe against the abuses of power and the worship of money that the very things he detested are the very things we now accept unconditionally as facts of life. *We* are the capitalists he's putting down. In retrospect, *Madwoman of Chaillot* seems hoarse in the throat from its old-fashioned message. Nobody's listening.

Forbes should have realized this problem and made a clearer distinction between fantasy vs. reality. Instead of Giraudoux's champagne-sparkly dialogue, however, the film is slow and draggy and endlessly talky. The madwoman's house looks like one of those scrubbed birthday cakes on the Avenue Foch but inside it is empty, covered with cobwebs and dead leaves. Has she been asleep for one hundred years? It's all very confusing. And even when Katharine Hepburn finally appears from its cavernous depths, she wears the mad clothes they make her wear, but she seems so crisply alert, so full of Connecticut common sense and starch that I didn't believe for a minute she hadn't read a newspaper in fifty years. Hepburn achieves an aura of elegant decay collecting her giblets and bones for the cats of Chaillot, but the script provides her with no eloquence—only a jack o'lantern costume party tawdriness. The other madwomen are Edith Evans, who seems to know what she's doing even though she doesn't communicate very well with the other cast members while doing it; Giulietta Masina, who hasn't the vaguest idea what she's doing and is hampered even further by having to wrestle with English; and Margaret Leighton, whose idea of eccentricity is to bob her head up and down and shake all over like a spastic pelican. Since most of the acting is on the level of some amateur community theater group, they really all seem like pathetic lunatics instead of lovable and humorous loonies. Their madness seems calculated, not dotty and delicious. If they ever *really* appeared on the streets of Paris, they'd be put away. The rest of the cast is expensive—Charles Boyer, Danny Kaye, Yul Brynner, Donald Pleasence, Richard Chamberlain, John Gavin, Oscar Homolka, Paul Henreid, Nanette Newman—but hardly memorable. Claude Renoir and Burnett Guffey are both listed as cinematographers on the project, which could explain why the film has two distinctly opposed physical styles that conflict with each other and consistently confuse and annoy the viewer. The result is boring and the point—make love not war—is repeated so often I felt as though I'd been clubbed over the head with it.

The Madwoman of Chaillot is about twenty years too late. But then I shouldn't be surprised. I'm told there are people in the picture business who still don't know we reached the moon because it wasn't written up in *Variety*.

Liza Minnelli must surely have been sent to us all from the kindly cauldron of some wonderful witch from Oz, for each time I see her perform on a stage or in a night club I experience a rare kind of magic spell not easily broken even after leaving the place. After *The Sterile Cuckoo* I'm afraid the damage may be permanent. It's an interesting, offbeat little picture about two students from neighboring colleges in upstate New York who are swept up in a tragic romantic interlude calling for a maturity of vision beyond their experience or capabilities. Liza is simply wonderful as Pookie Adams—a kooky, lonely misfit with no family and no place to go, who wraps herself up like a security blanket in a quiet, studious, square little fellow who lacks the maturity to deal with the serious emotional demands that are made of him. Finally, in one of the most disturbing final scenes since *Brief Encounter*, they lose each other and something of themselves as well.

Judging from the number of tearful eyes at the screening I attended, I doubt that there will be many people who do not in some way identify with the young people in *The Sterile Cuckoo*. There is nothing more touching than watching someone smothered with so much love that he eventually runs away. But much of the reason for the film's success is the way the kids are played by Miss Minnelli and by a likable, hesitant Pooh Bear of a boy named Wendell Burton. I've never seen more perfect casting. Together, they are ideal counterparts. I especially liked the way they played the scene in which they rent their first motel room in the deadly isolation of a lake community closed for the winter. "Didja hear the one about the two prostitutes going to the Navy Yard on Ground Hog Day?" bursts Miss Minnelli. "You don't have to be crass about it," nervously whispers young Burton, who is having a terrible time fumbling with his buttons. "I'm not being crass, I'm just trying to get this show on the road." That's the kind of endearing, stray puppy-dog character Miss Pookie Adams is—quite the most entertaining concoction since Holly Golightly, and played to the hilt by Miss Minnelli with big awkward horn-rim glasses, eyes like big chocolate jawbreakers, a twitchy nose like a bunny with hay fever, and a funny hee-haw cackle laugh that crashes through your heart like a flash of sun on a foggy day. It's the kind of performance that breaks hearts and wins Oscars.

Oh! What a Lovely War is a baronial splendor in which actor Richard Attenborough makes a thrilling directorial debut by turning Joan Littlewood's tiny theater travesty into a magnificently designed charade that chronicles the songs and events of World War I in a whirling festival of billowing skirts and flashing gold buttons, ending in a holocaust that cost the lives of nine million men. The entire film sings, dances, and clowns its way through a variety of British music hall skits and snatches about the bloody war years while an ugly computer gadget continually tallies up the casualty list. It's like some grisly sick joke that should never come off. And yet, in spite of its irreverence and cruelty, it *does* come off, because it has a true sense of what it is trying to say, both historically and theatrically, and communicates it with unequalled panache.

The evening itself is like a war. Credits flash across bullets, holsters, guns, barbed wire, and rifle butts. Gaudy Mardi Gras players accented in hats, Army caps, and finally even bandages rip and tear through such authentic songs as *Keep the Home Fires Burning* and *Belgium Put the Kaibosh on the Kaiser*. Drill sergeants, cockney chorus girls, recruiting posters, French and British generals so breathtakingly obtuse they make you wonder how any war was ever gotten through, dancing Limeys, war heroes, Red Cross nurses, tarts, wives, Johnnys packing up their troubles in their proverbial old kit bags, German limbs holding up allied trenches—it's all here, all sore reminders of how gaudy, how silly, how pathetic and purposeless all wars are.

In the midst of the horror, though, Attenborough's brilliant all-star cast keeps a stiff upper lip like 5 P.M. in Harrod's, and you know it's Gracie Fields time back at the Palladium. There's Laurence Olivier waltzing in his spiffy epaulets in a ballroom of white parachute silk done up to look like a Brighton pavilion. There's Maggie Smith, all powder and rouge, a one-woman recruiting officer, belting out *I'll Make a Man of You* from the footlights so persuasively that you just know she could. There's Vanessa Redgrave as a suffering suffragette, Susannah York and Dick Bogarde as pompous socialites ("Oh, the boys at the front simply adore it—I had a letter from Julian—says it's like a great picnic—nobody grumbles at him for getting dirty!"), and Michael Redgrave and John Gielgud and Ralph Richardson and John Mills and just about everybody else you ever heard of in the British theater, as somebody or other. It gets tedious. Maybe it's all very shocking and ribald to the British to hear Sir Douglas Haig called a bastard, but it doesn't mean much to Americans.

Still, war is repetitious, too, and *Oh! What a Lovely War* is a lot more than that: it is also funny and sad and thought-provoking and exasperating, and ultimately, so *true* that it makes more of a monkey out of war than all the Ernie Pyle stories or Bill Mauldin cartoons ever published. As a movie, it is frosted with imagery, pointed writing, improvisation, mimicry, and talent. As a hilarious bit of peace propaganda, it is born out of pacifist pride and an obvious contempt for Establishment greed. And it has one of the most gorgeous closing shots I've ever seen in any motion picture, as the surviving female members of a family of war dead dressed in lacy white crinoline walk through a military battleground marked by thousands of white crosses. A helicopter rises from the ground and the camera pans down on the battlefield as a military chorus sings Jerome Kern's "They'll Never Believe Me." It's a scene I'll never forget and *Oh! What a Lovely War* is a movie I intend to see again and again.

I do not intend to see *Cactus Flower* again. As a play, it wasn't much, but as a movie, it's a hopeless disaster in which absolutely nothing goes right. To begin with, Walter Matthau, a modestly pleasant but vastly overrated actor who looks and acts like Smokey the Bear sleeping through a four-alarm fire, gets star billing over Ingrid Bergman, a fact that makes no sense except (1) to demonstrate the suicidal confusion that exists in Hollywood these days about how much money people are worth according to whatever current spurt of overexposure they might be undergoing and (2) to prove the old adage that you are only as important as your last picture, which, in Miss Bergman's case, is not very.

The film also is very sloppily directed by Gene Saks. When, for example, a girl working in a record shop is motivated by the script to leave the room she tells the customer the record he's holding is out of stock and she must look in the stockroom to see if any extra copies might still exist. Ordinarily I wouldn't pay much attention to a scene like this, but so much is made of it that one's attention is naturally drawn to the record album jacket, just to see what all the fuss is about. When the record turns out to be *Mame*, there's reason to worry about directors like Gene Saks. And since *Mame*, by no small coincidence, was a Broadway show directed by Mr. Saks, who would also like to direct the movie version, and since the original cast album of that show is not only *not* out of print but selling nicely in stores all over the world—well, one can only wonder what men like these are doing directing realistic movies. Later, the same clerk takes a customer into a booth with an album clearly labeled as Laurindo Almeida guitar music, but when she puts the needle on the record, soft strings come out arranged by Quincy Jones. Nit picking? Small goofs to an audience that has come in off the street to get out of the heat, perhaps, but the sort of maddening slovenliness that has given old-fashioned Hollywood movies a bad name. And rightfully so.

Cactus Flower has no feel, no style, no tempo, no rhythm, none of the elements of timing so essential to the success of comedy. It is dreadfully acted, especially by Goldie Hawn, a listless little chickadee from *Laugh-In* who plays Matthau's mistress like an illustration for a bird-seed commercial. Maybe those wide-eyed one-liners and pregnant pauses work on television, but if Miss Hawn is to have any kind of future in movies, she needs to learn something about the rudimentary techniques necessary to sustain a comic scene without putting the audience to sleep. Ingrid Bergman is too attractive to ever be convincing as an old maid dental assistant (knowing what we all do about her, she could never make me believe she can't get a man) and Walter Matthau continues to draw top salaries by walking through his roles as though in an advanced state of hypnosis. Frankly, I don't blame him. Helps to get through movies like *Cactus Flower* without wincing.

December 1969

Out in Hollywood, they tell the story about the director at MGM who was making a movie about a schoolteacher. One day he looked at the dress designs and shook his head. "They're all wrong," he said, adjusting his viewfinder. "These costumes are too elaborate, too glamorous . . . after all, schoolteachers only make about four hundred dollars a week."

Norman Jewison's new film *Gaily, Gaily* is, similarly, a rather Walt Disneyish way of looking at those merry, hard-fisted, sharp-shooting, wise-cracking, beer-swigging American legends, the Chicago newspapermen. Chicago doesn't have many legends: it takes care of the ones it's got. And in Chicago, the name Ben Hecht is still as much of a legend as Mrs. O'Leary's cow. The Ben Hecht tales emanating from the Chicago city rooms get taller every time I hear them. His feats of Demon Rumming, wenching, and derring-do have become the *modus operandi* for every aspiring young journalist on the rewrite desk, his own autobiographical notes (in the pages of *Gaily, Gaily* and especially in the self-styled Hildy Johnson character Hecht wrote about in *The Front Page*) have added fever to the myth, and now Jewison's jolly carousel of a movie should make his admirers legion. I couldn't be happier about the whole thing, for newspapermen are a colorful lot. A few more young Ben Hechts wouldn't hurt the business. They deserve their own technicolor Utopia. People in the medical profession have Blair Hospital; now the world of journalism has *Gaily, Gaily*.

The setting is Chicago, 1910, and cinematographer Richard Kline has made it look like a wild and wonderful place to be. It was a time of string purses, starched collars, gaslights, Salvation Army missionaries, stockyards, slaughter houses, brothels that looked like the palaces of Ukrainian czars, and hot lunches for orphans. It was a time when people got hot under the collar about everything from the price of mutton to Maxim Gorky, and a pox on us all for missing all the fun. Ben Hecht didn't miss a thing, and Norman Jewison relates his lavish adventures in *Gaily, Gaily* with so much opulent dash and style that I can't think of anything in recent memory that has given me more pleasure. The film begins with some fine period stuff at a Fourth of July picnic in the leafy oasis called Galena, Illinois, and it is one of the finest segments of small-town life I've seen in any film since

Mickey Rooney drove Walter Huston down Main Street in his sparkling new Stanley Steamer in *Summer Holiday*. (Much of *Gaily, Gaily*, in fact, reminded me of the breathless happiness of *Ah, Wilderness!*, the Eugene O'Neill play on which *Summer Holiday* was based.) It then journeys with the wide-eyed young Ben to the raucous festal atmosphere of Chicago, chronicling his initiation into the world of booze and broads with more crispness and joy than the screen has a right to create.

Most of *Gaily, Gaily's* triumph lies not in its evocation of Hecht's ludicrous mishaps, but in the visual and emotional atmosphere he moves in and loves, making the absence of reality and the suspension of disbelief almost an integral part of the scene. It is really a satirical morality play seen through the eyes of a Mark Twain hero; between chases set to nickelodeon music, parallels are interestingly drawn between some of the political and social values of America in 1910 involving the wobblies vs. the anarchists vs. the Reform Movement. Jewison hasn't missed a beat, and he crowds it all in without a single moment of boredom. There are wonderful performances by Melina Mercouri as a cigar-smoking madam gotten up to look like a cross between Medusa and Belle Watling, Brian Keith as a red-faced, whiskey-soaked Irish reporter, and especially Beau Bridges, who plays young Ben Hecht with a jowly innocence and eyes like clear blue gumdrops.

I guess Chicago newspapermen haven't really changed all that much. When I saw the movie, I sat next to Roger Ebert, the bright, sassy young film critic for the Chicago *Sun-Times* who is doing his best to carry on the tradition. He laughed more than I did, which, considering the fact that I am practically allergic to most Hollywood comedies, produced a considerable amount of noise from us both. Occasionally he would punch me on the arm and exclaim excitedly, "What a great shot of Union Station" or "That's the Chicago Board of Trade" or "That's the Maxwell Street market" or "That's the way Lincoln Park looked before the riots!" You don't have to see *Gaily, Gaily* with a Chicago newspaperman, but it helps.

A different view of the Windy City is available in *A Dream of Kings*, in which Anthony Quinn plays a Chicago-style Zorba whose simple faith convinces him his son will not die if he can only scrape up enough money to fly him to the mountains of Greece where fresh air and a few ripe olives will undoubtedly cure his mysterious, unnamed illness. It's a labored, drawn-out affair, but Quinn's performance is hypnotic. It's the kind of thing he does better than anyone else—dancing to the bouzouki, kissing the old ladies, playing poker, and letching after the baker's wife (Inger Stevens) with the passion of an evangelist having a vision, all the while spouting philosophy about God and Man. Luckily, director Daniel Mann gives him center stage with the good sense of a man who knows when his show would be better off run by somebody else.

The movie is also beautifully photographed by the same Richard Kline who shot *Gaily, Gaily* (Kline should get some kind of medal from the city of Chicago for making it look much more interesting than it really is). There is a nice sense of mood and atmosphere and a crispy cold-wet look to the streets and sets. Irene Papas, that ruinously neglected Greek actress who walks through minor roles like a quiet bonfire, is brilliant as Quinn's long-suffering wife, but it is Quinn's movie all the way. In his powerful hands, *A Dream of Kings* becomes a tribute to the small, tough, faceless little people who would rather fly to the stars than buy a telescope.

The Adding Machine should have been burned. The movie they've made from Elmer Rice's abstract Depression fantasy is such a monstrosity of old-fashioned empty-headedness you can almost smell the mothballs it must have been preserved in. Phyllis Diller makes her dramatic debut covered in liver spots. She spits in a goldfish bowl, pours ketchup in her soup, and looks like something out of the Grand Guignol. The whole mess ends up in Heaven, which according to this picture, it's rather unsettling to discover, looks just like Upper Sandusky.

Less than ten minutes into *The Battle of Britain*, I got the message: it's not a movie about human beings at all, but a movie about airplanes, with a few closeups of movie stars in the cockpits. Like all movies about things instead of people, it's also an expensive, brainless bore put together with nuts and bolts (most of them rattling about in the head of the producer) featuring the usual war movie clichés—dummies falling out of planes attached to parachutes that won't open, British officers sipping tea as the bombs fall, etc. The Spitfires and the Messerschmitts and the Heinkels the research boys have collected are impressive to look at, but there's an incredible predictability to the way they are used. The battles all look terribly over-rehearsed. I could tell exactly which building and which plane would blow up long before the actual explosions occurred. While people are dying, the soundtrack blares a lot of irritating triumphal marches. Guy Hamilton's direction is so obtuse you see people get into cars, get out of cars, get into planes, fly the planes, land the planes, then get out of the planes, open doors, close doors; it's as though he didn't trust the audience to think for itself. Then, every time one of those endless doors opens and closes, there's a Big Star in a Cameo Role behind it saying things like

"Beware a hun in the sun" or "Winston gets carried away sometimes," and we're supposed to know that Winston is Churchill and not some cigarette manufacturer and chuckle at the thought. Only I didn't chuckle, I dozed.

There is no sense of time, like what year it is or how long the war's been going on, in any scene in the picture. Worse still, the Germans (who always appear to the accompaniment of slushy Mantovani-like strings) all look about as Aryan as Xaviar Cugat. (The film was made in Spain; the Berlin street scenes are really Madrid with swastikas painted on its kiosks.) The ineptitude of it all is really staggering. I haven't the vaguest idea what got into Harry Saltzman, who produced this trash, or why anyone would want to make a movie called *The Battle of Britain* in the first place, but watching it added ten years to my life.

The Royal Hunt of the Sun is a literate second cousin to *Cobra Woman,* with Christopher Plummer playing Maria Montez. The only difference is the words and there are enough of them in this knuckle-headed attempt to examine the differences between Christianity and Paganism in ancient Peru to make sane people everywhere support the Theatre of the Deaf. Some of the flowery dialogue is so rich you could plant geraniums in it. Whatever happened to those uncomplicated island epics where sulphur bombs went off while native girls did their thing on top of a volcano? The effects in this movie are so pretentious the Incas conduct their battles to flamenco guitar music while the color processing is so self-consciously arty the skies are pink one minute and navy blue the next. Robert Shaw is wasted as Pizarro (his speaking voice is still a thing of beauty to hear) and Christopher Plummer has a lot of guts to allow himself to be exposed to millions of people in a loin cloth, an Indian headdress left over from some old Buffalo Bill Wild West Show, long false fingernails, gold earrings, and enough Man Tan to color half the guest list at Miami's Fontainebleau Hotel on a Labor Day weekend.

January 1970

It's that time of year again, when movie critics make up their lists. Here's mine:

The Ten Best Films of 1969

Medium Cool
The Prime of Miss Jean Brodie
Last Summer
Easy Rider
Oh! What a Lovely War
The Damned
Truman Capote's Trilogy
True Grit
Tell Them Willie Boy Is Here
The Happy Ending

The Ten Worst Films of 1969

Candy
Angel Angel Down We Go
The Wild Bunch
Alice's Restaurant
I Am Curious—Yellow
Staircase
Hard Contract
The Secret of Santa Vittoria
Che!
Three in the Attic

The seasonal surfeit of holiday films produced more than its usual abundance of trash. *Hail, Hero!* was a misguided attempt to be "the first motion picture to deal with the sensitive issues of the Vietnam War and its relationship to the Generation Gap." It wasn't, but it did prove that Kirk Douglas's son Michael is an actor worth seeing more of. *Adalen '31* was a beautifully photographed Swedish film about a 1931 strike that helped to establish that country's Social Democratic party It was Bo (*Elvira Madigan*) Widerberg's blow for social realism. It was also a bore. *Coming Apart* was a *cinéma vérité* file of X rays about a psychiatrist named Joe who never has time to diagnose his own mental illness because he's always too busy romping around naked with psychotic women in various advanced stages of physical malnutrition. Rip Torn played Joe. He looks much better with his clothes on. And John Huston's *A Walk with Love and Death* teamed his daughter Anjelica with Moshe Dayan's son Assaf in a pastoral prayer for peace in the fourteenth century. I don't know if it should be taken as a compliment or not, but for what it's worth, the film *did* look six hundred years old.

Paint Your Wagon is a monument to unparalleled incompetence. First, they bought an expensive musical property and hired actors who can't sing or dance. Then they took a boistrous, rowdy score that is practically an American institution and cut out most of the songs. Then they decided to make up for the glaring absence of story, theme, plot, and character development by overloading the film with overdoses of natural Oregon scenery. I could almost forgive them that (I'm a nut on atmosphere) except that they then hired a director (Joshua Logan) who seems to have no real love for the great outdoors and proves it by shooting more than an adequate amount of the whole thing in closeups. It was those nostril-dripping closeups that destroyed *Camelot*. You'd think Alan Jay Lerner would have learned his lesson from that fiasco. Instead, he has once again hired Logan and thereby compounded the error. Now he has two fiascos instead of one painful memory. *Camelot* was only a fifteen-million-dollar disaster; *Wagon* cost twenty.

During the entire course of this seemingly interminable film, absolutely nothing happens. The old story about a prospector and his daughter who falls in love with a Mexican has been thrown out. Not hip enough. Now Lee Marvin and Clint Eastwood play two partners in the Gold Rush. Jean Seberg is a Mormon who drags into town and suckles another woman's baby while some disgusting drunks leer at her from the sidelines. Marvin and Eastwood shack up with her in a sort of American Gothic *ménage à trois*. Intermission. The second half is primarily devoted to telling the story of the corruption of a young farm boy to the music of the Nitty Gritty Dirt Band, with a few new André Previn songs thrown in gratuitously. They sound like rejects from the out-of-town tryout of *Li'l Abner*. All of it is padding; none of it has anything to do with *Paint Your Wagon*. Finally, the whole thing slides downhill in a paroxysm of slapstick as broad as a custard pie splattering across the face of Lou Costello.

Occasionally a lusty, brawling male chorus livens up the yawns with more action than a leggy line of chorines on songs like "Hand Me Down That Can o' Beans" and "There's A Coach Comin' In," but most of the numbers are so badly staged they might as well be performed by the Hall Johnson Choir. "They Call The Wind Maria," for example, suggests to me endless possibilities for spectacular staging. Instead, Logan again wastes good shots by zooming in on Harve Presnell as if to make use of the only legitimate voice in the film. The performances are corny, the photography stagnant. Lee Marvin falls down in the mud a lot, as though he doesn't realize that smelly old drunks lost all their charm and went out of style with Wallace Ford. His mugging seems to set the tone for the other miners, who do their best to upstage each other like a group of high school sophomores in a Thespian class version of *Tobacco Road.*

Everyone is so busy overacting all around Clint Eastwood they make it easy for him to walk away with what little there is left of the shambles. Walking through the loblolly pines in his comfortable, easy old Stetson with the sweat soaking through its brim, he has a casual, soft elegance that makes him an instant friend of the audience (things are so quiet when he's around, I found myself looking forward to his one-dimensional underplaying out of sheer gratitude). The Jean Seberg character is the strangest person in the film. She never laughs. There is none of the fire and none of the charm that might make two men fall in love with her at the same time. She is passionless. In fact, the film, for all its efforts to update what Lerner must have considered an old-fashioned show, is oddly prudish. Here is a *ménage à trois* that never kisses or embraces or has any kind of three-way conversation that goes any deeper than superficiality. The relationship between the two miners and the girl is never even momentarily believable. It's just ugly and offensive. And all that's left of *Paint Your Wagon* is a lot of noise and body odor.

Goodbye Mr. Chips is a lot of sentimental, dewy-eyed old muck about a starchy British schoolmaster who is transformed by love and left with nothing but memories when his wife is killed in an air raid. In 1939, when James Hilton's soggy novella was brought to the screen, it was saved by Robert Donat (who won an Oscar) and Greer Garson (who almost destroyed herself by playing the same part for the rest of her life). The climate has changed, of course, for that kind of movie, but Arthur Jacobs, who was responsible for *Dr. Dolittle* and therefore a producer who does not know the meaning of the word impossible, has revived it as a musical. I *guess* you could call it a musical, although to insinuate that Leslie Bricusse's plodding score is merely dreadful would be an act of charity. Still, it's a much better movie than *Paint Your Wagon,* and much prettier to look at.

For the new version, the wife has been made a West End musical-comedy actress, which gives Petula Clark a reason for playing it. I think I'm in love with her. If she had come along twenty years ago, when the screen knew a mercurial presence when it saw one, she would have been a much bigger star than she ever has a chance of being now. The playing is superb. Peter O'Toole is a prim and angular Chips who wears a look of permanent insecurity; Miss Clark is a soft, sweet-smelling dimpled doughnut with powdery cheeks and witty anxiety, like a new Jean Arthur. Together, they are perfect counterparts. There is also a delicious bit by Sian Phillips (Mrs. O'Toole in real life) that must go down in history as kind of high mark in campy panache.

In Herbert Ross, *Chips* has found a genius of a director who really knows how to open up the screen and let the sun shine in. Most of the credit for making this musty old tearjerker palatable in the harsh light of today must go to him. A former ballet dancer and choreographer, Ross is a man of intelligence and impeccable taste who believes in getting his people and his songs out into the fresh air where they belong. His prewar Brookfield School is full of rugby games, pillow fights, Saturday night baths, swimming championships, and atmospheric gentility. The way he stages the musical stretches in the film is rather like soliloquies, never intrusive and always bottled with warmth and dexterity. His camera is never idle, but unlike recent sensory disturbances like *Sweet Charity*, its constant movement never becomes a series of dizzying apologies for directorial ineptitude. One song in particular, "What a Lot of Flowers," is photographed through such a buoyant mass of rainbows, sunspots, and buttercup fields, it actually seemed much better than it actually was. (Just listen to the record, and you'll realize how badly this movie's pitiful score needed Mr. Ross's visual flair to bring it to life.) Bits of song lyrics are intercut with dialogue so that the film's structure is not imposed upon by music. Herbert Ross seems to be one of the few young directors newly introduced to the screen who is not afraid to combine the best techniques of the past (there is a strong Vincente Minnelli influence) with all the modern let-it-all-hang-out logos of now. He is not afraid to be called a square.

Goodbye Mr. Chips is, I'm afraid, very square indeed, but thanks to an idyllic cast and a magnificent director there is so much love and beauty in it that it made my heart stop with joy. I found it all quite irresistible. Goodbye, Mr. Chips. And hello, Mr. Ross.

Tell Them Willie Boy Is Here is that rare dark horse among films, a Western with a political, social, and moral conscience. It has none of the murky, heavy breathing of something like *The Unforgiven* and none of the silly, self-conscious pop-art cuteness of *Butch Cassidy and the Sundance Kid*. It is extraordinarily moving and technically stunning, the work of a brilliant filmmaker named Abraham Polonsky who, through the impotent destruction of the era now referred to as the McCarthy Laugh-In, has been blacklisted since 1949. This is his first film in twenty years and the screen is much richer for his return.

The film was originally called *Willie Boy*, but then somebody was reminded that Joe Levine had a property about Somerset Maugham called *Willie*. Consequently the new title, which sounds like something scrawled on a latrine by American troops in occupied Berlin. I hope it doesn't deter anyone from seeing the film, because it's an amazingly good piece of work. The setting is 1909 and the leading character is a Paiute Indian boy who runs away from a reservation with his bride-to-be after murdering some of her relatives. All of which is perfectly permissible according to Indian law, but considered a crime by the so-called "civilized" whites. With his father's goatskin shirt, her father's gun, and only fifteen dollars to survive on, they head for the peace of the hills while a posse led by Robert Redford takes up the chase. Stalked like wounded animals, they fire at the posse's horses to give themselves more time to get away. In confusion, the whites think they have been ambushed by a whole band of savages. Soon the press and the National Guard are descending upon poor Willie like he's the whole Indian Nation uprising. The press is furious, of course. "Goddamit, we gotta show our readers somethin'!" "Tell them we're all outta souvenirs," answers Redford, who defends the Indians. It is no small irony that it is the sheriff who has been taking Willie's side all along who finally kills him, only to learn later that Willie had no bullets in his gun.

The film is a bitter indictment against racial intolerance, but although it is based on true historical incidents, it substitutes visual reality for sanctimonious platitudes. In the way in which it shows society's eagerness to make a public circus out of a political and moral issue for the sake of a good *cause célèbre*, it reminded me of Billy Wilder's *The Big Carnival*. It is a powerful film, tightly directed, sensitively photographed by Conrad Hall with a nice feel for sand and wind and the way the desert really looks, and acted with sincerity and dedicated commitment by an outstanding group of actors.

Polonsky uses painstaking devices to relate the color of the film to its emotional content. Desert scenes are double exposed to whitewash the screen with a cloud of chalk. A black and white print has been made and printed over the color print at times, to give physical presences like water a jelly-like quality. But even more impressive is the way Polonsky directly relates the emotional style of the film to the physical styles of his actors, all four of whom bring to their roles unique individualities: Katharine Ross is miscast as the Indian girl (Polonsky originally wanted Genevieve Bujold, who was pregnant and unavailable) but her blue eyes and fair features add a diverting presence. Redford is a slow, method actor who works his way through each scene in "takes"—as the day rolls on, he finds his key. Robert Blake, as Willie, is a "prepared" actor, with a curious impatience and unbridled energy, always ready on the first take. Susan Clark is a theatrically trained actress. Polonsky does a great job of balancing these differences in style and composing a wholeness that is subtle and uniquely realistic. He designs a form for his actors, who then follow in certain behavioral patterns, combining a unity of thought, a total poem. Unlike most "actor's directors," Polonsky does not write the poem for his actors to then recite. They all create the poem together. Everything about *Tell Them Willie Boy Is Here* is selfless, filled with the quality of spirit from which works of art are born.

The Secret of Santa Vittoria is a brainless farrago of flying rolling pins and rotten vegetables filled with the kind of screaming, belching, eye-rolling, "Mamma Mia"-spouting fictional Italians only Stanley Kramer could invent. As the two paragons of bad taste who do most of the belching and screaming, Anna Magnani and Anthony Quinn give the worst performances of their entire careers, but at least they are a distraction from the rest of the movie, which is a ghastly mess.

And finally there is *Downhill Racer.* It's a non-movie about skiing. Sometimes people talk to each other in monosyllables but mostly they just ski. And ski . . . and ski . . . and ski . . .

February 1970

I am not at all certain I am capable of arriving at any kind of rational appraisal of Richard Brooks's new film, *The Happy Ending.* Its courage and sensitivity, coupled with the sincerity and brutal honesty with which it has been made and the beauty and talent of Mr. Brooks's star and wife, Jean Simmons, has extracted from me a reaction so emotional it has made me blind to all reason. It is a profound, heartbreaking film about the triumphs and failures of middle age as seen through the eyes of a woman who believes that ultimate reality exists above and beyond the routine procedures of conscious, uninspired, everyday life. It is also a movie about faith and why marriages go sour and the hypocrisy of youth worship in America and a lot of other things. It is a movie of overwhelming impact and the fact that it has been made at all puts us all in the debt of American movies in general and gives me hope for their future.

With combined gusts of bravura and subtlety, Jean Simmons plays the kind of American housewife we all know very well, whether we are honest enough to admit it or not. She plays her magnificently. When she falls in love in front of an open fire, sipping champagne with stars in her eyes (Conrad Hall has photographed her with such tenderness and respect for her bruised beauty you can almost feel the love flooding from his camera), or when she hugs her man in the icy snowfall of a bobsled slope, Miss Simmons embodies the immortal qualities of the bigger-than-life screen heroines before her. There are flashes of Hepburn, Leigh, and Garbo in her movements and in her affair with the camera that take the breath away. When she thinks of ideal love in the man she plans to marry, he's Clark Gable in *Susan Lenox*. When she walks down the aisle at her own wedding, her idea of marriage is Spencer Tracy giving away purity in the form of Elizabeth Taylor in her famous Helen Rose bridal gown in *Father of the Bride*. When she dreamily looks into the eyes of her new husband across a candlelit dinner table, he turns into Leslie Howard. After all, her mother has told her, in the good old American way, that the life stories of all decent people in love always have happy endings.

I have always believed that this kind of well-bred, well-intentioned middle-class country club philosophy might even have a grain of truth in it if it were not for one thing—breakfast. Even the most romantic affairs curdle with the sounds and smells of eggs frying, toasters popping, kids leaving for school, and early morning disc jockeys with Pepsodent mouthwash in their voices. Like most of us who grew up in the movies, Miss Simmons doesn't want to settle for that. She grew up in the school of movie love, where people woke to the blush of a kiss without the aid of Binaca, ladies wore creamy peignoirs to the breakfast table and the cereal always arrived already prepared by invisible hands on silver trays with a freshly plucked rose. Then she gets married and Brooks makes a brilliant transition. The scene shifts from early idyllic passion to a morning after sixteen years of marriage. The idealistic elegy is orchestrated wrong. It has degenerated into a symphony of buttered whole wheat toast and a kitchen full of plaid housecoats, hard boiled eggs, diet pills, and Jack LaLanne doing sit-ups on TV. Life has changed around her, but not inside. She clips travel ads for the Bahamas from *Holiday*. She orders tomato juice in a bar and asks to have it in a champagne glass. On planes, she asks dreamily if it's midnight anywhere in the world and determines that if it is, it must be Casablanca, which, after all, was her favorite Bogart movie and in which, after all, it always seemed to be midnight.

The other women in her circle of friends are also over thirty-five, but they march to the sound of another drummer, doing everything to "keep looking thirty and their husbands thinking dirty." They drink to stop the clock, because time is a daily collage of horoscopes, health clubs, silicone injections, face lifts, affairs, and Milltowns. They are not like her, even though she takes to filling her perfume bottles with Russian vodka. She believes in God, children, daisies, chewing gum, and happily ever after. She takes to turning on the TV set in the middle of the night for company: "Say something, baby—*anything*!" She feels alone in rooms filled with people. She travels to the Bahamas, only to discover that Nassau is filled with more middle-aged people running away from life who are in worse emotional trouble than she is. "All I ever wanted was to love and be loved," she tells an old college girlfriend who has ended up the mistress of a married businessman. "Is that all?" sighs the friend, brilliantly played with shockingly wise candor by Shirley Jones. "It's only everything."

And so *The Happy Ending* becomes a sober analysis of people who feel cheated by an older generation that taught them to settle for nothing less than storybook finales, people who are disillusioned and restless and don't know why, people for whom life holds no easy answers. And Richard Brooks does not provide them with any. When Miss Simmons learns that life is merely life, not art and not a romantic illusion that can be cut and edited into a deceptive reflection of life with a beginning, middle, and end, like a movie, she learns how to survive. There is no easy solution for her tragedy. She simply returns from her trip, knowing she will never find herself by running away to a magazine layout island. Yet like most women who are brave enough to recognize who and what they are, she is also smart enough to know she will probably not change. For this kind of woman, life will always hold some form of self-betrayal. Even if she were suddenly made a glamorous spy for the CIA, she would probably still order tomato juice and ask the waiter to put it in a champagne glass. So, in a never-ending search for self-renewal, she moves out of her respectable middle-class home and attends night school. At the end of the picture, her husband (John Forsythe), who has long since ceased to try to understand her, says, "I still love you." She turns on the wintry steps of the school. "If we had never been married, would you still ask me to marry you?" He thinks. (Brooks wisely kept the last line of the film from Forsythe because he didn't want him to think of ways to *play* it.) The moment is magnificent. She smiles. There is no happy ending.

The ideas behind a film of this delicate nature are difficult things to get across, because they depend so much on richness of detail and an abundance of dialogue that is small but intelligent. Mr. Brooks has provided the film with everything it needs. It is one of the few fully alive, fully rational films I've ever seen on the subject of loneliness, and one of its chief joys is the way it reveals the art that can be achieved by giving a free reign to men of taste and perception instead of hopping on whatever pop bandwagon is currently vogueish in an effort to make a killing at the cashier's window. Hollywood is currently being buried with a spectacular kind of death rattle, made by men who are running scared. I know. I just finished something called *Myra Breckinridge*. It was a monument to confusion. There were days when we never got our first shot before five in the afternoon. Expensive studio technicians, actors, dialogue experts, wardrobe personnel, and make-up artists would sit around for hours drinking coffee, waiting while men with only peripheral filmmaking experience, who didn't even believe in the project in the first place, poured time, talent, and money down the drain in an attempt to make more money on an unsound investment. "I don't know what the hell it means," said one studio executive after a day's rushes, "but maybe the kids will buy it." Running scared.

I don't often stand on soap boxes, but after observing at close range a three-ring circus like *Myra Breckinridge*, I am convinced that if American films are to have any future at all, they must be made on relatively little money (show me a producer who pays any actor in the world a million dollars and I'll show you a fool), by gifted professionals, in actual rather than imitated surroundings, without the bloated budgets and insane union-labor hijinks that hinder commercial work in Hollywood studios. *The Happy Ending* was shot in difficult locations, with technically tricky camera set-ups, with a cast of stars who ordinarily demand high fees for their services. Yet Brooks always got his first shot at 9 A.M., went through as many as ten scenes a day, many of which were printed on the first take, went home at 5 P.M., and brought in his film eight weeks under schedule for only $1.4 million—one-twentieth a fraction of the cost of a piece of trash like *Paint Your Wagon*. His actors worked for scale because they believed in him and wanted to contribute to a project that meant and said something. That is the way to make movies.

It has paid off. By exercising a firm creative and financial control over his property, Brooks has produced a personal statement of social art that is uniquely his own. Almost every minute of his film has a kind of magnanimity and deep, direct emotional wisdom that could never have been achieved in the hands of the rent-a-car salesmen and Diners Club computers and ex-television hacks who are now running the big studios without knowledge or experience. By being his own boss, Brooks has fused the film with flair and style and searing intimacy. It is exceedingly well-acted by Teresa Wright, Lloyd Bridges, Shirley Jones, Dick Shawn, and especially by Bobby Darin, as a gigolo down on his luck.

But it is really Jean Simmons who fires the heart and stings the memory. Because she can play literally anything with every required emotion known to man, she has never taken the easy audience identification route common to most movie stars who play it safe. Consequently, she has never received due recognition for her gifts because publicity eludes her and ticket buyers do not have a clear picture of any one thing she can do. (Anne Baxter was the same kind of actress in the Forties; her own versatility harmed her.) In *The Happy Ending*, I found myself continuously stunned by Miss Simmons's depth as a woman, by her warm, natural, intrinsic common sense as a person and by her range, skill, and maturity as an actress. One scene in particular—in which she is arrested for drunken driving, forced to walk a straight line in a sobriety test and eventually humiliated into a state of panic, shame, and hysteria that causes her to throw up on her clean white blouse—is one of the most nerve-crushing feats of dramatic acting I have ever seen captured on a movie screen.

The Happy Ending appears to have been assembled by people in every aspect of its delivery with a singleness of mind and heart and purpose. This quality of spirit gives the film a particular kind of radiance, and yet, at the very moment I write this, I am only too sadly aware of how slim its chances are of being a financial success. Films about the small, very real problems of sensitive, irregular people are seldom popular. It has no nudity, perversion, or cacophonous rock music. And it is not likely to get much support from the people it is about. They will find the usual reasons for disliking it—it's a soap opera, or it's too downbeat, or people don't talk that way, or why doesn't Jean Simmons just go out and get a job? But I long ago decided that life was really just soap opera without the organ music and I don't buy that guff about the burned-out woman being passé and old hat, either. What critics of the film will fail to realize, of course, is that the innocent idealists in society have no weapons. They don't know how to get tough. Why do you suppose there is such a wealth of advertising revenue derived from the daytime television market comprised largely of middle-aged housewives?

Oddly enough, I think *The Happy Ending* will appeal to the young people whom Hollywood, in its X-rated blindness, is trying to reach through sex, nudity, rock, and stagnant imitations of *Easy Rider*. They are the ones who have listened to enough hype to see its vision of truth. It will not appeal to the ignorant children of middle-class reactionaries who still think marriage is like *Pepper Young's Family*. Nor is it likely to find much of an audience among the people most familiar with what it is trying to say. But just remember: the people who dislike *The Happy Ending* are probably the ones who are made the most uncomfortable by it. They are the ones who, after it is over, have to go home and live it.

March 1970

Everyone's talking about the new *Fellini Satyricon*, but they're saying the wrong things. Like most works of art nobody understands, lavish attempts are being made to either overintellectualize it or dismiss it as the creation of a sick mind. Word of mouth will no doubt save it from the eggheads in the same way Kubrick's *2001: A Space Odyssey* was rescued by an audience thirsty for adventurous filmmaking. But I can't help but wonder if all the analysis won't in some way diminish the film's purity of escape and style. (Look how the sages wore out Tennessee Williams's welcome by reading Christ symbols into all of his decadent Southern Gothic heroes.) I hope not, because *Satyricon* is simply not a movie to be dealt with on any level other than entertainment. It is not Fellini's interpretation of Roman mythology any more than it is Fellini's projection of the end of the world, and if Fellini himself claims it is either, then he's a bigger fool than I think he is. The best favor I could ever do for any moviegoer is make no effort to *explain Satyricon*; it simply exists for its own self. It *is*, and that's all there is to it.

In a recent interview, Fellini said, "My ambition has always been to restore fantasy to the cinema." Beginning with *8½*, his work has been monogrammed with a crescendo of freaked-out passion; that quality of the beautiful and the outrageous for design and effect seems to reach a new zenith in *Satyricon*. The film is an explosion of madness and perversion, designed like grand opera of the absurd—a homosexual odyssey in which the creatures of Fellini's mind writhe about like sequined snakes toward some surrealistic damnation of the soul. Every frame is filled with lust, greed, avarice, sacrifice, pain, and human torture. Structurally, the film follows the journey of a Roman student, Encolpius, who is enslaved and carried off on a kind of Homeric acid trip. There's a gay wedding every ten minutes, interspersed with rapes, stabbings, animals having their throats cut, and mass orgies of the most elegant distinction, in a lavish exercise in how to get as many Italian extras as possible into as many zonked-out costumes on as many weirdo sets as possible. The whole film is so awash in a sea of greasepaint and choreography it is impossible to take it all in on a first viewing. Almost everyone looks stoned on grass; never before has there been such a persuasive attempt to wed the new *drug cinema* to the creation of a truly unique rapport between the mind of the audience and the visual potential of the screen as an arena of ideas. There is no point in trying to analyze *Satyricon* in terms of theme, plot, or character development. Scenes melt into each other without connection or cohesion. It is Cocteau out of Dali, an exercise in mind expansion which is a major requisite for anyone who sincerely cares about movies and the direction in which they are going. *Satyricon* is a trip I urge everyone to take. Years from now, I know I, for one, will still be talking about it.

Another important film I've enjoyed recently and which I do not hesitate to recommend is Irvin Kershner's new film, *Loving*. Like *The Pumpkin Eater*, *The Happy Ending*, and *The Arrangement*, it falls into that category of films about successful men and women bored by routine and frightened by middle age. In theme and content, it more closely resembles *The Arrangement*, yet comparing it to that masterpiece of lunk-headed lunacy is like comparing *Gone With The Wind* to *Getting Gertie's Garter*. *The Arrangement* is one of the dopiest pictures ever made, acted with unmotivated uncertainty by a cast of wasted talents and directed and written with unbridled hysteria by a new Elia Kazan who seems to have temporarily run out of steam. *Loving* is a deeply reflective film with its own style, its own inner rhythm. The trouble with most movies about how "You can't take it the way you really are" and "I can't stand the way I really am" is they never take the time to indicate how anybody really *is*. Personal statements on film that try to convince an audience of some fact of life must have something to convince people *of*. In *Loving*, George Segal is a commercial illustrator who spends his life running: into things, away from things, to catch the commuter train, to grab that two-martini lunch, to cinch that new magazine account, to look at the new house his wife has picked out. Always running, yet never going anywhere. The race for success has left him barren, emotionless, a horse in midstream. The whole film is an exercise in selfishness, haunted by people who aren't there. His children never hear him, his neighbors intrude on his privacy for personal gains, his broads make selfish demands on his emotions, his wife gauges her life by material gains that are diametrically opposed to his search for artistic expression. He is a man against the wall and the wall is made of Saran Wrap. In *The Arrangement*, I kept asking myself, "What is Kirk Douglas's problem?" In *Loving*, there is no possibility for confusion. The problem is so simplistic it is inescapable.

Don Devlin's script is a remarkable work of self-control that never exploits the rotten sentimentality often found in Hollywood films about failed middle-age. It is unaffected and poignant and filled with moments of rare and candid insight. Irvin Kershner's direction of these elements contains enormous common sense. He makes the actors extensions of themselves, allowing them the ease and introspection necessary (but rarely profited by in American films) to create a mood and an ambiance of total reality. In later scenes, the story goes questionable—I found it hard to swallow the scene in which Eva Marie Saint discovers her husband's infidelity with a neighbor's wife at a party via closed-circuit television—but for more than half of the picture, it is a joy to see people behaving like real human beings in situations that are basic, moving, and thoroughly understandable.

George Segal, for the first time, has been given a chance to examine and develop the nuances of a serious role, and he plays it with an impressive range of subtlety and circumspection. Notice his face while he tries to finish a magazine layout through a travail of interminable interruptions. The phone keeps ringing, the oven timer goes off, a neighbor boorishly insists he paint his house because it's a nuisance to the street, his agent's office drops off his latest batch of illustrations for a Western campaign, demanding revisions because "Indians have no eyebrows." His shaggy, unmade bed of a face breaks into an attitude of reserved detachment, then slowly folds up like a dried apricot. There are other fine performances, too—Eva Marie Saint, Keenyn Wynn, and especially the brilliant actress Diana Douglas, who makes a brief appearance of ruined beauty as a woman with a house for sale—that record the sufferings of contemporary people caught up in life and the defeat of life. *Loving* is a wise human, painful experience—a film of remarkable truth and beauty. Bitter medicine; but good for you.

Also playing:

Jenny. Big deal. Marlo Thomas takes out her breasts, folks, and suckles a baby on the screen right before your very eyes. She can't do *that* on TV. Otherwise, *Jenny* might just as well be another weekly installment of *That Girl*. Plot: nice girl from small town in Connecticut gets pregnant, meets seedy young pothead filmmaker taking pictures of an old hag rummaging through a garbage can in Central Park, and naturally (nice young girls from Connecticut being what they are today) decides to marry him. After all, she needs a husband to legalize her unborn child and he needs a wife to get a reclassification from his draft board. "We'd have to call my parents," she warns, "they'd probably want to meet you." Otherwise, what could be more natural and wholesome? For one thing, a plateful of rattlesnakes.

The publicity handouts on this thing call it "a uniquely modern love story about today's young people" but I found the whole sordid mess rather pitiful—an unbearably sad comment on American youth, burned-out before their time. It's supposed to be some kind of comedy, but what little humor I found in it came not from the script or direction (except for one nice bit about a breakfast cereal commercial with dancing raisins and shredded wheats walking into a giant cardboard bowl), but from the improvisational acting technique of Alan Alda, who looks and talks like Henry Aldrich on speed. Marlo Thomas has a nice whiskey crunch to her voice and plays the silly title role with all the sympathy she can muster, but alas, she's upstaged by the dancing raisins.

Cat and Mouse, from a novel by Gunther Grass, is the latest offering from Grove Press, the firm responsible for dumping on the world the vile and boring *I Am Curious—Yellow*. It's not vile, but it's just as boring. It was designed, no doubt, as some kind of psychological comment on the youth of Hitlerian Germany, but all I can tell you is that in it an ugly boy spends his lonely childhood masturbating on a deserted barge while the people and animals around him keep turning into papier-mâché dummies. Years later, he deserts the Fuehrer's army and returns to hide under the barge only to discover, after disappearing beneath the water with a sack of canned goods to keep him alive, that he's forgotten the can opener. I'd suggest

Grove Press dump this little abortion into some river too, but the waters of the world are polluted enough already.

Anne of the Thousand Days. Henry the Eighth and Anne Boleyn again, so you know how it all comes out. According to the program notes handed out at the screening I attended, it took Hal Wallis a year longer to assemble all this pomp and circumstance than it took Henry to divorce Katherine of Aragon. There were times when I was perfectly prepared to believe it. Still, Richard Burton has never been better. He's always good when he has a challenge to meet, and he's found one in young Canadian actress Genevieve (*Isabel*) Bujold. Both Henry and Anne were such loathsome monsters it is hard to work up any real feeling for either of them other than the casual interest one might muster for museum curios, but the way they are played by Burton and Bujold with a keen regard for the kind of studied detail that makes up the dark side of human nature, they flash to life with unexpected intelligence and wit. In supporting roles, Irene Papas and Anthony Quayle are magnificent, as always. The rest, as they say, is ancient history.

Topaz is a code name for a group of high French officials who pass on information to the Soviet Union. It is also the title of a film so abominable that it is hard to believe Alfred Hitchcock directed it. His films have gotten progressively worse since *Psycho*, but no amount of disappointment in a former idol could have prepared me for a disaster this total. If Hitchcock had any of his old pizazz left, he would have taken his name off *Topaz* and burned the negative. The spies in this movie are the kind of people who end up in Maxine Cheshire's column. "We are going to New York and we aren't going to see a single spy," says the wife of one of them. "We've done things for each other no other agents in this town would do —and I'd like to keep it that way," says the French spy. "You picked a helluva time to come to Havana—security is tight," says the Cuban spy to the French spy. I didn't even catch some of the most cornball dialogue. The audience was laughing too hard.

Just to remind you he is still at the helm, Hitchcock has thrown in a circus of frenzied effects—an escape in a crowded Copenhagen street, microfilm hidden in a ham sandwich, security risks, sassy Russians, top secret transactions in the cold storage vault of a flower shop—but, alas, they are like elongated TV teasers. There is none of the spirit that used to light up the best work of Hitchcock, not even the simplest thread of dramatic tension you'd find in a half-hour Hitchcock television show. The spies all look like ads for

Robert Hall and the Cuban revolutionists are played by the slimiest group of thugs with accents since Warners fired its whole Nazi repertory company. The whole thing is so ineptly directed that if any of the actors moved half an inch to the right or left they'd be out of the frame. And those "guest appearances" by the director are getting to be a bore. In *Topaz,* he's the one in the wheelchair at the United Airlines counter who gets up out of his chair and shakes hands with someone. The moment is dreadfully embarrassing, but it's about the best thing that happens in *Topaz.*

The Last of the Mobile Hot Shots has to be seen to be believed. I never thought I'd live to see the day when Hollywood would make a bad play look even worse on the screen, but the screenplay Gore Vidal has adapted from Tennessee Williams's flop about a dying transvestite who marries a Southern birdbrain on a TV show to keep his Negro half-brother from inheriting the rotting family plantation bears no resemblance to any human beings either living or dead who ever inhabited Uncle Remus country or anywhere else. On the stage, it was called *The Seven Descents of Myrtle* and it remained alive only long enough to showcase the blazing talents of Estelle Parsons. Although many talented people are involved in this pretentious, ridiculous disaster, the best thing to do is pretend this movie version never happened at all and wish everyone concerned better luck next time.

James Wong Howe's photography is so washed out most of the movie looks like it was shot with a Polaroid camera. James Coburn's idea of a decaying Southern aristocrat is to play him as a nincompoop in purple granny glasses and sandals who splits up blood all over his white ice cream suit. Robert Hooks, saying impossible lines like "Yewz a lot weaker, Jed, than yew wuz in da winner," seems miscast even as a Negro. Sidney Lumet, who usually exercises firmer control over his films, resorts to such currently fashionable visual clichés as slow motion flashbacks and sometimes even sinks his actors into rocking chairs in front of windows through which the light turns crimson red. (I know the sun gets mighty powerful hot down there under all that moss on da levee, Sidney, but at night? Before a rainstorm?) To merely label Lynn Redgrave's hopeless Southern floozie act as the most incomprehensible performance of the decade would be an act of charity. Her diction is so phony it makes her speeches sound like they've been cut into sections with pinking shears and pasted back together with spit and chewing gum. I couldn't understand a single word she said in the entire movie, but I jotted down a few bits of what I heard between bursts of phony harmonica music: "JimbbbdybleedIgrowupwomin."

"Maybe surpletarz zrylympzled lonesome." I walked out just as she was on her knees, pleading with the Negro not to seduce her on the kitchen floor: "I counderlieezas gowomensick boutamicoma Jed." The sky turned red for the fourth time, but I didn't stick around to see if they all died in the flood. Ihaddagetouttathere.

April 1970

When Hollywood goes to war, it usually drops nothing but bombs. The movies rarely use the theater of war as a theater of ideas; most war films are, in fact, only mere excuses for various studio technical departments to flex their muscles with the latest developments in scar tissue, crowd scenes, heavy machinery, and explosions. It was with more than a fair degree of sound loathing, therefore, that I approached the screenings of both *Patton* and *M*A*S*H*. Two new 20th Century-Fox war flicks, I moaned, from the studio that bored us all to death with *The Longest Day*? So I held out. Now I'm eating crow. They are both extraordinarily fine pictures that do more to raise the artistic level of the war-movie genre in the direction of serious filmmaking than anything I've seen in quite some time.

Patton is not really a war movie at all. It is a sobering study in character analysis and I, for one, couldn't be more surprised that the profile under inspection would turn out to be so fascinating. General George Patton, commander of the Seventh United States Army in World War Two, was both Jekyll and Hyde, a martyr one minute and a monster the next. He loved war and carnage and death and slapped down any man who didn't, even at the risk of alienating a nation that previously held him dear. He was such an egomaniac that he even sewed on his own ensignia before his promotions in rank were ever officially approved by Congress. He sacrificed lives and orders and military strategy for the sake of a little glory in the press, often giving journalists a field day with his outbursts ("Do you read the Bible?" "Every goddam day!"). He gambled with the lives of his men at the expense of military law just for a crap shoot to become a hero. In the light of what we believe today in the murky shadow of Vietnam, his actions as a leader were unconscionable and his attitudes as a man were intolerable.

Yet Patton was much more than a hack writer's vision of grim-jawed Defense Department madness. He was a subject fit for a poet's rhetoric. He was religious yet profane, brutal yet easily moved to tears. He was so flamboyant and theatrical that he even went so far as to design the uniforms of his tank crewmen. He was a romantic sixteenth-century *gallant* lost in the revolution of twentieth-century callousness. "God, how I hate the twentieth century," he'd say, because, quite simply, he wasn't part of it. He firmly believed he was reincarnated, and on many occasions on the European front, he'd remind his troops of former victories from previous centuries won on the same battlegrounds, at which he'd insist he had been present. He had a dry and appealing sense of humor, even in the red flame of tragedy. The defeat of Rommel became an obsession one might equate with a contest between Roman gladiators, with Patton at one point even proposing to send Rommel a combat invitation engraved in iambic pentameter. Fortunately, the script for *Patton* is so well-researched and brilliantly thought out that it examines both the faults and the virtues of the man without leaning too heavily in either direction. (There is one magnificent scene in which Patton is off in Morocco getting decorated with a lot of worthless medals and phony glory, while shots are juxtaposed of Tunisian Arabs stripping a field of eighteen hundred dead American soldiers of their food and clothing. The effect is hair-raising.)

Obviously, an actor of enormous stature and power was needed to bring all the conflicting nuances of the man to the screen in a believable way. (If someone simply told us about Patton, I doubt if we'd believe it.) Luckily, George C. Scott turns the task of believably portraying a basically unbelievable man into a towering achievement. Scott devours the screen in Attila-like mouthfuls, while everyone else crawls around under the table searching for crumbs. He has a mouth thin and tight as a platinum razor blade, eyes like cold wintry clouds, and a voice like a broken car muffler. There are times in *Patton* when he looks as though he is about to choke on some of the obnoxious philosophical pomposities about war and glory and battle, but he says them all magnificently. He chews on his tongue the way a hunter dislodges a piece of bacon gristle before the kill. And finally, when it is all over, when Patton is put out to pasture because he has outlived his usefulness in a time when war is no longer looked upon as fun and games, Scott still plays him to the hilt. Through all his moods and all his seasons, there is in the playing all the fire and burnished pride reserved for thoroughbreds.

The film has been mounted with such care and precision that I wouldn't be at all surprised, years from now, to discover it has not aged, but instead seems stored in a drawer with somebody's favorite wool mittens. It has a durability about it. Franklin (*The Best Man*, *Planet of the Apes*) Schaeffner, one of the most accomplished yet underrated directors working in films today, has charged it with insight and compassion and the kind of beautifully controlled artistic skill and intelligence seldom found in action films. Producer Frank McCarthy, who was an aide to General Marshall during Patton's reign and who was personally acquainted with Patton himself, has put the project together with an honest objectivity all too rare in Hollywood biographies made by friends of the subject. And Fred Koenekamp, a cameraman until now unfamiliar to me, has photographed it with such bursts of natural color and opulence that my eyes popped from taking it all in. I have never seen battle footage with such light and dimension, or such total regard for space and movement.

There will undoubtedly be those who loathe Patton and everything he stood for, but I dare anyone who sees this movie of his life to tell me he was ever a bore. *Patton* is an absorbing testament to the life of a unique human being and a war movie for people who hate war movies.

*M*A*S*H*, on the other hand, treats war like some kind of painless mass suicide. It is a riotous farce about a surgical unit in Korea and most of it is totally ridiculous, yet the style of its zany good nature is so relentless in its insanity that I found myself laughing more hysterically than I've laughed in any Hollywood comedy since *Some Like It Hot* (which, I might add, it in no way resembles).

Director Robert Altman obviously decided to deal with the obscenity of war by pulling out all the plugs and levelling the audience to its knees with lunacy. The result is like mating Abbott and Costello with the Ace Trucking Company. People step on each other's toes and have flat tires in the rage of battle. Nurses flirt outrageously over the operating table and use clamps to scratch their noses before applying them to erupting blood vessels. "I can't really see—it's like the Mississippi River in there," says a surgeon, peering into an open chest wound. When the electricity goes off in the surgical ward, all the personnel instinctively forget their dying patients and hum a snappy chorus of "When the Lights Go Out All Over the World." The blood bank is full of cold beer. The helicopter landing strip for emergency wounded is used as a golf course. Blood donations are taken from unsuspecting commanding officers in their sleep. Elliott Gould and Donald Sutherland are two hot-shot surgeons who, at one point, operate in golf shoes and Japanese kimonos.

It is all totally offensive, of course, but after a while it all makes a very heavy point about American humor and where it is right now. I found myself angry at first for having such a good time watching such irreverence. Then I got with it and I *knew*. War *is* obscene. War *is* offensive. War *is* a charade of vulgarity, an endless variety act of uncompromising stupidity. In short, war is a joke, and unless we can laugh at it, the joke's on us. The routines in *M*A*S*H* are outrageous; only the corpses keep changing.

I've never held to the theory that the theater of war could also conceivably be a theater of comedy. I took it all very seriously, because I grew up with bitter doses of the kind of patriotic slush people like General Patton had dished out. *M*A*S*H* is the kind of film that will hopefully change that kind of thinking for today's youth. They will like the Super Nuts in Ring Lardner's script because they are so full of impudent, anti-Establishment sass! And they will probably also accept the platform of ideas in *M*A*S*H* because it is chock full of the human goofs that make real life funnier than fiction. (There is, for example, this intercom, see, that gets so confused all the time that it keeps having to spell out words between Japanese renditions of "Darktown Strutters Ball." I can't tell you how refreshing that is, after all those endless Tyrone Power war movies in which the intercom systems always sounded as though they were being emceed by Harry Von Zell!)

*M*A*S*H* topples the American system of cornball idealism so perfectly that Korean War veterans are likely to picket the movie houses where it plays. But thank goodness for all those army football players smoking grass on the bench, all those nurse cheerleaders yelling "69 is Divine!" and all those idiots sitting around the Mess Hall table in a second City reenactment of the Last Supper. And thank goodness for Sally Kellerman, all passion and squeak in her ironed khaki uniform as an officer named Hot Lips. With all these ingredients at the front, America may go down for the count, but it will go down grinning.

Also playing:

The Virgin Soldiers. England's version of *M*A*S*H.* Any other time, this soft little tale of young British morons and misfits in a Malayan transit camp might have had a chance, but coming as it does on the heels of *M*A*S*H,* it is pale by comparison. Half *Carry On Soldiers,* have serious drama about wars and the pitiful unpreparedness of the young people who must fight them. Good direction by John Dexter; fine performances by Hywel Bennett and Lynn Redgrave, who does her level best to win back some of her self-respect after making a fool of herself in *The Last of the Mobile Hot Shots.*

Ma Nuit Chez Maud. An intellectual exercise in which two men and a divorced woman sit around and discuss religion, sex, politics, and the boring philosophy of Pascal. An almost totally conversational movie, *Maud* is a great success in Paris, where they like things talky, but I found it as stimulating to the demands of American cinema as the sight of a dead mule.

The Kremlin Letter. As far as I can see, a feeble, labored, and ultimately bewildering attempt on the part of John Huston to remake an old 1940s spy movie. Here they are: Patrick O'Neal as Humphrey Bogart, Orson Welles as Sydney Greenstreet, Nigel Green as Peter Lorre, Lila Kedrova as Gladys George, Bibi Andersson as Lauren Bacall, etc., etc. Unfortunately, everybody did it better in the Forties. According to the ads, "if you miss the first five minutes, you miss one suicide, two executions, one seduction, and the key to the plot." Well, I caught the first five minutes and I still couldn't tell you the key to the plot (or anything else about it) even under torture—which, come to think of it, was appropriately the condition under which I survived *The Kremlin Letter.*

The Molly Maguires is a multi-million-dollar movie about a coal mine. Richard Harris is a spy for an insurance company investigating a secret group sabotaging the mines in order to start a union for better working conditions. This is a plot idea, albeit a basic one, that should build suspense. (Once he's accepted into the fraternal order of the Molly Maguires, will he side with them and support their cause? Or will he report their illegal activities to the authorities? Does anybody care?) But Richard Harris has the attention span of a cocker spaniel and all the emotional depth of a plastic cabbage. He also has two distinct deliveries—mumbling or shouting—which leaves his poor co-star, Samantha Eggar, looking as though she is delivering all her lines to Dr. Dolittle's Pushme-Pullyou. I have never seen a movie with so much action—fights, explosions, murders, riots, a brutal rugby game—turn out so dull. I don't blame Miss Eggar. At least in *Dolittle* you could understand the animals. When they talked back, they made a lot more sense than the people in *The Molly Maguires.*

Out Of It. That old slobber about the goony high-school kid who can't make it with the girls because they've only got eyes for the local football hero. Complete with front-porch necking, locker-room horniness, double-dating, and philosophy over hot fudge sundaes at Howard Johnson's. Typical dialogue, as the little creep pulls a gun on the football star in the locker room: "Hey, this is no joke—fooling around with a loaded weapon—

before scrimmage!" Jon Voight makes a brief appearance as the gum-chewing stud, and Barry Gordon, as the Creep Hero of the piece, has the body of a Munchkin and the face of an old troll. This movie is not only out of it, it's six feet under.

May 1970

The Only Game in Town is a big, slick, expensive misfortune masquerading as a small, intimate misfortune. It's too bad, because if it had been properly filmed, in black and white, on actual locations, with a skilled but less generally known actress in the leading role instead of Miss Elizabeth Taylor, it might have been a sensitive and meaningful little film on the order of *Marty* or *The Savage Eye*. Instead, it's just another tally mark in the long and embarrassing line of glossy corporate mistakes that are bringing the Hollywood studios to their knees.

All the ingredients of good, solid dramatic conflict are here. The plot is a simple but appealing one, about weakness and loneliness and need, revolving around a love affair between a musician with a gambling sickness and a chorus girl unable to commit herself to another human being because of a terror of rejection. The theme is so old it's hairy, but the way it is developed by playright Frank (*The Subject Was Roses*) Gilroy, the situations are real enough, the characters moving enough and the problems involving enough for engrossing movie fare. Where *Game* falls apart is largely in its design and execution. The setting is Las Vegas, but because of some tax problem of Miss Taylor's, it was shot in Paris. Find me one art director in the entire world who can make Paris look like Vegas and I'll eat the Desert Inn for breakfast—cactus, roulette wheel, and all. George Stevens is still a keen enough director to make life look more entertaining with a camera than it does in broad daylight, and he has fused the film with an interesting regulation of light that gives a distinct feeling of the mixed-up night-and-day vampire routine of most Vegas performers. (When Miss Taylor's alarm clock goes off in the middle of the afternoon and she opens her blinds to be blinded by the hot Nevada desert sun, I must admit I did feel she was in Vegas and not on some Paris studio set, but it is still only a substitution for reality instead of the real thing.) Nobody has been able to photograph

Miss Taylor as well as Stevens did in *A Place in the Sun* and the way he handles her closeups in *The Only Game in Town* takes the breath away. She is soft-focused away under almost as many filter lenses as Doris Day. Her face is still glorious. Unfortunately, she also walks around a bit in the picture and what Elizabeth Taylor looks like below the neck is positively terrifying. There's only one word for it, friends. She's *fat.*

Now if Elizabeth Taylor wants to go around looking like a Good Year blimp pumped full of Chasen's chili instead of butane gas, that is her own business. But neither she nor 20th Century-Fox nor George Stevens nor anyone else should expect anyone who hasn't been permanently brain damaged to believe for one minute that she could be a dancer in a chorus line! And when we can't believe in her, how can we believe in the film? I was rather puzzled by her characterization, too. Even at her worst, she is always entertaining to watch, but nowhere in her performance is there any evidence of the commonness of a woman who, for five years, has been nourished by the neon of Vegas. Not only is she the fattest chorine in Vegas history, she is also probably the only one who ever ate a whole pizza with a knife and fork.

The film's real surprise is Warren Beatty as the piano player who keeps losing his shirt at the crap tables. I mean it quite sincerely when I say his work in *The Only Game in Town* is the best work he has ever done as an actor. He is so into his role, from the way he wears his cocky hat to the way he allows himself to be mothered by the girl (not so difficult, considering the fact that Miss Taylor looks twice his age and is so immense that when she asks him to pick her up and carry her to the bedroom, the audience is screaming with laughter), to the way he wears his grin like an inverted, sugar-coated asterisk, that he makes an instant friend of the audience and keeps it in his powerful grasp until long after the film ends (which, I might add, is not a moment too soon). I have never seen him work so hard or with such tenderness and emotional directness. Certainly I have never seen him work with so much skill or concentration. The result is one of the most appealing, many-faceted performances by an actor I've seen this year. It has stuck in my memory with a haunting pleasantness, the way the smell of rain and tobacco sticks to a wet pea jacket.

There are other good things: Stevens has energized the film with a nice feel for Sunday night fifteen-years-ago *Philco Playhouse* sentiment and two-people-in-a-room realism and tension; there are some nice boats furnished by the Chrysler Corporation. But some of the dialogue is arch ("How old are you?" "When you're 97, I'll be 94") and none of it is ever really amusing, the way oddball life in Vegas really is. One line, however, did break up the monotony—and the audience. Miss Taylor's fiancé, a ludicrous square from whom she hasn't received so much as a telephone call in six months, appears suddenly to present her with an engagement ring. "Oh," she cries, "don't tell me how many carats it is—I'd be too scared to wear it!" She may be a slob from the neck down, but for Miss Elizabeth Taylor to deliver a line like that with a straight face proves the girl still has a sense of humor.

I suppose there's no way to avoid some brief mention of *Zabriskie Point.* Michelangelo Antonioni is, in my opinion, one of the most pretentious directors in the world today, but because he has so successfully pulled the wool over the eyes of so many people who think a movie's importance should be related directly to its degree of incoherence, Antonioni movies have become *causes célèbres.* I find almost all of them (with the exception of *Red Desert* and *La Notte*) beneath the level of intelligent discussion. *Zabriskie* is hilariously awful. It's as though some foreigner came to this country for the first time, met two student demonstrators at Berkeley and said, "Tell me what America is like!" then went out and made a movie about it.

America is in trouble. I'm not questioning that. Big business has never had a conscience and it has none now. We've produced a bourgeois middle class the likes of which the world has never seen. They use and use and contribute nothing in return. The kids, who seem to have a clearer vision than anyone else, are becoming victimized by their own cross-purposes and the frustration of knowing they have nothing to say about anything anyway until they are old enough to vote. We are at the vortex of nadir, running helter-skelter down a path of destruction that is likely to have annihilating consequences. I could name three hundred things right off the bat that are wrong with America. None of them are shown in this movie, because this movie isn't even *about* America. It's about some plastic planet inhabited by monsters, a vast wasteland of industrial complexes, meat-packing plants, and garbage dumps, where a gun shop clerk advises his customers to buy nothing smaller than a .38 and if they kill people in the yard be sure to drag them inside before calling the cops to protect themselves legally. It is a land of freeways and stock market computers and smog inspection stations where the only place to make love and achieve an honest orgasm is in Death Valley at the bottom of a sand dune.

The heroine is a total zero and although the boy doesn't turn on with grass he does kill people and steal planes, which he flies perfectly the first time out. After some interminable walking and staring at each other, the boy finally gets back into the plane, which has been painted by a mysteriously unexplained hermit who lives in the desert and owns lots of cans of bright paint, and flies back to Los Angeles, where the entire city police force awaits him to fill him full of holes. (What else can you expect, since these are the kinds of cops who are so corrupt, they arrest associate professors of history and change their occupation to "clerk" on the police blotter.) The girl is left with her middle-class industrialist (I guess he is her lover, although that is never explained either) and his beautiful glass house. She is helpless to change things, so she drives down the hill imagining his house being dynamited into a holocaust of smoke that takes the form of the atomic bomb over Hiroshima. At the end, refrigerators, glass house, and swimming pool furniture are blown up and the air is left with flying watermelons and loaves of Wonder Bread to eardrum-shattering electronic rock music that sounds like garbage-can lids being smashed together.

I find all this simple-mindedness boring, old-fashioned, and juvenile. Worst of all, it is uninspired and phony. People who live in Frank Lloyd Wright houses with swimming pools are shown as the real villains who are destroying America. That's like saying all CIA workers are Communists, or all Southerners are racists or all Jews have big noses. It just isn't true. Yet that is the visual motivation Antonioni uses for the boredom and unhappiness of the film's young protagonists. He makes no attempt to explain or develop either of them, so I can't blame them for turning in two of the worst performances of the decade. His camerawork is unimaginative, his technique sleazy and amateurish. "Sometimes I feel like screaming my head off!" says the girl. I know exactly what she means. Happens to me every time I have to sit through an Antonioni movie.

After his love affair with obscenity and violence in *The Wild Bunch*, it is immensely pleasurable to see that Sam Peckinpah can still make a good movie. *The Ballad of Cable Hogue* is such a soft, likable movie it is almost certain to horrify the hard-driven Peckinpah addicts, but for those who hated *The Wild Bunch* as much as I did, it's likely to be a revelation. In it, Peckinpah returns to his earlier lyrical western style and turns out a work of beauty, wit and gentle honesty that is the best western I've seen since *Will Penny*. He uses music, comedy, and cracker-barrel charm to tell a disarming talltale ballad of a weather-beaten old horny-toad hero called Cable Hogue (Jason Robards), a whore with a heart of gold (Stella Stevens), and a sexually depraved preacher (David Warner) who turn a mudhole into a paying proposition in a sandy wilderness where water is worth more than gold. Soon the stagecoach line is using Cable's oasis as a rest stop, the bank is lending him money, and a saga unwinds about the durability and resilience of man vs. nature. Peckinpah still seems hung up on the murder of small things (there are closeups of a gila monster being blown to pieces by a shotgun and a fly being squashed with a newspaper) but in *Cable Hogue* violence is far outdistanced by poetry. Scenes are shot in a progression of moving frames so that whole time lapses occur in a series of interesting visual fragments. There is nothing boring or ponderous about it because the direction is so solid, the camerawork is so musical and the acting is so filled with gusto that the eye never has time to wander. By the end, when cars are coming in and stagecoach stops are giving way to gas stations, the friends meet again and it's like getting together with old classmates and catching everybody up on what they've been doing. I have seldom felt so intimately involved with characters in a film. Just watching the poignance and fragrant loveliness of the talented Stella Stevens ripen and develop under a real director's guidance is reason enough to thank Mr. Peckinpah for *The Ballad of Cable Hogue*. She has been wasted, neglected, and badly handled long enough. It is good to see her triumph, but it is doubly rewarding to see it happen in a movie as special and as admirable as she is. *Cable Hogue* is a reason for rejoicing.

Also playing:

What Do You Say to a Naked Lady? Hilarious nonsense from Allen Funt; a swell X-rated put-on containing all the things you always wanted to see on *Candid Camera* but couldn't. The best satire on pornography we've had yet, and underneath the laughter, a gentle exposure of some of the sexual hangups, psychologist's misconceptions, and cocktail party conversation topics running rampant today. Don't miss it.

Me. Maurice Pialat, a protégé of François Truffaut's, makes a brilliant directorial debut with this sensitive study of France's abandoned orphans and the people who try to find homes for them. A film cut from the fabric of real life, so totally absorbing you can smell the rooms and feel the grief and quiet heartbreak without the guilt that usually accompanies sad movies that make you cry. The acting is so magnificent I was never aware I was watching professionals. *Me* is a symphonic revelation in an age of cacophonous movies.

Tropic of Cancer. "A spit in the face of art" is how Henry Miller described this non-book about his life in Paris. Now Joseph Strick has tried but failed to turn it into a movie. Miller was a shiftless bum, a human leech, a wastrel parasite living off the tables and bodies of others. He also took notes that read like scribblings on the urine-stained walls of an asylum toilet. On film, they sound even sillier. "Oh, Tanya, I make your ovaries incandescent," etc., etc. The narration is like dialogue from an old Popeye screw book. Rip Torn plays Miller as though he is reading the Sunday comics on the radio. The women all look like dead prostitutes from a Transylvanian cemetery. *Tropic of Cancer* is execrable gibberish. The man who wrote it was sick. The people who made it into a movie are whores. The people who pay money to see it are fools.

June 1970

n what I've seen of the movies for summer, I'd say we're in for a tural dry run. I hesitate to mention *The Adventurers* and *Airport*, on e assumption that they've been laughed at by enough people already. movies are vulgar, witless, and dull, not even good camp movies on r of *Hotel* or *The Carpetbaggers* or *Valley of the Dolls.* I am much more offended by something like Pier Paolo Pasolini's new *Medea. The Adventurers* and *Airport* would soil the inside of a garbage can, but they are trashy movies that don't pretend to be anything else—cheap, glossy trash for the sake of trash, with no ambitions other than financial ones—while *Medea* is trash pretending to be art.

Darling Lili is anything but. This hopeless cornucopia of clichés about a singing Mata Hari (Julie Andrews) suffers from a lot of maladies, not the least of which is its own indecision about what kind of movie it is trying to be. Sometimes it seems like a very ordinary spy movie; at other times it bursts into music out of its own embarrassment with toe-stubbing clumsiness. Everything it does, however, is vulgar and imitative and self-conscious, and the love scenes between Miss Andrews and Rock Hudson are hilarious.

Women in Love comes thundering down upon us with the kind of praise from British critics that often sounds like cannon fire. A lot of intellectual pretension always surrounds movies based on classic books; audiences are made to feel threatened if they don't respond thoughtfully and seriously to films like *Ulysses* and *War and Peace.* But what if they turn out to be empty and tiresome, as *Far From the Madding Crowd*, or what if they overreach in the direction of effect and visual style at the expense of clarity and character development? Then you have a movie-from-a-novel like *Women in Love.* It is bold and erotic and filled with D. H. Lawrence's passionate search for sexual fulfillment and love expressed as aesthetic masochism, but there is little humanity in it and a great deal of hysteria. Ken Russell is a hypnotic director, full of flash and poetry, and in his handling of the massive emotions of the novel and in Billy Williams' lu photography, there is a gut full of the flavor of the scrambled and stiflir Victorian life Lawrence's libidos were trying to scramble away from, bu the complexities of their hangups are dealt with in an excess of heavy breath ing and hot, sweaty sexual matches that look more like the bull deer ir *Bambi*, locked in a death grasp. Pauline Kael has condemned the film as being drowned in a purple style, and I think she has said it all. *Women in Love* is chock full of Gothic horror and sexual frustration—a girl on a country picnic confronts a herd of long-horned water buffalo in a heat of sexual frenzy, two men wrestle naked in the firelight and speak of homosexual matters, a sculptress representing the Betty Friedan age jams a stick into the mouth of her new clay model—but th groundwork for understanding why the characters behave as they d is also an endless amount of silly talk about pistils and stamens, the sig of a nude girl washed up from a bog while the band plays "Oh You Beautiful Doll," and more sexual symbolism than anything since Genet's script for *Mademoiselle.* The performances are charged with tense, murky impressionism; I especially admired the brilliant Glenda Jackson as Gudrun (a character based on Katherine Mansfield). Miss Jackson wraps herself around each scene like a menacing anaconda, but nobody can say the lines she is forced to pant. When she asks Oliver Reed, "How are your thighs? Are they strong? Because I want to drown in hot, physical, naked flesh," she is as turgidly ludicrous as the most simple-minded whore in *Fanny Hill.* There are few clues to what kind of people these characters are and instead of developing Lawrence's theme (greed for self-importance in love *vs.* sexual freedom), Ken Russell throws the movie to clashing effects and bravura technical effects. The sex in the film is very hostile and ugly; the lighting and costuming flamboyant but heavy; the tone oppressive and unhealthy. The logic buried beneath these elements becomes unbalanced and although Russell is certainly an impressive showoff of a director, none of it ever comes to much more than a lot of horny perspiration. They should take all the pretentious dialogue off the soundtrack and call it *Women in Heat.*

The Magic Christian. More disconnected, fragmented Terry Southern gibberish, in which Peter Sellers and Ringo Starr take a saturnine view of the universe as a Tower of Babble. Sellers talks too much and Ringo can't act, but the rest of the film is only awful.

Woodstock. 400,000 sweaty potheads, almost three hours of cacophonous rock music by such prehistoric teen heroes as Sly and the Family Stone, and a dizzying sequence of split-screen visual trickeries muddy up this otherwise moving and compelling account of the events that made the August, 1969, youth festival at Bethel, N.Y., the *cause célèbre de paix* it now seems in retrospect. The nonmusical portions (frolicking naked in the mud, smoking grass the way families on the green used to eat watermelons on hot summer afternoons, fornicating while a PA system announces "Ed Smith please go to the medical tent—your wife has just had a baby!") do have an immediacy and give off a bit of the drug-drenched aroma of what it must be like to be young and crazy in the violent Sixties, but there is nothing in *Woodstock* of any dramatic value. And the music, which goes on and on until you realize how much better most groups sound on records, becomes an endurance test. Too much rock, and, I'm sorry to say, not enough roll.

The Boys in the Band. Crisp, biting movie version of Mart Crowley's brilliant play about eight homosexuals and one almost-ran who should have been. Director William Friedkin, who previously opened up Pinter's *Birthday Party* for the screen, here repeats the thing he does best—isolating a small group in the confining space of a single setting and getting the most out of each actor that is humanly possible. The cast is the original one and if I have any reservations at all, they center around my feelings that these actors have been playing their parts too long. An over-rehearsed "feel" to the film sometimes turns the natural flow of Crowley's scenes into unnecessary melodramatics too big and wide for the screen to handle. Still, the acting is rich, the script seems to have been written with rattlesnake venom, and the effect is nasty, hilarious, and gratifying.

A Walk in the Spring Rain. The kind of icky slumgullion that might have been published in the pages of the *Ladies' Home Journal* in the days before it was invaded by the ground guerrillas from the Women's Liberation movement. It's the sort of drivel Greer Garson used to turn out in her sleep—a slow, unconvincing study of a professor's wife trying to get some of her youth back with a backwoods yokel in the Smoky Mountains of Tennessee. With today's headlines ripe for dramatization, it is inconceivable to me why anyone would want to make such a corny movie in the first place, and even more appalling that Ingrid Bergman would consent to be in it. Not one line or scene is believably written or acted, and the direction (by Guy Green, who sent *The Magus* into orbits of oblivion) is so lazy it appears to have been mailed in during the postal strike. I shudder to think what kind of audience might respond to the naïve presumption that a sophisticated New York matron (especially one who looks like Ingrid Bergman) would fall head-over-longuette in love with a cracker-barrel hayseed whose wife says things like, "It's a night fo' wild dawgs" and "I'll be a lookin' at chee!," whose son has just tried to rape her on a dirt road, and whose only personal qualifications for romance appear to be a particular fondness for redbud trees and pet goats. Ingrid gives it that brave old painful Bergman smile, but Anthony Quinn, who is less accomplished at lying his way out of rotten scripts, bulldozes his way through this sea of ineptitude playing a chawbacon country lumpkin like Zorba at a quilting bee.

Bloody Mama. Ludicrous programmer about Ma Barker and her perverted boys, with a lot of homosexuality, violence, and needles in the arm thrown in to make a fast buck at the box office. Roger Corman's direction tries hard to borrow the best things Arthur Penn did in *Bonnie and Clyde*, but Robert Thom, who has been responsible for some of the most atrocious garbage ever turned out of Hollywood, has poisoned Corman and the poor, wasted actors involved with a script containing neither cohesion nor even the most remote attempt at character analysis. Just assembling the right period costumes and cars, shooting on actual locations in Alabama, and adding a lot of guns going off and a bit of hillbilly music does not make a movie worth making (or seeing). *Bonnie and Clyde* was a movie about criminals in which we got some inkling of how they got that way. The creeps in this gory exploitation flick are merely pinheads in a freak show, victims of a bastard script unworthy of dramatization. Worse still, *Bloody Mama* is a hateful movie in the true tradition of American-International, a studio that makes big money by grinding out B movies that are bereft of taste, substance, or intelligence, but bloated with sex, violence, and titillation. Every time it falls short on logic, style, theme, content, or the slightest thread of believability that might keep an audience interested, it throws a karate chop with a scene guaranteed to keep the audience in a state of nausea and shock: A child is raped. A mother has intercourse with her sons. A man is stomped to death. A sadist sexually molests a boy in a prison cell. An innocent girl is drowned in a bathtub in a grisly series of closeups. A squealing pig is used as live bait for an alligator, then the alligator is killed with a sub-machine gun. A man blows his own head off. It's enough to make anti-censorship liberals think twice about government control of the arts. Shelley Winters, Diana Varsi, Pat Hingle, and Alex Nicol are some of the respectable actors who, in this filthy movie, are temporarily seduced and abandoned by the panderers to cult tastelessness at American-International. It only proves how hard it is in Hollywood these days to make an honest living and hold your head high in public at the same time.

The Walking Stick. A quiet, pensive film about a crippled girl (Samantha Eggar) who falls in love with a corrupt, ambitious rake (David Hemmings) and becomes involved in a robbery. There is a wan and evocative use of the camera to suggest the psychological upheaval inside the girl while the conventional suspense-thriller atmosphere builds up around her; the performances are first-rate; Eric Till's direction is sharply edged and sensitive. A lot of talent and consideration has gone into the making of this movie and all of it shows. One of the year's most welcome surprises.

July/August 1970

Times being what they are, I guess we're in for a barrage of movies based on themes of social and moral unrest. In the past month I've seen no fewer than ten movies about student riots, abortion, the war in Vietnam, legalization of narcotics, and what are we going to do about the poor Indians. Most of these movies are nervous and unsure, as though their producers had one finger on the pulse of the times and both eyes on the box office. Filmmakers who are wise to the economic pressures of their medium know they cannot get away with any more old-fashioned banana splits like *Hello, Dolly!* and *Paint Your Wagon*. They must make movies with bite and gristle, like *Easy Rider* and *Midnight Cowboy*. At the same time, they don't want to offend that vast, unwashed movie public called the Silent Majority. So they wind up like double agents in James Bond flicks —horses in midstream, trying to please everybody by sending little handouts to all opposing sides. They play it safe and nobody wins.

Getting Straight is a perfect example. I wouldn't be at all surprised if it turns out to be a big hit, because a lot of critics will no doubt be intimidated by its direct-assault approach into thinking it is really a "topical" (i.e. "important") film. And the kids will no doubt buy it because they'd like their own student rebellions to be just as exciting, their own female liberationists to be just as pretty and smart as Candice Bergen, and their own student leaders to be just as teddy-bear cuddly as Elliott Gould. But they won't learn anything from *Getting Straight* they don't already know, because it is really nothing more than an old Max Shulman comic strip for Philip Morris with a few riots thrown in. It is Dobie Gillis with bombs going off, only the biggest bomb of all is right there on the screen.

This is a college in which students are numbers graded by computers. The reason you know this is that a simple discussion about what college educates the population to do after graduation is interrupted by a comic computer screeching and belching paper all over the place. The comedy is forced, but the point is driven home like a railroad spike on a crosstie.

The students themselves are walking clichés—too busy smoking grass, planning campus demonstrations and making a lot of smart-aleck talk to study five hundred years of English literature. And why should they? Their professors are so corrupt and insecure they even agree to change grades and fix examinations if the bright students in their departments, who represent threats to their positions, will only transfer to other majors. Into this zoo of comic depravity comes Elliott Gould as a kind of Jules Feiffer hero named Harry. Harry is a good student who just wants to be a teacher. His best friend is a pothead who changes from an Indian to a Buddhist while trying to marry a Negro chick with five kids—*anything* to get out of the draft. His girl is an uptight, liberated WASP with a big IQ who really wants only to settle down and have a nice house in a subdivision. And so forth and so forth.

The other students he must live with are busy circulating petitions for the SDS to establish referendums to legalize pot and support the Black

Panthers, and generally getting into all sorts of disorganized trouble that has nothing to do with college. Well, Harry has been to Selma, he's been to the Mekong Delta, and all he wants to do is discover a laundromat where he can find a quiet corner to study in for a quarter. It may be unforgivably decadent of me, but I cannot get much excited about all this, especially when the seams show through all the political speeches (*Getting Straight* is the talkiest, preachiest movie since *Anthony Adverse*).

All of it is hard to sustain any kind of belief in, but the most troubling thing is why these young radicals ever put up with a square like Harry in the first place. The way he is played by Elliott Gould makes him hostile, vulgar, and stupid. One minute he is doing a comedy routine, telling his girl, "You're not a woman—you're just a guy with a hole in the middle!"; the next minute he's taking on the whole faculty by comparing its counterproposals to student demands with the court of Versailles. One minute *Getting Straight* is a TV show, full of bright sex gags, the next minute it's as serious and horrifying as anything since *The Snake Pit.* Whatever it is supposed to be, Gould blows it by pulling out all the stops and doing everything required to build up to his punch lines. The most embarrassing scene in the film occurs when he faces the most ludicrously caricatured group of graduate-school English professors ever assembled by Central Casting. He is trying to ignore the bombs going off on the lawn outside the window. He is trying not to notice the bleeding student revolutionaries being beaten to death by police brutality on the other side of the glass. He is simply trying to pass his orals, but there's this psychotic moron who keeps insisting that F. Scott Fitzgerald was a homosexual. It takes Gould nearly a full five minutes to work up to his punch line, but he finally blurts out something about how it will be a shock to Sheilah Graham. Three people seated around me in the theater had already delivered the line. We knew what was coming because *Getting Straight* has that kind of predictability to it. It is filled with the kind of cute, phony, pseudo-intellectual talk you get on TV, yet these are the kinds of people who'd probably put down TV if you asked them about it.

The whole thing is maddeningly impossible to watch because Richard Rust, a new director whose work is unknown to me, seems to have just learned about the camera, and every scene is so tightly framed that his characters are in focus only when they speak, and out of focus whenever they are being spoken *to.* A new political or social topic is introduced every few minutes, but none of them is ever developed or explored, and although the student riots are well staged, it is never clear what anyone is rioting *about.* (At one point a cop beat some kid over the head with a club and the audience cheered—an indication that whatever the motives were in making *Getting Straight*, they seem to have backfired.)

In the final analysis, it is a deceitful film because it uses up the viewer's patience by being a lot of pseudo-hip propaganda that never comes to anything more than a lot of noise and confusion. Current front-page "problems" form a chic backdrop for what turns out to be only a conventional Sandra Dee–George Hamilton college flick in disguise. Harry blows his whole college career and runs off with Miss Bergen, who is very happy that he has bucked the Establishment. But if she's so smart, doesn't she also know she'll never be able to have that house in the suburbs if her husband has no college degree to pay for it?

At one point, Gould looks through the picture window and points to the juicily choreographed college revolution outside the dean's office. "See that kid—yesterday all he wanted was to get laid. Today he wants to kill somebody!"

After suffering through the naïve slobber of *Getting Straight*, I knew what he meant. The movie does make you want to go out and kill somebody, but I won't say who.

In *On A Clear Day You Can See Forever*, a singing kook from MahWah, New Jersey, who wants to break the smoking habit sits in on a hypnotism class, and before you can say Barbra Streisand she's going around claiming to be this Lady Melinda Winifred Moorpark Tentrees from 1814. All of which gives Miss Streisand a wonderful opportunity to wear all sorts of lavish costumes on all sorts of sumptuous sets and sing some tuneful ditties by Burton Lane and Alan Jay Lerner about flowers and ESP. Vincente Minnelli, one of the few directors with taste and vision to emerge from the Hollywood musicals of the 1940's, directed; Jack (*Easy Rider*) Nicholson and Larry Blyden are Miss Streisand's suitors; Cecil Beaton designed the dream sequences; Nelson Riddle orchestrated the music with all the polish and brass reserved for a Sinatra recording session; and all of it ought to add up to more than it does. But the lamentable truth is that *On A Clear Day* needs glasses. It is a hulking old haunted house of an idea badly in need of ghosts with some spunk to haunt it.

As a kind of Bridey Murphy with bunions, Barbra Streisand is in fine shape, working in and out of both centuries with accents that sound like Fanny Brice cross pollinated with Dame Sybil Thorndyke. But there are times, alas, when she's not around, and that's when the movie around her falls right on its face. Jack Nicholson's singing debut never takes place because his song has been cut, and what is left wastes him so criminally that he should have stayed in bed. The sublime dream sequences provide the best moments in the film, but somebody at Paramount must have found them dull because they are abruptly chopped up, and all that remains is a series of confusing, disconnected fragments that don't go on nearly long enough.

Cecil Beaton's period gowns are regal and appealing, but Arnold Scaasi's clothes for Miss Streisand's contemporary scenes accent all the wrong lines in her body so that she spends half the movie looking like a voluptuous but erudite duchess, and the other half looking like a collapsible Murphy bed. Her rooftop garden, where she makes plastic flowers grow without New York soot by reading them Walter Lippmann, looks like the plant store at Disneyland. And I'd like to know whose suicidal idea it was to hire Yves Montand to play the romantic lead. Based on his past record in Hollywood movies, I'd say he has about as much drawing power as a dead walrus. The only thing he's ever been able to play is French detectives in movies with subtitles. When he's not standing on top of the Pan Am Building, shot by helicopter with his arms outstretched, singing "Bleest your hide, heer me cull, Must I fight City Hull, cum buck do mee" in his *boulevardier* style, he's announcing "Daisy, somewheer in yoo is zee keey to all zis!" It's all Miss Streisand can do to keep a straight face.

In the end, she reveals in another dream that she will marry him about thirty years into the twenty-first century and goes away singing merrily the movie's title song. It is never clear what she has to be happy about. The suave psychiatrist is going back to his wife, she has lost both prospective boyfriends, she has all these people living inside her driving her wild, she is still smoking, and she is obviously going to die very soon if she's going to be reincarnated in time to be old enough to marry the French drip in the year 2038. But she goes home anyway to her flowered roof, flowered walls, flowered floors, flowered ceilings, flowered bed, flowered sheets and matching flowered nightgowns, happy as a bumblebee in heat. All I can say is *On A Clear Day You Can See Forever* is not recommended to anyone with asthma or hay fever. It gave me the hives.

Norwood is a peculiar little movie that tries to have its cornbread and eat it too. Glen Campbell returns from Vietnam to Ralph, Texas, where a nice little script by Marguerite (*True Grit*) Roberts has provided a lot of local color—like folks who eat cold pork chops and wash them down with Nu-Grape, drink bootleg booze out of Mason jars on Saturday night at the local skating rink, and shine their shoes with lighter fluid and a nylon stocking. Life is jes' plumb corny, so Glen sings a few country and western tunes and shags tail off to wicked old Green-witch Village to find his buddy Joe Namath and get on the "Louisiana Hayride" program.

I found this very odd, since the "Louisiana Hayride" program has never, to my knowledge, been aired in New York City, but this is not the kind of movie that bears close scrutiny. Anyway, he gets into all sorts of doldrums up yonder, and the movie begins to look like a cleaned-up attempt to cash in on some of the success of *Midnight Cowboy*. But no worry; it turns into the kind of formula Elvis Presley musical I've managed to successfully avoid for years, and Norwood ends up on a Greyhound bus with a pregnant girl, a wonder chicken named Joanne, and a switchblade-carryin' theatrical midget. Nothing else ever happens, and although I cannot imagine what kind of audience there is left in the world for this kind of nonsense, I'm told that Elvis Presley movies just like this one still make money in Carthage, Alabama.

The Grasshopper is what people in the business used to call a "sleeper"—a film from which nothing much is expected and a great deal is perceived. The story—bored girl gives up a middle-class life of safety and a boyfriend with a future at the bank for the pills, poppers, and fast, glamorous life in Las Vegas—is not so special. What is impressive is the realism with which the movie explores this transient, restless life style, and the quiet, tragic splendor with which Jacqueline Bisset plays the victim of it. There are shots of kids in the Vegas area riding out at daybreak on horseback to find beauty in a sunrise, chorus girls studying in real estate school, stewardesses collecting travel folders for that next trip to someplace different. Trying to get through life and avoid the clichés is what it's called. Wanting to be someone special. The world is full of girls like these—grasshoppers jumping from one spot to the next, always wanting something but never sure what it is, equipped with none of the talent, maturity, intelligence, or any of the other weapons necessary to make it all happen.

Jim Brown is surprisingly good as the black pro-football star turned token hero in the show-biz come-on world of Vegas neon, where a name on a restaurant means more than the beat of a heart. Jacqueline Bisset is simply astounding. She is an actress of such quiet, moody beauty and such overwhelming talent that she performs witchcraft on the screen. Her work is subtle yet sincere and filled with truth and understanding. In *The Grasshopper*, she turns an ordinary movie idea into a vital and compelling portrait of young Americans today, of their search for a beacon that will lead them somewhere without too much tragedy, and of one of the ones who got lost along the way.

And finally, for anyone with a zinc-lined stomach, that long-threatened sequel to *I Am Curious—Yellow* is here, like a garbage strike that finally becomes a reality. It's called *I Am Curious—Blue* (blue being the other color in the Swedish flag), and it stars Lena Nyman, the same obese leading lady. There's less nudity for the prurient in this one (be thankful for small blessings), but it's even more pretentious and deadly dull than its predecessor. Travel at your own risk, but take care to carry along an air-sick bag. You'll need it.

September/October 1970

When I go to the movies, I usually arrive fully armed with pencils and notebooks into which I jot down impressions, lines of dialogue, credits, and other such useful notations. Rare is the occasion on which I do not leave the theater or screening room carrying pages filled with my own often undecipherable handwriting in the dark, but after the movie version of Robert Anderson's play *I Never Sang For My Father*, I was amazed to discover I had not written one note to myself. The film is so absorbing and so powerful that I couldn't take my eyes off the screen for a single minute, and that is probably the highest compliment any critic can pay to any movie.

I Never Sang For My Father is a wonderful movie, but it is probably as difficult to write about or talk about as it must be for the press agents at Columbia Pictures to sell, because it requires a very personal commitment to its ideas or it just won't work at all. It deals with the subject of old age, it investigates the barriers that prohibit the proper amount of feeling most people think they are obligated to have for their parents, and it seeks honest and painful answers to the questions of where responsibility to one's parents ends and commitment to oneself begins. These problems are universal, but seldom explored on the screen. Audiences usually find ways to resist reflections of real life in movies that make them cry, but I am filled with horror at the thought of anyone missing *I Never Sang For My Father*, because I think it contains a lesson for every thinking, breathing human being unscarred enough by life in 1970 to still care about other thinking, breathing human beings. It is certainly the film I have been moved by more than any other I've seen lately and the one I feel I have learned the most from.

Death is an inescapable fact of life. It happens to us all. Mature moviegoers who have experienced a death in their families will recognize the beauty and vision of *I Never Sang For My Father* without any prompter's help from me, but I also feel that young people will respond to it because it is so straight-on honest. In its development of an emotional relationship that never ripens until it is too late, the screenplay Robert Anderson has adapted from his own play hits upon some of the moral issues today's young people are fighting for. Gene Hackman is a widower with a chance for a new life, a new marriage, and a new home in California with his bride-to-be. The problem is his parents. His father (Melvyn Douglas) is a self-made old curmudgeon lost in the glimmer of a TV set, the memory of his own past, and the staleness of his own jokes. Even at his own wife's funeral, the old man talks only of his own life; when he is put to bed, he is a frosty old snowman in freshly-creased pajamas. He won't hire a housekeeper, he rejects the aid of his other child, a married daughter (Estelle Parsons) who had the good sense to run away and find a life for herself outside the cloistered confines of her father's selfish and demanding prejudices. Barriers. The sister can't move the brother, the brother can't make his own needs clear to his father because the father is too deafened by the sound of his own voice, the house vibrates with tensions erected by the inability to communicate. Hate is discolored and diluted by respect; action is blocked by guilt. Any resolution will end in sadness and the tears that were shed at the screening I attended seemed to be tears of compassion and recognition.

I am probably not wise enough to find the flaws in *I Never Sang For My Father*, but I don't really feel the inclination or the obligation. I was too emotionally involved. I saw in Mr. Douglas' towering performance too much of my own father, in Dorothy Stickney's vulnerable poetry too much of my own mother before she died, in Mr. Hackman's plight too many of my own guilts about leaving home to make my own life when I felt a responsibility to the people I was leaving behind. The film is all but totally actionless and its direction, by Gilbert Cates, is sparse and direct, but it never lags or sags, because Mr. Anderson's writing is so human and shattering and the performances are among the finest I've ever seen on a motion picture screen. Great roles seldom are written for men these days, unless they are roles of a classical nature or movie biographies of famous people, but the humanity and sensitivity in the roles of father and son, and the way in which they are played by Mr. Douglas and Mr. Hackman, lead me to believe there is no need to search any further for people who deserve Oscars next season.

It is gratifying to leave a movie having actually *felt* something. There is nothing wrong with a good cry now and then, and *I Never Sang For My Father* achieves that fleshy tingle, that gnawing at the heart, and that throbbing sense of participation in the lives of others that rise warmly through the body until the body reacts through tears of humility and gratitude—achieves it all without sentimentality or insistence. This is not a movie one can be passive about, but then neither is life—unless life, like death, is impenetrable. And if that is the case, we've made our last wish and seen our last movie.

The rising body of Frank Perry's work in American films convinces me he is one of our finest directors. Like Fred Zinneman, he imposes on each film only the rhythms and textures it can support without that irritating monomaniacal ego stamp that many directors insist upon in order to make all their films look exactly alike. Consequently, his new one, *Diary of a Mad Housewife*, no more resembles his previous one, *Last Summer*, then Zinneman's *High Noon* resembles his *Man For All Seasons*. *Diary* is about a sophisticated young New York marriage that could well have been invented by J. D. Salinger if he were still an active member of the human race instead of a weird recluse haunted by literary memories. The husband is one of those dopey young East Side execs who could very well have been a later version of Selena Graff's brother's friend Eric from *Just Before the War With the Eskimos*. He is very precise. When he instructs his wife to pack some things for an overnight trip, the coat can't be just any old coat, it must be the coat from Turnbull and Asser. The Thanksgiving turkey must be stuffed with oysters and chestnuts chopped *just so*, the Christmas shopping must be done according to a specified list, the wine he orders must be 1964 Rominez St. Vivant, and his breakfast must consist of a four-minute egg, a scone, no butter, and damson plum preserves. He is a creep, and Richard Benjamin plays him as though he is eating steak tartare with his bare hands and doesn't care who sees him. The wife is one of those marvy-poo Eastern tweedy types who arrives to have an affair with a slightly depraved writer and walks around his apartment with a purse in one hand and a drink in the other.

Diary of a Mad Housewife is all about their world and it is sublimely delicious. The film has a pristine look that is as sophisticated and crisp as the crystal department at Bonnier's. The sets are perfect replicas of the kind of high-ceilinged apartments young affluent New York couples on their way up live in that make you want to move right in when the movie's over. Yet behind all the masks of sophistication and now-people affluence, it's as though Perry had hidden his cameras in one of those kinetic sculptures in the couple's apartment and trained them on the fragments of life as they pass in and out of view like TV executives through revolving doors. Beneath the perfect gloss is the chafe and gristle of life as it is lived on the neurotic New York scale. This movie could never have been made anywhere else because it is not *about* anywhere else. It keeps its finger on the pulse-beat of a particular kind of *locomotor ataxia* that exists nowhere but in New York. These people have read their Norman Podhoretz and they know all the names of the caterers who serve omelettes at those deadly little after-theater parties in the best New York tradition, and Perry knows their scene so well that he has been able to bring out all the manifestations of it with what looks like breathless ease. He has managed to make New York apartments look as dark and intimate as they really do at four in the afternoon, he has managed to photograph New York streets with the proper amount of dirty slate-colored light so that they really look like New York streets instead of ribbons of blue romantic gauze, and he has extracted fresh, detailed performances from two newcomers, a bruised young Rabelais named Frank Langella and a slightly Tom Wolfe heroine named Carrie Snodgress, who smiles like Maria Schell and sounds like Margaret Sullavan.

Diary of a Mad Housewife is so much about getting ahead without getting sick (or running out of gas in the traffic jam) that I am now beginning to wonder how well the film will do in sections of society outside the New York metropolitan area. I hope it flourishes, because it is a beautiful, studied, controlled, and dazzling piece of filmmaking, but my mind keeps darting back to the scene in which Mr. Benjamin and Miss Snodgress try to impress everybody by inviting people they hardly even know to a disastrous party they can't afford to give, and only succeed in alienating all the people they wanted to impress in the first place. Unless you've been to as many of those parties as I have, you can't imagine what those dreadful omelettes can do to wreck a New York marriage.

Also playing:

The Revolutionary. At some university of indeterminate origin, in some Kafkaesque country of no particular geographical definition except "somewhere in the free world," Jon Voight dresses like a bum, urinates in the street for no reason, writes on walls, quotes Robespierre, and actually behaves as though he knows what this deadly movie is all about. He gets suspended from college for his politics, but you never know what his politics *are*. "I didn't realize all these other things were going on," says a rich girl. All *what* things? Voight mimeographs some appeals for a peace-strike fund and there's talk of "a radical committee" and a bit of the kind of police brutality that is all the rage these days in movies that are trying desperately to make a point with nothing specific in mind to say, but none of it makes any sense and the pacing is so slow I can't imagine anyone staying awake long enough to care. All the actors are Americans, but the atmosphere is more like Dublin, and whatever revolutionary nature there is to the film seems more like the Boxer Rebellion than anything today. All I can say is that *The Revolutionary* is lucky to have Jon Voight, because he is the only likeable thing in it. Without him it would be intolerable instead of merely forgettable.

The Cheyenne Social Club. Cowboy inherits whorehouse. From there, the laughs can't be located with a telescope. Picture, if you have the heart, James Stewart and Henry Fonda, lying in bed with their toupees slipping down on their foreheads, and Stewart can't go to sleep, see, because Fonda is keeping him awake cracking walnuts with his bare hands, and we're supposed to actually laugh! Actors must take whatever jobs they can get these days, but it's a sad embarrassment when old pros like these have to sink to this kind of corny, old-fashioned material. Co-starring Shirley Jones and Rigor Mortis, who enters early and stays through the very last scene.

Something For Everyone. A first film by Broadway director Harold Prince that borrows much from the art and style of the films of pre-Nazi Germany to illustrate a funny, baroque, and visually enchanting exercise in black comedy. Angela Lansbury is magnificent as a fading countess with a castle in need of repairs, and Michael York is all beautiful, silky, deadly charm and lean, hungry ambition as the young Machiavelli who seduces each member of her family to social climb. There is a wonderful bit by the Greek actress Despo as Miss Lansbury's old family Lesbian friend, a neatly dissected performance by a round, dimpled parfait named Jane Carr as Miss Lansbury's Little Lulu of a daughter, and awesomely lush photography by Walter (*Tom Jones*) Lassally that floods the film with fresh air and gingerbread atmosphere. Yet beneath the sun and the chiffon, *Something For Everyone* is saturated with the clinical, howling humor of early Billy Wilder, and bathed in the rich, intelligent decor of Ernst Lubitsch. It is a monument to artistry and taste—an evil little film filled with perversely funny humor, leaving the taste of a raspberry tart on the tongue.

Borsalino. A slick and diverting French version of an old Warner Brothers gangster movie, set in Marseilles, with Jean Paul Belmondo as Bonnie and Alain Delon as Clyde. Some nice Thirties costumes and sets; lovely color photography with a rhythmic feel for the period it depicts; a $3-million budget that looks it; a wonderful comic scene in which the boys sabotage the Marseilles fish market; and an amusing opportunity to watch Belmondo and Delon good-naturedly trying to upstage each other. Otherwise, imitative, hackneyed, lazily directed, and riddled with more Hollywood clichés than bullets.

Quackser Fortune Has a Cousin in the Bronx. One of the year's major surprises—a movie nobody ever heard of, sneaked into public view without the aid of the usual public relations trumpets, and an unexpected triumph, about a lovable horse manure salesman in Dublin, his romance with an American student (warmly and realistically played by a beautiful and talented screen newcomer named Margot Kidder) and his revolt against conformity and computers. Heartwarming and offbeat, and Elliott Gould and Dustin Hoffman can move over because Gene Wilder, as Quackser, is a funny-tragic new kind of anti-hero who is more than just another pretty face . . . he's dynamite!

November 1970

Unlike the sages in Cole Porter songs who get no kick from cocaine, I've never even sniffed the stuff, but I doubt if the effect would be much different from viewing the latest Vanessa Redgrave movie, *A Quiet Place in the Country.* In this schizoid nightmare of seances and ghosts and eerie apparitions Miss Redgrave plays the benefactress of a painter (Franco Nero) who is slowly sinking into madness. As the first scene unravels, the screen is washed in white, as though the pigmentation in the print has been blotted out with a strobe light. Miss Redgrave chains Mr. Nero to a chair, sadistically brutalizes his mind and body, then stabs him to death in a tub of steaming water. It is a vision out of science fiction, but when he awakes she is calmly dressing, pulling her cool, fashionable blouse over her head, preparing for another hot summer day in Milan. "You just murdered me," he says. "Are the police after me yet?" she laughs. Then she gives him enough money to get him through the day, cracks her heels down the steps, and vanishes into the traffic. He is her prisoner; she pulls his strings. She appears on the street as a nurse, pushing him in a wheelchair. She wraps his body with electrodes and pulls the switch, charging his body with bolts of electrocution. "I've got to get out of here—I'm sick!" he keeps saying, but Miss Redgrave wants him to keep turning out profitable canvases and nobody else pays any attention to him at all. I can't say I blame them. The dubbing is so bad you can't understand much of what he says anyway.

A quiet place in the country is what he needs—a place to work, an escape. So Miss Redgrave rents him a villa near Venice. The problem seems temporarily resolved, but this movie is just beginning. Poor Mr. Nero, it seems, has moved into a ruin haunted by a poltergeist named Wanda. Ceilings cave in, floors collapse, and a demented gardener leaves fresh flowers daily at the spot near the wall where poor Wanda was machine-gunned to death in a red dress by Nazi terrorists. If all this sounds funny, believe me it isn't. Wanda turns out to be a nymphomaniac who begins to take over the painter's soul. He builds a shrine to her in an attic room where he can secretly act out his sexual fantasies, and when Miss Redgrave becomes suspicious he murders her with a shovel, chops up her body with a butcher knife, and freezes her remains in an icebox. From his room, the placid, green fields form a postcard view in which a valley of painters now sit splashing canvases of their own with brilliant hues of homage to the ghost of his obsession. Suddenly he rubs his eyes. They have become Nazis. They search him out in the empty house, pack him into an ambulance and take him away to an asylum. In the final scene, he watches from the madhouse as Miss Redgrave walks her dog and counts the paintings he has finished behind the bars of his cell. Has she planned the whole thing? Was the murder a fantasy? Has *he* become Wanda in his own mind? (There is even a shot of him kissing himself, suggesting a soul transfer.) What is fantasy, what is illusion, and what is reality?

A Quiet Place in the Country is one of the sleepers of the year. It's bizarre and wild and sometimes self-indulgent in its camera trickeries, but it is never dull and often quite brilliant. As psychological thrillers go, it is one of the best of its kind, at times resembling a perverted *Portrait of*

Jennie. Elio Petri, one of Italy's best young directors, manages to make the audience experience paranoid fantasy in terms that are realistic and terrifying. Wine dripping off a tabletop, a bee struggling to get off its back, the noise of a spider inside a wall—Petri uses these devices to crush the nerves of the viewer until the audience is overtaken with nervous horror. His quiet place in the country is crawling with unseen perils and his camera knows exactly how to juxtapose the hidden pulses of the characters overtaken by the terror with the tempo and build of the visual aspects of the film. Petri has worked with fantasy themes before, in *The Tenth Victim* and *We Still Kill the Old Way*, and he knows exactly what he's doing. The movie fairly drips with style.

Vanessa Redgrave, I am told, appeared in the film to insure financing for her friend Mr. Nero. It was completed two years ago and I am appalled at the lack of publicity with which the people at United Artists surrounded its New York release. The studio moguls apparently think very little of it, so it might be difficult to find throughout the country. But if you enjoy having the living daylights scared out of you as much as I do, search it out. *A Quiet Place in the Country* is to horror films what Château Grillet is to wine. If the hacks who run the movie companies had their way, they'd drink nothing but Manischewitz.

Well timed to hit the nation's screens simultaneously with the American elections is *WUSA*, a commercial Hollywood movie with strong and bitter doses of political propaganda. I have seldom felt more distressed after seeing a movie than I did after seeing this one, but I hope its depressing aspects do not discourage that vast heartland of moviegoers who might learn something from it. *WUSA* is not a great film, and some of its flaws are serious, but it packs a terrific punch and it does raise questions we ought to start facing if this country is to have the kind of future some of us hope it will have.

Paul Newman is a drifter who has seen enough of the rough side of life and its causes to want to turn off the problems of the world and drown his sorrows in a beer can. Joanne Woodward, playing the kind of Southern floozie she does better than anyone else in films today, is a vagrant, down on her luck, "too dumb for the phone company and too old for the five-and-dime." They waft into New Orleans at Mardi Gras and decide to stay awhile. Newman gets a job as a disc jockey reading editorials on a radio station with the call letters WUSA. The editorial messages stink of phony liberalism and pseudo-patriotism, but the job pays the rent, so what the hell. Into this nest of dropouts falls idealistic, naïve do-gooder Tony

Perkins, a young man with a history of mental illness destined to be a self-styled Miss Lonelyhearts, carrying the problem of the weak and the afflicted in society on thin shoulders. Perkins gets a job conducting a welfare survey to see why so many downtrodden illiterates in the black community are not receiving their welfare benefits from this Great Society of ours. What he discovers in his thankless job is that there *is* no survey. It's all a fraudulent sham, backed by the black power structure, to further the ambitions of a gang of crooked white politicians headed by the owner of station WUSA. The white bosses are anxious to get people knocked out of their welfare benefits to create publicity for an evil political platform. When he confronts Newman with his evidence, his friend gives him some bleak advice: there is no hope for the patriots of the world, no future for the Christian martyrs and the social moralists. Newman sides with the bad guys because it's easier to survive that way, but something desperate and righteous snaps in Perkins' head and he takes matters into his own hands. Nobody will listen anymore, so he shows up at a political fund-raising rally in a memorial stadium and attempts to assassinate the corrupt politicians. A riot breaks out, he is murdered by the cops, Newman delivers a phony speech over the loudspeaker system and in the chaos poor, bewildered, and disillusioned Miss Woodward is arrested with a purse full of her hippie friends' marijuana and sent to jail. Alone in the dark emptiness of her cell, with a felony charge and a former record, with no friends in high places and no way out, she hangs herself with a chain. In the final scene, Newman is leaving New Orleans. Don't take it out on yourself, counsels one of his Existentialist friends, America is going to fall apart anyway before long. "I'm a survivor," says Newman, over his shoulder. "Ain't that great?"

WUSA is an exercise in nihilism. The portrait it paints of America is tragic and hopeless, but it has a conscience. It is trying to show the tremendous hoax that can be pulled in the name of patriotism on millions of gullible people at cross-purposes with their own values. The American Way has always been the way of innocence. Give 'em enough cherry cobbler and they'll believe anything. Corner enough old ladies at a quilting bee and they'll vote for the most perverted demagogue in the state if they know his Aunt Tillie. This is the kind of country Americans have built for themselves, but is what we've got what we deserve? The film also, I think, attempts to make its audience feel the defenselessness of the helpless and victimized optimists who try to buck the system. If you try to wipe out corruption with the weapons of goodness and justice for all, you can get annihilated in the scramble of confusion.

I appreciate the intentions of the film and respect the sincerity and dedication of the people involved in making it. And I suppose its honesty and truth seem more relevant to me because it has been set in Louisiana, a state I know well, whose dirty political history is no secret. But the film is marred by its own theatricality. Reduce all these righteous elements of truth to a series of theatrical characters resigned to a series of plot manipulations that are more specific than general, and a few eyebrows are likely to be raised as the movie careens dangerously toward melodrama. It worried me that the only two sympathetic characters in the film (Miss Woodward and Mr. Perkins) were both emotional cripples who had no power to fight back. There are some good people left who see the evils and injustices of the exciting American political and social structure, young men and women with brains and money and power. There are young people running for office who are trying to get things changed. The Southern bigots in *WUSA* are like Tennessee Williams stereotypes from *Sweet Bird of Youth.* They still exist, but there are a lot of people around making it tougher for them. Also, the interiors are too stagey, like old plays set in Southern rainstorms. Even the riot scene seems planned, with none of the blinding and stomach-churning cinéma vérité immediacy of *Medium Cool.* This is the big climactic scene in the picture, the one in which all the characters face their own individual moments of truth, yet it is never really clear just why Mr. Perkins makes it so easy for the cops to kill him, and that, it seems to me, is the key to why Miss Woodward loses faith, sits down in the bleachers in a daze, and allows the police to subdue *her.* Everything happens fast, but either careless editing or loose scriptwriting has sacrificed the characters and their motivations and betrayed the audience by substituting action thrills for emotional coherence.

Still, these are small points to raise in a film of such noble intentions. Paul Newman is not likely to please his fans because there is nothing admirable or heroic about the role he plays, but it is the hardest part to play in the whole movie and he chews little bits of it away like falling crumbs from a Moon Pie, savoring the juices and tasting the possibility of each moment before swallowing. I have never seen him more subtle. The rest of the cast is first-rate, especially Cloris Leachman, as a crippled friend of Miss Woodward's; Tony Perkins, who breaks his Southern drawl into neurotic little beats and pauses and who, in one scene in which he confronts one of the New Orleans businessmen with fire and anger and fright in his voice in the middle of the Playboy Club, does some of the finest acting of his career; Pat Hingle, doing the Southern cornpone Pat Hingle bit as the vermin behind the all-American mask; and, of course,

Joanne Woodward, who almost single-handedly walks away with the picture. Watching her pass a fan blowing air over a bowl of ice, her bra showing through her bargain basement dress, I was thrilled to notice how she lifted her legs to let the breeze cool them off on her way out of the room. It brought back memories of deadly summer afternoons in New Orleans and the women I've seen there doing the very same thing. Miss Woodward is a consummate actress whose varied skills never cease to amaze and enchant me.

There are other memorable things: The script Robert Stone has adapted from his brilliant novel *Hall of Mirrors* is tough and vigorous (except for that riot scene, when it seems to give up); Richard Moore's camerawork accurately captures the rain and the soupy, heady heat of the French Quarter and nails its inhabitants like jungle plants in a rococo cage; Stuart Rosenberg's direction gives his actors room to breathe. All things combined, *WUSA* is a film of urgency and conviction, with a plea in its voice worth listening to.

Monte Walsh is a thoughtful, gently paced movie about the death of the Old West, set in a time when the West just wasn't happening anymore. The saloons were empty, the cattle herds were dying, the cowpunchers were getting laid off, and when they started fencing in the land and closing down the ranches, the legends known as cowboys turned into vestigial organs. Some of them dug fence posts, others opened stores in the one-horse towns where the railroads sprang up, still others became cattle rustlers and outlaws, shooting and stealing from their old friends out of desperation and paranoia—anything to survive in a world that was passing them by.

"Where did all the cowboys go?" is a question that has been explored in better movies than *Monte Walsh*—superior films like *Will Penny*, *The Rounders*, and *Lonely Are the Brave*. But even though it is so slow it is often dull, *Monte Walsh* is not a dishonest movie. It has been assembled by men of taste and talent with what looks like dedication, and the hard work shows. William Fraker, a former cameraman best known for photographing the famous car chase sequence in *Bullitt*, has taken a story by Jack Schaefer, the author of *Shane*, and milked it of most of its possibilities. He still has a way with a difficult scene (I was particularly impressed with a bronco-busting sequence which, I am told, took ten days to shoot at a cost of half a million dollars). He has extracted from Lee Marvin a performance of surprising dimension and subtlety as an aging drifter who doesn't know where to turn when the only world he knows grows out from under him.

There is a nice background theme sung by Cass Elliott, some realistic shots of the cowboys remembering old times in the bunkhouse at night, and sturdy performances by Jack Palance, Jim Davis, Mitch Ryan, and a saddle full of wonderful character actors, all of whom have faces that look like missing pieces in a jigsaw puzzle of a barren and weatherbeaten desert landscape by Remington. And when all else fails, as it sometimes does, there is always the magic of Jeanne Moreau in her first American movie. Playing that old sagebrush cliché, the whore with the heart of gold who dies of tuberculosis, Miss Moreau has very little to do or say, but although her purpose is clearly to occasionally divert the audience from the continual sight of all those battered old war horses, she works like a real actress instead of a dance-hall prop in a Sunday night TV shoot-em-up. Her first scene is played without dialogue, but in her sighs and in her smiles and in her tired, timeless movements, you know all there is to know about her. Moreau's face is musical, and even in a movie like *Monte Walsh* she plays its themes to the camera like a symphony of sadness. Without her, *Monte Walsh* might not be half the movie it is; with her, it seems a great deal more, I suspect, than anyone intended.

And finally, in case anyone cares, there's *Little Fauss and Big Halsy*, a sort of Batman and Robin on wheels. God only knows to what hellish degree the success of *Easy Rider* will affect commercial Hollywood film-making, but it looks as though we're in for a landslide of bastardized variations on the anti-hero theme about emptyheaded bike riders doing their thing. This one has songs by Johnny Cash, nudity, profanity, Lesbianism, and Hell's Angels girls in motorcycle outfits by Pierre Cardin. Robert Redford is the new-style stud Erroll Flynn played twenty years ago and Michael J. Pollard, a kind of duncey sidekick who looks like Mr. Peepers stoned on Acapulco Gold, are entering this big race, see, and . . . well, you get the picture.

December 1970

The Ten Best Films of 1970

Five Easy Pieces
I Never Sang For My Father

Loving
Diary of a Mad Housewife
The Passion of Anna
Three
The Landlord
*M*A*S*H*
Tristana
Ryan's Daughter

The Ten Worst Films of 1970

Myra Breckinridge and *Catch-22* (a tie)
Beyond the Valley of the Dolls
Getting Straight
Tropic of Cancer
The Magic Garden of Stanley Sweetheart
Bloody Mama
Medea
Burn!
The Magic Christian
Zabriskie Point

Bad movies that pop up continually, like buttercups along a highway, are almost always easy to write about. What is difficult in reviewing films is finding new ways to praise good pictures without getting sappy and sentimental. The problem reaches insurmountable heights this month because *Five Easy Pieces* is not only a good film, it's a masterpiece—and I don't know any other way to communicate the proper amount of enthusiasm I feel for it than to come right out and call it by its rightful name.

Like most works of art, it is an almost impossible movie to discuss. It simply has to be seen and felt. In a film so excellent, there are so many things to honor that I feel incapable of dealing with them all. To begin, *Five Easy Pieces* comes about as close to European filmmaking as Hollywood is likely to get. It's close enough. There is a triumphant purity about it; a silent tempo, like a throb in the temple, moving it quietly and subtly to its conclusion, that I find sadly lacking in most American films. It is quite simply the finest motion picture I have seen this year.

To merely say that it is a movie about a pipefitter on an oil rig who journeys back to the family of intellectuals he left back home in order to find the clues to what his life is all about would do the film a disservice. That is the basic plot, but *Five Easy Pieces* is more complex than that. A good bit of it is shot on the open highway, but it is also more than just another "on the road" flick. It is a film about people, about what makes them different from other people, about how they got that way. Nothing much happens in terms of action or histrionics, but it is totally absorbing, riveting drama, the stuff of life, and many things about it moved me to tears without the feeling that I was being manipulated in any way.

Essentially *Five Easy Pieces* concerns the life style (or lack of one) of a man running away from his potential. Jack Nicholson, the superb young actor who walked away with *Easy Rider*, plays Bobby Dupea, a man whose outward appearance suggests the stereotype of a small-town yokel: beer, bowling, and a waitress girlfriend with a henna rinse named Rayette, who sucks her thumb and listens to Tammy Wynette records. But Bobby is different. He is moody and bored. In a traffic jam, he spots a piano in the back of a truck, climbs aboard, and plays a Chopin sonata. Continual little defiances of his life style keep occurring to baffle his chums until he begins a long drive north toward British Columbia with Rayette in tow, and we begin to see what kind of roots he comes from. Life in the Victorian house of his childhood is sterile, fatuous, intellectual, pretentious. The corny simplicity of Rayette contrasted with the romantic idealism of a second girl he meets confuses him even deeper. In a futile attempt to reconcile himself with his mute and dying father, he explains: "I move around a lot, not because I'm looking for anything really, but 'cause I'm getting away from things that get bad if I stay. Auspicious beginnings, you know what I mean?" In a final scene reminiscent of Flannery O'Connor's heartbreaking story *The Life You Save May Be Your Own*, Nicholson drives his car into a gas station. He has once again turned his back on the intellectual atmosphere provided by his family of musical prodigies and now faces the future with the silly but loving Rayette. While the simple-minded, good-hearted Rayette goes into a nearby café for coffee, he watches his life pass before his aging eyes in an image of desperation and hopelessness in the men's room mirror. Thumbing a lift with a logging truck, he rides off down the highway once more, leaving behind in the frosty morning the girl who loves him, stranded in the lonely station.

Even in this bare outline, with none of the marrow to fill in its bones, I have done harm to the lyrical and poetic beauty of *Five Easy Pieces* because it is so much like a novel it is important to experience the myriad of details —ambiguous, outlined, embroidered, complicated—that make up the texture of its narrative fabric. Every scene is so honest and natural and right the movie seems unwritten, unrehearsed. Nicholson is a strange man, unable to find a niche in life, unable to commit or relate except in fragmentary incidence, and it is these fragments that give the film its literary quality. Bob Rafelson, a director whose only previous film was the way out, wonderful, and badly underrated musical fantasy *Head*, emerges as one of the handful of really top-echelon directors working in American films today. He places his camera in the right place, but in such a way that he gives each scene to the people involved in it. You are never aware of the mechanics of filmmaking in *Five Easy Pieces*; you see the scene and it moves you without being conscious of how it has been set up. I suppose there's a cliché of some sort to be drawn from that observation (something about art concealing art) but when it is all over the isolated moments add up so totally you could write a book about the character of Bobby Dupea even though he's a series of contradictions.

It would be impossible to over-praise the simplicity and deep, intrinsic wisdom of Jack Nicholson's performance. He is the great white hope among the current group of screen actors and this is the first film he has yet had the good fortune to appear in that has used all of his intelligence and artistry to the fullest of their capabilities. It is also good to see Rafelson's triumph over commercial casting in the use of people generally unknown to the public but realistically suited for their roles. *Five Easy Pieces* is so rich in an abundance of quality performances it would be impossible to single out everyone responsible for making even the most minute walk-on a cherished memory, but a special encomium of adulation goes to Karen Black, whose piggy pout, teased hair, seedy mascara and fake leopard-cloth miniskirts lend physical dynamite to the inner workings of a girl whose brain is soft but whose heart is full.

Simply everything about this film is a source of wide-eyed wonder, from the way its sets look as homemade as a patchwork quilt to the way its scenes have been written, as though the movements of its people had been worked out like notes on a sheet of symphonic score paper. *Five Easy Pieces* is that rarest event in the cinema—a movie in which absolutely nothing ever goes wrong. It breaks new ground in American films by photographing and communicating the messages inside the human heart and relating them to life in the style of art. It is *the* movie of 1970 to see if you are even remotely interested in the medium, and if you think all this is beginning to sound like a mash-note, you're right.

Because of *Holiday*'s combined December–January issue, it is impossible to review all the films I'd like to, but to round out the year, I'd like to mention a few:

Scrooge. Leslie Bricusse's musical version of *A Christmas Carol* is an

English pudding with sumptuous sets, hundreds of extras clog-dancing their way through Dickensian streets and back alleys that look like leftovers from Shepperton's *Oliver!* sets, a sob for every throat, a tear for every eye, and a smile for every face. Edith Evans is a crinkled and saturnine Ghost of Christmas Past, Alec Guinness is a campy Marley and an unlikely bit of casting has Albert Finney playing Scrooge. It's obvious from the direction that Ronald Neame had no idea what to do with any of it except to turn his cameras on and hope for the best, but even against such a stacked deck, it is fascinating to watch Finney assume the mannerisms of old age. In a movie with very few memorable moments, I nonetheless shall always look back with fondness on the sight of Finney—so laden with frown lines and wrinkles and asphalt-gray makeup he looks pickled in brine—as scabrous and crotchety an old skinflint as the brain of Lionel Barrymore could ever have conjured, shuffling through the Christmas market fleecing the poor, doubled over in meanness and rage, as he bursts into a fast chorus of a song called *I Hate People*. Delicious.

Homer. A warm, level-headed attempt to show, without bias or scorn, the reasons why kids leave home and why we have a generation gap that spans not just places like Woodstock and Berkeley, but also reaches the country hamlets and small farm communities in rural America as well. As *Homer* opens, a boy stands on an open highway with two signs in his hand. One says "New York," the other says "San Francisco." He's going somewhere and it doesn't much matter where. Any direction will do. The sheriff picks him up and takes him back home to his folks. They are good people, but they don't talk much and when they do it's usually about their son Homer's long hair or his messy room or his noisy rock music. They are the kind of parents who make the dinner table a psycho cage of "Pass the salt, please" and "Excuse me" and think the war is good for boys because it knocks some sense into them. Homer grows up, makes it with a local girl, plays a little guitar, swipes cigarettes and drinks hootch. He's shiftless, with no ambition. His parents give up. In the end, he's back on the highway, thumbing it on his way to a new life.

In the Forties, we had all the Italian street pictures, where everyone was rebelling against the Italian aristocracy in movies like *Shoeshine, Open City*, and *Paisan*. Today we have the American "road" pictures, where the youth of the country are leaving home in search of whatever it is they can find that is different from wherever it is they came from. *Homer* doesn't try to make any points or spout any philosophy, but it does open up new vistas of understanding for the stifled children of old-fashioned small town families. It is a lovely film, full of delicate humor and wise observations about human nature. When Homer scandalizes his parents by demonstrating against the war in Vietnam by chaining himself to the steps of the VFW Hall, it becomes a commitment for us all. John Trent, a young director worth watching, has guided *Homer* with a willful leisureliness that is gracious and touching, and the screenplay, by Claude Harz, constructs a series of vignettes of community life in provincial America that are realistic and refreshing without ever being cliché-ridden. (One carefully detailed and joyously corny sendoff for a boy on his way to Vietnam was so full of fresh air and natural charm it took me back to my salad days among the farmers and country neighbors of one of the many small towns I lived in as a child.) *Homer* is atmospheric and admirable, and Don Scardino, Alex Nicol, Lenka Peterson, and a wonderful young Canadian actor named Tim Henry are some of the people who make it so.

Adam at 6 A.M. This time a rich boy trying to make some sense out of the hypocrisy around him leaves the stagnant Beverly Hills swamps with their Japanese gardeners and heads out on the road in his expensive sports car to attend a relative's funeral near Kansas City, only to discover the "real" people out there are even more prejudiced and shallow than the affluent society he left behind. There is one great moment when a local hayseed demands an explanation of *Blow-Up*, but mostly it's pretty unbelievable stuff. A winning performance by Kirk Douglas' son Michael, who looks like a postcard replica of his old man right down to the chin-cleft; harmless but inconsequential entertainment.

R.P.M. The campus is rioting, and the only three mediators the violent radicals holed up in the administration building will listen to are Che Guevara, Eldridge Cleaver, and Anthony Quinn. Che is dead and Cleaver is obviously in secret conference with his publishers, so the poor, tortured board of trustees calls up Quinn in the middle of the night. "George who?—oh, hello, dean," yawns Quinn. "Tell him to shove it," says twenty-five-year-old graduate student Ann-Margret from the next pillow. But Ph.D. sociology professor Quinn gets on his motorcycle and heads for the faculty meeting. He wears tweed jackets and turtle-neck sweaters, eats Jello, jogs, and lives with Ann-Margret, so what's a little riot? Besides, he's written four books on social inter-reaction and he wants to see if it works. So he takes on the kids, who are making phone calls to Europe and crippling the university by sabotaging the IBM computers. But they aren't too formidable either, see, because they want to get this thing over with. Seems some of them have dates coming down from Smith on Saturday night . . .

Only Stanley Kramer, who brought the world *Ship of Fools, Guess Who's Coming To Dinner,* and the even ghastlier *Secret of Santa Vittoria,* could have dreamed up this escapist lunacy. He should be condemned to spend the rest of his days in a black screening room that shows nothing but his own movies, where the projector never stops turning, and there are no popcorn machines and no exits.

Trog. Try as I may, I can think of no better description of this ridiculous ordeal by disbelief than the publicity handout from Warner Bros. that accompanied it: "A troglodyte believed by scientist Joan Crawford to be the missing link is discovered in a subterranean cave. He's a killer and not too pretty but as a scientific find he's sensational."

First Love. The Turgenev novel, directed by Maximilian Schell, and photographed by Ingmar Bergman's cameraman, Sven Nykvist, with such a detached, icy casualness that it becomes hypnotic in spite of its own ennui. Brooding, cold, and pretty to look at, like an opium dream sponsored by Westinghouse.

The Act of the Heart. Donald Sutherland, the most obscure closet movie star in the world, is a monk who smiles at his own dialogue, and Genevieve Bujold is a weird girl who keeps seeing imaginary coffins burst into flames in the church aisle while Heavenly choirs sing Bach cantatas, in a pretentious, hysterical exercise in religious fanatacism that is even funnier than *The Song of Bernadette.* Sections of it are in French, but the subtitles are so clumsy only halves of sentences are translated, resulting in stretches of boorish tedium. Gorgeous photography of Canada in winter, good shots of winter sports. Chic trash, but certainly not a movie.

I Am Not Curious

The New York Times
March 23, 1969

The Trash Explosion is here, and *I Am Curious—Yellow* is at the bottom of the garbage dump. This genuinely vile and disgusting Swedish meatball is pseudo-pornography at its ugliest and least titillating, and pseudosociology at its lowest point of technical ineptitude, yet the thing that distresses me—and indeed should distress us all—is the way it has been received. Passing one of the two theaters in New York where this rotten little movie was playing last week, I was amazed to see the lines of suckers at the box office. "Must be somethin' dirty," said the cab driver, motioning to the crowd falling in, chow-line style, in groups of twos, all the way down the block. "Only thing people line up for in this town is somethin' free or somethin' dirty."

An instant later, two college types with a Connecticut license plate pulled alongside the cab. "Which way to the Cinema Rendezvous?" they asked, rolling down the window.

"That the dirty movie?" yelled the cab driver.

"Yeah, that's the one. The Swedish one."

"Back two blocks—you'll see the crowd out on the street waitin' ta get in." The two Joe Colleges licked their chops, whirled their car around in the middle of 57th Street, nearly causing three collisions, and headed back across town with a roar of exhaust. "Them crazy sons-a-bitches. Nearly get everbody killed just to see a dirty movie. What's the world comin' to?"

It's really not such a dumb question. Penises, Lesbians, and sadomasochist hairbrush spankers adorn at least one window in every block in the Broadway area. Bare behinds, fornication, and endlessly creative aberrations are appearing with alarming frequency in practically every movie and play turned out from Tokyo to Tallahassee. Out in California, Sal Mineo has restaged *Fortune and Men's Eyes* so the homosexuals now shower on stage; in the off-Broadway show *Geese* two actors portraying homosexuals strip naked, lick and kiss each other's bodies, and go to bed onstage—keeping their clothes on, however, during Sunday matinees, "so the children can come"; and only last week Sally Kirkland announced that yes, she would be only too happy to perform fellatio on Rip Torn in their new movie. That's all. No more of a problem than, say, instant coffee. Of course I'd like to ask all these dedicated people what they think fellatio and showering onstage could possibly have to do with acting, but the question seems too obvious.

Almost as obvious as *I Am Curious—Yellow*, which some critics are even giving favorable reviews. Which only proves, I guess, how gullible people are when they think something is good for them. *I Am Curious* was confiscated by U.S. Customs and found obscene by a federal court jury, and we all know federal courts are part of the Establishment and therefore knockable; therefore it is good for you. *I Am Curious* was later appealed and the original ruling reversed in another court, so it is now a triumph for hard-core pornography (often mislabeled by critics as "artistic freedom") and a milestone in the fight against censorship; therefore it is good for you. *I Am Curious* has an "X" rating from Jack Valenti's MPAA committee, and any committee old-fashioned enough to tell today's psyched-out kids they can't see a movie has to be attacked and ridiculed; therefore it is good for you. Well, don't you believe it. *I Am Curious—Yellow* is about as good for you as drinking furniture polish. Unlike *The Killing of Sister George* and *If* (which do *not* deserve "X" ratings), this is one crummy, lewd little 42nd Street peep show that justifiably deserves to be censored. Children *shouldn't* see it. It would bore them to death. In fact, I don't think it should be seen by any people of *any* age with I.Q.'s of 25 or over, unless they suffer from chronic insomnia. One thing I guarantee: *I Am Curious—Yellow* will put you straight to sleep.

Don't get me wrong. I have crusaded against censorship for as long as I can remember. I'm as much of a voyeur as the next guy. And I have nothing against horny pornography, either. Pornography can even be fun, as long as it doesn't pretend to be something it isn't. But don't show me a naked girl performing fellatio on a man's genitalia in the middle of a field or a man performing cunnilingus on a girl in the middle of the living room floor and pass it off as "social comment." I've read some pretty weird apologies for *I Am Curious—Yellow* (including the one by the man at the *Times*) but I really had to laugh at the defensive article by a writer named Richard Atcheson which Grove Press is sending out in the form of a publicity press kit. This article claims "the film contains many straightforward scenes of sexual intercourse in a variety of *tableaux vivants*, a feature that has given rise to the assumption that *I Am Curious* is a dirty movie." Oh, c'mon, already. The movie is out and it's no longer an assumption. This IS a dirty movie, and if fornicating on fence rails, in lakes, tree trunks, and various other public places, or performing fellatio, cunnilingus, and anal intercourse on screen are "perfectly straightforward," then the ladies everybody got so upset about in *The Killing of Sister George* were merely two nice Radcliffe co-eds making mudpies. The people who are lining up to see *I Am Curious—Yellow*—victims of advertising exploitation and suckers willing to shell out advanced prices for a cheap thrill (at the theater where the film is playing in Greenwich Village, they're charging $4.50 on a reserved-seat basis and taking mail orders)—are not going to all that bother because they are looking for another *Lassie Come Home*. They want smut. Of course what they get is such simple-minded, badly photographed, crudely directed textbook sociology with pretentious overtones of seriousness that they could easily stay home and make the same movie themselves. Call it "CBS Reports the Social Fabric of Sweden Today" and subdivide it into three segments:

(1) "How To Make a Home Movie." Here we have a director named Vilgot Sjoman, who, John Simon has already informed us in a recent Sunday *Times* article, is a "serious" director because he studied under Ingmar Bergman (he was an assistant director on *Winter Light*); but whose three works I've seen (*My Sister, My Love, 491,* and now this crud) prove only that he is a very sick Swede with an overwhelming ego and a fondness for photographing pubic hair. Because he has no visible idea of what coherent moviemaking is all about, he has used that hairy old "movie-within-a-movie technique to splice together several disconnected impressions of things on the minds of most reactionary Swedes today and label them sociology.

As the film begins, he is sleeping with a part-time actress with a double chin named Lena Nyman. They invent an idea for a new film in which she will star, thereby inabling her to hike around Stockholm asking people silly questions about Martin Luther King, nonviolence, class consciousness, the draft (yawn), etc., etc. This Lena is not only a fat pig who looks a bit down in the ankle; she's a real intellectual *poseur*, too. During a Yevtushenko lecture, she turns to Sjoman and says, "In Rio de Janeiro you can screw for free." Quick cut from Yevtushenko to a mongoloid child banging its head against the bars of an iron crib. In this same "home movie" segment, add a lot of nudity and playing around (you'll have to find an actress (?) who doesn't mind playing around, which shouldn't be difficult) in Lena's room, which is full of "I Am Free" posters, filing cabinets, Coke bottles, and enormous portraits of Franco on the wall—everything to suggest one of the naïve little Dumb Doras in the mid-Thirties who joined the Communist party because it seemed like a swell place to meet their friends. Add a lot of talk about socio-economic reform, show Lena carrying a bunch of "Boycott Spain" or "Message to the Colored People—Be Prepared! The Whites Are Staggering!" signs, or whatever is current and fashionable that week, and—presto!—you've got a home movie *and* a social comment, Swedish documentary style, all grainy and badly photographed like the worst of American television, and all ready for American critics to call "art."

(2) "How To Conduct a Meaningless Interview." Begin each scene with an obvious political slur. You know. Something really snappy, like "The conservative party leader has had a nightmare!" Accompany it with the time of day and a weather forecast. Have the Swedish national anthem sung while panties are being lowered and pants flies unzipped. Then have the two leads sit on top of each other and fornicate on a balustrade of the Royal Palace while a chorus sings a military song in the background. Intercut the sexual intercourse with a superficial, banal interview with the King of Sweden. Intersperse the nudity, voyeurism, and sexual perversity with "serious intellectual attitudes," like applying the purpose of the Nazi criminal trials in Nuremberg to United States intervention in Vietnam. Just so people like Richard Atcheson won't think it's a dirty movie. Then by all means throw in newscasts and election returns on TV during the fornication scenes, interrupting the telecasts with clever knee-slappers like the announcement: "We'd Like To Inform Our Viewers—The Bad Picture Is Due To An Erection Fault."

(3) "How To Put the Audience On by Making Them Think They Are Seeing Something Shocking." In the previously mentioned publicity handout from Grove Press, Mr. Atcheson is also quoted as saying, "I suppose persons for whom sex itself is dirty would find scenes of sexual intercourse incorrigibly offensive, wherever they might occur and in whatever context . . . for me, it confirmed the integrity of the director and the players and projected an unexpected aura of wholesome candor." Now let me tell you about this wholesome candor. At no time in this movie does the sex act suggest reality or become even mildly wholesome. Almost every sexual act known to man is committed by people who are not only so physically repulsive that to be even slightly titillated by their grotesqueness would

suggest to me the need for consultation with a reputable psychiatrist, but who actually seem to *hate* what they are doing.

The girl Lena is so tortured by the idea of being a sex object for men who behave like dogs that she has fantasies of tying up her lovers and castrating them. And if you need further proof of how phony the whole movie is, examine this: after all the huffing and puffing, the boy, shortly before having his genitals cut off with a kitchen knife ("youth and earnestness," I believe Mr. Atcheson called it), rises from a particularly exhausting round of anal intercourse on the floor. He doesn't appear to be physically aroused in even the most miniscule way. It's like the girls in those low-budget grind house flicks who roll around on the beds in cheap motel rooms licking their lips a lot, but never perspire. All this pretentious, revolting, cheapjack Grove Press sideshow proves, in the final analysis, is that there are as many stupid and provincial no-talents trying to make a fast buck in Sweden as there are in every other part of the world. They're just more devious about it in Sweden; they call it *art* there.

The thing that gives me cause for concern is not the silly people who pay their hard-earned money to be flim-flammed by all this rubbish, but the effect it is likely to have on the movie industry in general. Quick to catch on to the fast-buck idea, Anthony Newley has now cornered the market on Hollywood-style pornography with *Can Hieronymus Merkin Ever Forget Mercy Humppe, etc., etc.* in which, among other assorted nauseas, he dances in the nude, performs cunnilingus on a naked girl underwater, sings a song called "What a Son of a Bitch I Am" and, for the crowning blow, actually allows a dirty old letch to run his hand up his own baby daughter's dress in a scene that has to win some kind of award for the penultimate in rotten bad taste. Asked "why" in a television interview, Newley said, "It's what the public wants." Have we become so corrupted in our search for the liberation of the arts that nothing is sacred?

Germs are spreading, and the critics (the state of criticism being what it is today) are not always wise enough to detect and diagnose them properly. At the screening of *I Am Curious—Yellow* I attended, several critics talked loudly back to the screen, moaned, and made other gratifying noises. Some even dozed off soundly. When the film ended, we all cheered with relief and headed for the elevator. Suddenly the projectionist came runnning out of the projection booth, excitedly and apologetically announcing that one of the reels had been mislaid. Would we all come back into the screening room and see the extra reel, which had just been found? All of us (including the man from the *Times*) trudged back into the room and another reel began. Several critics asked aloud where this added reel was supposed to fall in the logical sequence of events. Since the movie had been incomprehensible anyway, nobody seemed to know. I walked out somewhere between the point where a man urinated on the screen and the point where the leads discover they have "the itch" and visit a venereal disease clinic. Many others left too, declaring they had suffered enough punishment for one day. But some of the critics who confessed they didn't know where the missing reel of film belonged later published rave reviews. So don't ask me about critics.

The title *I Am Curious—Yellow*, by the way, comes from the Swedish flag. It is yellow and blue, both colors symbolically representing two different sides of the Swedish character. Sjoman has made two versions of this same film. That means that after Grove Press has made all the money it can make on this drek, there is somewhere, in some outhouse, an *I Am Curious—Blue* waiting to be unleashed on us all. Remind me to miss it.

Movies in Paris

Paris
March 1970

The French hate water. For years, Americans visiting Paris have had to ask indignant waiters for water in French restaurants, and for years I've been wondering why. Now I know. They don't like it and they don't drink it. In fact, they hate it so much they seldom even wash with it. That is why French perfume is popular and French cinemas smell as they do. Paris is probably the only city in the world where you can see a cowboy movie and smell the horses at the same time.

I am in Paris waiting for a Russian visa that may never come, and like most people in Paris with a lot of free time, I eat and go to the movies. The food is great, but the movies? Well, at least they're popular. Next to New York, Paris is probably the most movie-going city in existence. Cinema magazines with both large and tiny circulations seem to flourish from every available loft big enough to hold a desk and typewriter. The French talk movies, eat movies, make movies with handheld cameras and engage in loud, frantic arguments over the politics of movies everywhere from the Deux Magots to the Crillon bar. It is now that time of year between Christmas and Cannes—a good time to be in Paris. Daily snowfalls are drenching the city with a mixture of excitement and *tristesse*, and the French are out in droves, heading for cinemas the way New Yorkers headed for their neighborhood bars during the blackout. If, at the moment, there is a national spirit under Pompidou, it meets at the movies.

In the last three days, I've seen seven films—six French and one American—that demonstrate, to some degree, what is happening here in terms of mood, taste, and temperament. The biggest success in Paris is, unquestionably, Visconti's *The Damned*. The lines are so long they are bottlenecking traffic on the Champs-Elysées. I know some French film buffs who have gone five days in a row and discovered such traffic jams and crowds they can't get close enough to the box office to find out when the feature changes. Everywhere I go I am confronted with the same puzzled questions. The French don't understand why this "*oeuvre maitresse de Visconti*" has not been nominated for American Academy Awards. They seem even more dissatisfied with American intelligence when I tell them I don't understand it either.

Throughout Paris, a growing dissatisfaction with Hollywood as a fool's paradise of frivolity and wastefulness seems to be a uniformly expressed sentiment at the moment. *Butch Cassidy and the Sundance Kid* (called *Butch et le Kid*) and *True Grit (100 Dollars pour un sheriff)* are enjoying a moderate success because the French love westerns, but although old Vincente Minnelli musicals still draw big crowds at the Cinémathèque Française, American song-and-dance spectacles are generally spat upon with horror. *Hello Dolly!* is a disaster. Ever since *West Side Story*, probably the most successful musical ever shown here, the French have lionized Natalie Wood, so they are going to *Bob et Carole et Ted et Alice*, but few of them have anything good to say about it. They find it vulgar and naïve; after all, what this film's *ménage à quatre* cops out on in its squeamish final scene is something the French have been going through with for years. They can't see what all the fuss is about. *Alice's Restaurant* is also a catastrophe, as well it should be. The French frown on American hippies and have no understanding at all of young people preoccupied with Yogiesque withdrawal from war or social unrest. As one leading Paris critic noted: "This film has had both wide critical and financial success in the U.S., which could make one wonder about the state of that nation." Amen.

So what do they like? Well, they love the new René Clement film, *Stranger in the Rain*, a very mixed-up psychological thriller about the neurotic wife of an airline pilot whose frantic life is filled with such daily upsets as rape, Lesbian seductions, murder, escaped maniacs, bodies being thrown off cliffs into the sea, chases in the Eiffel Tower, gangland tortures, and missing red TWA bags filled with stolen fortunes. For every plot twist there are two or three new and equally confusing subplots, and by the time all the mysteries are unraveled, the film has lapsed into unrelieved tedium. As a mysterious sleuth *qui s'appelle* Harry Dobbs, Charles Bronson, who has been knocking around for years in American movies, turns in a fine, sturdy performance (although his French is a bit like Jane Fonda's), and as the housewife with never a dull moment, an outstanding young actress named Marlene Jobert is a kind of gutsy French Shirley MacLaine. I doubt if there is much here to interest America, where whodunits are a dime a dozen, but

Joe Levine has just bought it for the other side of the Atlantic. Even if it flounders, Miss Jobert will undeniably make a splash.

The new François Truffaut film, *The Wild Child*, is *The Miracle Worker* with escargot on its breath, in which Truffaut himself plays Anne Bancroft. It opens in a French forest in the Tarn in 1797. A woman gathering mushrooms is frightened out of her wits by a black monster who scurries into a hole in the ground. Aroused to a frenzy, the panicky villagers chase down the creature with vicious dogs that nearly chew its limbs off, capture it in a net, and commit it to an asylum. It comes to the attention of a doctor, a young disciple of Rousseau, who uses the savage infant as a guinea pig to test his innovational theories of education. The rest of the film shows how, with patience and compassion, he civilizes the child and turns him into a functioning member of society. The story is a true one, and by combining large doses of documentary detail and narration, Truffaut's customary delicacy and style are synthesized into a film of taste and nobility that is certainly impressive and convincing, but sometimes also repetitious and dull as well. What seems missing is the human element (all that back-breaking toil in *The Miracle Worker* was worth sitting through because, after all, we knew *that* little savage child would someday turn out to be Helen Keller). And in the same way that Patty Duke stole that film from accomplished performers several times her age, Mr. Truffaut is sweepingly upstaged by a tiny thunderbolt of energy and imagination named Jean-Pierre Cargol who, as the *enfant sauvage* of the title, turns in one of the damnedest feats of human skill to come out of the French cinema in years.

Then there is the hotly discussed Maria Callas *Medea*, directed with typical confusion and pretentiousness by Pier Paolo Pasolini. It is not quite as ridiculous as *Teorema* but equally offensive to the intelligence. This is a *Medea* that would make Euripides cut his own throat. The Italians, who are wise to Pasolini, threw cabbages at the screen, but in Paris, the French yelled "La Diva!," "La Divina!," and the local critics hurled raves for Madame Callas's debut as a movie star. For my money, it is a movie of indescribable incompetence, directed with unrelenting hysteria and performed with unequalled amateurishness. It begins with a lot of stomach-churning closeups of human sacrifice, but to what purpose (or what that has to do with *Medea*) I don't know, except perhaps to establish the fact that she comes from a barbaric country. (When she gets to Greece, it looks more barbaric than the land in the Caspian Sea she came from.) Nothing is motivated. The stealing of the Golden Fleece is never explained, since

Pasolini never even introduces Medea to Jason at any point in the film. The murder of Medea's brother is incoherent, because she is never shown falling in love with Jason except for one closeup of the famous Callas nostrils flaring intensely. (Callas is the best nostril-flarer since Susan Hayward.) The entire *Medea* legend is given short shrift and it soon becomes clear that in Pasolini's mind the Fleece (which looks like an old Mardi Gras costume) signifies a symbol of forbidden sanctity, like the apple in Eden, and what happens to Jason (who has almost been demoted to the status of a bit player) seems to represent broadly the downfall of mankind.

Instead of plot, there is a lot of loco philosophy spouted at intervals by a sexy centaur; some phony music that switches in derivation and construction from mock-Chinese to mock-Turkish to mock-Indian raga; and some bizarre sets that look not at all like Greece but very much like Indian cliff dwellings in New Mexico. The Jason of the piece looks and acts alarmingly like Howard Keel in *Jupiter's Darling* and his Greek cronies behave and sound disconcertingly like Italian pasta-rollers on the Via Veneto. Medea is a role that cries out for a Papas or Mercouri; here, it is choked to death in the hands of a woman with the emotional range of an electrical fruit juice machine. The pitch of Madame Callas's singing voice is regulated too high to adapt to dialogue of animal passion, so what screeches out from the screen instead is what the French call a *voix à la domestique*. She sounds like a chambermaid, and her movements suggest she is not so much performing a classical role as posing for the paparazzi. I realize the great Callas singing voice may not be what it used to be, but I do not think it unwise to suggest that in the future she restrict her acting to the shower.

Finally, there are three other less important but still respectable French films currently bidding for the big sail to America—the new Chabrol film, *Le Boucher*, a Hitchcockian horror film about a quaint French village and the local butcher who murders women in his spare time; *La Horse*, with the indefatigable Jean Gabin as a peaceful Norman farmer who takes on a gang of heroin-peddling gangsters; and the new Claude Lelouch film, *Love Is a Funny Thing*. The French are fed up with Lelouch. They consider him old-fashioned and one-dimensional. I agree that his last few efforts have been weepy, shallow catastrophes, but this one has a supple charm all its own. Jean Paul Belmondo is a composer scoring a film in Hollywood who runs into a French actress (Annie Girardot) laboring over a role in English. Together, they rent a car and see a bit of America. They are lonely and far from home and their own sensitivities, orchestrated against the rush and bark of western America, leads them into an affair that is alternately amusing and touching. Back home on familiar ground, after promising to meet at a designated airport in Europe, the girl finds the courage to leave her husband, but it is the man who doesn't show up. It is a sad film, but its style is more that of a jazz waltz than a violin concerto. The photography is magnificent (it took a French director to be the first to shoot the Grand Canyon, Las Vegas, and New Orleans the way they really look) and Belmondo and Girardot are like two beautiful colts romping through their first spring rain. Not a great film, but likable.

Last, and definitely least, there's *Honeymoon*, a vile, humorless 1942 fiasco that should never have been released then, much less allowed out of America *now*, but which, for reasons understood best by those who laugh at plagues and suicides, the French have seen fit to resurrect and admire. It is a big hit here and although threats of bamboo shoots under the nails could never force from me a synopsis of its maddening plot, I will recall the instance in the film at which the audience laughed loudest. Ginger Rodgers, a chorus girl who has married a Nazi, discovers on the eve of the fall of Poland, that her maid is being sent to a concentration camp. Of course poor Ginger doesn't even know what a concentration camp is, but she's certain the food must be terrible, so she does her job for her flag. She stamps her own photo in her maid's passport and in her finest furs and jewels, waves goodbye in the terminal full of boxcars full of Jews going in the opposite direction. Later she is arrested, along with Cary Grant, a radio reporter, who is also suspected of being a Jew. They end up in a series of concentration camps and are finally led by a menacing Gestapo from the RKO Nazi repertory company to a room marked for sexual guinea-pig experiments. Well, this is too much. Ginger gets mad. "Call the American ambassador!" she yells. The movie goes on like this for hours, with an endless parade of tastelessness and phony flag-waving Leo McCarey patriotism masquerading behind the ruse of comedy-cum-social comment. We forget what unconscionable monuments to obscenity Hollywood turned out in its heyday, but you can find old stinkers in Paris, pickled in lysol.

Not much to cheer about. But with customary cinematic optimism, expectations are high. It is impossible to look in any direction without seeing treetop-high billboards announcing the year's most publicized French film—and the one guaranteed to quench the French thirst for crime and violence on the screen. It's called *Borsalino* and is being trumpeted as a French *Bonnie and Clyde*, with Alain Delon and Jean Paul Belmondo. No one is sure which one plays Bonnie and which one plays Clyde. The French don't care. They'll go anyway. They'll survive the body odor; they'll sit through the interminable intermissions between features called *séances*, during which hawkers walk along the rows of seats selling popsicles while miles of badly photographed, amateurishly made commercials unreel on the screen advertising everything from foot powder to refrigerators; and when it's over, they'll walk up the aisles while loudspeakers play "Home on the Range" by the Norman Luboff Choir. I've got news for Pauline Kael: when the French say "I lost it at the movies," they really *mean* it.

Miscellaneous Movie Reviews

Dear John is probably the best film to come out of Sweden since the early days of Ingmar Bergman, from whom it derives absolutely nothing. But if it lacks the dark brown taste and moody inversion of the Bergman films, it also lacks the self-conscious cuteness of the new Swedish cinema (Jorn Donner's *To Love* comes to mind instantly). Director Lars Magnus Lindgren has embroidered a lacy love story between the lonely, unmarried mother of a four-year-old child and a moody, restless sea captain with a touch that is just old-fashioned enough to tug at your heart (if your heart is not too jaded to be tugged at), yet modern and breezy enough to make sex swing.

The people in *Dear John* could just as well live on the coast of Maine. The location is unimportant, except that Sweden just possibly photographs better than Maine; I haven't seen too many good pictures photographed there lately. It's what they do and how they are spied on by Lindgren's camera while doing it that matters here. Relationships are not merely photographed, they're allowed to happen. Lovers walk slowly along a reef as a lighthouse flickers on and off in the foreground. The film takes its time with a scene. A little girl licks an ice cream cone. A bug crawls slowly along the handle of a teakettle. Yet there is none of the Italian boredom. None of the French treetops. The experience is unique. The people are real. When the lovers pinch under the sheets, you feel it.

Dear John is also one of the most erotic films ever made, because it makes sex seem so healthy and appealing. This is done primarily through the use of two of the most exciting actors I've seen in years—Jarl Kulle and Christina Schollin. Miss Schollin looks like a radish-cheeked, slightly plumpish Lee Remick, which is quite a change from the usual nudes we get from Sweden, with their greasy hair and black circles under the eyes. Kulle is unlike American actors, because he is neither vaselined and movie-starish nor chiseled and un-movie starish. He has sandpaper skin, soft sun-specked white hair, a continually impish grin and big sad eyes, and when he looks down into Miss Schollin's eyes as she offers him money, saying "Nix baby" in broken crooked-tooth English, the screen turns several shades lighter in color.

If *Dear John* had been made in Hollywood, those bed scenes would inevitably have led to pregnancy, suicide, madness, blackmail, abortion or—worse still—marriage and a tearful ending. But somebody would have paid for all that fun. In Lindgren's film, the captain simply sends a box of chocolates and ends up in another port, where he rushes to a telephone and calls her up to say hello. There will be a next time, just like real life. It's a lovely present tense illusion with a keen eye for space, size, and light—next door, I'd say, to perfection. See *Dear John*. But don't expect a movie. Expect an experience.

Loving Couples. Also from Sweden, though not even in the same league as *Dear John*, is *Loving Couples*, the first film directed by Swedish actress Mai Zetterling, who deals with her subject matter with more brooding murkiness than is actually called for. This suffocating, semi-paralyzed little epic about three mothers awaiting childbirth in a Stockholm hospital has moments of real energy and a few hot flashes of talent, but they are too few and far between. Mostly it's just Strindberg with a hangover. Having already created quite a stir in Europe, the film will probably get a limited release in America, because it shows, among other things, two dogs having intercourse while a gaggle of silly girls titters on the sidelines, a homosexual parading as a woman in a feather boa, a Lesbian attacking an innocent schoolgirl, and the actual birth of a baby. These scenes seemed hardly as upsetting as the dreary canyons of silence around them, as though Director Zetterling had nothing really solid to offset her shock effects. There's plenty of thread, but not much of it ever gets through the eye of the needle.

The picture looks like a costly one and most of the actors are first-rate. The always hypnotic and forever versatile Harriet Andersson is impressive as a model who first is raped by a lecherous old man and later marries a homosexual artist, but I've seen her photographed better in other films. Gunnel Lindblom, Eva Dahlbeck, and several other members of the Ingmar Bergman repertory company do their best to stomp Miss Zetterling's script (co-authored with her husband, British novelist David Hughes) into the ground, which, I'm afraid, is pretty much where it belongs.

The Young Girls of Rochefort. A curious phenomenon exists today in France. Charles de Gaulle's rabid anti-Americanism has poisoned most Frenchmen with an alarming resistance to everything we do, from hemlines to hairlines. On the other hand, the French secretly copy us in many ways. They dance in western cowboy-style bars like the Crazy Horse Saloon, they crave hillbilly music and American rock-pop groups (you almost never hear a record in French in any Paris discotheque), they scream for self-defrost refrigerators and American cars, and the most "in" spot in Paris for teenagers and businessmen alike is an American Main Street replica of an apothecary shop called Le Drugstore, where you can buy everything from *Playboy* to a Blue Plate Special. Not surprisingly, then, the one area in which the French idolize us most is the Hollywood musical. Every time the Cinémathèque Française holds a "Festival de Gene Kelly" you can hear the mippie-weenies dancing down the St. Germain des Prés at midnight with garbage-can lids on their feet singing "I Got Rhythm" in bad English, their faces lit up in technicolor. No wonder then that Jacques Demy is a Deity among French film directors.

Demy loves musicals. He knows every scene from every MGM technicolor musical ever made and in recent years his greatest success has been *The Umbrellas of Cherbourg*. The French loved it, because finally they had a musical of their own, and so did many Americans. To me, it was a thumping bore, because Demy took his clichés so seriously that his film became the very thing it parodied: the American soap opera with subtitles. In *The Young Girls of Rochefort*, he does not appear to take himself so seriously and the result is much more fun.

This is a movie so pirated from old Hollywood film clips that to make sure nobody misses the point Demy even has Gene Kelly doing a guest appearance in a music shop takeoff on the "Slaughter on Tenth Avenue" number from *Words and Music*, all in wedding-cake white, with Françoise Dorléac playing Vera-Ellen. But it is filmed with such an artist's eye for color and sound and lush visual detail, and it is such a tribute to music and dance (two art forms that have all but disappeared in our own movie musicals) that I found the entire experience a perfect delight, rather like one of those magnificent super-colossal Walgreen specials.

Demy's plot is one of those mistaken identity, love-is-just-around-the-corner, everything-comes-out-O.K.-in-the-end affairs involving luscious looking people (the way people used to look at MGM before Hollywood found out about the great unwashed masses), sumptuous whitewashed sets, and an unbeatable formula for instant success: when in danger, bring on the girls. And the girls are worth bringing on. They are France's answer to the Gemini twins—Catherine Deneuve (looking more like Grace Kelly every day) and her sister, the freckle-faced Lorelei, Françoise Dorléac, who died tragically in an automobile crash soon after the film's completion. The film is as much a valentine to them as it is to Hollywood musicals, but the combination is a creamy one. American dancers George Chakiris and Grover Dale team up with the girls on one number in which everyone dances around a lavish apartment playing musical instruments that reminds me of old Gene Kelly-Donald O'Connor-Debbie Reynolds-Jane Powell movies. There's even a takeoff on the Jane Russell-Marilyn Monroe "Little Rock" number from *Gentlemen Prefer Blondes*, with the girls decked out in red sequins with slits up the side. The actors go through their paces like vitamin-injected carousel horses, the boys in orange and blue shirts and white pants, and the girls in pale pastel pinks and lavenders. Around every corner is a street filled with Jerome Robbins ballet dancers whirling through the town like dolphins, in costumes designed to match the peppermint colors of the port of Rochefort.

What Demy has done is cut out all the boring stuff that used to plague me between musical numbers and keep all the numbers. The result is a kind of jazz opera with fabulous Michel Legrand music and the Swingle Singers scat-singing through the soundtrack while the townfolk sing and dance on motorcycles, on modern-jazz-ballet basketball teams, and in front of majestic white fountains. None of it makes any sense (it isn't supposed to) and the result may not be everybody's cup of hemlock. But I don't care about everybody. I had a wonderful time and I went away, after gorging myself, feeling the need for a Bromo-Seltzer. That's better than going away feeling nothing.

The Singing Nun, with desperately pious effort, asks you to like—and believe in—all-American Debbie Reynolds as a guitar-plunking, motorcycle-riding Belgian nun who takes time out from her duties in the convent to make hit records, sign autographs, and even do a little flirting with a rival rock-and-roll team who record for the same label.

In an attempt to present nuns as golly-gee-they're-just-like-everybody-else types, the picture runs aground in a tidal wave of clichés. (Old Boyfriend Chad Everett to Debbie, when he discovers she is a nun: "Good Lord!" Debbie: "Exactly.") There is every kind of nun, from typically sour (typically sour Agnes Moorehead) to a Mother Superior with false eyelashes (Greer Garson). As for Debbie, she sings (songs by Randy Sparks of New Christy Minstrels fame), clowns, dances, prays, and bounces about like a penguin with the hiccups. A harmless, worthless little distraction, *The Singing Nun* draws a fine line between Heaven and Heavenly Hash.

A Big Hand for the Little Lady. Joanne Woodward has an intriguing way of inhaling just any old line, sloshing it around in her mouth like Lavoris, and puffing it out through her nose like cigarette smoke. She may not be Kim Stanley, but she is a much more interesting actress than a picture like *A Big Hand for the Little Lady* deserves.

Although this heavy-handed Western comedy never quite comes off, the appetizing idea behind it is admirable. Under less hoked up circumstances it might even work. Six men have bet three thousand dollars apiece on a winning hand in the biggest poker game in the prairies of 1896. While Joanne (decked out like the midwife on a Mormon wagon train) is off at the local blacksmith shop having the family horse's shoes resoled, husband Henry Fonda bets the family fortune. Before he can play his hand, he suffers a heart attack and Joanne is left to win the pot or lose her pretty shirt. She wins, of course, with the aid of a blubbery banker (Paul Ford) and all the crusty, snaggle-toothed, rattlesnake-tongued losers saddle off with heads dancing full of sugar plums of honest womanhood.

The picture doesn't stop there. It goes on and on. The "little lady," it develops, in a surprise "twist" ending, is no lady at all, but one of the best poker players in the West and a member of a gang of chiselers. Even her nine-year-old son is a crook. A good joke, once remarkably well turned in an hour TV show on which the film is based, is milked sour by enough scene-padding and facial mugging to fill three college varsity shows, with a little left over for the Hasty Pudding revue.

Fielder Cook's direction is lively enough, though somewhat hampered by all those people sitting at that poker table. Jason Robards, as a loud-mouthed bore, is merely loud-mouthed and boring, proving once and for all he is *not* America's finest actor. Henry Fonda hides his bald head under a red toupée with annoyingly girlish bangs over the forehead. Mainly the whole thing is just too overcooked for serious farce, too underplayed for howling comedy. Somehow, it just lies there, in-between, like last night's cornflakes.

Up the Down Staircase is a gingersnappy comment on the American educational system based on a wildly successful book by Bel Kaufman, who was a schoolteacher in a New York blackboard jungle for seventeen years and knew what she was talking about. The picture could have been another of those Look-at-me-while-I-make-a-point movies, but Director Robert (*To Kill a Mockingbird, Inside Daisy Clover*) Mulligan and Pulitzer Prize-winning writer Tad (*All the Way Home*) Mosel have fashioned a story so touching, so chock-full of human frailties and so rich in schoolroom detail that it achieves a reality transcending the limitations of its overworked genre.

A young teacher named Ellen Barrett (played by Sandy Dennis with such an uncommonly gifted eye for detail that she even wipes her hands each time after closing the window) stands on a crowded Harlem-slum street corner looking up at the bleak, forebidding pillar of learning called Calvin Coolidge High. Given a rousing educational send-off of six years in college, Ellen is ready to conquer the teaching profession with dedication and love. Instead, she is sent to a "problem-area" school with 3,000 students crammed 44 to a room built to hold only 33, where the other teachers are like computers, the kids are the cards they punch, and everything is so run by organized, symmetrical custom that on the first day the guidance counselor warns the new "teach" to "please watch for latent maladjustments and send them to me on alternate Tuesdays."

The miracle of teaching turns out to be such a colossal collage of accident report blanks, lateness room cards, Delaney cards, age-level reports, accident and health reports, and IBM cards that there is no time left to call the roll. Big-city schools, says this film, are not institutions for molding young minds but asylums for after-school faculty meetings that turn into fiascos because of the subway rush, kids who can't do their homework because they "had to get married," nurses who are forbidden by law to doctor a wound, and teachers who can't even *find* the wounds. When one troubled girl leaps from a window, for example, the school is very upset because her "punch-card record shows she was an excellent blackboard monitor" and because she also "has a library copy of *Idylls of the King* which is already fifteen cents overdue."

Staircase exposes the waste, the ineptitude, the stupidity of the system, and it also explores the frustrations between students and teachers, making it a personal as well as social document. It also hints not-so-subtly at why more and more teachers are turning to private schools with white columns and green lawns, where kids who pay large tuitions can still afford to let their teachers shower them with love. There's no risk involved.

The picture is notable primarily because it never preaches, it merely reminds with wonderful good humor and a few scenes that are even hilarious. (What happens when Miss Dennis defies the "system" by starting her own suggestion box, or holds an informal class discussion of *Tale of Two Cities*, is the stuff that makes it one of the year's most ingratiating films.) It is also distinguished by Director Mulligan's resistance to Hollywood casting, with the result that the movie's "faculty" (made up of Broadway actors) seems so inspired by the realistic surroundings (shot on location in the New York City schools), the "students" (all portrayed brilliantly by amateur kids from public schools), and by the highly intelligent intention of the film, that they turn in the most immaculate set of naturalistic performances I have ever seen in one movie.

But the film's major triumph is Sandy Dennis—all thumbs and mistakes as the teacher who can't even quit because they keep sending her retirement forms instead of resignation forms. It is a role full of charm and luster, and she plays it like a limp pudding turning into an elegant, full-bodied baked alaska.

Hawaii is pure corn out of the same Hollywood fields that turned Alaska into *Ice Palace* and Texas into *Giant*. Worse, because it cost more. Another of those wide-screen epics at road-show prices, it starts out tracing thirty years in the lives of the first missionaries who arrived in the Hawaiian Islands to teach Calvinism and stayed to rape a virgin country, rob its people of their innocence, their land, their sugar cane, and their self-respect. The story is an interesting one in outline form, but at these production costs it could only go in one of two directions: Margaret Mead or Edna Ferber. *Hawaii* chooses the latter and the results are, of course, horrendous.

The missionaries are pictured as an insulting, arrogant, brainless group of jackasses and the natives are such phony bowing-scraping-easy-to-convert ethnic examples they seem as insulting to Hawaiians as Uncle Toms are to Negroes. None of this is helped much by George Roy Hill's clumsy direction: characters arrive by boat and are never seen again. Others age considerably in the changing of a frame, while some remain the same. In the midst of Julie Andrews's breech-birth labor pains, when you don't know if she will live or die, the scene suddenly switches to two young Hawaiian lovers talking about incest with English subtitles. The queen of the village dies in the middle of a whistling wind that nearly destroys the town, yet the next morning the minister surveys the damage and straightens the tombstone on her grave. With scenes like that, you'll never get bored in the 3½ hours it takes to sit through *Hawaii*. You'll be too busy laughing.

As the long-suffering minister's wife, Julie Andrews is largely wasted, but tries hard to win another Oscar in that birth scene. In the kind of totally unsympathetic and highly unbelievable role that went out of style when they stopped writing scripts for Lionel Barrymore, Max von Sydow creaks through the film looking like Molière's *Tartuffe*. Von Sydow is a stunning actor whose appearances in Ingmar Bergman's films already qualify him for a kind of movie immortality. He was probably lured to Hollywood with enough money to retire on a farm in Sweden for the rest of his life. Another film like *Hawaii* and he may have to.

A Funny Thing Happened on the Way to the Forum is every bit as vulgar, witless, and dull as the burlesque Broadway musical upon which it was based, except for a few added excesses that were impossible to show onstage, namely an endless parody of the chariot race in *Ben-Hur* in which the entire cast gets battered, bruised, and knocked out in a sadistic free-for-all combining all the worst qualities of a Woody Woodpecker cartoon.

The film is a prime example of a director (Richard Lester) clashing head on with material for which he appears to have no sympathy or fondness. Lester, who directed both Beatles films and the far better *The Knack*, chose to treat the bawdy banality of the stage play with campy, far-out, free-swinging direction, ignoring plot and the mugging of star Zero Mostel. He does both, but the result is such a grab bag of camera tricks, visual gimmicks, sky pans, sherbet colors, and fast cuts that you are dizzy trying to keep up. Two scenes—one in which Mostel pursues Jack Gilford in drag on a spattered, death stained, fly-specked funeral bed, and a running gag in which Michael Crawford chases various horses through the streets to fill a goblet with horse sweat (which the other characters eventually have to drink)—are in nauseous bad taste.

The sight of all those old men knocking each other down and parading around in women's clothes is embarrassing and the shots of a gray-skinned Buster Keaton running up and down hills and crashing into tree trunks shortly before his own untimely death is too painful to watch. Zero Mostel is wasted and Stephen Sondheim's songs (the Broadway show's saving grace) are all but thrown away. It's Richard Lester's play toy all the way and he hits you between the eyes with it like a wet brick.

Georgy Girl, which won the grand prize at this year's Berlin Film Festival, is one of those heartbreaking movie experiences that are becoming rare as blue butterflies. Georgy is one of those too-big, too-ugly, unloved misfits who live in other people's spotlights. When her roommate has an unwanted baby, Georgy has the labor pains. You know the type. As played by Lynn Redgrave, the youngest member of England's famous Redgrave acting family, she is unforgettable.

Economically directed by New Waver Silvio Narizzano with a minimum of talk and a maximum of the kind of sincerity that comes from a man who cares, *Georgy* is perhaps the best keyhole-view of London's 1966 Mod world to date. It is a more successful film than *Darling* because it leaves its characters alone. They don't become movie stars or live in Italian villas. They are never manipulated to get the movie going. Narizzano controls *them*, they don't control their film. Georgy's philosophy is, "God's always got a custard pie up his sleeve." Howling like a banshee in the rain, then sitting all alone crying while watching natural childbirth on the telly, she becomes the most endearing heroine since Julie Harris played Frankie Addams in *The Member of the Wedding*. Narizzano tells her story without sentimentality, flashing scenes of humor and impact: the pregnant roommate and her boy friend on their way to get married, their footsteps echoing in the hall past the "If you need help" sign, or Georgy desperate and confused on a Thames River tour boat. (The baby is being sent off to an adoption agency and nobody cares but Georgy, and still the driver keeps talking about Christopher Wren's red brick house.) The script is a flawless gem of underwriting, leaving time for character development through the camera's eye with an economy of dialogue.

And then, of course, there is Lynn Redgrave to watch: a large, schmoo-like girl with kooky speech patterns, a voice like a boy soprano, skin that looks like an ad for Johnson's baby powder, and a blazing bonfire of a future.

Any Wednesday is a good example of the movies taking everything that is crisp and human about the stage and turning it into everything that is loud and vulgar and boring about Hollywood. Simply everything is wrong with this loud-mouthed movie based very loosely on Muriel Resnik's warm and funny Broadway play. The story of a thirty-year-old mistress who never grew up (played with strokes of vulnerable cotton-candy brilliance and big feet by Sandy Dennis onstage) gets all but stomped on with cleated boots by Jane Fonda. She is about as funny as a manic-depressive having her first nervous breakdown. She screams, weeps, beats the furniture, picks at her cuticles, and when she has no lines she just pouts and fusses with her fright wig. Her kooky little-girl apartment with its closet full of balloons has been turned into something that looks like the storage room of a Third Avenue version of the Salvation Army. Her taste could be described as early fag. Her keeper, who was once a charming man with a sense of humor onstage, is now a leering, lecherous magnate on the cover of *Time* magazine who yells and belches without a trace of "real person" quality in a performance which suggests that Jason Robards has tired blood.

To Sir with Love is *Blackboard Jungle* with tea and crumpets. Although less polished than *Up the Down Staircase*, it is similar and equally amusing. This time Sidney Poitier is the young teacher from British Guiana who enters the Mod world of the East London slums and changes the lives of the hardboiled little asps he teaches. Like Sandy Dennis's school, Poitier's is a den of iniquity where the kids bait and insult the teachers, read nudie magazines in class, and rock-and-roll during recess. There is little supervision and no punishment. Through his enormous personal magnitude, however, he soon has them convinced their hair styles are two hundred years old and their clothes are right out of the Roaring 20's and—you guessed it—before it's all over the movie insists the swinging hipsters of the younger generation may be the freest in years to rebel without chastisement, but they are just as fraught with anxieties, frustrations, and troubles as their elders.

In spite of a foundation as shaky as that to wobble along on, *To Sir with Love*, in its curious, old-fashioned way, says more about kids today than all the Beatles lyrics or shapeless Richard Lester films put together. It is acted with enormous exuberance by a daisy-fresh cast of London teenagers and directed with promising skill by James Clavell, who wrote the novel *King Rat*. The results are sweet-tempered, unpretentious, and quite likable.

Hombre indicates, hopefully, a new trend toward humanizing the American Western. In it, you are asked to believe in Paul Newman as a saddle-leathered white man raised by Apaches in the squalor of Arizona's San Carlos reservation and turned out, after years of deprivation and Indian schooling, to make his way in white society. Credit Martin (*Hud*) Ritt's double-barreled, unflinching direction, or possibly Newman's extraordinary skill as an actor, but I was with *Hombre* all the way.

I suspect it was really a combination of the two elements, coupled with an attitude posed in the first reel and carried through to the finish, but this is a picture demanding attention because it is about a great deal more than it seems at first glance. Never mind the fact that in the closeups the gauze comes loose around Newman's temples exposing his Apache hair as a hairdresser's wig. And never mind the totally unbelievable final scene, in which Newman abandons his philosophy about white men being bastards to save the hairy crew he is holed up in a mountain shack with, losing his own life in the process, shortly before a daguerrotype fadeout on the photo of a small boy standing with a group of Indians à la Roman Polanski's ending in *Repulsion*. These are eyebrow-raising points to quibble about, but they are overpowered by more good elements than bad.

I liked, for instance, the idea behind the screenplay, in which a man who is treated like a second-class citizen for rejecting his own people suddenly finds himself facing the dilemma of whether to save the people he hates and die or whether to live and let *them* die. (You can almost hear the whispers rise above the crunch of popcorn: *What would you do?*) *Hombre* raises the question of where a man's responsibility ultimately lies, to himself or to his fellow man.

I also liked the way Ritt gets around the problem of the old stagecoach theme (crowd eight people with colorful, complicated stories into a confined space, let them react to each other in the face of tragedy, and—*presto!*—a drama good for twenty shoot-em-ups). But in *Hombre* the only hero is a dead man. Nobody falls in love and walks into a cinemascope sunset. They end up in just as much trouble as they started with in the beginning. I liked the dialogue which, possibly for the very first time in a Western, allows people to talk the way they probably really talked in the West instead of the way they are forced to sound in John Ford movies. (Says disillusioned Barbara Rush, whose husband, Fredric March, is a Department of Interior official on his way to Mexico to escape detection for cheating the government out of money designated to buy meat for starving Indians: "When I was seventeen, and a student of his, I heard him read Robert Browning—now I'm thirty-five and I hear him cough up phlegm.")

I also liked the serene camerawork of James Wong Howe—and a special boquet to a cast of gargantuan talents: Newman, Richard Boone (doing his Freddie Ferocious bit), Barbara Rush, Martin Balsam, and specifically England's Diane Cilento, who in her first American role, sounds more authentically checked gingham than anyone else.

In all these capable hands, *Hombre* only looks like a Western. It's really a portrait of life nailed on a much broader canvas, thankfully unrelated to the sagebrush sagas Tex Ritter sings about.

Chappaqua, a first film by a young man named Conrad Rooks, is already a sensation in Europe where it is being compared in impact to the early films of Cocteau. Now ready for American release, it gives the distinct, slimy impression of what it might be like to go directly to Hell by sliding down the tongue of the devil himself. It is the kind of experience Andy Warhol and the super-punks of the underground school always dream of creating, but—due to a total lack of talent, imagination, technical knowledge, and poetic vision—never do.

Rooks is a thirty-three-year-old Missourian who became a narcotics addict as a teen-ager while being treated for pain by the use of morphine.

The addiction led to a ten-year syndrome of heroin and alcohol that ended in a chateau-sanitarium in Switzerland, where he was cured and where he began to visualize an autobiographical film—financed entirely by himself—which might deter other teen-agers from the hippie world that ends up on a slab in the morgue. Rooks almost went broke making *Chappaqua*, but the result is a classic exercise in the subconscious exorcism of a man struggling to find a new meaning in life and overcome a condition that threatens to cancel his existence.

Magnificently photographed in both lush color and moody black and white, Rooks's film contains more excitement than it is possible to relate, but of chief importance is the freedom it creates both for the filmmaker and the audience: freedom from images, illusions, language. It creates its own uniquely flavored opium-eye view of the world, enveloping the viewer by its structure as well as its eerily bloody content. Here, in a supreme psychedelic fusion of mind and matter, is an extraordinary film shot in the form of an LSD hallucination. As such, it overlaps the real world, in a smattering of juxtaposed styles—Bergman, Pabst, Franju, German surrealist, *March of Time*, Bela Lugosi, John Huston, Warners' '40 gangster mellers—to the dope-addicted sound track of the world of junk—clutters of barroom chatter, Ravi Shankar music, Allen Ginsberg mutterings, The Fugs, Donovan, Bach's *St. Matthew Passion*, Trude Heller's Buttercups, and the Indian drums of Peyote-eating ceremonies. Rooks's vision at times actually extends to the film itself, so that the addict (played with both guts and gusto by Rooks himself) thinks he is blinded by the cameras while the sound track is really turned on to record the sounds of the crew setting up a scene. The weaving of reality and illusion becomes a fascinating game, and the entire film becomes as close a thing to what it must be like under the influence of drugs as the average viewer is likely to get without actually taking them.

The logic used is the logic American kids are raised on—American movies, motorcycles, speed, cars, 42nd Street. Rooks becomes Dracula in a meat locker full of frozen carcasses hanging on hooks. Rooks becomes Little Caesar machine-gunning his foes in a deserted warehouse. Rooks becomes the lone cold-fish eye of the addict in search of a contact on a crowded Paris street with all the noise erased except the sound of his own footsteps. Finally, after we wander with his own mind through the world of needles and syringes and pushers and funk, through Stonehenge, a Negro church in Georgia, a deer park in Montana—we leave with Rooks in a helicopter, cured and clean as a newly waxed floor. Then, the final comment:

as he soars above the chateau, he sees himself doing the frug on the steeple in a strait-jacket, far, far, below. In that bizarre instant, blood-curdling though it is, there is a final irony for the man who has just been released from purgatory. He leaves part of himself behind in every experience.

Chappaqua has already won the Silver Lion at the 1966 Venice Film Festival, and if there is any justice left among the people responsible for such things, it seems safe to assume that the awards are just beginning. It's a bit long and could stand slight editing (too many train whistles and closeups of neon signs for my taste) but *Chappaqua* should establish Conrad Rooks as a cinematic Hieronymous Bosch.

The Wild Bunch. I have often been accused of being too passionate about films. The criticism is justified. I *am* passionate about what I believe in. I *do* react strongly to what I dislike. I am almost never middle-of-the-road, and if I am, I just sit back and wait until something comes along to stir the old passions again. There are plenty of critics around who cannot be accused of these crimes. Read them. They need your support. But if you are going to read *me*, you'd better get used to the passion, because I do not know any other way to write.

And yet, even with the admission of all this, I still almost hesitate to write about Sam Peckinpah's new film, *The Wild Bunch.* I'm afraid the revulsion I feel for it will be misinterpreted. In view of the reviews it has received (it's gotten some good ones) and considering the general climate of America today (pretty damned sick, if you ask me), I'm afraid any attack on violence will make it only too easy for the muckrakers to get out all the old labels. If you hate bloodshed and corruption, you're in trouble, pal. And if plunking down hard-earned money to see naked fannies, pubic hair, and entertainment aimed at the baser instincts of human beings is not your idea of the way you want to spend your time, you are most definitely either a fag or a Communist or a left-winger or a right-winger or a John Bircher or a member of the K.K.K. And you will never make friends of Sam Peckinpah fans. Well, Sam Peckinpah fans, I say up yours. *The Wild Bunch* stinks and I don't care who knows it.

This is the most pretentious, most violent blood-letting it has ever been my grave misfortune to witness on a motion picture screen. It is also the most pointless. But the violence is not what I object to as much as the obvious glorification of violence as titillation. Peckinpah's philosophy of life appears to be that the world is totally corrupt, that there is no decency or morality left in society, and therefore the best thing to do is blow everyone's head off and have a great time doing it. He's a man to be pitied, not admired. In his first scene, before the credits are even over, he zooms in on the happy, innocent smiles of a group of children who are torturing two scorpions by feeding them to a colony of carnivorous red ants. The camera intercuts the sweet smiles and the hiss of the creatures as they are being stung to death and eaten alive. It's only a preview of things to come. Ten minutes later, the "wild bunch," a gang of cut-throats and creeps who look like they've just come from doing a Burma Shave commercial shot in a pig sty, ride into town and murder three hundred women and children in a massacre of violence one critic poetically but stupidly described as a "blood ballet." Fifteen minutes after that, the same children from the first scene are back, driving home the point that even babies are evil and corrupt, by setting fire to the red ants that have just eaten the scorpions. The camera moves in (heaven forbid that you should miss a single juicy second) for a closeup of the ants burning alive.

In the interminable amateur night that follows, people are whip-lashed, girls are shot through the breasts, young soldiers are blown up by dynamite, limbs are severed, and blood spurts three feet in places, occasionally even splashing across Peckinpah's camera lens like ketchup on a steak. All of which gives the *auteur* critics—you know, the ones who still go to twenty-five-year-old John Ford movies without falling asleep and consider Jerry Lewis the best actor in America—the chance to embrace *The Wild Bunch* as an art film, because the blood squirts in slow motion. And every now and then there is a witty line like "That general'd just as soon kill us as break wind," which is a sample of the kind of gutter dialogue Peckinpah fans love to support as "western honesty," although how the hell they'd know how people talked on the Mexican border in 1913 is beyond me.

It all looks like a movie that smacks of desperation to me. Peckinpah's reputation as a director, negligible to all save a few fanatics like the *Cahiers du Cinéma* crowd, has been in trouble for some time. His first three films—*The Deadly Companion, Ride the High Country, Major Dundee*—were all financial and artistic disasters. He needed a hit. And what better way to have a commercial jackpot than a movie that would be so controversial people would go because they couldn't afford not to see what all the commotion was about? How else can anyone explain the isolation of each throat-slashing by use of the slow motion technique? It's not even an interesting film technique, but it does drag out a desired emotional reaction. It will make an audience gag to the point of being so nauseated they'll leave the movie house talking about what has upset them so. You can't miss the blood and gore when it gushes slowly. I just wish Peckinpah would admit he has turned out a trashy movie exploiting violence to make a fast buck. Even that would be a legitimate reason for perpetrating an insult like *The Wild Bunch* on the movie-going public. I'd have more respect for him. As a con artist.

I still would not admire him as a filmmaker, however. *The Wild Bunch* has a kind of feeble-minded plot. Something about two gangs of slimy bad guys trying to annihilate some equally slimy Texas railroad bounty hunters while smuggling guns to a third slimy group of immoral Mexican bandits. Most of it is incomprehensible, which proves Andrew Sarris's comment in his book *The American Cinema* that "since Peckinpah considers himself too intellectual to tell a story, it remains to be seen whether he will be forceful enough to develop a theme." He hasn't learned yet. The storytelling style in *The Wild Bunch* is often sentimental and sloppy, usually turgid and rhetorical, and always dull. I wouldn't even mind it if the movie pitted good guys vs. bad guys, with all the bad guys killing off all the good guys. That would at least make some kind of valid point, demonstrating the Genet theory of good vs. evil to which Peckinpah seems to subscribe, with evil always triumphing over good. But in *The Wild Bunch* everyone is corrupt, soulless, and inhuman. The only character with a sense of decency throughout the film deserts his own conscience in the final scene for absolutely no discernible reason, then joins up with the only slime left standing after a slaughterhouse of carnage the likes of which I have never seen equalled in any medium. I don't get it.

The film is not so much directed as it is phoned in. The actors are efficient but totally forgettable. The camera work is adequate but hardly impressive. There isn't one scene in the picture I haven't seen mounted better in some other film. And simmering underneath it all, like a rotting fungus, is the hateful knowledge that Peckinpah has had a good leer at the expense of a gullible public that likes to be outraged. For sheer pretension, I can think of no better way to describe the praise that has greeted *The Wild Bunch* than to quote one less-than-reliable critic who urged, "This is a film you must see, as a basis for cocktail-party chitchat on the subject of violence which is all the rage these days."

And you still think this country's in the very best of hands?

The Pumpkin Eater. Penelope Mortimer's exasperating, highly controversial 1963 novel, *The Pumpkin Eater*, was an intriguing study of a woman slowly losing contact with reality while approaching the change of life. But for all its imagination, its literary weaving of past and present, and its relentless pursuit of the elements that make up the feminine mystique, it never became more than a kind of gilt-edged *Stella Dallas*. Knife-edge direction by Jack Clayton (*Room at the Top, The Innocents*) and a meticulously detailed, almost painfully analytical script by Britain's top young playwright, Harold Pinter, have turned *Pumpkin* into an odd, sensitive, luminous film about the disintegration of a modern marriage.

As the film begins, a woman in a plaid coat stands by an upstairs window, her face a mask of paleness and apprehension. The telephone goes unanswered, the tea things untouched. We know she has a problem, but nothing more. The camera follows her like a silent eye as she sinks into a serious depression; walks sadly through the city streets; wanders, expressionless, past rows of glossy refrigerators and TV sets; finally breaks down in Harrod's department store.

Slowly and methodically, the pieces of her puzzle are fitted together by scenes of past and present. The past reveals she is the rebellious, carefree, only daughter of an upper-class British family; a victim of two marriages who once lived in a ramshackle barn filled with cats, children, and scattered toys. Her third husband was at first a fledgling writer who packed up her brood and moved them into London. The first person she ever really loved, he has made life all lollipops and nursery rhymes.

But as the years go by, the children increase (the number is never mentioned, in book or film, though I counted eight in one scene), and the husband becomes a highly successful film writer. With financial achievement come fine clothes, hairdos, cocktail parties, and nannies to take care of the children—all intrusions on her private world of carefree happiness. Her husband rises to prominence and her mother-wife image becomes less important. Her position has slowly changed, but not her attitude toward life. In addition, the past reveals that her husband has impaled himself on the horns of a domestic dilemma by having an affair with a woman boarder.

It is revealed, through analysis, that she thinks sex is lewd without reproduction. The husband doesn't understand her. To him, loving her is like loving an eye with a cataract on it. Time has changed his love and made him restless. He finds himself seeking other affairs. Finally, he learns she is to have another baby—a final threat to his freedom and his marriage. Fed up with noisy children, petty jealousies, blaring phonograph records, he persuades her to have an abortion. Just as the new pregnancy evolves from a desire to hold onto him, its termination and her eventual sterilization are performed through fear of losing him.

Faced with the cruel reality of a husband who no longer loves her as he once did, and a family growing up who seems to no longer need her, she retreats from the pain of conscious living to the solace of a deserted, country windmill, the proposed site of their future house. At the end of all her years of marriage, she stands on the border between girlhood anxiety and middle-age boredom. Her problems will never end like the Pumpkin Eater of the children's rhyme, her future will never be resolved. Perhaps this coming to grips with oneself in the end is what life is really all about.

In a framework so laden with the earmarks of soap opera, Jack Clayton has directed the story unconventionally and without sentimentality: the past and present are fused in a kind of Faulknerian style. Characters repeat themselves to make points. One scene, in which the wife pays a return visit to her second husband, is run backwards, so that the smoke drifts cloudily back into a cigarette that becomes longer instead of shorter, in an endless passing of time.

Pinter, whose previous works have delved into the baroque, misshapen distortions of the human soul, has remained as faithful to Mrs. Mortimer's novel as a cocker spaniel. His script has the same flair for dialogue (many scenes are transferred almost intact), the same situations and characters. Yet the movie is better, because it has something more—a grasp of dramatic construction. Mrs. Mortimer's climax was uncertain. Her characters suffered anemically from lack of development and her structure ached for strength and form.

Pinter's screenplay is a caustic, realistic mirror that sweeps away the conventional gauze surrounding marriage and psychoanalysis, and probes into the reasons why people do unforgivable wrongs to each other in the name of love. His characters are diffuse, yet so carefully etched they ring true with bleeding urgency.

The performances are works of art. As the wife, Anne Bancroft has already won a Best Actress award at the Cannes Film Festival, and an Academy Award nomination seems certain. Clayton has had the good sense to hold down her usual rough-edged, overbearing personality, and the result is one of the finest pieces of acting ever captured on film. With hair shaggy as moss and eyes as big and dark as Japanese plum seeds, she crumbles beneath the weight of each sigh, only to come surging to the top of her power at the beginning of each new moment, each new breath, each new awareness. All this, and yet she is ever conscious of her place, her surroundings, her fellow players. Staring quietly into a London street through a dirty window, or thumbing aimlessly through a magazine while contemplating her husband's indiscretions, she tosses atoms with her eyes. Pitching strength and defiance into a burst of throaty laughter when she learns she can no longer bear children, she brings film acting to the top of its form. Watching her perform under a good director is like a pastoral painting one moment, like the taming of hydroelectric power the next.

Peter Finch, an actor who has thrown away a few previous roles with the detached boredom of a man working a crossword puzzle, is perfect as Bancroft's male counterpart—virile, exciting, breathing fire and foam and tearful helplessness into each movement. James Mason is terrifying as a vicious, filthy mouthed weakling who spits obscenities over a deceptive glass of lemon tea; Maggie Smith comes close to stealing the first part of the film as a woman named Philpot with whom Finch has an affair; the late Sir Cedric Hardwicke in his last screen role, Alan Webb, Richard Johnson, and the rest of the distinguished cast are believable and touching in finely detailed characterizations.

Blue. Two years ago a young director named Silvio Narizzano made a sensitive, funny, with-it little low-budget film called *Georgy Girl*. The inevitable happened. Success went to everybody's head and now Narizzano, having fallen prey to big-studio filmmaking, has turned out his first four-million-dollar Hollywood Western. It is called *Blue* and it is a disaster so total I pray for the professional futures of everyone involved. The same thing happened to French director Serge Bourguinon who followed his *Sundays and Cybèle* with a big-budget Hollywood shoot-em-up called *The Reward* in 1965. Like Bourguinon, I hope Narizzano is safely back in Europe. The trouble is, he should have scrapped *Blue* before the print on the negative was dry.

This is one of those sociological Freudian art house horse operas about a white boy whose folks were social outcasts, see, so this here boy just ups and runs off to the Texas plains near the Mexican border in 1850 and gets adopted by Mexican bandits hell-bent on burnin', rapin', pillagin', and causin' all sorts of general concern for the white settlers. The bandit leader, a no'count named Ortega (played with a lot of heavy panting by Ricardo Montalban, who should know better) names him Azul, which is Mexican for "blue," see, on account of he has blue eyes. Needless to say, this causes jealousy among the ranks, composed of the largest collection of method Mexicans this side of the Actors Studio.

Azul decides you can take the boy out of Brooklyn but you can't take Brooklyn out of the boy, so to speak, so he decides to desert and stay with this young pioneer hellion played by Joanna Pettet, whose future seems in serious jeopardy if she keeps saying lines like "Possess yoreself Jess, you make too much of a fuss pleasurin' yoreself over a girl." Anyway, everybody gets all riled up over Blue because that Ortega is an ornery cuss. Like he holds grudges. There's a lot of cornpone dialogue among the so-called "civilized" settlers dreamed up by people who obviously have never been any closer to Texas than the Bel Air Country Club during which everybody debates whether or not to trust Blue, who got them into this mess, to get them out. "I tell ya, Emma, he coulda killed my boy and he didn't—I say we trust him." Like that. Needless to say, everyone survives except Blue and that ornery Ortega, who die in each other's arms in the middle of the Rio Grande with all the Mexicans on one side and all the settlers on the other. Big symbolic death scene, floating downstream in each other's arms. Men without a country and all that. But even the final shot, in which the film fades out on Blue's blue eyes, is a cop-out, stolen as it is from the last scene in *Hombre* when the film faded out on Paul Newman's white man raised by-Indians blue eyes.

Blue is a curiously disobedient movie that continually refuses to be what it's supposed to be. At times you almost think you see why Narizzano was attracted to the idea of doing a Western. He has crammed his period piece with enough beautiful effects to fill an exhibition at the Museum of Modern Art—shots through tall corn growing against the parched and bleeding sky, handshakes between silhouetted figures on an American Gothic horizon, clusters of dramatic guitar music. And in photographer Stanley Cortez, he found the perfect cameraman to record the peppermint clouds and adobe earth of Utah, where the exteriors were shot. But even here he has been foiled by the Hollywood hacks. For every beautiful daytime exterior, there is a lousy night scene shot back in the studio full of process photography chock full of skies that turn from painted Indian violet to bright orange (in the same evening). There is even one perfectly beautiful green sky. It may sound like nit picking, but I have never seen a green sky in Texas or anywhere else and I don't think anyone else has, either, unless he was taking LSD at the time. And for every attempt to turn the corny script into a social or psychological comment on what's going on behind those blue eyes (closeup of Blue playing a piano in a settler's cabin as the camera keeps zooming eerily in on a family picnic scene on the wall as he remembers his youth) there is a lot of pretty unbelievable dialogue that keeps getting in the way.

Not the least of the trouble is the chief miscasting of Terence Stamp in the title role. Stamp is a good actor but trying to be half-savage, half-gringo, he is always overcome by an oddball Cockney English Teddy boy accent that makes him look as scratchy and out of place as a tortilla in Alaska. Even if he did live with Mexicans, where, in the Texas of 1850, would he find peroxide? Stamp has black hair on his chest, as well as a black moustache throughout the film, yet the hair on his head is a badly dyed lemon-streaked straw color. The effect is ludicrous. He becomes a strange kind of Billy Budd of Mexico who turns *Blue* into a very good comedy routine but a not-very-convincing piece of social significance.

I don't know which is worse: bad cowboy movies or bad *arty* cowboy movies. *Blue* is both. Gene Autry was never very convincing in horse operas either, but at least he would never have been caught dead *or* alive with peroxided hair.

Years of Lightning, Days of Drums. Let's get one thing straight right now. *Years of Lightning, Days of Drums,* the eighty-seven-minute commercial about John F. Kennedy, is a thumping bore and an archetype of bad documentary filmmaking. Joseph E. Levine, in the pretentious full-page ads he's been taking out to ballyhoo the film, claims "there are no words . . . it is just something you feel . . . its impact sweeps through every emotion you have ever felt . . . it is, in a word, unforgettable." In a word, *hogwash.* The two years and ten days of Kennedy's administration are adequately outlined in a rather mangled assemblage of newsreels, but with almost no reference to the man who made them happen. The pieces fall into place in old-fashioned documentary style—Kennedy watching a rocket launching, Kennedy speaking to the Peace Corps on the White House lawn, Kennedy sending troops to Thailand, Kennedy asking for a nuclear test ban treaty with the Soviets, Kennedy on the Bay of Pigs invasion, Kennedy delivering his famous Berlin Wall speech, Kennedy exalting Costa Rica for being "brave" and "vital," while the voice of Gregory Peck gushes, "The President would never again stand on the soil of Latin America."

There is a lot of souped-up soundtrack dialogue about "Peace" and "Happiness" and "Hope" abroad, but no mention of how the Americans at home were (and are) being taxed within an inch of their lives to pay for all these big-hearted projects, while the rest of the "brave" and "vital" countries sit with their hands out. Rarely does the film reach out past its history-book documentation and touch the human heart, as did that masterpiece, *The Eleanor Roosevelt Story.* What it needed, perhaps, was a writer of the caliber of Archibald MacLeish to fuse its ideas with the materials assembled to illustrate them. It has neither. The editing is so careless that the senses are never moved or jarred, merely confused; *e.g.,* the one black and white shot of segregated schools shows white children leaving the exits of an attractive school with their laughing Negro schoolmates, but the soundtrack is busily grinding out somber talk about the horrors of racial prejudice. Technically, the color shots look no better than color TV on a bad day.

Luckily, the film does not try to goad its audience into a response, but the result, unfortunately, is that you are left with none. It is cold, unemotional and dull and sets the cause for the documentary back to the gloomy days of the *March of Time*. Can *The Queen Elizabeth Story* be far behind?

Lord Love a Duck is about the most revolting piece of draff the smoker-room of George (*Paris When It Sizzles*) Axelrod has yet produced. It is amateurish, excessive, pornographic, illiterate, and—worse—unoriginal, borrowing heavily, as it does, from: *How to Stuff a Wild Bikini*, the American-International beach pictures, *Darling*, Jayne Mansfield, *Lolita*, the old Sid Caesar TV shows, *What's New, Pussycat?*, Madison Avenue, *How To Murder Your Wife*, Dobie Gillis, Max Shulman—Philip Morris cartoons, *Playboy* magazine, *Oh Dad, Poor Dad, Mama's Hung You in the Closet and I'm Feeling So Sad*, and half a dozen old Jerry Lewis throwaways.

The plot, if you can take it: an effeminate, seventeen-year-old moron named Mollymauk (played by Roddy McDowall, who looks about as much like a high school senior as Ghidrah, the three-headed monster) meets and hypnotizes a baton-twirling Trilby-like nymphet (Tuesday Weld) into believing all her wishes will come true in her senior year. He manages to make her chief cheerleader, gets her married to a sex maniac majoring in "marriage counseling," and lands her a part in a beach-party movie by introducing her to a lecherous old producer (Martin Gabel, who refuses to take screen credit, and I don't blame him). Her mother (Lola Albright) is a cocktail waitress-prostitute-alcoholic who commits suicide. Tuesday's mother-in-law (Ruth Gordon), under Roddy's hypnotic aid, also becomes an alcoholic, and together the three of them try every trick in the book to murder Tuesday's husband so she can become a big star.

Finally, after smashing him up in a car accident, Roddy drives his wheel chair to the center of the football field during class commencement exercises and runs down the helpless cripple with a bulldozer. Tuesday becomes the star of *Bikini Widow*, and Roddy is driven away to the psychiatric ward of the Los Angeles jail, as a monotone rock and roll group screams the title tune off-key behind the closing credits. Isn't that funny? Additionally, it's all laced together with obscenities such as a drive-in church run by a fairy minister and his wife "Butch" (Axelrod's nod to the

Hollywood "in" crowd, no doubt) and a rather shocking bit where Miss Weld gets a secretarial job to the principal of the high school by sitting on his desk and playing with her breasts while he proceeds to scrawl "69" on his memo pad—drool running down his chin—then calmly eats his pencil.

Most scenes have no beginning and no real end, and the actors are allowed, through Axelrod's inability to direct even the simplest action shot, to wallow in excesses that would embarrass the Three Stooges (one scene, at a drive-in restaurant, shows two characters so redfaced from their own dialogue that they collapse into a fit of unrehearsed laughter and smear each other with ketchup and mustard). The late Wolcott Gibbs, during an unhappy sojourn as a movie critic, once lamented that most Hollywood comedies are so "vulgar, witless and dull it is preposterous to write about them in any publication not meant to be read while chewing gum." Too bad he didn't see *Lord Love a Duck*. Even the gum doesn't help.

Born Free. With the predicament movies are in today, it seems less than remarkable that a British import about a baby lion turns out to be much more moving, believable, and charming than most of the ones about human beings. But *Born Free* gets into trouble only when the real people get into the act, and not very much then, since the leads are played by the superb husband-wife team, Virginia McKenna and Bill Travers. Miss McKenna is Joy Adamson, wife of the senior game warden in the northern province of Kenya; and the story, taken from Mrs. Adamson's enchanting novel, involves a lioness named Elsa, which the Adamsons raised as their own child. The film pinpoints with uncanny insight the love between Elsa and her "family" and the confusion and unhappiness on both sides when she is turned away from home to make her own life.

Mrs. Adamson's husband, George, acted as technical adviser, and the director, James Hill, and his marvelous crew worked with the cooperation of the game preserves of Uganda to authenticate the story the way it happened. It is not particularly a valuable or even monumental film, but its energy, its exquisite regard for form and detail, its warm, unhampered use of color—and just about the damnedest animal performance ever captured on film by the lioness who plays Elsa—make *Born Free* a vastly progressive and entertaining experience.

Harper is a leaden, heavy-handed spoof of the old Sam Spade private-eye stories, and *The Big Sleep* in particular. Not bad on its own terms, but not very good, either. Still, it's a pleasant change of pace from the garbage heap of James Bond-style supersonic spy spoofs. Paul Newman is not a very good substitute for Humphrey Bogart (who used to do this sort of thing very well), but Julie Harris is wonderfully miscast as a heroin-addicted jazz singer who gets tortured by having cigarettes stamped out on the bottoms of her feet.

The Trouble with Angels is an Ida Lupino-directed series of vacuous little vignettes mixing up some pious (and unconvincing) nuns like Rosalind Russell with some nauseating little brats like Hayley Mills. The result is harmless, but about as indigestible as cold tea at a wedding breakfast.

Promise Her Anything is incredibly simple-minded pap, filmed in Europe, with a Greenwich Village set that looks suspiciously like Great Windmill Street in Soho. It has an aging, baggy-eyed Leslie Caron playing second fiddle to Warren Beatty, who seems as scratchy and uneasy in his first comedy as an ex-novitiate in her first Minsky's chorus line.

The Heart Is a Lonely Hunter. There was this girl, see. She was never very pretty—her nose was too big, her teeth were crooked, and her slip often showed—but you loved her anyway. Then one day you saw her again for the first time in years. She had a two-thousand-dollar nose job, her teeth were capped, and somebody had bought her a subscription to *Harper's Bazaar.* In her copy of a copy of a copy of Dior, she just wasn't the same girl.

That's how I feel about *The Heart Is a Lonely Hunter,* the film Hollywood has made out of Carson McCullers's brilliant and disturbing Gothic novel about loneliness in a hot, bumble bee-sticky Southern town in summer. All gussied up in James Wong Howe photography and shining in frosty technicolor like a tinsel-wrapped Christmas bangle, it just isn't the same enchilada. It involves, but it doesn't haunt.

Part of the problem is the elusiveness of Mrs. McCullers's own peculiar genius. *The Member of the Wedding* is the only thing she ever wrote that adapted well in any other medium. It was a masterpiece on stage and with Fred Zinnemann behind the camera, it translated magically to the screen in one of the few really perfect films ever made in this country. But although she enjoyed movies and seemed eternally fascinated by the language of film, Mrs. McCullers did not write with the screen in mind. Her novels and short stories had the evasive quality of a lightning bug on a starless summer night. One minute you saw the brightly charted course, flickering with knowledge and truth, the next minute you had to search for the path once again, unaided by a compass. The marvelous, labyrinthian way in which she guided her readers through the dark brown prose of her journey into the hearts and souls of tormented, isolated people worked on paper. It doesn't work well on film, where a movie without action is like toast without butter.

The Heart Is a Lonely Hunter presents an even greater problem. How, they were asking last autumn when the film was being shot in Selma, Alabama, do you make a movie in which the leading character is a deaf mute who never acts, but merely reacts to the characters revolving around him? The answer is they didn't. They only made a valiant effort. I don't mean to imply *The Heart Is a Lonely Hunter* is a bad movie. A lot of it is very good indeed. It has been constructed by people with taste, talent, and an obvious dedication to Mrs. McCullers. Tom Ryan has structured a reverent screenplay that never compromises or cheapens her original work. But, in order to provide the audience with a movie that is both aesthetic (as her writing was) and visually tangible (as movies must be these days if they are to make money), he has crowded enough vignettes into the framework of the film to make three more. The result is often a patchwork quilt, where Mrs. McCullers's literary weaving was more like embroidery on fine linen. James Wong Howe has photographed the work subtly and sensitively. Robert Ellis Miller has directed it with compassion, preventing the depressing quality of the novel from oozing onto the screen drenched in sadness and sentimentality. And although the acting is largely amateurish and disappointing, a few of the performers have actually gotten down to the nitty-gritty of what alienated, sensitive Southerners groping for identification were all about on the printed page.

Alan Arkin is simply magnificent as the mute. Like the Dilsey character in Faulkner's *The Sound and the Fury*, he is the catalyst who makes the other characters' hearts beat. Arkin has filled an actionless role with a multitude of nuances, from the Old Spice next to his orderly shaving kit to the little watchfob he carries in his neatly arranged pocket. Every detail, from the notebook he writes messages in to the ball-point pen he wears on his coat, is filed down to the quick like a too-carefully manicured fingernail. Whether he is trying to look the other way so he won't read the lips of a teen-ager's boy friend or dulling his eyes with a Halloween glaze, pursing his lips and groping out in the agony of an unfulfilled lack of communication, his performance is masterful and wise. And weirdly gripping.

The two children in the film who bear remarkable resemblances to the Frankie Addams and John Henry characters in *The Member of the Wedding* are played by unknowns who, if there is any justice left in such matters, won't be unknown long. Jackie Marlowe, a red-haired, freckle-nosed, rhubarb-cheeked youngster from Birmingham is Bubber, and he plays the part with the natural abandon of a new Butch Jenkins. Mick Kelly, the tomboyish teen-ager so desperate to belong to something outside her own stifling little world that she pulls her little brothers through the town in a wagon just to hear the music coming from other people's houses, is played by a creamy, dreamy-eyed girl from Shelbyville, Tennessee. Her name is Sondra Locke and in all her innocence and passion she comes closer than anyone else in the film to capturing the spirit of Mrs. McCullers's lonely, barren world.

Every attempt has been made to photograph that world. Mick and Bubber live in a decaying old gingerbread house the color of vanilla ice cream very much like the one Mrs. McCullers lived in when she died prematurely at the age of fifty in Nyack, New York. Selma has provided a perfect re-creation of the steamy town in rural Georgia where most of Mrs. McCullers's novels were set: everything is there, from the smell of the bacon drippings to the Thirsty Boy signs peeling in the dusty breezeless summer afternoon. James Wong Howe slides his camera up the drainpipe and through the lacy window curtains like a lazy lizard. An X-ray machine announcing the end of an old and used-up life fades into the white-hot sun shining through the treetops on the awakening of love in a young *new* life.

And yet, with all the love that has been poured into it, the movie misses. It misses because the dark recesses of the human soul so sensitively described in Mrs. McCullers's novel cannot be photographed by a camera even if it is operated by James Wong Howe. "Sometimes I think that's what my life is all about—not really *bein'* anything, just lookin' at a lotta pictures," says Miss Locke. And that's the problem nobody has been able to solve. With a minimum of success, movies have often been able to show what life is all about, but not what life is *not* about. *The Heart Is a Lonely Hunter* provides a series of interesting scenes, but they rarely have any relation to the unseen, the unprotected, the unfelt telegrams in Mrs. McCullers's heart of hearts. We see things happening, but we never know to what purpose or to what end they are happening. The movie becomes artless. Too many stories are going on at once, but not one single idea. All that bright color (the movie should have been in black and white) and the misuse of a seemingly interminable number of annoying closeups add to the problem by breaking up the flow of Mrs. McCullers's pen and diluting her pervasive theme of loneliness. There are wonderful moments of individual splendor, but the final result is disappointingly unmoving.

I'm glad everyone tried and I respect them for it. But *The Heart Is a Lonely Hunter* remains a try. Like childhood girl friends, some things in life are better stored away in memories, unchanged by fashion and untouched by time. In a moment of quiet and unexpected candor, Carson McCullers once told me the best thoughts were the ones unspoken. Similarly, maybe the best movies are the ones left unmade. It may be presumptuous, but I think if she had lived to see *The Heart Is a Lonely Hunter* she might agree.

Funny Girl. No more cracks about Barbra Streisand's nose. After *Funny Girl,* they'll be as obsolete as Harold Teen comics. It took the combined efforts of God knows how many people to do it, but I'll be damned if they haven't made her beautiful. In the most remarkable screen debut I will probably ever see in my lifetime, the toadstool from Erasmus High School has been turned into a truffle, and I, for one, couldn't be happier about the transformation. Every age has its Super Lady. Other ages had Lillian Russell and Sarah Bernhardt and Gertrude Lawrence and Helen Morgan and Judy Garland. Well, we've got ours. Her name is Barbra, and whether we like it or not, all those monstrous things she keeps doing to people out of fear and insecurity only make her more exciting onscreen. When all that talent comes to a boiling, raging, ferocious head of fireball steam, as it does in *Funny Girl,* bad publicity pales in the glow of her extraordinary genius. Unfortunately, Streisand is the only thing extraordinary about *Funny Girl.* The rest of the movie is chopped liver.

Fanny Brice, as anyone who has ever read *The Fabulous Fanny* knows, had a love affair with the world and the world loved right back. The thing everyone connected with *Funny Girl* on Broadway and in the film seems to keep forgetting is that she was a fabulous character, and she deserves a better valentine to her memory than the old-fashioned period soap opera William Wyler has fashioned here. Nice Jewish girl wants to go into show business but everybody discourages her because she's ugly. Nice Jewish girl does it anyway, meets dashing backstage playboy gambler, talks playboy gambler into marrying her, has a baby, and finds true happiness while her star rises and his luck disintegrates. Playboy gambler gets sent to prison and walks out on nice Jewish girl who by this time has become a nice Jewish star in the Ziegfield Follies. Nice Jewish star, loved by millions, goes onstage in best show-must-go-on tradition, and sings the blues with tears streaming down her face like Mrs. Norman Maine in the last reel of *A Star Is Born*. The End. The formula is so old it's hairy. Fanny Brice's life was more complex and interesting than that. The movie they have made of it is merely vague and pedestrian. With Barbra's unquenchable flair, *Funny Girl* should have them lined up at the box office for the next five years, but it does nothing to forward the cause of the musical movie biography in terms that can in any way be called innovational.

The Film: very little has been done to progress the stage play and/or expand it into larger and more visual terms for the screen. The only improvement I can see is "Don't Rain on My Parade," which took ten days to film, starting out in the abandoned Jersey Central Railroad Station, continuing through the Battery, and ending up with Barbra heading out past the Statue of Liberty in a tugboat while the camera rises in the air taking in the New York harbor from a helicopter. It's an electrifying number, providing a bang-up lead-in to the intermission. Otherwise, the production numbers Herb Ross has staged seem disappointingly familiar. The much-ballyhooed "Swan Lake" number, for example, which took more than three months of intensive rehearsal and ten days to film, is a total wash-out. Not only is it boring, it is also intercut with shots of the gambler husband losing at cards, which only breaks up the audience's concentration and minimizes the comedy genius of Fanny Brice onstage.

Although Harry Stradling, who photographed Garbo, has framed Streisand with all the care an adopted parent could shower on a war orphan and so much respect that she often looks ethereal as a lady madonna, the rest of his camerawork is technically uninteresting. Isobel Lennart's script seems as uninspired as it did on Broadway, providing only the anatomy of a biography, but leaving out the red corpuscles. Most upsetting of all, William Wyler's direction of the dialogue scenes (he didn't have much to do with the musical numbers) seems downright prehistoric. (At times even sloppy—I noticed one scene in which the match shots were so uneven Barbara and Omar Sharif actually talked to each other in different colored lighting.)

The Songs: Jule Styne and Bob Merrill's score has been so butchered that, in an effort to make Barbra the focal point and do something "new" at the same time, most of what they started out with onstage has been all but destroyed. Barbra's new roller skate number, one of those new-chorus-girl-wrecks-number-but-audience-loves-her-for-being-so-clumsy routines, seems distinctly *déjà vu*. (There's an almost identical number in the forthcoming Gertrude Lawrence biography, *Star*, which leads audiences to believe that all great theatrical legends got started by being perfectly terrible performers but too lovable for the boss to fire.) The "Rat-Tat-Tat-Tat" number, which has been dropped from the original score, was a much funnier Follies number than any of the production numbers in the film. "If A Girl Isn't Pretty," the song Fanny's mother sang with her cronies, has almost been entirely dismissed in the movie. It wasn't a shattering song, but it was important because it showed the odds Fanny had to overcome even at home to break into show business. One quick chorus in the movie and there's a fast cut to her first job. "My Man" is a brilliant inspiration for a tear-jerking finale, hokey as it is, but it needn't have ruled out the inclusion in the film of the score's best song, "The Music That Makes Me Dance." The absence of that song in particular leaves a gap in the film that is never fully bridged. "People" and "My Man" are, along with most of the other songs, shot in an annoying series of disturbing and irritating closeups. Closeups ruined *Camelot.* You'd think directors would learn from each other's mistakes. Don't they ever see each other's films?

The Actors: the film is so completely tailored for Barbra's colossal debut as a movie star that everyone else has ended up on the cutting room floor. She is the whole team. Luckily, she carries the ball beautifully, but all the other wonderful people who gave Fanny Brice a story worth telling are sadly missing. I'm amazed that such fine performers as Kay Medford (as Fanny's Mama) and the versatile Lee Allen (as her friend Eddie Ryan) agreed to appear in the film at all, even though they had both played the roles onstage. Their songs have all been cut and their juicy stage roles sliced into nothing. Walter Pidgeon, as Flo Ziegfield, does the Walter Pidgeon bit. Anne Francis, one of the most criminally neglected actresses in Hollywood, is wonderful in her one or two moments as Fanny's chorus girl friend in the Follies, but all of her best scenes have been deleted with no explanation for her character's presence. Admittedly, Nicky Arnstein is a thankless assignment, but the way he has been written here, Omar Sharif has no choice but to play a stage prop. He has absolutely nothing of any importance to do or say except to react to Barbra's best scenes, so he plays the heel in a lot of ruffled shirts and he smiles sexy. At these salaries, you don't expect cardboard.

That leaves a movie that would be a total zero without a very great ego to put glue in all the cracks. Fortunately, Barbra meets the challenge in a head-on collision unequalled in movie history. She is almost never offscreen in a role the length of one of June Havoc's marathon dances. Whether she is bouncing through her Mama's saloon munching a pickle, dancing down

Henry Street with her dreams up in lights, or stealing the spotlight from the naked showgirls as a bride pregnant as a water oxen, she breathes witchcraft into a medium desperately in need of some. She pouts, she cries, she looks quietly at other people in moments of quiet splendor, she makes funny faces, she makes funny noises, she gobbles up the part like it was lobster thermidor and she was eating for two with her fingers.

People are always asking me for a definition of star quality. Barbra has defined it for generations to come. In *Funny Girl* Irene Sharaff has draped her in enough fur and chiffon and diamonds to put Dior out of business, but the only thing you see is Streisand. Gene Callahan has surrounded her with wall-to-wall mirrors, ivory staircases that rise out of the floor, cellophane curtains that seem to stretch to the stars, cockatoo feathers, velvet walls, cut-glass chandeliers, marble statues, and enough gilt-edge furniture to build a moat around Fort Knox, but the only thing you really ever watch is Streisand. Never, at any time in this film, does anything else catch your eye. That's star quality. Through some mysterious biological magic, she has turned into an orchard harvest of ripening womanhood—warm, moving, soft, sensual, and mature. Every scene reveals a new facet of her ravenous hunger for perfection.

According to the gossip from Hollywood, she drove practically everyone connected with the filming of *Funny Girl* bananas. Maybe she knew what she was doing. The search for the right lipstick, the right camera angle, the right lighting—it has all paid off. When Sharif tells her he is leaving for what seems like the thousandth time, it's like something she's hearing for the first. The lips curve out, the blue eyes fill with tears, and she makes a tiny smacking sigh that is perfectly timed to coincide with the closing of her eyes. The effect, which probably took all day to shoot, is like that of a child raised on vanilla and tasting, for the first time, rum raisin.

When Streisand is around, she turns *Funny Girl* from disguised technicolor wide-screen hokum into something bordering on art. With her voice, with her walk, with her emotion, and with the passion of her hydroelectric power, she makes tickets something worth buying. Everyone else should have stayed in bed.

The Chase. Ignoring the fact that such things are completely out of style, out of fashion, and out of date, Lillian Hellman has set her screenplay (the term is used loosely, because that is how most of it is written) in the most wife-swappin'est, blackheartedest, gun-totin'est, possum-huntin'est, nigger-hatin'est town in Texas. I guess it's in Texas, because there is a lot of talk about driving to Houston for breakfast. That's how you have to piece things together in this film. Then there's some more talk about a real bad hombre named Bubber (Robert Redford) who has escaped from a chain gang because they tried to make him eat some rotten pork. Bubber is on his way to town, and this worries just about everybody in sight. His wife (Jane Fonda) is playing around with the sissy son of a local Big Daddy-type land baron (E. G. Marshall), and everybody jes' knows there's gonna be trouble. That's about all the story there is, except for several subplots involving enough town whores, adulterous husbands, alcoholic wives, hopped-up teen-agers, mistreated Uncle Tom–type Negroes, and gospel-chanting lunatics to make Tobacco Road look like Berkeley Square in bloomers.

The action all takes place in one night that is so badly lit I often had difficulty seeing just who was talking. It's a peculiar night, too, because everybody in town is drunk. Is it New Year's Eve? Or Mardi Gras? You are never sure, but there *is* a party in every house on every block, with lots of shots through lighted windows showing the citizens writhing on rugs with their neighbors' wives, smashing bottles against walls, women screaming and men breaking up the furniture. It's a busy night. Some local hoods, who work in the bank in the daytime, beat the Sheriff (Marlon Brando) to a bloody pulp and there is one rather odd shot of a group of men arriving from God-knows-where for a dental convention. Then there's a crazy, toothless old hag who keeps entering dramatic scenes shouting "So burned Sodom, so burned Gomorrah" (is Miss Hellman trying not so subtly to make a point?). Finally everybody finds out that Bubber is hiding out down at the Negro junkyard on the outskirts of town, so there is a traffic jam that looks like a film clip from the last New York transit strike, with the whole town throwing gasoline torches into the wrecked cars, and rolling lighted tires and firecrackers off the top of the hill into the city dump. The sheriff arrests Bubber and it makes the townspeople so mad they blow up the junkyard, kill the son of the town patriarch, and march down to the sheriff's office, where an unidentified Madison Avenue type in a button-down collar who has been sulking throughout the film saying "I hate niggers" pumps several slugs of lead into the scared jackrabbit body of the captured but innocent Bubber. That's just about all, except that the next morning the town looks like the morning after the closing of the World's Fair and Sheriff Brando, after being beaten, kicked, mauled, pistol-whipped, and almost murdered the night before, drives out of town forever, pouting dejectedly and wearing one Band Aid on his chin. There is no dialogue in this last scene, but it doesn't matter. At the preview I attended, the audience was so hysterical by this time the hisses and boos made even the end-title music inaudible.

The question is why? I tremble to think what this picture cost. I shudder even more to think about the disintegration of playwright Lillian Hellman. In joining the vogue for turning bad trash into artful mass entertainment she has failed even in the first step. She has not been able to write even one trash scene that bites or stings or even makes coherent sense. The fact that the film is so ludicrous can be largely credited to her, though the ineptitude of Arthur Penn's high school thespian play direction contributes heavily to the holocaust. Although I never cared for the souped up Actors Studio hysteria of Penn's first film, *The Left-Handed Gun* (Billy the Kid seen as a kind of six-gun Lee Oswald), I found his second, *The Miracle Worker*, to be a work of beautiful introspection, showing what can be done to expand the stifled dimensions of the stage proscenium on film. And in spite of occasional lapses of self-consciousness, *Mickey One* was overpowered by his strong kinetic flair for making scenes burst with visual vitality. Up to now, his work has been among the best to come out of American films in recent years. But with *The Chase* the great white hope of American directors falls so devastatingly low I wonder where his future lies.

The photography is so bad that most of it looks like old Republic serials, the lighting is poor, the shots are old-hat (endless two-shots that make the actors look like daguerrotypes), the technical flaws too numerous to mention, and the sets so tacky that even the town, phony down to its movie marquees with made-up names, looks like it was built at cost by Sears, Roebuck. Marlon Brando, who gave up acting shortly after *On the Waterfront*, is now simply a balding, middle-aged, pot-bellied man driven to undisciplined excesses that are clearly inexcusable on the screen. In one scene, he becomes so enraptured in a love affair with his own thumb that he actually appears to forget his own lines. The embarrassment on his face when he is forced to say Miss Hellman's lines is understandable, but most of the time he sounds like he has a mouth full of wet toilet paper.

The rest of the acting is mostly objectionable and absurd, unless you are pervertedly amused by the sight of Martha Hyer collapsing on the top of an automobile and swallowing a handful of pearls in a drunken rage. Angie Dickinson, whom I know to be one of the loveliest women in America, looks like a cadaver. James Fox (the splendid young actor in *The Servant* and *King Rat*) has dyed hair, an accent as authentically Texas as a penguin in the Panhandle, and more pimples on his face than years to his age.

Miriam Hopkins, as the convict's mother, evokes guffaws when she runs down the center of the street wailing and gnashing her teeth with nothing on her mind but a possible Oscar nomination. Only Janice Rule rises above the banality, treating the nonsense around her like she was just emerging from a refreshing hiatus in a Chinese opium den. Everyone else looks drawn and quartered by the cameraman.

Unfortunately, unlike Miss Rule, I was unable to consider *The Chase* as a hallucination. Hollywood does a lot of back-slapping and trumpet-blowing these days, about how movies are better than ever, about how top writers, directors, and stars from Broadway are turning to films, where "art and talent pay off." Well, a lot of stage people may wish they had a job when the public gets a good hard look at this one. There's a lot of talent here, and it should have all stayed home. *The Chase* is the worst thing that has happened to movies since the year Lassie played a war veteran with amnesia.

Fahrenheit 451. The critics have treated François Truffaut's *Fahrenheit 451* as though somebody walked in and spat on the floor. What will emerge, in the process of evaluation and reevaluation, is a film for future ages to think about. It will take time. But on a first meeting, it rises like Everest, crystal-pure and shiny, towering above the hills of mediocrity and trash the movies have turned out lately to become (in my opinion) one of the most interesting films of the decade.

The time is the square root of now and the direction is the one in which the world is heading. People live in fireproof houses, so the firemen no longer put out fires. When children hear fire engines they clutch their mothers' hands in terror and shout, "There's going to *be* a fire." They're right. Books are unlawful and it is the duty of these firemen-of-the-future to root out hidden libraries full of Tolstoy and Shakespeare, annihilate them with flame throwers, and arrest their owners. Not only the bookcases are empty: people live in numbered blocks and watch giant wall screens on which bloodless women announcers bleat the news and viewers participate in the broadcast when a red light flashes above the screen. Child-bearing is discouraged, sex is taboo, men read comic strips with no words, and women privately stroke their breasts like dried pomegranates. Individuality is forbidden and noncomformity is out. "Mop-up squads" patrol the streets and arrest young boys on streetcorners for wearing long hair. There is no music, no laughter, no love.

Into this X-ray dream floats Oskar Werner (who could make you believe it even if it were *not* a great movie), playing a fireman with a mind full of question marks. In a dual role, Julie Christie plays both his emotionless wife and a young teacher with a cache of classics hidden in her uncle's house. With a rediscovery of the printed word, there is a rediscovery of emotion, a luxury punishable by death. But in the world of Ray Bradbury (on whose novel the film is based), there is, as in all worlds worth living in, a beam of hope: a place of silvery birches near a shimmering stream where the special people escape with books memorized inside their heads, where they are forced to live like tramps with the visions of poets, hoping for the day when books will once again be printed.

In the hands of Hollywood butchers, this could have been a ridiculous science fiction fiasco on the caliber of, say, George Orwell's *1984*. But Truffaut is a genius of seemingly limitless poetic dimensions. With a minimum of dialogue, he turns his own screenplay into something bordering on the lyrics of a lute song, fashions his actors into trembling prophets who are vulnerable and human and, most of all, believable. There is one wonderful scene in which an old woman who wants to die as she has lived burns to death in the flames of one of the last Victorian houses on earth. The camera peers down the stairs into a holocaust that licks her beautiful wallpaper as *Othello* and Emily Dickinson and *Mein Kampf* and hundreds of volumes of the greatest books of the centuries burn to ashes and the screen turns orange with fire.

Truffaut also triggers the emotions of the viewer with moments and actions that are deceptively simple, but surprisingly moving. There is, for example, something unexpectedly heartbreaking about watching a closeup of the pages of *The Catcher in the Rye* curling up into black charcoal next to Dickens. Equally intriguing is his use of color schemes that are in themselves designer studies (orange and chocolate brown rooms; a sterile powdery street with a flaming gold-lettered red firehouse). Then there is a final scene, in which the book people (about fifty of them left in the world in exile) stalk through a snowfall reciting pages of Sartre and Jane Austen and *Alice in Wonderland* and dozens of other books, that is one of the most chilling visual stanzas ever captured on film. They speak like wounded madmen with eyes full of Halloween glaze, crying out to be heard in the loneliness of an asylum. Their madhouse is their reality, their insanity the only hope for survival. And they cry alone, the last remnants of civilization.

Truffaut has delivered a eulogy with blood on his tongue—a frightening revelation that the knowledge of the future lies in a remembrance of the past.

The Game Is Over. Roger Vadim's concoction *La Curée*, which for some obscure reason known only to the label fixers of Hollywood has been absurdly retitled *The Game Is Over* for American distribution, is the updated, jet-age version of a classic Émile Zola tale about a man's revenge on his unfaithful child bride who has seduced his own son. In the hand of Vadim, it turns into a combination Southern Gothic horror fable and half Cocteau's *Les Enfants Terribles.* Although much of it is borrowed from other directors, it has everything a decadent study in perversion should have to make it look like more than it really is: a house like Xanadu transferred to the heart of Paris, surrounded by thickets and complete with a steam bath, a Garden of Eden for Jane Fonda (Mrs. Vadim) to prance about naked in, a goldfish pond for Fonda to swim naked in, and the most vicious group of German police dogs since the early Sherlock Holmes movies. It also has a dark, brooding Heathcliff master of the house who wears hunting jackets and leaves town a lot on mysterious business trips; a beautiful Rapunzel of a bride, reduced through boredom to playing a game with her sexy stepson. They dress up in Genghis Khan costumes, smear each other with cold cream, drive sportscars into rivers, set their bedclothes on fire and put them out with champagne, break up the furniture, smash up the gilt-edge mirrors (there are lots of gilt-edge mirrors, because it's a Vadim picture and he loves gilt), and even shoot at each other with rifles. Soon the game becomes reality, masquerade is life itself, and son and stepmother are between the sheets instead of on top of them.

None of it ever gets very deep, but Vadim makes it all so painlessly air-conditioned looking that it's worth a look. There are some of the most indescribably sensual love scenes since the walls melted in *Phaedra* (including one in which a hot sax purrs seductively as Fonda dances behind a smoked glass with her face covered by white cream), and endless shots in which the actors hop around in the buff (I counted seven full-face bare breast shots of Fonda, whose father must be purple-faced with embarrassment). Vadim handles her as though she were the Venus de Milo and even demonstrates, whenever possible, her American influence on *him.* Simple French idioms like "*à table*" turn up in the subtitles as "chow time" and at one point he has Fonda arriving at the breakfast table singing Comden and Green's "Good Morning" from *Singin' in the Rain.*

The best thing about the picture (aside from Fonda's breasts) is Claude Renoir's lush camerawork, which is remarkable even in a picture of such simple dimensions. Vadim's films are always better photographed than directed, but this must surely be his most beautiful to look at. Everything is shot as though color had just been invented, and the shots of a factory at Lacq (borrowed though the idea is from Antonioni's *Red Desert*) turns the screen into great walls of sulphur in pastel yellow against white smoke rising into a purple sky. *The Game Is Over* is easy on the brain and easier on the eye, but all of that half-hearted upper-class sexual depravity is enough to make one long for the dear departed days of Walt Disney.

Night Games. When Mai Zetterling's *Night Games* was unveiled at the 1966 Venice Film Festival, forty armed policemen kept everyone out of the Cinema Palais on the Lido except the international critics and the resulting hysteria equalled anything Il Duce ever provoked during his reign of Fascist terror. Too sexy to show in public, cried festival officials, canceling out the purpose of both criticism *and* film festivals. Now the film has found its way to America (in plain wrapper, no doubt, and without a seal of approval) and after a first glimpse there's reason to consider the banned Italians pretty lucky critters.

Miss Zetterling gave up acting after falling victim to some dreadful Hollywood films, and now seems hell-bent on directing her own projects to show a woman's independence in transferring to the screen subjects no man would dream of photographing. *Night Games* tells the story of an impotent man so haunted by memories of his monstrous, degenerate mother that he is unable to consummate his own marriage. Past and present fuse as he tries to exorcise his inhibitions in the castle of his childhood. And what a childhood: Miss Zetterling shows orgies in which slobbering, lecherous men shoot holes through his schoolboy maps with rifles. A hairy-chested homosexual tries to seduce him. His mother (played brilliantly, as always, by Ingrid Thulin) gives birth to a stillborn child at a costume party while the guests look on in their greasepaint, a monk peers down through her knees crying "What a beautiful motif!" and a saxophonist plays progressive jazz over the bed. Then the dead fetus is christened with champagne and destroyed. (Sell *that* to the Legion of Decency.)

Later a man draws musical notes on a woman's buttocks, the hero vomits on the screen three times in plain view of the camera, and a crazy old woman who looks like Jean Cocteau builds the city of Paris out of newspapers, sets them on fire in the boy's living room, and watches as the room catches fire while she plays the harmonica. The child plays with cockatoos and wears his mother's earrings, lipstick, and false eyelashes. The mother caresses his growing, naked body as he plays with her legs, then she forces him to masturbate while she looks on. All of this madness for the sake of madness has a kind of queer fascination, but it becomes tiresome as the camera tricks get trickier and the dialogue pretentious ("You like compliments," says one of the mother's lovers. "I prefer vomit," she replies, "it's more honest.") All of it is very shocking, but it doesn't mean anything.

Miss Zetterling turns out a *scandale* that has the taste of persimmons, but it is filled with such incredibly juvenile Freudian pap that audiences are more likely to giggle than gasp. She simply has nothing to say. The film is devoid of any real theme, plot, or character development. There are wonderful moments of isolated depravity, but the erotic scenes recur with no direction toward any kind of well-defined purpose. Finally, the young man feels the death bed is too late to wake up, so he blows up the castle and frees himself of his past *and* his obsession and the film ends with the young couple dancing gaily in the snow.

If Miss Zetterling is suggesting impotence and pseudo-homosexuality brought on by a lifetime of sexual anxiety can be cured by a keg of dynamite, her naïveté is too embarrassing to provoke further discussion. If she is not careful, she may turn out to be Andy Warhol in skirts.

Hotel is a good, expensive, old-fashioned movie kind of movie cut from the same bolt of cloth as *Grand Hotel*, *Ship of Fools* and—all right, you asked for it—even *Stagecoach*, demonstrating once again the never-failing trick of putting a miscellaneous group of people together in a dangerous, suspenseful situation and watching them like hamsters in a cage as they work their way out. All the sturdy hotel types are here: sexy French mistress, wily hotel magnate, decent grandfatherly older-generation hotel owner who wants to keep his hotel from the vultures, a Duchess with a spineless Duke for a husband, the hotel thief, crooked blackmailing house detective, convention whores, tough cocktail bar vocalist. You know the types. None of them doing much of importance, when you come right down to it, but making everything enjoyable because they look like they have decided ahead of time to play every scene right to the finish without giggling, and every scene comes off that way.

Directed with tense control but no special artistic distinction by Richard Quine, it is a picture that is nothing but entertainment, yet on a purely superficial level it does make a point in its diatribe against the New Architecture, which is turning all the old-fashioned, comfortable hotels into automatons with punch-card brains and lubricating oil for blood. There are some sincere performances by Merle Oberon, Rod Taylor, Karl Malden, Melvyn Douglas, and Richard Conte, and one really super performance by Kevin McCarthy, as a junior-league Conrad Hilton, patting his naked chest and negotiating for the destruction of all that is old and elegant and replacing it with all that is synthetic and cheap. I haven't thought much about *Hotel* since, but I had a lot of fun while it was on the screen. In this day and age, when most movies are no more interesting than the screens they're projected on, that's an achievement.

The Quiller Memorandum is an exercise in simple-mindedness that shows a momentary lapse of intelligence on behalf of both Harold Pinter, who wrote it, and the good natured but brainless wonders who had the bright idea of casting George Segal in the leading role. It pretends to be a suspense story about neo-Nazis in modern Berlin, but Pinter shows them as a group of leather-jacketed pseudo-sadists straight out of an old Republic horror serial, living like cat people in the bombed-out cellars of Gothic mansions, capturing victims and torturing them with hypnosis and hypodermic needles, when everybody who has read the newspapers in the past six months knows the *real* neo-Nazis are bland, hand-shaking businessmen being elected to the Bundestag and proud of it.

There is also the problem of Segal, an actor who chews his dialogue, winks cutely from the sides of his eyes, rubs the fatty tissue around his chin, and looks like a newly powdered model from a label of baby spinach. Everything about this film is absurd, from the sexy Nazi schoolteacher who takes Segal to bed purring, "How much do you know about these bad people?" to the self-centered, cardboard comic-strip dolts Pinter presents in his anti-Establishment attitude toward Her Majesty's spies. Max von Sydow plays the leader of the underground Nazis like Captain Queeg and George Segal plays the good-natured slob of no particular ability or intelligence who gets involved in the spying like a good-natured slob of no particular talent.

Marat/Sade. Movies are often attacked and berated for ignoring the truly mature audience. The question of just *how* mature the audience for film really is and the question of whether the audience under consideration is really undeniably interested in films as an intellectual visual art or whether it only pretends to be may be determined once and for all by how many people turn out to see England's Royal Shakespeare Company in Peter Brook's staggering new film version of Peter Weiss's play, *The Persecution and Assassination of Jean-Paul Marat as Performed by the Inmates of the Asylum of Charenton Under the Direction of the Marquis De Sade*. For this, unquestionably, is the supreme achievement in modern cinema—a film that transcends vanguards, fashions, eras, accepted cinematic standards, even the very celluloid on which it is recorded. It is a picture for those who care enough to see the very best.

Onstage, *Marat/Sade* was a theatrical triumph *and* a box office smash, but I had little hope for its success as a movie. Certainly I scarcely expected anything so overwhelmingly masterful as the picture Brook has come up with here. Not only has he stripped the play of the inhibitions forced upon it by the proscenium stage, but he has defied every artificial barrier imposed upon the movies by conventional filmmakers. Onstage there was so much action you couldn't follow it all. Every time De Sade had an important speech, some brilliant actor would be busy in some obscure corner of the stage writhing in madness or clutching at the nuns who streamed by with great clanking keys around their wasits. The production was ear-splitting and eye-boggling and it was impossible to take it all in at once. In the film, Brook broadens the dimensions of the stage and at the same time emphasizes the details of his production through his uncanny use of the closeup: faces through bars, hands on organ keys bound by chains, the hidden insanity in the face of De Sade suddenly blossoming in the rays of sunlight shooting through a window in the bathhouse.

Isolated by the camera, Brook's screeching monsters, with their eyes running and their mouths foaming, teach the audience more of De Sade's philosophy than it was possible to discern on the cluttered stage: death is only a process of nature. Only the most extreme actions matter. One feels the passion of pleasure in the sweetness of pain. And by having his lunatics enact the French Revolution for another audience, one not seen in the theater but visible in the film in the blackness of a room outside the bathhouse cell, Brook makes the filmgoer even more aware of the questions Peter Weiss meant to raise in his original text: What is freedom? Who is sane and who is not? By allowing the mad vegetables of the asylum to speak up in the camera's eye, the viewer becomes painfully aware for the first time of De Sade's life premise: that locked cells within the human body are a thousand times worse than all the dungeons of the world.

But aside from its considerable intellectual content, *Marat/Sade* is a smashingly visual film on its own terms. In towering performances that defy written description, Brook has enlisted every one of the forty-one members of the original London cast as slobbering mongoloids, murderous straight-jacketed schizophrenics, syphilis-scabbed sex maniacs, and festering catatonics, turning the screen into a sea of slimy, slithering cobras, weaving in and out of songs and pantomimes and blood-curdling horrors with dazzling effects. In all my years of sitting through films on every level of merit, I have never seen more stunning ensemble work, but special mention must be made of the particular brilliance of Glenda Jackson's extraordinary Charlotte Corday. Trembling across the sweat-stained floorboards, her face swollen and cracked from the terrors of sleeping sickness and melancholia, her head bobbing like a rotten cabbage on a stick, Miss Jackson gives the kind of performance that should send every American member of the Screen Actor's Guild back to drama school. If she is not nominated for an Academy Award in the forthcoming season, the American movie industry is sicker than even I thought possible.

The film also utilizes choreography, music, improvisation, costuming, and symbolic imagery in a symphony of hypnotic precision never before equalled in films. By turning on the steam valves and blurring the inmates into a swirl of blood-stained bandages and drool, Brook turns Marat's nightmare scene into a ghoulish assault on the senses. In this and every other scene, he uses two color cameras, like huge bloodshot eyes, roaming through the asylum, stalking the inmates like Baskerville hounds, and photographing the madness without missing a detail. The entire spectacle is witnessed through bars, with the color pigmentation sometimes practically wiped out by floods of light, followed by darkness, in a startling chiaroscuro effect. Eerie camera angles focus on backgrounds and blur the foregrounds to heighten the pace and frenzy of the emotional turbulence.

There is simply no way to adequately relate on paper the total amount of greatness in this fantastic motion picture. It must be seen to be believed, but its very existence makes movies grow several inches taller in importance, in stature and in achievement. And the most wonderful thing of all—it'll never be shown on television.

Dutchman. I am tired of LeRoi Jones and his jaundiced, narrow impressions of the white man. Call him Whitey, call him Mister Charlie, he is nothing like the characters in playwright Jone's sour little exercises in self-destruction. I am also tired of being sold racial prejudice in such outrageously medicinal doses, like a bitter cough syrup, when it applies (as Mr. Jones sees it) to such an exaggerated, un-representative few. In *Dutchman*, a new film made in England by Americans who were refused permission to shoot it in its actual New York locale, the white race is symbolized by a filthy slattern in a clinging striped Mod dress who lusts after a Negro man on a subway train, lasciviously taunts him with promises of sexual intercourse, lewdly rubs him with her thighs, then at the height of his passion, stabs him to death and goes unpunished to the next train and the next Negro victim.

Hard to take either as drama or as reflected truth, simply nothing about *Dutchman* convinces me that this is what being white and being Negro is all about. The girl's scenes are written with a rising action, a height of passion, then a decline of emotion. Then the Negro, first pictured as a grinning Sambo, suddenly bursts into flame and beats up practically everyone in the subway car. Nobody leaves. One man, whose newspaper is ripped into shreds, continues to read half a page without looking up. A woman passenger, having been baptized with orange juice and pelted with flying apples from the girl's shopping bag, continues her journey looking straight ahead. This is Jones's way of saying that in New York nobody cares about anyone else unless directly affected. (Witness the Kitty Genovese murder, in which a woman was killed in full view of her neighbors.) I think he even means the film to be representative of the entire world, but surely even Jones must understand that New York is not now and never has been representative of anything but what is uniquely New York. The way of life —from the taxis to the dirt to the neurosis that is its particular trademark— has very little to do with the rest of the world at large. And even in New York anyone who has ever been on the subways knows they are frequented by people who look like inmates of an asylum anyway, constantly moving about from car to car like restless zombies, but at the first sign of trouble (like getting pelted with apples) they flee like bats out of hell.

Because it is written with an ear for the realistic speech of troubled people and acted by method actors who make each line overly natural, it is impossible to take *Dutchman* any other way but realistically. Yet I do not think anyone connected with the film means for it to be realistic. It is supposed to be a *surrealistic* nightmare dramatized on a train that never stops and acted by two extreme symbols of humanity who act out their racial, sexual, and psychological fantasies on each other. This is another of its failures—it gets its styles mixed up.

Shirley Knight and Al Freeman, Jr., turn in stunning performances. With an absolutely bare minimum of action and only a thread of dialogue, they squeeze more juice out of the script than out of Miss Knight's oranges. And Miss Knight's husband, Gene Persson, has produced the film with great economy, shooting it for $65,000 in only six days in a London studio on a subway set drawn and constructed by British artists from photographs. It all looks remarkably authentic and proves that films need more people like these, who are willing to pool their talents and money and go out and thumb their noses at Hollywood's ridiculous production costs. I respect the people involved in *Dutchman*. I only wish I could swallow what it tries to preach so vigorously.

Oh Dad, Poor Dad. I never cease to be amazed at the agility with which Hollywood manages to make sex seem so vulgar. Who ever thought the brainless hacks of big-budget boobism would so distort and cheapen as kooky, fresh and far-out a bauble as Arthur Kopit's off-Broadway lampoon, *Oh Dad, Poor Dad, Mama's Hung You in the Closet and I'm Feeling So Sad*. But cheapen it they did. Will the real villain responsible for this chamber of horrors please step forward?

Is it Rosalind Russell, who plays Kopit's take-off on Momism with "false fingernails made in Calcutta from ground Yak powder," slashes of nasty lipstick, and hoods that look like Vampira on her way to a Halloween party? She used to be funny, but she seems determined lately to destroy herself and her career by playing every role she touches like a cross between Auntie Mame and the Bride of Frankenstein.

Is it Jonathan Winters, as a talking corpse, whose own writers have written in gags to be dubbed in over the soundtrack between lines of dialogue spoken by the other characters? Sample: when the son offers to help Mama hang his cadaver up in the closet, Winters says, "Let Mumsy do it herself, son, it is my fondest wish to give her a hernia." Sick. Unfunny. Embarrassing.

Is it Robert Morse, who plays the emasculated son without charm in red eyeliner and white pancake makeup, slobbering like a member of the *Marat/Sade* cast applying for an award at a school for retarded adults?

Is it Broadway's lovable schmoo Barbara Harris, who is much too fat to roll about on top of billiard tables in lace bikinis like a baby hippopotamus in diapers?

Is it Richard Quine who, by shooting it in lush trappings in Montego Bay and inserting what amounts to a comedy act for Winters, seems to have completely missed the point?

Or is it playright Kopit himself, who should have suspected the worst when he sold the property to Hollywood?

I suspect it is a combination of all these poor misguided people who, with dubious teamwork, have turned this once delightful spoof into a witless monstrosity so inept that, although the year is young, it just might be the worst film of 1967.

The Bible. Christians, Jews, or Zoroastrians—there should be something to offend just about everybody in *The Bible*. Cecil B. De Mille, who—according to Pauline Kael—once laid claim to having falsified history more than anybody else, can move over. He has a new rival in John Huston. Even the title of Huston's film is a falsification (the picture really deals only with selected short subjects in the Book of Genesis). Some shrewd observer must have pointed this out because the ads have now been altered to read: *The Bible . . . in the beginning*. It's not much help.

With a few rare exceptions, like Pasolini's *The Gospel According to Saint Matthew*, religious films have been largely insulting to the audiences who care for them, high camp to the audiences who don't, and money in the box office till from both. *The Bible*, which pretends to be the biggest and most spectacular of them all, is the latest, longest, campiest, and most ludicrous. It should pave the streets of Beverly Hills with gold.

Like *The Greatest Story Ever Told, King of Kings*, and other patently absurd wide-screen spectacles before it, *The Bible* is so dazzled by its size and budget that it fills the width and length of the screen with God and this magnitude in itself represents an achievement to the public. (It does have one advantage over its predecessors: nobody has to play Jesus.) Hollywood producers, like dope peddlers selling bennies to babies, are perfectly willing to invest millions in this two-way self-destruction. The drive by economic necessity to give the public what it wants does not make these men villains in themselves; the audiences who pay for reserved seats to feed their own 70-mm. DeLuxe Color habits have created their own monsters.

In the Forties, the public had been gorged with enough anti-Nazi films to make everyone sick of Hitler. It was time to bring on the girls. Now, with explosions still ringing in the ears from bombs like *The Robe* and *Esther and the King*, it's time to wave that white flag again. Is there nothing that will pacify the Huston ego? What happened to the economy of talent that turned out *The Maltese Falcon*? Or the poet who made *The Misfits* ten years ahead of its time? Wasn't his misguided departure into Tennessee Williams country in *Night of the Iguana* enough to teach him to stick to the simple things? Apparently not, for now we are faced with enough awesome Huston ego to turn Abraham into a driveling, navel-scratching method actor, set Noah's Ark afloat as a multilingual *Titanic*, make a pretentious ballet out of The Creation, and produce a Tower of Babel expensive enough to pay the production costs of *The Shop on Main Street* and *Darling* put together. And out of it all he gets the least possible results, like casting a reel into the Great Lakes and catching goldfish.

The saddest thing about *The Bible* is that, like most Hollywood biblical epics, it seems to have been made without love. In the age of astronauts, when anthropology courses deify Darwin and chastize Jesus, the Bible can be accepted at best as Divinely Inspired. Huston sees it as merely Divine. He pictures a Garden of Eden that looks like a garden party in Bel Air, with so much vaseline smeared over the camera lens it is impossible to see anything. (If you're paying all that box office money to get a prurient peek at the much-publicized nudity of Adam and Eve, forget it—you can hardly see the grass, much less the people.) The Creation (which gets credit on the screen for its own special second unit director) is a gimmicky bit of business out of the old Val Lewton horror films, with a giant wind machine whooshing through the dust to uncover a moldy looking mound of clay that later turns into—yipes, Charlie!—a living thing. He has an Adam (Michael Parks) who looks like a reject from the Hell's Angels motorcycle gang and a dewy-eyed, fawn-like Eve (Ulla Bergryd) who luckily says very little. Then there's a very funny bit involving a serpent dressed in a sort of harlequin costume who slithers menacingly up and down the trunk of a tree that looks like it was stolen from an old Wizard of Oz set, complete with plastic apples. The serpent is credited with "choreography by Katherine Dunham" and occasionally whispers "Eee-ve" and "Aaa-dam" through several echo chambers, and it has been reported by the 20th Century-Fox publicity department that the role was turned down by Rudolf Nureyev after he read the script. (Admittedly, it was a better role in the book, but then *everything* was better in the book.)

There's an impressive Noah's Ark sequence marred only by some second-rate rear-screen projection (every time a dangerous animal enters the boat, the screen around Noah turns purple and begins to shake). Then there's the problem of those accents: every member of Noah's family is dubbed from some foreign tongue, with Noah (Huston himself) booming loud and clear through the sound track in that greased, bass clef Iowa cornfield drawl: "C'mon, everybody, get on board!"—a large moan, accompanied by some *religioso* violins from the studio pen of someone named Toshiro Mayuzumi.

The final blow comes in the Sodom and Gomorrah sequence, which seems thrown in for shock value and nothing else, since it bears no relation to the rest of the film, and since it really can only be described as a kind of production number staged inside Carlsbad Caverns. Pop-art sets and papier mâché people who look very much like the cast of *Marat/Sade* on a movie holiday slink venomously in the background as three angels (all played with a kind of screening-room pallor by Peter O'Toole) march zombie-like through the sinful caverns hovering under the brink of a tottering halo. Skinny purplish men hold hands in the background and witchlike women with black teeth and sequin eye-shadow hiss like lobsters in boiling water. The effect is so garish, it's funny. Everyone has a vision of what

Sodom was like, but Huston can't really believe it was like *that* . . . or can he?

The film runs three hours (plus intermission) and in that time the only real surprise is Ava Gardner, who plays the barren, childless Sarah with staggering beauty, control, and dimension. She is no longer the beautiful female wolf the MGM press agents taught her how to be in 1950, but she has matured beyond all expectations into something much more exciting: a real person, able to bring real levels of emotion to roles that deserve her. There is also some interesting work by George C. Scott as Abraham—a craggy, windswept man with a voice that sounds like it has been massaged with brandy—but when he takes his son up to the top of that mountain for the sacrifice, it becomes clear that he needs a stronger director than Huston to keep him in line. A good scene becomes spoiled by the kind of inaudible crunching of dialogue and gnashing of teeth one usually gets only from Orson Welles on an uncontrollable day.

All told, at a time when religion needs all the help it can get, John Huston may have set its cause back a couple of thousand years. In his hands, *The Bible* looks like the Hebrews' answer to Greek mythology.

Rachel, Rachel. Like the cows Pet Milk comes from, Paul Newman and Joanne Woodward must be very contented creatures. As actors, they are two of the most admirable members of a profession that often neglects its own. While everyone else's salaries go up, the Newmans are among the very few who will gamble on a Broadway play they believe in to keep their pride alive. They have always maintained a high creative performance level, even when saddled with Hollywood slag far beneath their dignity or ability. Yet through all the commercial junk, they have remained individuals, with firm grips on their identities and their knowledge of their craft. And they both have minds of their own, in a business where actors tend to think collectively.

It would take two nose-thumbing, tasteful, anti-Establishment rebels with strong convictions to make a film like *Rachel, Rachel,* and the Newmans have done it. It wasn't easy. Every major studio in Hollywood turned them down, sniffing with typical chaotic irrationalization, "Newman's a star, it's too big a gamble to let him direct; Woodward's not a financeable name." They both had to commit a chunk of their lives away to get Warners-Seven Arts to finance their little film, but they have now surprised all the skeptics by delivering their package for less than $800,000 (a feat unheard of these days with names like the Newmans involved). And they have surprised everyone even more by turning out not an adequate little movie, but a thoughtful, provocative, moving, undeniably brilliant movie—one of the best movies, in fact, I've seen in years.

Rachel, Rachel is a small, touching, *Marty* kind of movie—the sort of film that has never been promoted or understood in Hollywood's box office lingo. Yet, like *Marty*, it is vastly more important than nine out of ten of the top grossing junk collages the studios grind out yearly like cheese sandwiches. It deals more with the inner workings of the human heart than it does with telling a big story in terms of action and panorama, yet its power lies in the way it involves the viewer in much the same way a good novel involves the reader. Everyone knows a Rachel. There's a Rachel in every town and a Rachel in every family. Sometimes she's a librarian, sometimes a school teacher. People seldom get to know her well, because she's usually something of a bore. But in Newman's film, we have no other choice. There she is, on the X-ray table, warm and sad and vulnerable and appealing in a loyal, cocker spaniel sort of way, exposed by the camera in her every nuance.

Newman's Rachel is a thirty-five-year-old spinster life has passed by without even a smile. Her father, a small-town New England mortician, has been dead for fourteen years, but she still lives with her widowed mother above the Japonica Funeral Chapel, surrounded by the smell of formaldehyde and haunted by childhood memories of being teased by the cruel chants of "Slaughter, slaughter, undertaker's daughter." Like the pages of a book, Newman unfolds each layer of his character's psyche. Each scene allows the audience to know her better. He *cares* and his camera knows how to take its time in developing a flesh-and-blood person instead of merely photographing one. Rachel hums in her tiny schoolroom as her pupils have their slumber period. Silently, she sends a slow child to the principal. Cautiously, she reads her way through a page of sheet music on a musty old piano badly in need of a tuner. "Anyone who teaches school is an absolute saint," coo her mother's friends; "I think Rachel is an absolute saint."

And that's how it goes as Rachel's summer comes on. She forgets her mother's Hershey bar on her way home from school. She eats a cold pork chop and daydreams of what might have been. Or might still be. "I'm going to paint my apartment lilac. I'm gonna get a good suntan." But illusion gives way to reality; "No, I'm not. Every summer I buy tons of suntan lotion and at the end I'm as white as a mushroom." If somebody pinched her, it wouldn't hurt. "I'm in the middle of my life," she says,

"And this is my last ascending summer." Her friend, played with pathos and dowdy charm by Estelle Parsons, tries to bring her out of her shell. "Every time we've gone for an ice cream cone, you've ordered vanilla—that's not the only kind. There are thirty other flavors and a Flavor of the Month!"

There are occasional respites. Rachel tries religion and the screen fills with the throbbing fever of a tent revival, as a Bible-preaching evangelist builds the scene to such a thrashing crescendo your stomach turns and the dust of the stomping feet and clapping hands fills the nostrils with suffocation as Rachel reaches out for love. It is a powerful scene, like a group therapy session, in which I was alternately repelled, repulsed, nauseated, exhausted, and moved to tears. And, eventually, there is even a man—an old school chum of Rachel's, who plays on her sensitivity and clumsiness to selfishly fulfill his own fleeting sexual drive. The tragedy is he's the only kind of man a girl of Rachel's age and station can get. The others are all married or queer. Yet even here her frustrations take wing in flights of fancy. She thinks she's pregnant. Her life takes on new meaning. In her imagination, she rocks her baby carriage in the park while myriads of happy children play nearby. But it's only a cyst.

The film has no end, because there is no real solution to the problems or the sadness of the Rachels of our society. There is simply always another day. So Rachel takes a Greyhound bus to a new hope and Newman ends his film like Truffaut's *The 400 Blows*. The problem becomes ours.

Joanne Woodward, one of the most underrated and sadly underexposed actresses of this era, deserves a valentine for a performance of such monumental character and strength it is hard to describe. There are really *two* Rachels in the film and she plays them both magnificently. She is the Rachel of the naked eye, taking quiet walks through pastoral meadows, past tractors, and barns, searching for her own symbiosis in an isolated world she is too shy to combat. Juxtaposed with her physical presence, there is also the subconscious Rachel, the alter-ego of unfulfilled passion.

Newman's direction of his wife is so detailed you not only see the expressions on her face, you also see the motivations behind them. Miss Woodward has done a thorough research project. She knows so much about Rachel (from the way she wiggles across the room in front of a TV set afraid to disturb whoever might be watching it to the way her slip shows beneath her cotton dress to the way she takes her date dress gingerly from its plastic cleaners bag to the misty, red-lidded sadness in her eyes) that she actually *is* Rachel. Her painstakingly accurate anatomy of a middle-aged spinster is agonizingly brutal, yet poetically rewarding.

But then nothing about *Rachel, Rachel* is sugar-coated or placebo-flavored. It will undoubtedly have to struggle to find an audience as sympathetic to its intentions as I am. But I found it to be almost as enriching a social comment on the search for love as *The Member of the Wedding*. For the ostriches who don't want to recognize the Rachels of the world in each of us, there are other movies to bury their heads in. But they'll find no sand in *Rachel, Rachel*.

La Guerre est finie is certainly Alain Resnais's clearest film to date and the one that should win him a wider and more important audience than the dilettante crowd which flocked to *Muriel* and *Last Year at Marienbad*. The story tells of a professional revolutionary in Paris trying to fashion an organic coherence out of the political underground in Spain. Resnais has always been interested in political expatriates, but because this film is a less personal statement than his *Hiroshima, Mon Amour*, his often confusing directorial techniques don't tend to get mixed up with what he is trying to say. This doesn't mean *La Guerre est finie* is less cerebral than *Hiroshima*. It just makes better sense.

In his best performance to date, Yves Montand is an activist involved in the Spanish war (don't ask which one; there's always a war of some kind in Spain). Instead of settling down and forming a future with his lovely wife (Ingrid Thulin, brilliant as always), he fakes a positive attitude while getting mixed up with a group of intellectual French terrorists trying to locate a friend behind the Spanish border. But is any man involved in other people's causes instead of his own life really a whole man? He fears death and sweats when he passes cemeteries, refuses to say "I love you" in bed, avoids any action that will indicate a commitment.

Resnais tells the story in a style that is more conventional than usual. Still, nothing about his work has ever been ordinary. He cuts in such a way that action is interspersed with conscience, straight narrative juxtaposed with indications of past and future tense. He insists his films don't borrow from each other, yet certain patterns do repeat themselves. His films are intellectual rather than physical. His camera is carefully controlled rather than allowed to follow its nose. His scripts are like dignified chess games instead of games of life. What is new about *La Guerre est finie* is his use of "flash forwards"—projections not of the past, but of the future. Scenes-to-come flash across the screen before they happen to the hero because to Resnais that is the way a militant mind works: always figuring out the next move, making plans ahead of time, visualizing what each set-up will be like before it occurs. The audience watches a conventional action shot and sees what flashes across the character's mind at the same time. In this sense, Resnais uses his camera to produce a human mosaic rather than an autonomous statement.

This technique is exciting filmmaking, but it is not without its flaws and ambiguities: (1) it is unclear whether the narration is the voice of the character played by Montand or of an outside narrator; (2) some of the "flash forwards" tend to confuse as to whether they are actually happening in the next room or imagined; and (3) the ending is hazy. Will Miss Thulin head Montand off at the border before he is captured by the Spanish? The indication is an optimistic one, which shows that maybe Resnais is growing mellow. If he is finally getting around to telling the world that people are more important than causes, the sign is a healthy one.

Two for the Road is perhaps the best American movie of 1967, even with its occasional lapses into Hollywood formula lushness. But overlooking its oversized budget and some of Director Stanley Donen's self-conscious camera trickeries (they are fewer and less noticeable than in *Arabesque* and *Charade*) you will be rewarded with a moving, disturbing, strikingly adult comment on modern marriage written by Frederick (*Darling*) Raphael, and by two of the most brilliant performances—by Audrey Hepburn and Albert Finney—ever captured on the screen. Hepburn and Finney are such a dream combination that they visually achieve such revelations of character, atmosphere, and emotion that their freshness and originality give the film a kind of vitality and continuance that seems easy. It is only much later that their brilliance begins to overtake you. They are aided, of course, by Raphael's script—funny, warm, juicy, rich—with serious undertones of now people and now relationships.

The film is intercut to show three different stages of a married couple's life—the year they met hitchhiking through Europe, the year they returned to tour with a family of epicene young suburban Americans, and the year when they have finally become successful, jaded, and bored with life and each other—as each stage continually meets and crosses at the intersections of various roads through the European countryside. Between road signs, the characters grow and change with the ease characters seldom get time to use in films. They have affairs, lose face, grow apart, yet they stay together through sticktoitivity, the glue that holds most modern marriages together. At the end, they *loathe* each other. They *love* each other. They drive their expensive car toward a ferry landing like the couple in Polanski's *Knife in the Water*. Will they divorce or survive? "Bitch," says Finney to the elegantly gowned Miss Hepburn. "Bastard," she says back. And they drive off together, still two for the road. Just like in real life.

Thoroughly Modern Millie is, I suppose, what has come to be regarded by Hollywood standards as a family picture. It should also be revered, a few critics have pointed out, because it is the first musical out of Hollywood in years. So what? MGM used to turn them out at the rate of two a month and nobody cared. Most of them were better than this hot-fudge sundae with whipped cream and double on the pistachio nuts. So steeped in gooey schmaltz is this technicolor, reserved-seat, advance-priced drugstore special that practically nobody has paused to notice how like one of those ghastly Max Liebman TV specials it is, or how old Mary Tyler Moore and Julie Andrews look in their girlish flapper costumes saying lines like "Gee whiz, your friendship is so precious to me," or how none of the spastic musical numbers thrown in to break up the monotony are very well executed (not to mention the fact that they have nothing whatever to do with the plot). There is a nice job by Carol Channing, the original Jazz Baby herself, who seems so giddy and bullet-brained she gives the impression she might be living in the wrong age off-screen. Most of the other unfortunates involved in this mess look like aging, lipsticked mannequins let out of their boxes to whoop it up after the store has closed down for the night.

The Happening. The really awful thing about *The Happening*, aside from the fact that nothing much ever happens, is the depressing spectacle of having to watch a talented director like Elliot (*Cat Ballou*) Silverstein and some capable actors like Anthony Quinn and Faye Dunaway in hand-to-hand combat with an outrageous mish-mash of overcleverness that backfires into something much more square than anyone intended. Silverstein started out with a dramatic script about a Miami businessman kidnapped by college kids of the Fort Lauderdale variety and faced with the tragic destiny of watching all his friends and relatives refuse to claim the body. A good idea, but Silverstein turns it into social satire, gimmicking it up with such heavy-handed right hooks as Mafia members who say "don't kill us—we'll kill you"; a series of ridiculous scenes involving Milton Berle as—are you ready?—a cuckold; contrived pacing; "in" gags that don't come off; Keystone Kops and Beach Party Bikini movie take-offs; and unbelievably amateurish performances and direction. Most of *The Happening* is ludicrous, and a good bit of it is worse than that.

You're a Big Boy Now is an experimental movie directed by a twenty-seven-year-old boy named Francis Coppola as his master's thesis project at UCLA. With Hollywood so desperately crying out for young blood to turn its sagging industry into something fresh and bearable again, Coppola's effort should be applauded even though it fails. As a fairy tale about a nice boy who suffers through labyrinthian growing pains of wicked witches, domineering mamas, pontifical-pompous papas, and assorted sideshow gnomes and goblins before he finally ends up with the sugar-crusted princess right there at home under his nose the whole time, *Big Boy* really isn't much different from the old Mickey Rooney—Judy Garland sarsaparillas MGM used to whip up in cluttered profusion. But Coppola is infected with a severe case of Richard Lesterism and in his future movies one can only hope for a quick cure.

Because he has no story worth mentioning, he sudses up his film with endless pop-art clutter involving quick pans of Times Square and all its bawdy glitter (including seemingly endless closeups of pretzel machines). Then to spice up his lagging action, he makes all the people in his film run a lot. Some of the people who run are Julie Harris, as a crazy old-maid landlady who gets her leg broken by a woman-hating rooster; Geraldine Page, as a crazy mother who emasculates her son by sending him a lock of her hair every day until she is bald; Elizabeth Hartman, as a crazy beatnik sadist discotheque dancer whose prize possession is the wooden leg of an albino hypnotherapist who raped her in her youth; Rip Torn as a clichéd father who looks suspiciously like William Jennings Bryan after a silver debate; and a sheepdog named Emily. All the people who run are miscast beyond salvage. The person they are always running after is a young Canadian actor named Peter Kastner, who is also miscast since he plays a virginal lad but continually displays a heavy stubble of five o'clock shadow.

No, *You're a Big Boy Now* is not exactly the answer to Hollywood's problems, even though it *was* filmed in New York. But as a class project, it deserves at least a B+ for a good old expensive college try.

Hurry Sundown. Critic Wilfrid Sheed wrote recently in *Esquire* that "no movie is ever so bad that you can't find some virtue in it." He must not have seen *Hurry Sundown.* This Otto Preminger absurdity about the nigger-hatin', fornicatin', wife-beatin', chitlin' and cornbread eatin', white trash infested South is so unique in its own uniform brand of raunchiness that it must not go ignored. Nobody has accused Otto of any particularly noticeable talents in recent years, but this time the Big O (as he is called by his co-workers) has pulled out all the stops in supreme bad taste. Except for *Laura*, Preminger's films have always been smelly examples of banality, badly directed and clumsily photographed, but shrewdly sold as items of controversy. In all of them, he has riddled some poor victim with phony bullets in the name of box office: in *The Cardinal* it was Catholics, in *Advise and Consent* it was Congress, in *The Moon Is Blue* it was virgins, in *In Harm's Way* it was the men in uniform, in *Bunny Lake Is Missing* it was Noel Coward and Laurence Olivier. Otto needed a new villain. Villains can't be Japanese any more. People are tired of Russian and Nazi villains. Hey, how about all those lecherous white Southern judges and those whore-mongering Southern white trash women and those pore ol' Uncle Toms and those dirty-faced li'l pickaninnies?

Well, he did it. In a time when the South is trying desperately to make some kind of sense out of itself, he has had the raw audacity to belch up a piece of filth that bears absolutely no resemblance to any kind of reality anywhere—a slimy, crawling, pitiful obscenity in which the "syphilitic ol' niggers" have nothing to worry about because when the sheriff and his Klansmen come to lynch them they are too busy singing and dancing like Sambos in a cornfield to the tune of a production number with music by Hugo Montenegro to notice. One fat Negro woman sticks a hot chicken leg into the sheriff's mouth and he licks his lips ("The blacker the berry, the sweeter the juice") and takes her off to bed. But then the white folks are all such mangy, degenerate critters that they are too ignorant to notice anything too, what with Michael Caine (swallowing every syllable with a Cockney drawl so thick it is possible to decipher only about every fifth word) stealing everybody's land in between drivin' his little boy into a state of plumb mental ree-tardation by locking him in a hotel room, see, and driving his wife, Jane Fonda (just as scratchy and ill-at-ease in drama as she is in comedy roles) into a sexual frenzy so powerful she jes' falls between his knees and puts the butt of his saxophone right in her mouth with the slobber fallin' down her chin and all. 'Course there's plenty of other uppity white trash too—all hell-bent on drink, miscegenation, slappin' uppity colored girls' faces 'cause they been to Harlem and done slept with white men too, tearin' up evidence, beatin' up on the key witnesses in one of the funniest courtroom trials in the history of movies, blowin' each other up with dynamite, and puttin' on airs. But don't worry. You won't be able to see much of this drek (it's so badly edited it is impossible to see where the action is half the time) or hear it either. At the screening I attended, the audience was hissing, booing, and throwing popcorn boxes at the screen with such nasty vigor I almost missed the scene where the judge spit into the church communion cup. Unfortunately they quietened down long enough for me to hear Jane Fonda gurgle, "I was ten years old 'fore I learned damn and Yankee were two different words."

Preminger's direction of all this silliness is laughable. Not that there is anything to direct but insulting dialogue and some of the worst actors this side of the old Monogram serials. But a man who has been calling himself a director as long as Otto should know better than to end a scene by having Burgess Meredith (who'll do anything for money these days—from *Batman* to this is strictly the bottom of the scum pot) open a door only to be shoved in the face by an unidentified hand. That kind of clumsiness is simply amateur night in Poughkeepsie.

Blow-Up. The only explosive thing about *Blow-Up* is the title. Otherwise it is just another exercise in petrifying boredom from Italy's Nihilist director Michelangelo Antonioni.

Whatever happened to movies that used to be *about* something? Antonioni's disciples insist his films are indeed about the isolation of the human soul in a society where nobody loves anything. Fine, but does his camera show it? No, it merely insinuates. His films involve scripts that are no more than blank pages of white paper blowing in the wind and people who are no more than minority-group bores made of papier-mâché. *Blow-Up* could have been an ingenious thriller, but it is ruined by Antonioni's inability to tell a story simply or with compassion and by his refusal to use movies as anything but an intellectual device to relieve his own frustrations.

One-third of the film follows the script's antihero, a smashingly successful London Mod photographer (based, perhaps, on David Bailey?) around London as he takes pictures of everything from naked girls to old men. When his camera finally accidentally records a murder, the audience jerks to attention as the picture begins to make sense. But no, a couple of teenyboppers come into the studio and for no apparent reason the whole movie turns into a seduction scene of naked breasts collapsing into a sea of blue paper. Does the antihero care about humanity? About life? About law vs. society? About death? About the murderess (played with helpless annoyance by Vanessa Redgrave, like a lady caught in public with a hangnail and no emery board). Is she really the murderess? Was there ever really a murder at all?

None of these, or any of the other questions that pop up with alarming precision, are ever answered. In the last scene the antihero is tossed a ball by a group of Marcel Marceau–like revelers in clown whiteface, playing silently on an eerie tennis court. He holds the ball a moment, clinging to all the unexpectancy of life, then tosses it back. The movie ends. Antonioni grips the mind, then loses his stranglehold.

In *Eclipse* he became so disgusted with people he spent the last ten minutes of the movie with his camera focused on treetops. *Blow-Up* is at least more concerned with anatomical devices that pretend to pass for human beings, no matter how dull they are. Still, he shies away from anything that might involve an old-fashioned use of the cinematic medium: He will not, for example, film the simple composite frame of a car being parked on a city street. Instead, he trains his camera on the curb or on a shop window or on two young fairies walking their poodles the way it would appear if you were looking through the car window while it was *being* parked. It's a good way to put the spectator into the picture, but it is also excruciatingly dull to watch.

For all its metaphysical mumbo-jumbo and all its unexplained action, *Blow-Up* is lovely to see in color. The cinematography, by Carlo di Palma, is fashioned in designs of basic eggshell white with an occasional splash of lavender. There is more color than he used in *Red Desert* (he even hand-painted the grass a brilliant kelly green) but the effect is less interesting because it isn't used to evoke any particular response in the viewer. More often than not, it seems stripped of its pigmentation.

Most of the actors (especially poor David Hemmings, who might be a good actor for all I know, but who seems here more like a rummage-sale Terence Stamp) seem to have been shoved in front of the camera and told to "do something—*anything*!" The discotheque and pot party crowd scenes (which Antonioni has never been able to do well) are as phony and unconvincing as anything ever staged by Hollywood. Every time Antonioni's fable almost but not quite makes a point, he clutters the screen with silly sex scenes that are supposed to suggest an interjection of man's desire to relieve himself of responsibility, but they only serve to cheapen his statements. Consequently, *Blow-Up* looks like the work of a man who spends most of his life reading *Playboy* and never really learning what life is all about. It is spoken in English, but in any language in the world it has the unmistakable sound of a big fat yawn.

Grand Prix cuts right to the heart of the most expensive sport in the world—automobile racing—and finds it full of heartworms. It is directed, with the most imaginative use to date of Cinerama, by John Frankenheimer, whose track record (*Manchurian Candidate, All Fall Down, Seconds*) just about makes him America's most energetic and cold-eyed young director. In *Grand Prix*, Frankenheimer staggers the senses and boggles the eye with imaginative photography, incisive viewpoints into the kind of madness that inspires the racing fever and the kind of breakneck breathlessness that drives the crowds at Le Mans and Monza into a frenzy. He fills his Cinerama lens with spectacular kaleidoscopes of whirling wheels, grinding tires, and dizzying ribbons of highway. He breathes life into the Maseratis and Aston-Martins and Ferraris and Hondas and Alfa Romeos until they seem as human and as dangerous as the men who drive them. He splits his screen into TV-size collages of what the driver is thinking as he accelerates to supersonic speeds with cameras attached. He crowds his frames with effects that send both cars and spectators into a blur of thrills and he balances the thrills with a smashing performance by Eva Marie Saint and arresting—if uneven—work by an international cast headed by Brian Bedford, Jessica Walter, Yves Montand, and Genevieve Page.

Regrettably, what Frankenheimer fails to do is conquer the banalities of a 3½-hour script that sinks the picture into a peat bog of clichés whenever the cars are forced to share the screen with people like Hollywood's great stone face, James Garner, or France's Françoise Hardy, who continually announces to the press that she is "not an actress at all" and proves it. The big screen seems too overwhelming for these people and it certainly proves too much for former TV scriptwriter Robert Alan Aurthur's screenplay. Frankenheimer builds up the audience with beautifully mounted scenes of racing, shot on authentic locations along the seventeen-race course held yearly in Europe. Then Aurthur's screenplay tears down the sport by emphasizing the crudeness and immaturity of its drivers. It is a disheartening conflict that seriously distracts from an otherwise beautifully filmed *Grand Prix*.

Negatives. From the looks of some of the recent movies from England, the young British filmmakers must be leading some pretty far-out sex lives. Take *Negatives*. It's a mind-blower about a husband and wife who run an antique shop (there must be something psychological in setting these nightmares in antique shops—I remember at least ten British horror films in recent memory all set in similar surroundings, as though nothing unnatural ever happens in, say, Regent Park). Anyway, this couple finds sex a physical impossibility without dressing up on Sunday afternoons in costumes of another era and simultaneously assuming the identities of other people. The young man becomes the notorious London murderer Dr. Crippen and the wife becomes Crippen's mistress, wife, and male traveling companion. They are bored, mundane people with no flair or talent for life. When they ride on a bus, they sit separately, pretending to be strangers. OK. I'll go along with that as a premise for an interesting, offbeat movie. But that's not all. A bisexual German photographer shows up, makes Lesbian advances to the wife, and talks the boy into becoming her *own* personal sexual fantasy. She doesn't see him as Dr. Crippen at all, but as Baron von Richtofen, the German World War I flying ace.

At about this point, the film begins to fall apart. When he becomes a different fantasy, he no longer wants Dr. Crippen's fantasy playmates. His fantasy differs now from his wife's, and there can be no further communion. So he begins his own one-man charade, buys an old red Tiger Moth airplane, sets it up in the flower garden, dons a German pilot's uniform, cuts his hair Hitler style and parts it down the middle, and enters a world of Snoopy-like daydreams. When his wife tries to destroy the plane, he beats her up and sends her to the hospital, then embarks on a final mission that leaves him riddled with bullets from imaginary enemy planes. The last shot shows his corpse sitting in the cock pit with blood running from his mouth—the final von Richtofen stigmata. He has never left the flower garden.

Negatives might have been quite a good movie if its thirty-one-year-old director Peter Medak had not tried so desperately to make a point. I'm not sure what the point was, unless it had something to do with the fact that one sexual fantasy is quite enough, thank you very much. But the beautiful color photography and the brilliant actors and the way the film has been paced like a minuet makes for an interesting film that never comes to much of anything in the expensive final analysis. The fantasies keep getting in the way.

Peter McEnery is a droll and private kind of actor who seems to have the right idea of the tempo the movie intended but deserted along the way. Diane Cilento, as the photographer, is harnessed with a silly blonde wig that looks like it was purchased at auction in the Chelsea Flea Market, but she handles the role with delicate shadings. Glenda Jackson, as the wife who is visibly upset by all the carrying on, is the magnificent actress who played Charlotte Corday in the London, Broadway, and film versions of

Marat/Sade. *Negatives* gives her little more to do than gnash her teeth, but she has eyes dark as black olives and a mouth that makes sad, desperate little bites out of her words. She is one of the most exciting actresses the screen has discovered in a very long time and the opportunity to watch her work is reason enough to buy a ticket to *Negatives*. She plays crazies beautifully.

Eulogy for Forgotten Films

The New York Times
February 2, 1969

Movies are living things. They can live forever if they are treated with respect and cared for properly, but they can also die off faster than Indian extras if they are kicked about by jaded critics, deserted by the film companies that spawned them, and left to survive at the mercy of today's fickle, TV-brainwashed audiences. Standing by helplessly and watching a good movie die is like losing a friend to an incurable disease, yet through the years I've lost a few. *The Member of the Wedding, All Fall Down, The Goddess, Monsieur Verdoux, Mickey One, The Savage Eye, The Joker, All the Way Home, Red Beard, The Wanderer, Paths of Glory, Carnival in Flanders, Les Enfants Terribles, Remember the Night, Blood and Roses, The Misfits, Vampyr*—movie history is littered with the discarded corpses of great films few people ever saw. I will never understand why great movies go overlooked any more than I understand the critics who, in 1968, foamed at the mouth with glee over a socially irresponsible, cinematically useless, politically simple-minded, and artistically banal and amateurish waste of time like *Weekend*, or why audiences who have been warned against it by the worst set of notices in years are still flocking to trash like *Candy*. When the tallies are in, 1968 will be a year in which a rotten movie like *Wild in the Streets* made a lot of money, while outstanding films like *Will Penny, Isabel, Pretty Poison, Targets, Fist in His Pocket,* and *The Bofors Gun* are hardly remembered even by the film buffs who supported them. Talk to fifty different movie executives about why their quality products failed last year and you will never get the same answer twice. Yet it was a bad year for good movies.

I sat in a dark screening room last week with a lump in my throat and a general feeling of disbelief, while a projectionist ran one of the best pictures I've ever seen, *Will Penny*. Like nearly everybody else who missed *Will Penny* the first (and last) time around, I was turned off by one of the worst ad campaigns ever dumped on a movie. Without ever getting the message that it was an intelligent film, people took one look at the tacky, nebulous ads (Charlton Heston, showing more cleavage than Jane Fonda and holding a smoking sixgun), assumed an immediate attitude toward the picture ("Oh, here's Heston again, chucked his monkey suit and his Michelangelo smock and now he's a cowboy!"), and stayed away in droves. What they missed was one of the most luminous and penetrating films ever turned out by Hollywood, with a thoughtful and tightly written script by Tom Gries that shows with subtlety and detail that cowboys are anything but the embodiment of the songs Burl Ives sings.

Under Gries's direction, it is one of the few Westerns ever made that takes its time with a scene, constructing atmosphere and character development rather than inflated plot mechanics, without trying to brag on its budget or reel up stock footage simply to lengthen itself into a main feature. In cameraman Lucien Ballard, it found one of the few people who has ever been able to photograph the west in color the way it really looks, instead of a pale resemblance to a Santa Fe railroad poster or a glossy illustration in *Arizona Highways*, adding willful leisureness to the marshmallow clouds, peppermint skies, and adobe horizons of California's high Sierra country. *Will Penny* also shocked me with a sensitive, many-faceted performance by Charlton Heston that will probably be overlooked when Hollywood's subcellar mentality sets to work at Oscar time, but which, in my estimation, is the best work in an extremely difficult role I've seen by any actor this year. As a windswept cowpoke who faces respectability, love, and the first human emotion of his dried-up life, then turns his back on the responsibility of such an emotion because he just can't cut it, Heston was moved within each shot to seem as simple and spontaneous as the character he played. Contrasted with the introspective style of the very underrated-but-brilliant Joan Hackett, the details in Heston's powerful performance seemed manly and touching. Teaching a child how to shoot, learning his first Christmas carol, or awkwardly trying to explain to a lady what cow chips are, he became the hound-dog quintessence of the western hero, so natural and believable it became impossible to accept him as a fictional character. *Will Penny* makes *Shane* and *Hondo* and all of its other oaty predecessors seem phony by comparison, and it raises the genre of Hollywood moviemaking several niches in the direction of art.

Yet *Will Penny* didn't make a dime. Radio City Music Hall rejected it without comment (although later the same "showplace of the nation" didn't seem to mind showing a lurid, witless little teen-age sex film called *The Impossible Years*, which brought the biggest tornado of hate mail from angry parents in the theater's history) and poor *Will Penny* ended up on the neighborhood circuit. The only thing that can save a movie after it loses a first-run booking is critical praise, especially from *The New York Times*. There is no way to estimate the power wielded over films by a *Times* review. Most movie studios are so unsure of their own product they haven't the slightest idea whether a film is any good or not until the *Times* passes an official sentence. The Times review then determines, especially in the case of foreign films, whether the film will ever get a general distribution anywhere outside New York. The insanity of this kind of thinking is best proved by the fact that a New York booking represents only one-seventh of a film's gross in America and only one-fourteenth of a film's gross in the entire world. Yet if a film is to survive, how it opens and how it is reviewed in New York are of grave importance to the men behind the potted ferns in Hollywood. In the case of *Will Penny*, it was overlooked by critics who had already been influenced by its pathetic ad campaign (Renata Adler devoted more than half of her review to reviewing the theater in which she saw it). Consequently Paramount lost interest in bringing the film to the attention of the kind of audience that might have enjoyed it, and one of the best films of 1968 ended up in a vault.

More good movies have been killed by the *Times* than by bad actors, yet the wrong kind of theater can be just as deadly as a bad review. *Isabel* was another Paramount release that opened, this time to enthusiastic notices, but in a theater so far off the beaten track, in a residential neighborhood, that the art film audience never got there. Too bad, because it was a modern Gothic horror story that turned out to be a small classic, about a neurotic girl who returns home for her mother's funeral on the seldom-photographed Gaspé Peninsula and uncovers all the ghosts in the family closet. But more than that, it was a haunting examination of the contrasts between the old traditions that rule our life styles and the stirrings of new traditions that form our futures, with a wonderful feel for light, texture, and sound, beautiful white wintry photography, and a warm performance by Genevieve Bujold as the girl who is exorcised by the forces around her.

Isabel is a good example of a movie destroyed by its own studio. Paramount financed it for very little money, then refused to give it proper sales and advertising. It's an equally typical example of the absurdity of Hollywood logic. Studios would rather spend a million dollars promoting a five million dollar picture than spend one hundred thousand dollars on a small-budgeted film brought in for half a million. Consequently a dog like *Blue*, which no amount of publicity could save, and even three blockbusters like *The Odd Couple*, *Rosemary's Baby*, and *Barbarella*—which didn't need the ad campaigns—got all the money, while *Isabel*, *Will Penny*, and the independently purchased Peter Bogdanovich film *Targets* were treated with a go-to-hell attitude. When will they learn that it is folly to add to the budgets of big films that have already cost a fortune to make and that already have built-in publicity in terms of word-of-mouth, when the chances are healthier to make a wider profit margin by investing more money in less costly products that need the exposure in order to catch on? Fox learned its lesson with *Star!* I hope some of the other studios learn too, before they all lose their shirts and most of the good movies along with them.

Then there's the unfortunate movie for which absolutely *everything* goes wrong. This year it was *Pretty Poison*. Here was an offbeat, original, totally irreverent examination of violence in America, refreshing in its subtlety and intelligent in its delivery. It had energetic and lyrical performances by Tony Perkins (his best work in years) and Tuesday Weld (re-establishing her, by the way, as a major talent—although, like Charlton Heston, if you mention her name people look at you like you're crazy!). It had masterful, crisp writing by Lorenzo Semple, Jr., and more craftsmanship for less money in the technical departments than nine out of ten of the films currently running in New York's first-run houses. Yet it was a bomb from the beginning, and *everyone* was to blame: First, there was the provocative title, *She Let Him Continue*, which some studio dum-dum changed to *Pretty Poison*. Already it was in trouble.

Then, as far back as March 1968, the Fox people who believed in the picture as a rare and conscientious American film tried in vain to search for a New York booking. Most exhibitors are morons with very little taste who only understand one thing—the sound of money. Not one exhibitor would show something with the awful title, *Pretty Poison*. Then the sales department decided to detour New York's artsy-craftsy critics and open it in Los Angeles. Hah! The worst mistake of all; try to sell art in Los Angeles before it has been officially approved by New York and you might as well hang a black crepe funeral wreath on the door. The film flopped, as expected, so back in New York the publicity department began a campaign to save the picture. Media reaction was all negative: "Tony Perkins and Tuesday *Weld*? Ugh! You gotta be kidding!" Fox couldn't even get them booked on that old standby, the *Tonight Show*. One publicity girl sent out screening invitations and not one single reviewer bothered to respond or even show up. To make matters worse, the two stars didn't believe in the film and refused to help promote it, which must be some kind of "first" in the field of self-destruction right there.

Word got out that Fox was keeping the film in a drawer with Darryl Zanuck's old wool socks. Like kids who can't get into an X-rated movie, nothing arouses the curiosity of the so-called "intellectual" New York critics like a property Hollywood is trying to keep them from seeing. So finally, when *Pretty Poison* opened October 23 in the usual dreary round of neighborhood grindhouses to unenthusiastic notices from the daily papers, the magazines leaped to the rescue, lavishing it with praise. It was already too late. The Fox sales department, with rave reviews in hand, were still unable to interest a single class-A art house booking (which says something for the influence of arty critics, I suppose). The same houses that leaped at the chance to show mindless gibberish like *Joanna* and *The Magus* turned a deaf ear. Fox, in a final plunge of desperation, sent *Pretty Poison* down to a couple of quaint "art cinemas" in Greenwich Village. Big deal. You need an ESSO map to find it now. One of the best films of 1968 remains a pleasant memory to the few of us who were lucky enough to see it.

There were other forgotten films that towered above the commercial drivel that will unfortunately go down as 1968's most popular offal. Peter Bogdanovich's *Targets* was a raw, energetic blend of social comment and movie-buff nostalgia that paralleled the headline-making activities of an all-American boy-turned-sniper with the retirement plans of an aging horror-film star. In spots it was crude and cornily *cahier*, and in general there was much too much footage from godawful Roger Corman movies to be of much interest to the general public, but Bogdanovich got a fantastic performance out of Boris Karloff, and *Targets* will still go down in my book as one of the most exciting movie ideas of the year.

Fist in His Pocket, a masterpiece that I first saw in Venice in 1965, was a first film by Marco Bellocchio, about a family of epileptics. It drew a fascinating portrait of Italy's dying bourgeoisie. It also featured some of the most unusual camerawork of the year to show madness and torment from *inside* the mind, and it provided the screen with one of the most brilliant acting debuts by a young inexperienced actor (Lou Castel) I have ever seen. It was the best-kept secret of the year.

Last, but not least, I admired a grim, unfriendly item from England called *The Bofors Gun*. There was nobody in it named Bofors and it was not about a gun. Instead, it was a small, tightly structured, and very aggressive film about class structure in which a group of mutinous, psychotic artillery guards test their sensitive, frail commanding officer in a series of blistering, drunken army violations until they eventually destroy themselves and their decent but frightened superior as well. Instead of superstars, it had real actors like Nicol Williamson and Ian Holm, but on every level it seemed doomed commercially.

The only reason I can think of for labeling a film with the poisonous title, *The Bofors Gun*, is professional suicide, something film companies have been committing with startling frequency for years. At the screening I attended, a particularly outspoken lady critic launched into a tirade on the subject. "Well," said a press agent representing the film, as though no other alternative seemed possible, "would you rather we called it by its original title—'Events While Guarding the Bofors Gun'?"

You can't argue with logic like that, any more than you can go out and force people to see good movies massacred by stupid ad campaigns, *recherché* critics, or exhibitors and distributors who play silly games for profit, buying and selling movies like they were green peppers. All you can do is remember where the bodies are buried, and send flowers on alternate Thursdays.

The Cannes Film Festival

1970

"Venice," the film buffs used to say, "is where you go to get educated. Cannes is where you go to get laid."

The first thing you see is the Mediterranean, curling lazily and blue as a cornflower, licking the yachts that dot the harbor like happy sugar cubes on their way to Monte Carlo. The next thing you see is this lethal traffic jam on its way to the Carlton Hotel, which time and Hollywood public relations have declared the official headquarters of wheeling and dealing each spring at the Cannes Film Festival. The Carlton is an enormous white monstrosity that looks like the Brighton Pavilion and the Luna Park penny arcade all rolled into one and this is where the action is. Here Harry Saltzman can buy a real martini and for 10 francs the concierge will give you Grace Kelly's private unlisted phone number. Up and down the Croisette, which is the oceanfront street along the Riviera that is similar to the boardwalk in Atlantic City, the flags of all the nations entered in competition at Cannes fly boldly. The only two flags missing this year are Russia and Japan. There are no Russian or Japanese entries because Robert Favre LeBret, the founding head of the Cannes bash who has been choosing and rejecting movies here for twenty-three years, decided he was tired of Slavic spectacles and Japanese samurai flicks. The Japanese were highly insulted by this gaffe. The Russians, who had sent the expensive *Tchaikovsky*, were even angrier. The Festival selection committee (which is only a formality, since everybody knows Favre LeBret makes all the final selections himself) took too long to make a decision on *Tchaikovsky*, so the Russians took it back. They also took back a member of the jury, Sergei Obrazov, head of the famous Moscow puppet theater. That left Cannes with only eight jurors instead of the usual nine. Too bad, because in addition to throwing the voting off, it also means there will be no Russian parties this year. "The Reds give the best parties," says a Festival spokesman. "Plenty of caviar." The president of the jury is Miguel Angel Asturias, ambassador of Guatemala in France and a 1967 Nobel Prize winner; the other judges are Kirk Douglas, Karel Reisz, French lady producer (don't ask me what she produced) Christine Renal, playwright Félicien Marceau, Czech director Vojtech Jasny, an Italian critic named Guglielmo Biraghi, and somebody from Germany named Volker Schloendorff. Impressed?

There are 10,000 people in Cannes, representing the most incredible combination of artifices known to man—from two-toned dentures to hookers walking poodles through the Carlton bar. One thousand visitors to Cannes 1970 claim to be members of the press, and half of these are highly suspicious. Each member of the press pays ten francs (about $2.00) for the key to a post office box into which tons of flotsam are pumped each day—screening notices, synopses of Algerian films written in Italian, instructions on how to get into pornographic movies shown at midnight, discounts at local barber shops. Invitations to the more than 2,000 cocktail parties that will be held are also promised, but one thing Cannes needs is some kind of organization, because nobody knows who anybody is, especially the Americans, and the result is that even top critics seldom get invited to anything. In a way, I can hardly blame the French for this oversight. Walking along the rows of boxes, I noticed "press" representatives from such well-known American publications as *Movie Show, Cinema Talk,* and *Screen Digest.* I don't know how the freeloaders, hippies wandering through the Riviera, and tourists on vacation get away with it, but the Festival lets them all in free. I guess it's just as difficult every year in San Francisco to check out the man from the *Lourdes Gazette.*

Cannes used to be a carnival of pulchritudinal splendors. Starlets jumped naked into the sea and the flashbulbs never stopped popping. It was the playpen of the international jet set and the Cinema-à-Go-Go of the cigar-smoking Jewish czars from the hills of Beverly. It still is, in a way, but now the excitement is all on the screen. In the old days, before the New Left took over, Cannes was the place where Gisèle Pascal, the former mistress of Prince Rainier, took out her revenge on him for refusing to marry her after finding out she was sterile, by having an illicit affair with Gary Cooper, photographed in living color by the paparazzi. A young actress named Grace Kelly, in Cannes to plug *To Catch a Thief*, was trying to get into the pages of *Paris-Match*. The idea was to get her picture taken with Rainier. They met in the Carlton bar and the rest, as they say, is history. And people still talk about the *scandale* the year Simone Sylva, an Egyptian starlet with phenomenal mammaries, took off her bathing suit while being nibbled by Robert Mitchum. She later committed suicide. Things don't always work out at Cannes.

All this is for the memory books. Two years ago there was a revolution against such headline-grabbing frivolity. François Truffaut, Jean-Luc Godard, and a dozen revolutionaries from the *nouvelle vague* school of French directors launched a riot that closed down the festival. Revolution spread like the measles and one night Geraldine Chaplin even stood onstage at the Cinema Palais, where the films are shown, and held the curtains closed with her bare hands to keep the Festival from seeing her own film. (Cannes may have its no-nos, but hypocrisy has never been one of them.) All the gasoline in Cannes was stolen and there were no cars, buses, trucks, planes, or mule carts out of or into the city. People were even jumping into the Mediterranean and swimming out to Sam Spiegel's yacht to get out of Cannes—figuring, I suppose, an uninvited boat ride was better than an invited trip on a rail. It paid off. What used to be a circus staged by Barnum, is now just one main tent and a series of compromising sideshows staged by a disorganized Bailey. In addition to the official films in competition, there is now another section called the "*Quinzaine des réalisateurs*" in which the Young Turks or Maoists or New Left—call them what you like—can show movies that reflect the new styles and attitudes in movie-making. Then there is a "critics section" in which critics nobody ever heard of select films not commercial enough to be accepted by the Festival but interesting enough to be seen anyway. Add to all this, short subjects, sex movies, underground movies, and the hundreds of films being shown in the cinema marketplaces around the *palais* in the hopes that distributors will buy them for worldwide release, and there is an estimated 500,000 miles of celluloid to be traveled by eye—more than 400 movies to be seen in 14 days. There's talk of following the Festival with an optometrists' convention.

The first thing you do in Cannes is hide your American cigarettes. The second thing you do is find Margaret Gardner. Head of Rogers, Cowan and Brenner in Europe, she is more famous and beloved here than any of the stars she handles and she is the only woman in Cannes with enough power to get you a decent hotel room, an American typewriter, an invitation to the major events, or a doctor in the middle of the night. This year she was the only person in Cannes who could get an extra ticket to *Woodstock*, and at $50 a ticket on the black market, that took power that had nothing to do with flowers. The third thing you do is put on your glasses, take an Excedrin, and head for the movies.

I arrived too late for the opening night film, for which I am told I have reasons to be grateful. It was a French film by Marc Allegret called *The Ball of Count D'Orgel* and, according to the early arrivals, it contained dialogue by Françoise Sagan, gowns by Balmain, handsome color photography of Maxim's by Christian Matras, and very little substance. (Opening nights in Cannes are generally considered a waste of time; too few people have arrived that early so the Festival usually reserves a film out of competition that is spectacular but superfluous. Last year they showed *Gone with the Wind,* after which MGM threw a dinner party on the beach where, between mouthfuls of salade niçoise, the guests could look out to sea and watch a $50,000 re-enactment of the burning of Tara.)

Sunday, May 3. The morning after the opening. The press is in full swing. The English journalists are briskly preparing for the day's entry from Great Britain, *Leo the Last.* Peppery, freckled-faced Alexander Walker, from the *Evening Standard*, is in deep consultation with hatchet-faced Penelope Mortimer, author of *The Pumpkin Eater* and film critic for the posh *Observer*, who occasionally comes out with brilliant observations about movies, such as "Alfred Hitchcock is relatively new to the cinema, having made his first film in 1948." The people to avoid are the cheery Israeli TV reporters who are always picking the other journalists' brains about what to ask in the press conferences. Jean-Claude Brialy, star of the opening night film, is brooding in the Carlton bar over the reception of hisses he got the night before. At 11:00 everyone heads off to the *palais,* or Festival Hall, for an Italian entry, *Investigation of a Private Citizen*, about a chief of police who murders his mistress in a certainty that he will never be suspected because police officers are above suspicion. It shows grimly that Italy is politically corrupt and it has an outstanding performance by Gian Maria Volonte, but I found it pretty tedious stuff. Said one American journalist: "The Italians ratted on the Germans in the First War and ratted on the allies in the Second; now they've made a movie ratting on themselves."

Everything at Cannes is attached to snob appeal. The most popular luncheon spots are the beach bars; this year "Maschou" is the "in" beach with the French film stars, while the Americans stick to the Carlton. The English have their own beach, where the British Film Producers Association has set up a good-will center to introduce critics and directors to each other with hopes for optimistic results. Here Karel Reisz, Richard Lester, and John Boorman smile gallantly and drink Guinness, creating an ambiance much more pleasant than that created by Boorman's film, *Leo the Last,* about as mannered and pretentious a load of twaddle as I've ever seen on the screen. Marcello Mastroianni is, if you can believe it, an exiled member of British royalty, who returns to London and sets up a rehabilitation center for blacks in Notting Hill Gate. It is very patronizing to the blacks and is filmed in a chic charcoal color that soon gave me a swimming stomach-ache. The French gave it a big ovation. They love vulgarity mixed with zoom lenses. This film was followed by a press conference during which a black minister sang protest songs and two stars of the picture, Billie Whitelaw and Glynna Foster-Jones, admitted they didn't have a clue what it was about either while they were making it or after. Like Katzenjammer Kids, some actors really should be seen and not heard.

Monday, May 4. The official Egyptian film, *The Earth,* has been received acidly. Many walkouts and boos. "Cannes is changing," says the critic for *France-Soir* sadly. "In spite of the revolution, the press still wants the faded glamour. It used to be a wonderful showcase for films from little countries that otherwise never got a chance. Now the press wants Jane Fonda and Bardot. It has become very commercial."

When the big screens in the *palais* are silent, there are movies everywhere that go until 2 A.M. These are usually pornographic films, but they include documentaries, independent low-budget American flicks, and Andy Warholish amateur experiments. Last year the big hit in this off-Broadway market was *The Secret Sex Lives of Romeo and Juliet.* This year it's *The Notorious Cleopatra.* I found it at four in the afternoon on a little side street near the Carlton in a cinema that was showing *Winning.* More press showed up here than for the official Egyptian film that morning. It turned out to be a slap in the face of the Arabs, a Hollywood smoker full of naked Egyptian slave girls with appendicitis scars and horny Roman warriors with vaccination marks and pot bellies who delivered lines like "Egypt is ripe with pleasure, but Rome awaits my coming!" I recognized the advertised "cast of celebrated Hollywood professionals" as extras from the orgy scene in *Myra Breckinridge.*

7:45. The big black tie and limousine lineup begins at the *palais* for the world premiere of *The Strawberry Statement.* This is the Festival's first American film and MGM seems to have sent representatives from every country where it maintains even a typewriter. Already it has aroused a storm of controversy from the agitated press and a fashionable riot has been promised. "They think it's a fascist film," says Herb Solow. "With the whole campus at Santa Barbara in chaos since the kids burned down the Bank of America and thousands of kids rioting everywhere, they think it isn't true. That's great. Let them riot in the streets. It's when they *don't* talk that we have to worry."

I don't know what all the fuss was about, since *Strawberry* turned out to be a naïve little comment on student unrest complete with a horrid theme song by the boring Buffy Sainte-Marie, a group of college revolutionaries so immature they think a Communist cell is when everybody drinks out of the same orange juice bottle, some political double talk delivered like an Elaine May comedy routine, and an anarchist hero who takes over the dean's office and can't even fix the Xerox machine. "So how does it feel?" asks the creep-hero's girl when they get carried away in a police wagon. "Nice—not terrific, not fantastic, but nice." It's all a cheery, amiable game, like "Red Rover Come Over," but except for a nicely staged bit of brutality in front of the American flag, there is not a moment of persuasion in it that might convince an unsympathetic audience that there is any honor in the student movement. Real revolution and real reformation is a full-time job. Cleaning up America is a full-time job. None of these employments have room for part-time dilettantes who take time out to listen to bad rock songs or zoftic lame-brains who strip behind the mimeograph machine and announce: "Did you know Lenin liked big breasts?" Twenty-eight-year-old director Stuart Hagmann is going to be a major talent and his two young actors, Bruce Davison and Kim Darby, are first-rate performers, although I must admit I found Miss Darby saying "I'm into Women's Liberation" about as believable as Margaret O'Brien in *Little Women* saying "No, Marmee, I don't have a cold" just before she kicked the bucket. MGM insists it did not make *Strawberry Statement* to hop on the box-office bandwagon, and to prove it they threw a big party after the film at the Playboy Club.

Tuesday, May 5. Spain comes to the rescue with the new Luis Buñuel film, *Tristana*, the best thing shown so far. Alas, it is out of competition. The big directors do not like to compete for prizes and one can hardly blame them, considering what they're up against. *Tristana* is a beautifully made, sour romance between a barren young amputee (Catherine Deneuve) and the lonely old man (Fernando Rey) who takes care of her. It is Buñuel at the top of his form—magically directed, impeccably photographed, tightly written—and nothing else has come close to it in the direction of art at this Festival.

Today the action is in the cafés. There is even a snob atmosphere here. The Festival café (to the right of the *palais*) is snubbed by the aristocrats and ends up patronized by the Germans and the bourgeoisie. The intelligentsia heads for the Blue Bar, where Susan Sontag and Richard Roud are engaged in God knows whatever kind of pseudo-intellectual bull it is that makes it possible for them to program the New York Film Festival at Lincoln Center. I tried to eavesdrop, but they were on some wave length that couldn't be picked up on a Geiger counter. The *Cahiers du Cinéma* man is conducting a psychological discussion of the Camus film while Vassilis Vassilikos (author of *Z*) is noisily waving away the gypsies who flock to Cannes each year to beg, steal, and fleece the tourists. Pale, wild-eyed, and looking like miniature Maria Ouspenskayas, the gypsy children promenade the Croisette asking for centimes. If you motion them on, they steal your sugar cubes and scream mind-spattering gypsy threats and curses at you. Greta Garbo would hate Cannes. When you are not being bothered by gypsies, you are being besieged by roving photographers with baby tigers and lion cubs. The French government is threatening legislation to curb this cruelty, but so far nothing has been done and probably won't be, since this sidewalk amusement is good for Riviera business. The cubs are drugged, stuffed with candy, and handed about so much that they must be killed at the end of each tourist season because no zoo will take them if they are too domesticized to protect themselves from the other animals.

On the Croisette, William Wyler is talking to Betsy Blair, whose husband, Karel Reisz, is on the jury. Maurice Ronet is being photographed by the paparazzi. The Cubans are having a press conference. The wife of some cigar-smoking Hollywood producer has discovered a baby lion and is having her picture taken. "I thought it was an MGM lion used as a publicity stunt," says the haughty producer, who wasn't invited to the *Strawberry Statement* party the night before. "I thought it was Leo the Last," chuckles Philippe de Broca.

Bosley Crowther looks not-so-lean but very Cassius-hungry on top of the boardwalk. Crowther is here scouting for films to buy for Columbia. He gazes nostalgically at the press badges of the passersby. Remembering poorer but better days, perhaps. At the Maschou Beach grill, the *Strawberry Statement* group is hotly discussing the morning reviews. The film has been massacred by the English and American press, praised by the French (for obvious reasons). An MGM representative snubs Tom Curtiss, the American critic for the Paris-based *Herald Tribune* who has just called it "a Busby Berkeley version of a campus revolution, only more Busby than Berkeley."

Having, in the past twelve hours, survived a Japanese sex film, a Russian documentary about Leningrad in October, a Roman Polanski movie about an old alcoholic and a five-year-old child on a beach, a Yugoslavian film about the underworld of a socialist state, three Middle Eastern films of the boy-meets-tractor formula, a Pasolini film called *Ostia*, about religious anarchy, a dramatization by conductor Herbert van Karajan of the La Scala Opera production of *Pagliacci*, a suspenseless French detective drama, *The Last Jump*, about a paratrooper who murders his unfaithful Oriental wife, and three short subjects about the Black Panthers, the press is exhausted. "There are four hundred films—you can't see even half of them," moans Gene Moscowitz of *Variety*, who likes them all. "I have had a headache for three days," says Irwin Shaw. Shaw is covering Cannes for *Harper's*. He's the last one out of the bars at night and the only man at Cannes who wakes up every morning and asks, "What's playing today?" I like him for that.

It's becoming clear just who comes to Cannes. First there are the *vedettes* (French for movie stars). (Sounds like a cross between a bidet and a Rockette and there are painfully few this year.) Then there is the "sales force" that comes to sell the *vedettes*, followed by the revolutionaries who come to complain, the serious film buffs who come to criticize, the buyers and sellers who come to make deals, the bikini-clad starlets who come to do a bit of tax-free business of their own, and the big industrial magnates who come to look at them all. In two days I have met *the* Mr. Heineken, whose tummy looks as though he's been drinking up his own profits; the Vaseline king; and the refrigerator king of Italy, who drops $1,000,000 a season at the crap tables in Monte Carlo. These men are treated with more honor and respect at Cannes than Bergman, Buñuel, and Godard combined. And finally, there are the socialites, who come to be seen and go to all the parties.

1970 will be known as the year of inflation at Cannes. Bar bills are down ten percent and there aren't as many parties. Last year the most lavish party was thrown by Commonwealth United: people were flown in by private jet, lavished with champagne, caviar, and lobsters, treated to entertainment and a fireworks display, and then all the ladies were given 100 francs to drop in the casinos, which is probably one reason why Commonwealth is now under new management and its stock down to 78¢ a share.

This year the talk along the beach is all about the Freddie Fields party. Fields is flying in by private helicopter to throw a bash in an ancient villa in the mountains. Not all of the faces upturned toward the sun are waiting for a tan—some are watching for him to land on the Carlton roof. The party promises to be so lavish that seventeen cops have been hired to keep gate-crashers out.

"He is married to Candy Bergen?" asks a lady from *France-Soir.*
"No. *Polly* Bergen."
"Qui est Freddie Fields?"
"He was married to Judy Garland."
"Ah, c'est ça."

Wednesday, May 6. The international contingent is beginning to arrive. Claude Jade, Pierre Brasseur, Eddie Constantine, Sweden's Bibi Andersson, Kim Darby. Bruce Davison has also arrived after MGM flew him to Philadelphia to pick up his birth certificate so he could get a passport. (Maybe *Strawberry* wasn't as knuckle-headed as it seems; the morning papers also carry headlines about the Kent University students and MGM is beaming commercially on the beach.) Stuart Hagmann dips into his strawberries and confides: "When Jim Aubrey saw my film he called in to say three things. His first question was 'Is there ever a scene where we get to see the boy balling the girl?' His second question was 'Well, is there any way we can get some more sex scenes into the picture?' After I answered no to both, his third remark was, 'No further questions.'" (Applause from surrounding tables.) Eddie Luntz, a French director who made a film in Brazil for Fox that has never been released, chimes in: "Darryl Zanuck made me take sixty people instead of twenty, by the time I hired all the friends of his friends, he made me shoot in Brazil because Fox had money tied up there that couldn't be taken out of the country. By the time I made all the compromises and finished the picture, Zanuck came with his girl friend and she didn't like the leading lady (grownup Patricia Gozzi, of *Sundays and Cybèle*) so he walked out without saying goodbye. So the next thing I know two days later I receive a letter saying he will cut the film himself. I sued and now the court awards me a victory that sets a precedent in France—no producer can ever have the final cut of any film in France. Unfortunately they can still do whatever they like in America, but I will never again work for an American company. Zanuck is senile and knows absolutely nothing about modern cinema, but he still is surrounded by a lot of yes men who are afraid to say anything to him. Hollywood is committing mass suicide—they deserve everything they get." (More applause from the surrounding tables.)

The first film of the day is Ingmar Bergman's *The Passion of Anna* and it is a masterpiece. It is also not in competition. Four variously neurotic people work out their problems of commitment to humanity on an isolated island where a maniac is at work hanging dogs, burning horses, and slaughtering sheep. Each actor has a chance to step out of the film and be interviewed, which gives the audience a chance to look in on the characters' souls, hear their difficulties and the problems of the actors in playing them, and discover the performers' own projected hopes for how the film will be resolved. It is perhaps Bergman's most introspective work and his second film in color. The camerawork is magnificent—giving the film actual emotional textures against which its action is played, feelings through light and color that change with the film's moods. I found it totally absorbing; the other critics were rocketed into transports of delight. It's beginning to look like a Festival.

This was followed by a Hungarian film, *The Falcons*, about these birds, see, who are trained to kill herons, and therefore an allegory about the suppression of anarchy in the animal kingdom. During the two hours it takes to get these medieval falcons into the air, there is one bit of action when the game warden has a few salty words with some peasants who have been marking up his "Keep Out" sign, but the rest of the movie is strictly for the birds. They must really be backward in Hungary. They never heard of scarecrows.

Thursday, May 7. Everybody is talking about an underground film, *Celebration*, an hour-long documentary about the Chicago 7 and their radical activities during Nixon's inauguration, including the group's "counter-inaugural ball" held in a circus tent the size of a football field.

11 A.M. From Brazil, *Palace of Angels*—a cynical, hypnotic film that dynamites the old theory that Brazil only makes folk legends and movies about peasants harvesting sugar cane. A sophisticated, cosmopolitan study of three nice girls in a São Paulo office who decide the only way to survive on a grand scale and defeat boredom is to go into the prostitution business, the film traces their rise (using computers and other modern business methods) and eventual descent into perversion and decadence. I thought it was rather like *Golddiggers* rewritten by Jean Genet, but the French obviously didn't find it pretentious enough, because they gave the Brazilians a very hot time in the press conference that followed. They yelled "*Scandale!*" and asked the actresses how their mothers felt about their roles, the kind of question that went out of style with Louella Parsons. "I could go to Baia and make lush travelogues that exploit island folklore that the European critics would like more," said Walter Hugo Khouri, the director, "but I want to make films that are about the times we live in. People in Brazil don't still dance the carioca and eat bananas." Amen, and I hope *Palace of Angels* finds an American distributor to spread the news about what an interesting new outlet for films Brazil is becoming.

The only thing all these press conferences proves is that the audiences at Cannes don't understand the movies. At the Israeli press conference after

The Dreamer, the French parrots kept trying to insist it was a war picture about Israeli aggression against the Arabs. It was simply a slow, languorous study of a simple-minded oaf who works in an old folks' home. Maddening.

No festival would be complete without its dose of Godard, so even though his newest effort, *Wind from the East,* was violently rejected as trash by the Festival committee, it got an "off-Broadway" screening at a local cinema. Three hundred students and a few brave critics marched into a dark, foul-smelling hole that seated 150, and what we all got for our curiosity was two hours of monomaniacal slobber in which a grating, screeching voice read a do-it-yourself lesson in how to stage our own Marxist revolution while a group of talentless amateurs dressed up in old Halloween costumes and shouted obscenities from the screen, most of which was totally black a good deal of the time. I can't imagine the most radical Godard fans, who liked his work even when he still knew how to make movies, standing for such gibberish. However, there was scattered applause among the boos and screams of "Merde!" at the end, indicating how, at Cannes, there are still some film buffs willing to suffer the gravest indignities as long as the projector keeps turning.

Friday, May 8. Had coffee with Vincent Canby, who just arrived after a stopover in Paris and is still suffering jet lag. He is complaining that he is falling asleep in some of the films from fatigue, something he never does in New York. He's not alone. During one particularly endless Argentine film, I sat a few seats away from Kirk Douglas, who seemed to be nodding off himself. Of all the judges I've talked to, Kirk seems to be taking his job the most seriously. Even the jury has a right to doze under this kind of strain. I've been snoozing a bit myself.

Canby is trying to see everything he can to meet his deadline. "I've got to see ten movies by tomorrow night." Last year he waited until the festival was over to telegraph his copy, the official cable office was closed, and it cost him $125. An extra burden is the translation. All films are shown in their original languages with French subtitles. Earphones are provided for dumb Americans like me, but nobody has provided a translator for the translator, an English lady who has become known to the English-speaking press at Tokyo Rose West. She thinks she is an actress and performs along with the actors, making it impossible to decipher what she is saying. Sometimes she goes out for a sandwich and leaves the earphones totally blank. Try that in the middle of a philosophical Czechoslovakian movie full of Socialist dream sequences and see where it gets you.

Between *Harry Munter,* a Swedish movie about a boy inventor who turns down an offer to work for an industrial firm in America in order to stay home in Sweden and protect a weird street girl from the clutches of an evil pimp, and *Don Segundo Sombra*, an Argentine spectacle about stoicism among the gauchos, speculation begins about the awards. "The Italian will win for *Investigation of a Private Citizen*," insists a French press agent. "He's a Communist—they always give prizes to Communists." To which Tom Curtiss replies: "That reminds me of a story about Emil Jannings. He was very popular when Hitler came to power in Germany, so he stayed on. After the war, he tried to deny having been part of the Nazi regime. A producer handed him a photo and said, 'But Mr. Jannings, what about this photo of you and the Fuehrer with his arm around you after pinning a medal on you?' 'Oh *that*!' he said. 'That happened during a lunch break.' "

Innocents Abroad Department: Vassilis Vassilikos, the author of *Z*, tells me he was paid only $750 for the book by a shrewd American publisher. For the movie rights he was paid only $10,000 and no percentage. For his new book, he was paid only $3,000 for the hardback rights. All this to a poor Greek refugee whose work is expected to gross an estimated $50-million. "Do you think I did wrong?" he asks meekly, bumming a True cigarette. I promise to introduce him to Irving Lazar.

10:30 P.M. The limousines climb through picturesque villages to Freddie Fields' castle surrounded by a moat. It looks like a movie set from something by Zeffirelli. There are telephones in all the bathrooms and long distance calls are coming in on all of them for Freddie Fields. A jazz band from Marseilles plays *Blue Moon* while 120 guests drink champagne and nibble *pâté de foie gras*.

"Freddie, how many multimillion-dollar deals have you set tonight?"

"Samantha Eggar, have you met Irwin Shaw?"

"How did they get all those uniformed police out there in the middle of the night?"

"It's called *l'argent*, baby; it's the same the world over."

"Long distance call from Joanna Shimkus from the Beverly Hills Hotel!"

"Agnes Varda, this is—what's your name again?"

"Jacques Demy."

"Miss Varda, Monsieur Demy."

"He's my husband."

"I saw this wonderful Danish film today about a man who marries his father's mistress only to learn she's also his mother's boyfriend. Now if we re-work the script and get Raquel Welch to play both parts . . ."

"Is that Romy Schneider over in the corner eating strawberries? Romy, darling, it *is* you . . ."

"Did you see Betsy Blair? She looks like she's wearing the living room curtains from some old stucco bungalow in Santa Monica. And under *that* she's got on sandals with *socks*!"

"Betsy was never a snappy dresser."

"Well, she got two million dollars of Gene Kelly's money; what did she spend it on?"

"Obviously new living room curtains . . ."

"What did you think of the Buñuel film?"

"I wanted Deneuve to go off with Franco Nero . . ."

"Don't be silly. Franco Nero would never go with her after she had her leg amputated . . ."

"I don't come to go to movies. I play the crap tables with Mike Frankovitch."

"What did you think of the Bergman film?"

"Won't make a dime. Too goddam intellectual."

"I saw the Jorn Donner film everyone's talking about. He plays a pornographic filmmaker who walks into one scene with an honest-to-God *erection*! I consider that something of a breakthrough."

"Don't tell Tony Newley about that."

"There's Kirk Douglas. I want to ask him what he thought of *Strawberry Statement*."

"The jury isn't allowed to discuss the films until the voting is over, honey."

"Oh, Kirk'll tell *me* . . ."

"Pia Degermark can't get a room in Cannes."

"That's all settled. David Hemmings may not come, so they're giving her *his* room."

"What if he shows up later?"

"I guess they'll have to share it."

"I'm calling Miss Rona. It's 6:30 in Hollywood. We can get it on tonight's show."

"Freddie, is the drawbridge down? I'm too tired to swim any goddam French moat tonight!"

"What this place needs is Sue Mengers . . ."

Over the weekend, people begin trying to escape. Everybody who is anybody heads for La Voile D'Or, the most fabulous hotel on the Côte d'Azur, near Somerset Maugham's villa, where swell types like Melina Mercouri, Federico Fellini, and Lord Snowden are holed up. The big sport driving along the coast is to look for Monaco license plates. If you see one ending in 77, it belongs to Prince Rainier. He has twelve cars and they all end in 77. I went to the Grand Prix in Monte Carlo, so I missed the note of sadness when, on Saturday afternoon, the Festival unveiled Sharon Tate's last film, *12 plus 1*, but I returned in time to catch *Sweet Hunters*, a monument to waste and confusion in which Sterling Hayden, Susan Strasberg, and Maureen McNally stagnate on a deserted island full of fog and mud while awaiting the approach of an escaped prisoner, played by Stuart Whitman with the kind of puzzled hysteria usually reserved for people who wake up in foreign hotels with their travelers checks missing. There is a lot of heavy breathing, a symbolic shot of two crabs locked in mortal combat, a sermonette on octopuses, a speech about a mulberry bush, dialogue like "My beloved and sweet-breasted wife, don't forget to take in the washing, it might frighten the sea gulls," and a closeup of Hayden looking like an insane Abe Lincoln fingering the blood and intestines of a newly slaughtered goose, while the sound track plays Gregorian chants. You can't even call it pretentious, because to call a movie pretentious you must first know what it's pretending to be. All you can do about *Sweet Hunters* is pray for the professional futures of everyone involved.

Woodstock caused a mild sensation when director Michael Wadleigh announced from the stage that it was dedicated to the four American students "murdered by the American troops" and to all the many deaths to come in the name of world peace. He then asked everyone in Cannes who supported "peace against the oppressors in Washington" to join the more than one thousand hippies who had invaded Cannes that afternoon (many of whom turned out to be hired by Warner Brothers as a publicity stunt) by wearing black arm bands. The packed Festival Hall reacted with a tidal wave of boos, hisses, and flying programs and Wadleigh had to be taken to safe cover by guards. I still don't know what to make of this little demonstration, but I do know that after an hour, you could sit anywhere you pleased. There were that many people walking out of *Woodstock*. Maybe the silent majority doesn't all live in America. The best comment of the evening: "I am in full agreement with these kids, but why doesn't somebody stage a Woodstock with Ella Fitzgerald, Frank Sinatra, and Tony Bennett? Then I'd pitch a tent right alongside them."

On Sunday, Marcello Mastroianni appeared in a second Festival entry, making a shoo-in favorite for Best Actor. It was a silly Italian farce called *Drama of Jealousy* (in America it will probably be titled *The Pizza Triangle*) about a *ménage à trois* between a smelly street worker, a flower girl (played wittily by Monica Vitti), and a pizza cook. This was followed by a beautiful French film, *Les Choses de la Vie,* about the images and events of a man's life flashing through his mind in the black moments hovering between life and death following a fatal automobile accident. It has crisp, detailed direction, lush camerawork, and heartbreaking performances by Michel Piccoli, as the man, and Romy Schneider, as his mistress. It received a standing ovation.

If you can survive the first week at Cannes, they tell me the second week is easy. By Monday, May 11, events were being scheduled at the rate of forty-three a day. It becomes a blur in the mind now—an interminable projection of allegories and political sermons about socialism and revolution that numbs the senses and deadens the brain. The monotony was temporarily relieved when Otto Preminger greeted the press with his usual sulphuric demeanor. He was in rare form, insulting his interpreter by saying, "Your French is worse than mine, so I might as well answer the questions myself," and putting down the journalists on general principles. One could almost admire him for that, considering how fatuous and labored the press conferences were throughout the Festival. On the other hand, one could also hardly blame the critics for their reciprocal hostility at the press conference considering the film that had just preceded it. *Tell Me That You Love Me, Junie Moon* is one of the most demented movies ever made. The fact that it concerns a *ménage à trois* between an epileptic, a crippled homosexual with a distinct yen for black bellhops, and a girl whose face has been burned off with acid by a sex maniac is disagreeable enough. The idea is strange and certainly offbeat, all right, but instead of making it believable or acceptable or in any way palatable in the sensitive direction of, say, a Carson McCullers tale of survival among the misfits, Preminger (with the aid of a deadly script by Marjorie Kellogg) has chosen to accent all the bizarre aspects of her novel and none of the poetic ones. The result is that *Junie Moon* is just plain repulsive. There are so many technical flaws in it, so many sleazy disregards for coherence, so many holes in the script and so many tired clichés that I haven't the space to list them all. I might add, however, that I've seldom seen more incompetent lighting and cinematography, and although Liza Minnelli, Ken Howard, Robert Moore, and Kay Thompson struggle bravely to make flesh-and-blood characters out of one-dimensional creatures, even good actors need a director, and if there was any direction on *Junie Moon* they must have been phoning it in from the next town.

Monday night was the French gala, La Nuit Française. Generally considered the event of the year, the American press is usually uninvited. Out of 10,000 people only a favored 400 are asked to attend and even Margaret Gardner can't get an extra table. I should have stayed in bed. Photographers flash away while you try to eat; for food, there was cold chicken soup, American chicken and dressing and raspberry sherbet; for entertainment there was French cabaret performer Annie Cordy doing a takeoff on Al Jolson, some American rock group singing "The Flight of the Bumble Bee" and Sacha Distel doing an imitation of a French music hall star who got carried off in a strait-jacket, followed by a fireworks display and complimentary gifts of salt and pepper shakers. Quel clinker.

But through it all, the movies and the aspirin never stop. There was an Italian film about labor troubles a century ago in Florence; a wonderful British film called *Kes*, about a slum lad and his pet falcon; a new Polish film by the great Andrzej Wadja about the liberation of a Nazi concentration camp after the war; a lovely English film by Robert Ellis Miller, *The Buttercup Chain*, in which four young people are unable to commit themselves to reality until they are brought to their senses by the death of a child; a retrospective of the films of Josef von Sternberg; the loudly booed American *Putney Swope;* a lushly mounted first directorial effort by Maximilian Schell that turns Turgenev's *First Love* into an enriching cinematic experience; *Hoa Binh*, a moving study by Raoul Coutard of the lives of two Vietnamese children in Saigon; and when you were satiated with movies you could watch Roger Moore, Anne Heywood, Genevieve Page, Curt Jurgens, Helmut Berger, Mel Ferrer, Pia Degermark, Charles Aznavour, or Monica Vitti on the beach.

Candy Bergen arrived, announced, "It's the Trenton of the Riviera," and promptly began taking pictures of all the photographers taking pictures of *her*. The M*A*S*H people arrived and got thrown out of the screening of their own picture. The paparazzi went wild over Sally Kellerman, who nibbled marzipan lobsters, smiled like Carole Lombard and walked like an anchovy. "Bonjour, Sally!" yelled the French and Hot Lips Houlihan yelled "Mercy bouquet!" and gave the peace sign in high-heeled sandals, a Lois Lane purse, and an Aztec Indian headband, stealing the thunder from Viva, who competed for attention in high-heel black patent leather shoes, white ankle socks, a fake purple Pucci print, and a thin feather boa. Hasn't anybody here ever heard of *Women's Wear Daily*?

On the last day, you had your choice between *The Sex Serum of Dr. Blake, Eldridge Cleaver in Exile*, or some Rita Hayworth picture shot in

Salaria. Most people either slept all day, conserving energy for the awards ceremony that night, or drove off to Villefranche, an old fishing village where Cocteau decorated a chapel used by fishermen to pray for calm waters, in which all the angels look exactly like Jean Marais.

Awaiting the announcement of the prizes is as much of an event each year at Cannes as the awards night itself. Press agents and movie executives move about the Carlton bar with the kind of excitement usually reserved for a public hanging. The jury is locked away on a yacht in the harbor, but by 3 P.M. everyone in Cannes knows the results. The back-stabbing, offers of bribes, and the lobbying would draw envy from the most hard-nosed Congressman. One year a famous French film director was expelled from the jury after trying to influence voting for a film he had financed himself; another year a leading French critic wrote a vicious review of a particular favorite, hoping to sway opinion against it. Later, it was discovered that the same critic had been employed secretly as a press agent for the other competing film.

The awards ceremony itself must be seen to be believed. By 7 P.M. there are lines all the way to the Carlton with mounted police to hold back the onslaught. More than one hundred photographers push and shove. The women are given free samples of Coty cosmetics at the door. Inside, it is like a sauna bath turned to "high." There were not enough seats, so actress Joanne Pflug ended up sitting on Robert Altman's lap. (Here was the Grand Prize winner and he not only had to sit *with* somebody, but *under* somebody—which should give you some idea of how disorganized the whole thing is.) Then Gig Young came out and wiped his brow, saying "I don't speak French, but I feel your warmth," which got a laugh from the English-speaking audience and a stony silence from the French. Then Candy Bergen, who looked gorgeous and spoke French like Charlie Bronson, gave a special award for "best new director" to *Hoa Binh*, directed by Raoul Coutard, who has been in the movie business for twenty years. Third prize was a tie between Hungary's *The Falcons* and *The Strawberry Statement*. Second prize went to Italy's *Investigation of a Private Citizen*. Best Director went to John Boorman for all those filter lenses in *Leo the Last*. Best Actress went to a terrible actress who had a minor role in one of the Italian films that was shown at 8 A.M. Best Actor went to Marcello Mastroianni, and the Grand Prize went to *M*A*S*H*, which was greeted by lots of boos and angry shouting from the French and bravos from the allies. After each prize is announced, there is the scratchy sound of a needle being placed on a phonograph record, followed by a distant blast of bugles, like the sound track from *Ivanhoe*. The awards look like menus from the Tour d'Argent and the women get an additional prize of an enormous glass jar that looks like a water pitcher. "How do they ever pack those goddam things in their luggage to get them back home?" asked a lady reporter next to me. Vanessa Redgrave didn't bother. The year she won for *Isadora,* she dropped it on-stage and it shattered into a million splinters. They had to cancel the next act, which was a ballerina dancing *Swan Lake.* Winners are usually invited back the next year, but in Cannes 1970 Miss Redgrave was among the missing.

After the prizes, they showed *They Shoot Horses, Don't They?* and ABC threw a glittering dinner party, where a producer signed one of the photographers to a motion picture contract and a gate-crashing truckdriver on his way to Amsterdam with a load of fertilizer got introduced as the son of the French prime minister and ended up the next morning on the front page of *Nice-Matin.*

After Cannes, it'll be hard to laugh at the Oscars from now on.

Index